Baghdad ER:

Fifteen Minutes

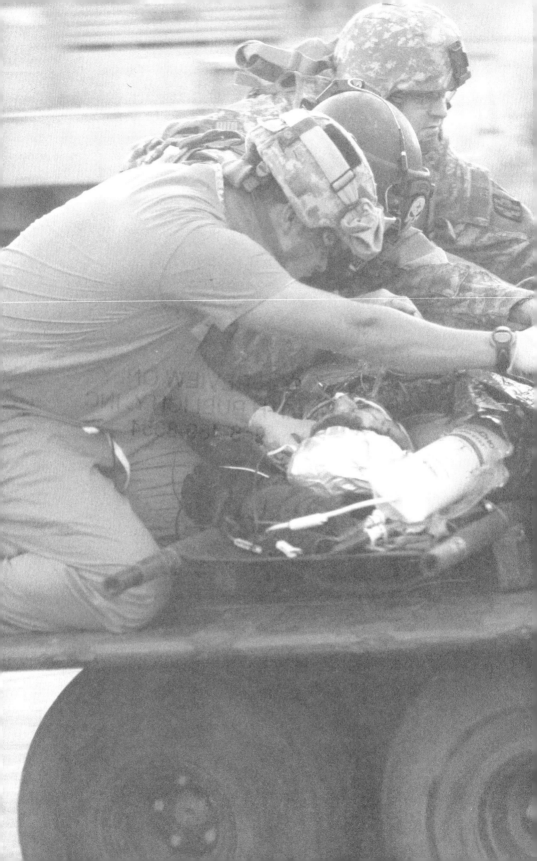

BAGHDAD ER:
FIFTEEN MINUTES

Todd Baker, MD

Gray Fox Publishing
Branson, MO

www.BaghdadER.net

Printed in the United States of America

ISBN 978-0-578-06992-0

Cover photo: U.S. Army Capt. Mike Berriman, left, 1st Lt. Matt Lynes, second left, Command Sgt. Maj. Rodney L. Greene, second right, and Lt. Col. Johnnie Johnson, right, of Task Force 4-64 Armor salute a seriously-wounded comrade as his medevac helicopter leaves Ibn Sina Hospital in the Green Zone in Baghdad, Iraq on Thursday, Dec. 13, 2007. The soldier, who was wounded by a roadside bomb in Baghdad, was transferred to the Air Force Theater Hospital for further treatment after being stabilized at Ibn Sina. (AP Photo/Maya Alleruzzo)

Title page photo: U.S. Army medics rush a seriously wounded civilian contractor to the emergency room at Ibn Sina Hospital in the Green Zone of Baghdad, Iraq on Sunday, Dec. 9, 2007

Contents

America Will Never Forget

We will never forget your
Contributions
We will never forget your
Dedication
We will never forget your
Loyalty
For you are the very
Reason, America is free.
America will always
Remember
The Soldier
Who gave not just their love
For the country
But their life for the
Country
America Will Never Forget!

Author Unknown
Posted in U.S. Morgue
Ibn Sina Hospital
Baghdad, Iraq

Introduction

Baghdad ER: Fifteen Minutes is dedicated to every American soldier, sailor, airmen, marine, and civilian who has put themselves in harm's way to protect our freedom. Without your dedication, determination, and selfless sacrifice, we would not have the freedom to tell your amazing stories. All of us serving behind the lines honor and salute you and the sacrifices you have made.

Likewise, we honor the line medics, corpsmen, and medical professionals who ride in many of the same vehicles, sit in the same shelters, and pay many of the same sacrifices that our brothers in the combat arms branches do. Without your presence, the mission would not endure. You provide the security blanket that gives our warriors on the street the confidence to fight bravely, knowing that you will be there for them, day or night, if they fall in battle.

Baghdad ER documents the medical care of hundreds of wounded American service personnel, contractors, foreign nationals, and Iraqis. As an emergency physician, in my day-to-day practice I rarely receive feedback on patients I have cared for once they leave the emergency department. Likewise, many of the patients mentioned in this book are not followed once they were admitted to the hospital or left the EMT. As an emergency physician serving in Baghdad ER, all I could do was my best for each patient I cared for, the rest was up to God.

Listed Below Are Those Who Served in the EMT of the Eighty-sixth Combat Support Hospital, "Baghdad ER" during Operation Iraqi Freedom Rotation 07–09

MEDICS

Sgt. Nicole Brunelle

Spc. James Crawford

Sgt. Jonathan Desillier

Sgt. Adam Estep

Cpl. Raymond Hasty

Sgt. Sion Ledbetter

S.Sgt. Matthew Longnaker

Sgt. Matthew Mitchell

Spc. David Raffler

Sfc. John Richard

Msg. Robert Schueck

Sgt. Rony Soltis

Sgt. Justin Ubert

Sgt. Kelly Yates

Sgt. Thomas Clise

Spc. Michael Degnovivo

Spc. Christopher Eichert

Spc. Dacia Gilliam

S.Sgt. Emily Hobbs

Spc. Steven Lockwood

Sgt. Fernando Medina

Spc. Tyler Nash

Sgt. Amy Rice

S.Sgt. Michael Schantz

Sgt. Gary Scott

Spc. Joshua Stewart

Spc. Lamond Williams

NURSES

Cpt. Kristy Bischoff, RN

1st Lt. Heather Brown, RN

Maj. Katharine Frost, RN

Cpt. Samuel Matta, RN

Cpt. Patrick Smith, RN

Cpt. Robyn Stafford, RN

1st Lt. Marc Brinsley

Maj. Debra Chappel, RN

Cpt. Ann Gockley, RN

Maj. Katharine Richardson, RN

Cpt. Megan Solberg, RN

PHYSICIANS

Maj. Todd Baker, MD
Cpt. Jason Cohen, DO
Maj. Martha Roellig, MD

Rotators and Volunteers Who Spent Time

Working in Baghdad ER

Medics

Sgt. James Alford

Spc. Kelly Barr

Cpl. Jonathan Bowman

Sgt. James Buscampbel

Cpl. Terry Dilday

Spc. Anastasia Efstration

Sgt. Keith Francis

Sgt. Erick Garcia

Spc. Russell Grant

Pfc. Anastasha Haynes

Spc. Ashley Howell

Spc. Hunmin Lee

Spc. Juan Martinez

Spc. Justin McFarland

Spc. Kevin Nakata

Sgt. John Offiner

Sgt. Jennifer Pertler

Spc. David Schmidt

Spc. Derik Shires

Spc. Charles Southard

Spc. Aaron Baldwin

S.Sgt. Matthew Betke

Spc. Bradley Burkley

Spc. Michael Dierich

Sgt. Mary Duncan

Spc. Terry Emslander

Sgt. Sekiah Freeman

Sgt. Jeremy Graham

S.Sgt. Stacy Hayletts

Spc. Elizabeth Heckman

Spc. Muhammad Lawson

Sgt. Pedro Lopez

Spc. Kyle Mason

Spc. Andrew Milone

Pfc. Joshua Novey

Spc. Victoria Parrish

Sgt. Reece, Cole

Spc. Chris Shelton

Spc. Andrew Smith

Spc. Amy Steele

Sgt. Victor Stepper
Pfc. Patrick Sullivan
Spc. David Tate
Sgt. Justin Waynick
Spc. John Williams
Pfc. Katreena Yesbeck

Spc. Jonathan Strand
Pfc. Lisa Tabary
Spc. Jason Vanwickler
Sgt. Brian Weser
Sgt. Patrick Witt
Sgt. Michael Zeir

NURSES

Cpt. Melanie Bowman, RN
Cpt. William Bosompem, RN
Victoria Hoban, RN, New Zealand
Cpt. Kim Karnowski, RN
Maj. Dave Volbrecht, RN

Cpt. Michelle Chador, RN
Cpt. Stefen Gambino, RN
Cpt. Christopher Johnson, RN
Maj. Irene Tallarico, RN

U.S. ARMY SPECIAL FORCES MEDICS

Drew
Dave
Dennis
Rich

Nate
Mike
Chuck

PROVIDERS

Maj. Andrew Beckmann, DO
Cpt. Scott Benson, PAC
Cpt. Aaron Buzzard, MD
Cpt. Christopher Crowell, MD
Maj. Garrett Gore, MD
Maj. Robert Hennesy, MD
Cpt. Guyon Hill, MD

Cpt. Stephen Beckwith, MD
Cpt. Scott Bier, MD
Cpt. Joseph Campbell, MD
Cpt. Ramon Fry, PAC
Maj. Mark Guffey, MD
Cpt. Erik Hermstad, MD
Cpt. Clinton Keilman, MD

Maj. Donald Kraft, MD

1st Lt. James Lorenz, PAC

Maj. Stewart Mccarver, MD

Cpt. Robert Nolan, DO

Cpt. Abigail Raez, MD

Cpt. Kevin Schwecten, MD

Maj. Williams Smith, MD

1st Lt. Emily Wyatt, PAC

Lt. Col. Larry Leventhal, MD

Cpt. Tara Mazza, DO

Lt. Col. Robert Monteleone, MD

Maj. Bruce Ong, MD

Cpt. Kathleen Samsey, MD

Maj. Walter Simmons, MD

Maj. Samuel Urso, DO

Civilian and Coalition Volunteers

Paul Bellamy-UK

Aaron Cutbush-New Zealand

Roger Erickson-U.S.

Ralph Greenaway-UK

Mark Iroha-UK

Jorgen Vestergaard Jensen-Denmark

Robert "Tex" Marshall-UK

Rasmus Pedersen-Denmark

Paul Reeves-UK

Pte McKenzie-UK

Curtis Simpson-UK

Curt Collins-U.S.

David Dana-UK

Christopher Gonzales-U.S.

Brett Holbert-U.S.

Michael Jensen-Denmark

Kenneth LeBow-U.S.

Hans Gram Novrup-Denmark

Jesus Rodriguez-U.S.

Anthony Steele-UK

Dane Richardson-UK

The Wait Is Over

September 30, 2007

The drive through Tennessee was beautiful. Colorful deciduous trees stretched as far as I could see, rolling hills reached across the horizon, and meandering roadways wandered off the beaten path. The drive up Highway 49 was very surreal. It reminded me of my past home in Arkansas, prior to my entry into the world of military medicine. Surveying the beautiful landscape, I could not help but think about my future home in Missouri, where the colors would be bursting from the seams just as they did this day. En route to Fort Campbell, Kentucky, I could feel myself begin to get nervous, already working myself into "business mode," focusing on what my first move would be after arrival to my new unit. After a few moments of trepidation, my mind relaxed and wandered back to the lazy highway and the mountainous kaleidoscope of color stretching endlessly before me. The time had finally come.

I had been waiting for this day since March 2003. As senior emergency medicine resident physicians at Fort Hood, Texas, my classmates and I watched as our staff physicians were deployed to war one by one. Within a matter of months, only three or four staff docs were left at The Hood, and the rest were doing what we were training to do, what we lived for—saving lives in the heat of battle. We would hear stories about one doc treating heatstroke in the back of a M113 armored personnel carrier, then moments later putting a chest tube in a traumatized soldier while calling for the Blackhawks to come in and carry him away to a higher level of care. They were heroes. America called, and they put their lives on hold and answered. Many were in the line of fire, but most were not. After all, as physicians, the point in battle is that we do not get caught in the line of fire. Who would provide care if we got hit? But whether our staff docs were in immediate danger or not did not matter to those of us back home, waiting our turn. They were there to take care of Joe. They were there to keep Joe safe. They were there so that soldiers, marines, and other American military personnel could do their mission and not have to worry about "what if?" They were there in the sandbox, and my seven classmates and I knew we would be following in their footsteps soon.

On our standardized in-training exam each year of our residency, the Darnall Army Community Hospital emergency medicine graduating class of 2004 scored first in the nation amongst all emergency medicine residency programs, civilian and military alike. Our scores and ranking reflected the dedication and commitment my classmates and I shared; we would be the best and accept nothing short of that. Upon graduation, we were scattered throughout the country, spreading out to army installations including Forts Drum, Campbell, Gordon, Stewart, Hood, and Lewis. There was even a lucky one sent to "Fort Puke," otherwise known as Fort Polk, Louisiana. That lucky one would be me, the new regimental surgeon of the Second Armored Cavalry Regiment, *Toujours Prêt! (*Always Ready!). While my classmates and I were graduating from residency in May 2004, the Second ACR was completing a twelve-month tour of duty in Iraq, only to be informed they had been stretched an extra three months to help deal with uprising in Najaf, Iraq, led by the radical Shiite cleric Muqtada al-Sadr. I did not know at that time how much pain and suffering al-Sadr's forces would cause during our time in Iraq. The Second ACR was attached to the First Armored Division and was among the first units in the army to be extended to a fifteen-month tour in the Iraq War. With their recent extension in theater, I assumed I would be thrown into the mix first, deploying before any of my classmates. I would get to test my skills first, and I thought my chance to shine had arrived. However, after the proper training, I arrived at the unit in August 2004, only two weeks before they returned home to Fort Polk, Louisiana. There would be no deployment for me, at least not right away. I would have to wait my turn.

I spent the next two years serving as the regimental surgeon for the Second ACR, relocating with the unit to Fort Lewis, Washington, in December 2004 and helping the unit build into a Stryker Brigade Combat Team. Since the unit was building, it did not deploy to Iraq or Afghanistan during that time. My job consisted of sick call each morning at 6:30 AM, and then office work with an endless array of emails and phone calls. Usually the day ended with long meetings. There were no emergencies, at least not the kind I was trained to do. Having spent the past seven years of my life preparing to be an emergency physician, I was ready to enter the hospital to treat patients. But it was not to be, at least not until I sat at a desk and put out fires for two long years. It was a valuable and memorable experience, as I had the opportunity to ride in Stryker Combat Fighting Vehicles, fly in Blackhawk helicopters, and do other "green" things that the docs stationed at the hospital did not get to do. But I also did not get to deploy. I had no chance to be a hero.

My classmates had it differently. Dr. Jake Roberts was deployed to Mosul, Iraq, by December 2004, just a few months after graduating residency. He spent ten months in a small aid station and was known as the "cowboy" doc of Mosul. Equipment was limited, and he only had a portable ultrasound machine to play with. Utilizing the emergency ultrasound skills he learned in residency, he quickly adapted to a more austere environment and taught himself to make lifesaving decisions with the technology he had. Decisions were tough: "Who should I fly out first? Who should get intubated or a chest tube prior to evacuation?" Jake made those decisions and came home a hero. Dr. Floriano Putigna served three months with a combat support hospital (CSH) in New Orleans during the Hurricane Katrina disaster and then turned around and spent twelve more months with the CSH in Afghanistan. Drs. Tim Laseter and Laurie Pemberton went to Ibn Sina Hospital in the Green Zone, Baghdad, Iraq, referred to in the HBO documentary "Baghdad ER." There they saved lives on a daily basis, making a difference in the war on terror. Dr. Brian Hall went to Iraq with the Tenth Mountain Division as a flight surgeon. He was able to get to the combat support hospital nearby, where he worked daily to provide emergency care for his soldiers. Dr. Jason Christensen went to a CSH in Tikrit, Iraq, the birthplace of Saddam Hussein, and did amazing work. Dr. Raymond Brovont went to Fort Stewart, Georgia, as a brigade surgeon, a job identical to mine. He deployed in late 2004 and oversaw the healthcare of over four thousand soldiers, spending time in Baghdad ER when he could get free from his desk job. By June 2007, all seven of my residency classmates had not only deployed, but had also returned home to their families. Some had Bronze Stars while others had Meritorious Service Medals, but all of them had saved lives and made America proud. Everyone had deployed and come home a hero, everyone but me.

I left the Second Cavalry Regiment in June 2006 and landed an incredible teaching job at Madigan Army Medical Center, located at Fort Lewis, Washington. It was a dream job, and I enjoyed every minute of it. The two years I had spent "on the Green Side" had set me up for this opportunity. I have always loved teaching, and I was voted the 2007 Teaching Staff of the Year by the residents, an honor of which I am very proud. However, still no deployment, no chance for me to serve. I volunteered to go to my superiors on a weekly basis—not so much as to be in Iraq or Afghanistan, but more so as a chance to prove to myself that I could do it. I felt I could not look my classmates in the eye because I had not paid the price and deployed. When spending time with my fellow staff physicians, I would count right-arm combat patches. More often than not, I would be the only one in the room without the mark of deployment, the mark of the hero. I would hear about units that needed a doctor from time to time, and I would carefully consider the pros and cons of deployment with each. Did I want to go with this or that unit? Realistically, it was not up to me anyway, as my boss would make the decision as to when and where I would go. I had no say in the matter.

Finally, in late 2006, news trickled down to me that I would deploy with the Eighty-sixth Combat Support Hospital, or Eighty-sixth CSH, out of Fort Campbell, Kentucky in summer 2007. The wait would finally be over. My wife Laura and I had been mentally preparing ourselves for years for the combat tour; it was a relief to finally be able put a date and time on it. It would lead right up to the time I was to get out of the army in June 2008, the same time as many of my colleagues in residency. These three years of waiting, not being able to make plans three or four months ahead of time, not knowing when I would be called upon, waiting to begin more waiting, and the feeling of miserable procrastination, would be over in summer 2007. My time was going to come, or so I thought.

In April 2007, the secretary of defense announced that army combat tours would be extended from twelve to fifteen months as part of the "surge." This pushed back the Twenty-eighth CSH, the unit we were to replace in Baghdad, by three months. Our deployment would be delayed and then extended by three months. Great, more waiting! This news, along with a new stop-loss policy for physicians, meant that I would linger until the fall to deploy to Iraq, and then would not get out of the military in June 2008 with my classmates. I would be held over until the unit's deployment was over, presumably in February 2009.

That summer was long as my wife and I prepared for a painful good-bye. We moved from the Fort Lewis, Washington, area to the vicinity of Little Rock, Arkansas, so she could be around her family while I was gone. The weeks and days slowly ticked away, until the day finally arrived. After a tearful good-bye with friends and family, which extended over several days, my wife and I finally said farewell. Driving away from my new home to go to war was by far one of the hardest moments of my life, one I will never forget.

After kissing my five-month-old baby girl, Laura, and two beagles good-bye, I drove from central Arkansas to Fort Campbell to meet up with the Eighty-sixth Combat Support Hospital. We were not sure how long exactly I would be gone. But I traveled that day so I might get on with the rest of my life. No more waiting. No more feeling inadequate because I did not have a deployment patch on my right arm. Now I would get my chance to do my job, a chance to save lives. I was finally able to move on and quit waiting for the inevitable.

—————

Our first day of in-processing went relatively well. We stood and waited in different lines for a few hours, but overall it was not bad. We received briefs from combat stress control, the judge advocate general, and military intelligence personnel. We learned that we were not supposed to fraternize with our subordinates, shoot innocent detainees, or give away big military secrets. I remember pondering that the last time I checked, these things were pretty much common sense but, this being the army, I was sure we each would hear the information several times.

Three hundred of us were placed into platoons and sections to be organized for travel. Our emergency treatment team, or EMT, would consist of about thirty soldiers, from the 68W lower enlisted medics to lieutenant and captain nurses and docs. Deb Chappel, a major who had been serving as a nurse supervisor over the past few years at Fort Sill, Oklahoma, would be our head nurse. She had civilian trauma experience, but many of our medics and nurses were young, and trauma would be new to them. We knew we would have to train quickly to get prepared for what we were about to experience. As we assumed charge of our mission, I had no doubt that people were going to suffer due to our inexperience, and lives would be lost. We had to quickly learn the equipment, teamwork, and essential skills necessary to run the craziest trauma center in the world. However, the priority at the time was to reinforce to our crew the basics, like stopping bleeding, stabilizing cervical spines, and functioning as members of a trauma team.

For some reason, our CSH was assigned four emergency medicine physicians to replace six when we got to Iraq. One of our guys, Cpt. Rob Nolan, was traveling to Mosul in northern Iraq, where he was to replace two ER docs on his own. None of us were certain as to how that was going to work out. He just wanted to be able to take a shower sometime without having to worry if the EMT was covered, but at this moment, he did not expect to get that luxury. We knew something would have to be done; someone was going to have to help him out, but we were not sure how.

The other two emergency medicine physicians, Cpt. Martha Roellig and Cpt. Jason Cohen, were to be joining me in Baghdad. We would be replacing four physicians; being short one doc, we also were trying to figure out how to cover. We were all convinced that we would not be getting any midtour leave at that point. We had mentioned this concern to our command several times, as early as six months prior to our arrival at Campbell, and knew that we would need to continue engaging them about this situation. With only three of us in Baghdad and just Rob in Mosul, we expected to be crushed and were not sure how long we would last both mentally and physically.

The next day, we lined up to receive our RFI, or rapid fielding initiative. About 250 of us were herded through several stations and given everything from hot and cold weather boots to gloves, sleeping systems, Gerber multitools, long underwear, and reflective belts. It was very well organized, although it lasted almost six hours, from 6:00 AM until around noon. I wished they had told us to eat breakfast first! It was a long, painful day that ended up with us loading, inventorying, and inspecting our gear. We then packed our tuff boxes into huge containers to be shipped by boat to the Middle East. They were to arrive about a month after we had boots on the ground in Baghdad. I placed several DVDs, books, extra clothes, my alarm clock, scrubs, and other items in my box. It would be a nice package to receive after we were settled into our new quarters. Dr. Cohen had a Nintendo Wii packed in his, so we would be especially happy to see his tuff box arrive.

After a long week of 6:00 AM formations and days lasting until 9:00 PM, Saturday finally arrived. At the time, I was very impressed with the organization of the Eighty-sixth CSH. They had split all 250 or so of us PROFIS (professional filler system; those of us who come from other hospitals and units all over the world) into several groups, with each group performing different activities each day. Some would draw their nuclear, biological, and chemical, or NBC, suits, while others would go to a family-readiness briefing or related events. We also were divided into two task forces, TF Baghdad, comprising about 80 percent of the hospital, and Task Force Mosul with the other 20 percent. Each morning, we would come together at formation as a hospital and then separate into our different task forces. The base CSH personnel stationed at Fort Campbell had rented several vans for those travelling from different installations. Those in the vans were riding from the motels we were crashing in to post and back, but they began to bicker with each other and leave people behind at different places when the group did not want to wait. The command got so frustrated with complaints they eventually took control of the vans and tightened up the movement of the personnel. I thanked God every day that I had my truck!

The command of the CSH was also very concerned with marksmanship. Everyone drew an M16 rifle, and lieutenant colonels and above also received an M9 pistol. Unfortunately, as a major, I did not make the cut, so I would have to be lugging a rifle around with me every time I went to eat a meal, trek to the Porta John, or do anything outside of the building. Most of the soldiers who actually belonged to the CSH stationed at Fort Campbell received a pistol if they were a sergeant or above. After a day or two, many of us realized that we did not draw pistols because we were clinical officers rather than administrators. I remember being frustrated, but thinking, "I guess there are worse things in life, like being in Iraq without a weapon!" I asked my first sergeant if he thought the command would let me carry my deer rifle or shotgun, but of course I already knew the answer to that. I was happy to get to know an M16 and excited about the time we would spend on marksmanship.

The first day at the range was eye-opening indeed. I had always enjoyed shooting, but you should have seen these people! Many of the senior officers had not fired a rifle in many years, much less in all their combat gear, or "battle rattle." Having been an avid hunter since childhood, I had always thought of myself as a good marksman, but the truth is I had shot with a riflescope and had never qualified for the peep sights of an M16. The thought of this medical crew going to the range reminded me of my officer basic course in 1998 at Camp Bullis, Texas. We went to the range as a rag-tag bunch of medical students and fired M9 Beretta 9mm pistols. I was used to shooting a pistol, so it was not a big deal to me, but it was scary to watch many of the students fire! Dirt was flying twenty feet short of the targets, fifty feet behind them, and some people were even shooting other people's objects. The command of the CSH was surely aware of this; they had scheduled a great training program, the same program used by the infantry soldiers of the 101st Airborne Division. We were hard pressed for time, but nevertheless, we devoted several days to marksmanship. My old regimental commander, Col. Jon Lehr of the Second Cavalry Regiment Stryker Brigade Combat Team, always said that he wanted the rifle to be "an extension of the trooper's arms." I believe our command had the same idea, and even though we were not a combat unit, we knew all too well that it was not only the combat units who were being engaged by the enemy in Iraq. I was quite pleased with the time and effort we spent teaching our medics, nurses, pharmacists, and physicians to defend themselves. I kept trying to weasel my way into getting to fire a SAW or larger M240 machine gun, but to no avail. Sunday was to be range day for us, so we were scheduled to meet on post at 5:00 AM.

The day before, we took our physical fitness test at 6:00 AM. I had always passed my tests over the past six years of my army life, but I still disliked them. I always pushed myself to do the maximum number of push-ups and sit-ups, which would make me more tired for the two-mile run. It actually did not matter how many push-ups I did, as long as I performed to the standard. I had turned thirty-two years old the previous April and had relocated to the age 32–36 bracket, making my minimum standards a little lower than they were during the earlier years of my army career. Nice. I was thrilled with my new standards of thirty-nine push-ups, forty-five sit-ups, and the run within seventeen minutes and forty-five seconds. Nothing to it. I remember wondering, "If we fail the test, what really happens?" Lower enlisted soldiers who failed got extra PT time each week to get into better shape, but my job did not allow time for that. For the first time ever on a PT test, I was able to stop myself and not push it to the max on each event, affecting my other scores. Fifty push-ups, stop. Fifty sit-ups, stop. I was then able to finish my two miles in fifteen minutes, twenty-two seconds, which was about a minute faster than usual for me. It was great to have that done, and it was nice to not feel guilty for eating ice cream later in the day!

I had made several new friends since my arrival, and although I liked our crew of nurses we would have for the EMT, I did not know how good they would be clinically at that time. We did seem to get along well, and that was an important start. My two colleagues, Jason Cohen and Marti Roellig, were great, and we befriended a couple of the other docs from the outpatient clinic. Dr. Pat Hickey was a pediatric infectious disease specialist who would be with us for six months before going home, and Dr. Dena George was a family medicine doc I knew in residency. She would get to stay and play for the duration with the rest of us, and eventually become The Doctor to the Stars, as she would take care of all our VIPs, both American and Iraqi alike.

It had been seven days since I had left my new home, and of course I missed my family deeply. Most days were good, but when I talked to Laura and learned how our five-month-old daughter Avery was doing and that our dogs were okay and playful and that things were rolling along without me, I missed home. In my motel room, I had a nice framed picture of Laura and me—she in a beautiful flowing black evening gown, and me in my dress blue army uniform and Stetson hat from my days with the cavalry. But I had to pack the portrait in my tuff box soon after arrival so it could meet me in Iraq. I missed seeing her face, but I still had a wallet picture to remind me of how lucky I was. I did have a stunning picture of Avery that jumped out every time I opened my wallet and warmed my heart each time I glimpsed at it. It did make this much easier knowing that I was blessed with an unbelievable family. From my wife to my parents, siblings, in-laws, and incredible friends, I knew I was not to go on this journey alone. "It will seem to take forever, but as with all things, this too shall pass. Thank God it's begun and I don't have to feel like I'm procrastinating anymore!" I repeated in my mind continuously. However, it had only been a few days, and the finish line was nowhere in sight. It was way over the horizon, over mountains as tall as the Rockies, oceans as wide as the Pacific, and a distance as far as the moon it seemed.

On our day off, Jason Cohen and I went to see *The Kingdom*, a movie about FBI agents investigating a terrorist attack in Saudi Arabia. The lead character Jamie Foxx wore a boonie hat the whole time, and it looked like it was really hot there, making me realize that I needed to get a boonie hat for Kuwait. A "shoot 'em up in the Middle East" movie was not what we should have been going to at the moment, as every time someone got shot or injured all I could think of was "what emergency medical procedure does this guy need?" At least I was in the right mindset.

I normally love to get up at 4:00 AM on Sundays, but not this time. Usually the alarm waking me that early meant I would be getting dressed, eating a bowl of cereal, and then jumping in the truck to go duck, deer, or some other type of hunting. Living in the Great Northwest, it may even mean I was about to go sturgeon or "combat" salmon fishing. On this Sunday, however, getting up at 4:00 AM meant being in formation an hour later and drawing weapons. Naming my personal weapon Betsy for some unknown reason, we received our M16 assignments and loaded up in the vans for a trip to the range. It had been unusually warm for October along the Kentucky-Tennessee border, and this day was no exception. We were at the range all day, hanging out in our body armor in the 93-degree heat.

The heat actually served two purposes. One was to get us ready for the 130-degree heat we would face in the next year, and two was to build our empathy for "Joe," the slang term for the common foot soldier. Regular soldiers wear this crap all day every day and do their jobs without complaining.

When in Iraq, they would only come to us to gripe when they had been blown up, shot, or found themselves in some other bad situation. We decided it was no big deal that we *had* to wear our body armor, even if it was hot!

We were placed into groups and were taken to the "zero" range first. I had never fired a M16 for accuracy, with my only M16 experience being a range at Fort Lewis with my old unit that was more about tactical firing positions and movement rather than precision. After firing several groups of five shots, and making several adjustments, I had to bend my front sight pin back to a vertical position because it was bent 20 degrees to the right when I drew the weapon. One of the weapons specialists, Spc. Chapman, helped me out and let me know that he hailed from Hot Springs, Arkansas, a town just thirty minutes north of our college town and where Laura and I had our first date. He was the second person in the Eighty-sixth CSH I had met from Arkansas.

After zeroing our weapons, we shot up man-sized silhouette targets, and then we fired on the pop-up range. The green pop-up targets were shaped like the torso and head of a person, and I was told that during the Cold War they were called "Ivan" to represent a Russian soldier. I did not know if we had a different name for them at this point, so I unofficially named them "Osama." Trying to represent my roots and the great state of Arkansas, I was disappointed to find that I did not shoot expert, but for my first-ever range I did fair, shooting thirty-one of forty and hitting all the distant targets. The most distant "Osamas" were three hundred meters away, and while I could never imaging shooting at a deer from three hundred meters with iron sights, it was indeed easier than I expected. We were then bused back to the armory, and we got to sit and clean weapons for the next few hours. All in all, it was a fun day but a very long one. I probably shot over two hundred rounds, and I was feeling it the next day in my right shoulder.

The following morning began SRP day (soldier readiness profile) and was a fun-filled day of standing in line to get our affairs in order, including medical, legal, personal stuff, and more. However, the day began with the Task Force Eighty-six hospital photo, with about four hundred of us crowding in front of the Fort Campbell Air Assault tower for a massive picture. It was interesting watching the two first sergeants struggle to herd and cram us all into the frame, then attempt to rearrange us by height using military formation commands many of us had never heard. Every time one would call a new command, I would watch the enlisted people around me and follow their lead. I was sure they thought I was pretty clueless, but I did not really care. As I continuously told my nurses and fellow docs, I was more concerned about our abilities as a trauma team than our knowledge of army commands and formations.

A few of us from the EMT (The CSH term for the ER) were going to a video teleconference with the hospital command, so we were front-loaded into the gym where the SRP was held. After a short briefing, we went to different lines and got moving. My favorite station was the immunization station, where I received a typhoid booster and my first anthrax immunization in my right arm, and a smallpox vaccination in my left. Good times indeed! It really did not hurt until about three hours later when I was convinced I could not drive my truck back to the motel. At least the PT test was done! Hours later, we were done with the SRP and off to the video teleconference and more briefings.

It was during this drive across post that we solidified the nicknames for our group, at least for the time being. I wanted to eat at a fast food burger joint, so I was called Fatty even though I am a thin guy. Jason Cohen made some comment that reminded us of the television show *The Office*, so he was named Faggy. During one episode of the sitcom, the boss Michael Scott, played by Steve Carell, accidently insulted a homosexual office worker and then tried to talk his way out of it. He just continued to dig himself into a deeper and deeper hole throughout the episode. Dr. Dena George wanted to eat at the Cracker Barrel restaurant, so we called her Cracker. A month or two later, her name would be changed to The Doctor to the Stars, but we did not know that would be her role at the time. Pat Hickey was a normal sized guy who wore a size large chemical weapons mask, so we decided to name him Melon Head. And last, Dr. Martha Roellig was a former drill sergeant in the army, giving her the appropriate name Drill Sarge. We were

sure these names would change as we got to know each other better, but at
the moment that was the best we had.

Whenever our task force or company was called to attention as a unit,
we were supposed to shout "Eagle medics, hooah!" with "Hooah!" being a
common term for *esprit d'corps* in the army. It essentially meant anything
other than no. We were trying to create a motto for our EMT section, one
that was just for us and something we could put on T-shirts or coffee mugs.
We enjoyed slogans with cynical humor such as "We didn't kill 'em," meant
to be said while shrugging your shoulders and acting as if we were innocent
of wrongdoing. It sounded terrible, but it was an example of the very dark
humor medical providers and staff routinely used to cope with the stress
of working in an ER. Our everyday job is to save lives, to prevent death
and morbidity, but we can only do so much. As my mother-in-law Bernice
Burns always told me, we do one-third, the patient's body does one-third,
and God does the rest. It is always in his hands. We all hoped we would
not require too much dark humor to cope with the daily struggle for life
and death we were about to dive head first into, but only time would tell.
We knew we just needed to focus on doing our third, and let God and the
patient do the rest. I liked the slogan "Eagles out front," since we were the
receiving and stabilizing area for our hospital. I knew that soldiers would
be in bad shape when they got to us, and we would stabilize them and then
move them into the hospital, into the rear. Of the Eagle medics, *we* would
be the first to care, and *we* would be out front.

A few days later, I journeyed to the Laundromat on post. It had been a few
years since I had been to a public washing facility, but usually they were
nice places, and this was no exception. I know it is strange to say, but since
my college days I have always enjoyed spending time in the laundry while
waiting on clothes to wash. That time allowed me to slow down and pick
up a good book or do something else relaxing. I could stop worrying about
my list of things to get done and just chill. People have always told me I am
easily entertained, as evidenced by my enjoyment of stupid movies, dumb

jokes, and such. My brother Carl and I always agreed that a movie does not have to be realistic, or even have an award-winning plot, it just has to entertain us. And just like an entertaining movie, I was always happy to have an excuse to take a break from my Type A personality and just sit and wait on laundry to dry.

I was informed the next day that Jason Cohen and I would room together at Ibn Sina Hospital in Baghdad, a discovery with which we both were very pleased. While I was a staunch conservative and Bible-thumping Christian, he was a wonderful Jewish man with a great personality who loved his family greatly. We seemed to mesh well, despite our differing viewpoints. We were convinced we would have great political and spiritual discussions, and we did indeed learn and benefit from each other throughout our tour.

We later met up with many of our nurses and medics in the Emergency Department at Blanchfield Army Community Hospital, and we had two hours to get to know each other and begin our progression into a trauma team. Of our fifteen or so medics, exactly two had been in real trauma situations, with one E-4 specialist having worked at Ibn Sina with the Eighty-sixth CSH during their first deployment and another doing trauma with the First Brigade, Twenty-fifth Infantry Division Stryker Brigade Combat Team based out of Fort Lewis, Washington, my home station. The majority of our nurses had very little or no ER or trauma experience. That was worrisome, yet not uncommon as similar CSHs deploying before us consisted of a similar makeup. In one way, it would be a good thing as most of our crew would not have preconceived ideas or bad habits, and we would be able to mold them into a team much quicker and more efficiently.

I gave a quick trauma overview, with some of the new ideas that were being implemented in theater, and followed it up by running through a quick trauma with me as a patient. However, much to everyone's dismay, I would not let them put a bladder catheter in me! After this, all of our medics practiced putting IVs in each other. We only had two hours available to practice, but it was two more hours than our command had planned for us to train. Our schedule looked much busier the next week, and we did not anticipate a chance to do more training, if any, before we left for

Kuwait. We wanted to get a chance to put our nurses and medics through a suturing class, but we did not get the opportunity.

That night, we rented a triple fish cooker from the Morale, Wellness, and Recreation Center, or MWR, on Fort Campbell and obtained thirty pounds of large shrimp. Using a recipe taught to me by my friend Justin Powell, a veterinarian in my hometown of Texarkana, Texas, we put together a Cajun shrimp boil for the officers of the EMT. We wanted to invite our enlisted personnel, but it would have been simply too expensive, so we stuck with the nurses and docs. I used spicy Cajun seasonings to heat the potatoes, shrimp, and corn, and we all pigged out. Only one or two of our crew had done this before, so it was a novelty to almost all of them, and it went over very well. Some told me I should start a restaurant and serve this as the only item on the menu! Others told me it was the best meal they had eaten in weeks, and that it was better then any restaurant shrimp they had ever had. It was very flattering to say the least.

I have always gotten a kick out of cooking for people. I am not an accomplished chef by any stretch of the imagination, but I *love* to grill and cook. To be honest, I am terrible at cooking normal things like burgers and steaks, but if you want some deer, duck, saltwater fish, or some other type of exotic game, look out! I thought the shrimp boil was a great coming-together for our crew; it was the beginning of an experience that we hoped would have more positive memories than negative ones. We were determined to keep up our spirits and our level of camaraderie throughout the fifteen months to come. Many of us had already been trying to figure out how to get to cook some exotic stuff once we arrived in Baghdad. I doubted the Iraqi government or the United States military would be happy with me going out into the wilderness of Iraq to obtain some sort of wild game to prepare (camel anyone?), but I imagined we would come up with some way to get good food to grill while we were there. After supper, we all kicked back and enjoyed cigars, a tradition at our destination of Ibn Sina Hospital in Baghdad. We were told many of the doctors and nurses would go to the rooftops of the buildings to smoke cigars and relax while watching the explosions in the distance. We hoped there would not be too many for us to watch during our time, but if the last five years were any indication, then we knew we would get quite a show at some point. We were right.

I missed Laura and Avery more and more each day, and it had been only two weeks since I had left home! One Thursday, Laura received flowers from me, with a card in my handwriting. She kept trying her best to discover how I could have pulled that off, but I would not give her any hints. I was sure she would figure it out at some point, and she eventually surmised that I had set up a deal with the local florist to deliver fresh flowers every Thursday and had prewritten all of the cards—but I so loved to surprise her and keep her guessing. She was and is the love of my life and the thought of her smile kept me going. The video Web cam we had purchased before I left home was a lifesaver, and I hoped and prayed we could continue to use it in Iraq. We had been able to have Web conversations two or three times during my stay at Fort Campbell, and they had been a huge morale boost for me. I was even able to watch Avery almost crawl for the first time on the Internet! She could get up on all fours but did not quite have the coordination to crawl. I figured she would be crawling within the next two weeks, and that was a pretty close estimate. I hated to miss it, but I was so happy and proud of her. I cannot imagine the soldiers from past wars who had nothing but snail mail to communicate with their loved ones!

A week after our long day at the range, I did a quick Internet search and found a local church, Grace Christian Community, which met in a local high school. Attending their service kept me singing the praise songs all day. The pastor had a great message: continuously work to become the person you want to be, no matter what you are doing in your life at that time. It was a great message for someone about to deploy for fifteen months!

After church, I went by Toys-R-Us to pick up gifts for my daughter's six-month birthday, buying her six presents, one for each month. I then drove to the local riverside park. It was a beautiful, warm, and sunny day, and Little League football games were in full swing. Five- and six-year-old cheerleaders were cheering their hearts out, likely not even paying attention to the team they were cheering for. The constant noise of whistles, parents, and coaches yelling filled my ears. Walkers and joggers were all over the trails, and the river was full of boats. Every couple of minutes, a boat would go by, one with fishermen, another with skiers, and some with people simply joy-riding. Bringing up the rear was a couple of tugboats pushing huge barges. I sat in a swing and read a book from cover to cover, *From Baghdad, With Love*, by Marine Corps Lt. Col. Jay Kopelman. It was a great book about his attempts to rescue his unit's canine mascot from the streets of Fallujah, with the story moving on to Baghdad and eventually reaching his home of San Diego. It was an enjoyable book, but the day was about more than reading—it was about my last chance to enjoy wonderful weather, kids playing without fear of attack, live football, and everyday Americans enjoy-ing the beautiful outdoors that God had given us. We have all been lucky enough to be born in our wonderful country, and many countries in the world do not have the incredible beauty that we take for granted daily. I routinely do so myself, but not this day. This day, I appreciated America. I had a feeling, after living in a city of several million people for fifteen months, that I would appreciate America even more when I returned home.

Three weeks after arriving at Fort Campbell, we had completed our training and were ready to get the show on the road. One of the only events of the last days was a theater policy briefing, with directions on how to wear our uniforms, when to wear what, how to keep our weapons clean, and those types of things. Much to our chagrin, we doctors realized we would have to lug around our M16 everywhere we went. Who would have thought that, in the most dangerous city in the world, we would have to take our personal protection with us? I laughed at this; apparently, a few years ago some of the docs at Ibn Sina took apart their weapons and stored them under their bunks throughout their tour.

Just before we left for Kuwait, we heard from the emergency medicine docs whom we were to replace in Baghdad, telling us we needed to find a replacement for our fourth physician as soon as possible. They said that when multiple patients from a suicide bombing or improvised explosive device attack arrived, it was very hard for them to keep control of things, as there was only one ER doc on shift at a time. I had already mentioned this issue to our deputy commander for clinical services, or DCCS, our hospital's chief physician. Col. John Rowe seemed to be a great guy, and I looked forward to working with him. He was aware of our plight, and I told him that I thought we three ER docs in Baghdad would last about eight weeks before we went crazy from exhaustion, trauma, anger, or a combination of everything with no relief. He acknowledged this and thought about loaning us docs from the outpatient clinic, but of course, he could not commit until we had arrived and assessed the situation. Clinic providers would not be trauma-trained physicians as Jason, Marti, and I, but we thought that maybe we could work out something. I thought his stance at the moment was not unreasonable, since none of us had deployed to Baghdad and we did not know what we were getting into. I attempted to contact my consultant to the surgeon general, the colonel who sent all the ER docs in the army to their assignments overseas. However, he was not available, and I received no replies to my inquiries. It looked like we would be on our own.

The next day arrived, and we were one day closer to heading overseas. We had formation at 6:30 AM, ate breakfast together, and then had nothing to do until 3:00 PM. We ran errands and began tying up loose ends with personal stuff like auto insurance, cell phones, and the like, but I could not help but feel that I would much rather have spent this down time with Laura and Avery rather than sitting in a motel room. Anyway, at 3:00 PM we had to be in formation to have our body armor inspected. The personality of the EMT stood out at that time; as sergeants formally inspected the other platoons, we grouped in a large circle and played hacky sac, kicking a small beanbag around. Watching the poor guys stand at attention for thirty minutes while they were inspected one by one, with the sergeant turning right angles and doing everything formally and "the right way," really gave us a good laugh. I felt bad for them, but I thought, "That's the real army." In the EMT, we planned to stick to our motto that we would focus on patient care. We had our armor checked as well, but we had a lot more fun doing it. I think this was the day that we all realized that our group would be "special" when compared to the others.

The calendar moved forward, and we finally made it to the day before our departure. We endured the departure ceremony by lining up in a huge formation and dressing up for the VIP crowd. It was sunny and warm, but it could have been a lot worse. The ceremony lasted about thirty minutes as we stood at attention or parade rest for the VIPs. Many of us were not looking particularly forward to it, as we had no family there and had no real reason for the pomp and circumstance. But we knew it was army tradition, so we drove along. No big deal.

I later went to the emergency department at Fort Campbell to see my former classmate, Dr. Tim Laseter. Like all the others, he had deployed overseas and long since returned, and he was planning on getting out of the army in June 2008, the same time I had expected to be discharged prior to my stop-loss for deployment. I had seen a million pictures of mutilated bodies with limbs missing, huge chunks taken out of their torsos, and the like previously. However, Tim displayed two pictures to me that day that caught my attention. One was a soldier with the lower half of his face blown off by an improvised explosive device (IED). He was awake and fully alert, and he had not seen a mirror so he had no idea how bad his injuries were. Tim told me that when he was intubating and placing a breathing tube in the soldier to put him on a ventilator, he could not define any of the normal anatomy and just "searched for the air bubbles." I had heard of similar scenarios with people trying to commit suicide by placing a shotgun under their chin and shooting upward, only to have the weapon facing too far forward, thus blowing off their face but sparing their brain. I had seen related pictures, as they are part of my job as an ER doc. But this day got to me. These pictures flustered me. He also showed me photos of clam-shelled patients, meaning they had died of their wounds in front of him so he or the surgeon had cut their chests open and exposed their hearts, hoping to be able to restore circulation or clamp the aorta just beneath to prevent exsanguination, or bleeding to death. I then realized that it was coming, and coming fast. It was almost put-up-or-shut-up time. It was almost time to go to battle in the effort to save lives. It would be what I was trained for and, despite having a moment of weakness when looking at the pictures, I knew I was ready. We were to leave for Kuwait in a day or two. The plane could not arrive fast enough.

The day arrived; we were ready to roll. The excitement of the awaiting adventure led to a difficult night's sleep. Three and a half years of anticipation had finally lapsed, and I could move on with the mission. It was time to put my training, attitude, aptitude, and leadership to work. I could now stop the waiting and the feelings of inadequacy with my peers. Hooah!

Breakfast proved to be our last chance to sit down to enjoy a restaurant meal, so along with the others, I went all out at the Cracker Barrel restaurant with a great feast of pancakes, eggs over medium, and a nice tall glass of orange juice. Later, we loaded our gear into cargo vans and began hauling it to post, where we would reload the bags into milvans for transport to the airfield. The excitement was palpable; you could feel it in the air. A spirited van ride into post turned into a lively and anxious collection at the company arms room. The family readiness group had tables set up with drinks and snacks for all, and there were approximately two hundred family members present to see their loved ones off. I made several phone calls to Laura to update her on my status, but I was happy she was not here. Saying good-bye three weeks prior had been the worst day of my life. Now, as I watched children cry, wives and husbands hold each other, and parents try to keep it together in front of their kids, I felt the impending loneliness of deployment, even without my family present. The anxiety and fear of the unknown was palpable. We drew our boonie hats and extra patrol caps, and then we had a couple of formations for accountability. To my surprise, the hospital was 100 percent present and ready to board the plane. Over the past several years, while I had been working in the army's emergency departments, I had seen many soldiers miss movement on their day of departure. Many missed movement because they were in jail, intoxicated, having emotional breakdowns, or for some other reason. I was certain that out of the 250 of us, at least one would not show. I was wrong; we were all ready to go.

We then drew our weapons, slings, butt stock magazine holders, and magazines. Several NCOs were around to help us figure out how to put our new toys on our rifles. While I was not fired up about dragging an M16 around everywhere I went in the Middle East, the slings were sweet and allowed you to keep the weapon in front of or behind you as you went. There was a quick release mechanism that allowed you to snap the weapon up to the firing position rapidly.

At the next formation, we had another accountability check, and still there were no elopers. The atmosphere grew more tense, exciting, and alive. It reminded me of the hour before kickoff at a college or NFL football game where the crowd slowly builds itself into a frenzy, with the only relief being the opening whistle. Upon kickoff, the crowd goes crazy and delivers that pent-up energy in the form of screaming, stomping, and cheering. We were getting closer and closer to kickoff.

While in formation, we watched several old school busses creeping toward us. Forming by platoon, we crammed into the buses using a single file line. Our marksmanship NCO, Sgt. First Class Fenlason, from the 101st Airborne, stood in line and shook each of our hands as we got on the bus. We were very impressed by this gesture.

We rode the busses to the airfield under the cover of darkness, with a starry sky watching over us. At the airfield, an air force C-17 waited with engines running. I was thinking, "It's gonna be a long flight on that!" Air force cargo planes do not have the creature comforts of a passenger airliner. But we were not about luxury; we were about accomplishing a mission for Uncle Sam.

Driving past the C-17 and leaving it behind, we arrived at our next staging area. Horded into a huge open bay, we were briefed and then led to a quick, last-minute SRP process, making those of us who had received our smallpox inoculations nine days prior feel fortunate. Those who had pregnant wives or small children had to wait until they left their families to get their smallpox vaccine. "Stinks for them," I thought. After the quick SRP, we were fed a free meal of hamburgers and hot dogs, by a fired up and jovial civilian staff. It was so nice seeing all of these people out there, excited about their jobs, and excited about their country at eleven on a Sunday night.

We formed into a large hanger with an enormous twenty- or thirty-foot wide American flag in the background. Like many deploying units, we were supposed to receive a deployment speech from a general officer, but our post commander was out of state, so our hospital commander Col. West delivered it. Afterward, our chaplain, Maj. Felix Sermon, stood in front of the formation with the flag at his back and delivered a quick message. He read from the book of Psalms, chapter twenty-three, the well-known writing of King David, "Though I walk through the valley of the shadow of death, I will fear no evil, for you are with me." As he led us in prayer, not a sound could be heard other than the resonance of the aircraft arriving from the night sky; the plane that would take us to our destiny as it landed on the runway behind us. At that moment, I do not think there were any atheists or agnostics in the room. It was an unbelievable time I will never forget.

The hanger we staged in was separated into three large rooms, each holding about five hundred chairs. Room A was empty, we were in B, and C was filled with forty-three marines. Each room had a door to an outside courtyard and smoking area, with the tarmac and our plane in the background. Each courtyard was surrounded by security fencing, separating the staging area into sections. It was an interesting site with the army soldiers and marines segregated from one another by a fence. It was eerily similar to visions of penitentiaries I had seen on television, with the different prisoners separated by chain-linked fences. The marines were flying to Kuwait as well, and then on to who knew where. They were all lower enlisted as far as I could tell; there could have been a few NCOs or junior officers, but I did not see any. I could not help but wonder where they would end up. We all knew the marines did much shorter combat tours than we in the army, but they also did a lot of the fighting. I wondered if I would I find myself putting a chest tube in one of those kids sometime in the next few months, intubating him, cracking his chest open, or worse, pronouncing him dead. Hopefully, we would never see them again, and they would go fight hard and be back in the U.S. long before we came home. But if they needed us, if they needed me, I would be ready. I promised them that.

We formed up in alphabetical order and headed out of the hanger straight into a receiving line of brass, with colonels and sergeant majors alike, as they shook everyone's hands and cheered for us. We walked about two hundred yards across the tarmac, were greeted by the rear detachment crew that loaded our gear onto the plane, and climbed on board of the large civilian plane that was chartered for our flight.

The World War II generation is commonly known as the Greatest Generation. They rationed gas, tires, food, and every other luxury that we take for granted as part of the war effort. The soldiers kissed their wives, children, and parents good-bye and boarded trains headed for the coast, followed by weeks and months at sea on ships going to Europe or Asia. They left home months before they even reached the battlefield, and they stayed until the fight was done. No seven-, twelve-, or even fifteen-month deployments; they only got to come home for one of three reasons: they were wounded and could not fight any more, they were in a body bag, or the war was over. That was it. The only contact they had with their loved ones were letters that took months to arrive. They had no idea what was going on in the United States. They only knew their mission: stay alive and make the other guy die for his country.

Even with the amazing respect I have for the Greatest Generation, getting on that plane, I saw those same characteristics in our soldiers, airmen, marines, and sailors today. The Iraq War to that point had no doubt been an up and down affair, mostly depending on what the media decided to report that month. However, despite the volatility of public opinion, there were three constants to me. One, progress on the ground had been slow since the surge began, but there was progress. Two, our leadership in the White House and the Pentagon, while obviously making many mistakes, blunders, and errors, had shown great resolve to that point. If they had it their way, America would win this struggle. Our leadership would not give up on the Iraqi people. As a soldier, while I had no desire to leave home for sixteen months, I appreciated this resiliency. I assumed at the time that some of the candidates campaigning to be the next president would change America's position, but to that point it had been steadfast. Third, our young men and women in the military had answered the call. They had deployed multiple times on short notice. They had gone on patrol time after time while staring death in the face. They had done their part to win this war with unbelievable professionalism, compassion, resiliency, and an unstoppable will. I write this not to be a political statement or diatribe, but I thought then and think now that it is imperative to point out that our current generation of leaders and servicemen answered the call, in our own way, just as the Greatest Generation did some seventy years ago.

Once I boarded the plane, I was thrilled to see two empty seats near a very warm air vent in the rear. While everyone else crammed in front of me, I gladly decided to be a little warm in order to get to spread out for the trans-Atlantic voyage. The flight was fantastic, with a two-hour layover in Germany. I got a chance to check email and send Laura instant messages on the Internet during our time in Europe. She was not around to get them at the time, but that was okay as I was just happy to let her know I was safe. I was able to fly all the way from Fort Campbell to Kuwait with great food, great comfort, and great sleep. What a great day indeed! After several years, I was on my way.

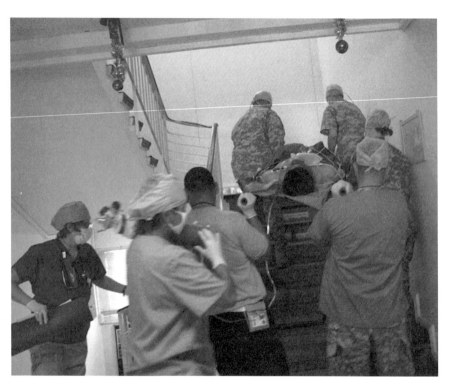

In this photo taken on Dec. 7, 2007, a patient is carried upstairs to the operating room atthe 86th Combat Support Hospital, the U.S. military hospital in the Green Zone in Baghdad, Iraq. (AP Photo/Maya Alleruzzo)

The Other Side of the World

October 22, 2007

There were no trees to be seen once we landed in Kuwait. At Camp Buehring, there were copious quantities of three things: sand, heat, and water. The sand was fine, silty, and likely the closest I would ever come to a lunar walk in my life. The highest temperature over the first few days was only 97 degrees Fahrenheit, not too bad for the Middle East, but still hot just the same. There were literally thousands of cases of bottled water all over the post. At the corner of most tents, inside just about every building, everywhere you looked, there were cases of water. There was a choice of cold water from a cooler inside or nice warm water from a corner pallet beside each tent, baking in the sun. Like most of the others, I usually opted for the cold ones. After dawn on October 22, 2007, we arrived and were released to our tent assignments, spending the next two days resting and acclimating to the heat and our new time zone. The tents were shared with several men, but I had a great crew so I could not complain. Dust covered everything, both inside and out. My boots, shoes, and anything else that came close to the ground were covered in a fine layer of brown.

Many soldiers complained about their tent assignments or whatever else they could think of to whine about, but it could not be the food, at least not in our first week in the Middle East. We ate like royalty, with an incredible selection of cuisine at every meal. I wondered how any of us, even a skinny guy like me, could leave Kuwait without gaining weight. There were United Service Organization (USO) and morale, welfare, and recreation (MWR) tents, telephone trailers, and Internet centers everywhere. I was able to call Laura on my first day, using a phone and calling card provided by the USO.

Rumors out of Ibn Sina were telling us that the carnage was down considerably in October. Whether it was due to the troop surge punishing Al Qaeda, the time of year, or the lack of people wanting to blow themselves up in the name of Allah, it did not matter; it was a good thing. The *Stars and Stripes* newsletters, printed and distributed daily, had also reported zero American deaths in both Iraq and Afghanistan for two days in a row. Could the surge be working?

It came as no surprise, but when we woke up the day after our arrival to Kuwait, it was still hot and sandy. I was spending a lot of time attempting to catch a glimpse of my first camel spider or desert scorpion. I learned that Iraq and Kuwait, unlike the U.S., had several types of dangerous scorpions. In America, only the bark scorpion has potent venom that can cause significant morbidity, especially in younger children. In Southwest Asia, there were three or four types of scorpions known to have toxic stings. I hoped I would get to see one firsthand at some point, but not too close.

Later in the morning, we did have some excitement. Just as we sat down to enjoy breakfast, the air raid sirens began to wail. When we were trained on this back home, it was obviously a drill and not a big deal, but in a combat zone our attitude was somewhat different. After stuffing our pockets with cereal, we followed proper precautions and procedures and got into position to receive whatever weapon was coming from the sky. The sirens then stopped and an announcement was made, "This is not a drill. Repeat, this is not a drill. There is a suspicious package on post." Other instructions were given, and since the location was not close to us, we decided to go back to enjoying our breakfast of eggs, bacon, cereal, and juice. The sirens kept repeating, but we were not concerned. After eating, we walked out toward our formation area and noticed most of our hospital colleagues crowded in the outdoor concrete bomb shelters. Man, it must have stunk for them as they sat crowded in the stifling heat! Either they did not get the message that there were no explosives en route to our location, or they were just following procedure. I was thankful we were in the dining facility, or DFAC, and did not have to sit in bomb shelters.

Moments later, we were ordered to put on our body armor and combat gear—a great time for a bunch of medical guys who were not used to this. Once again, it made me feel for our soldiers who actually run around in the heat wearing all that stuff. Afterward, when the all-clear was given, we were able to return to our normal routine and attend our training classes for the day.

Concrete barriers, similar to the Jersey barriers used by the highway department to section off roadways and shoulders during construction, were all over Camp Buehring. However, many of the hundreds of these barriers at the camp had a unique feature: they were used as murals for army units to paint, representing their presence at Camp Buehring prior to rolling into the combat of Iraq. Some were painted haphazardly and crudely, with just enough indentifying information to figure which unit did the job. Others were exquisite, with unit crests, commander and first sergeant/sergeant's major names, aircraft, soldiers, tanks, sabers, and more. These murals were unique works of art, displaying the concerns and passions of each soldier who painted there. On my first day, I found one Jersey barricade decorated with an Arkansas state flag along with information on the Thirty-ninth Infantry Brigade of the Arkansas National Guard. Another was painted in the colors of my old unit, the Second Cavalry Regiment, as they staged there prior to heading to Baghdad just a few weeks ahead of us. These murals are just one of the many interesting facets the military uses to demonstrate their unending pride in unit, job, and country.

Similar to the murals painted on the concrete barriers by the brigades, companies, and battalions, the Porta Johns represented another side of the military, but with more of individuality. Chuck Norris jokes covered the inside of the toilets all over post, mostly by people trying to explain why they thought Chuck Norris was tougher than anyone else in the world. It was almost as if the anonymous person who could write a joke about the martial arts master suddenly became as tough as Chuck, at least until he or she was bested by someone with a better joke. On the flip side, I would have been happy without the pornographic drawings and writings. But that is what you get when thousands of twenty-something-year-old warriors have to each explain in their own way why the army is tougher than the Marine Corps, the Marine Corps is tougher than the army, who is the "real" infantry, and why the air force is full of pansies (not my words). With the good came the bad, but I did learn some great Chuck Norris jokes.

In *Stars and Stripes,* we noticed that we had made it another day with zero American deaths in both Operation Iraqi Freedom and Operation Enduring Freedom. I knew we could not get our hopes up, but we could not help but feel good about these three days at least, especially when combining the news with the latest Osama Bin Laden tape asking the insurgents in Iraq to quit working with the Americans and reunite to terrorize the Iraqi people and the world again. He wanted them to continue the jihad, and soon we would see the results.

We awakened the next day to more sand and sunshine. It amazed me how a place so desolate could be so close to Mesopotamia, the Garden of Eden, and the beginning of civilization. It was a barren wasteland, and if there was not oil and gas beneath us or relatively close by, I was not sure why anyone would ever want to be there. It was the hottest day we had seen yet, but still only around 100 degrees Fahrenheit.

We later attended classes regarding IEDs, vehicle-borne explosive devices, and other devastating instruments used by the enemy. The classes were interesting and insightful, and I learned a great deal. It was amazing how the bad guys would strike with a certain type of bomb, we would counteract it, and then both sides would adapt and change tactics as quickly as possible in order to outwit and defeat the other. However, it was equally amazing to see how low these fanatic people were willing to go in order to hurt Americans, Iraqi civilians, or anyone else who stood for freedom. I could go on at length discussing the fiendish methods these people utilized to attack our forces.

Many British soldiers as well moved through Camp Beurhing, and we were briefed about fratricide and the danger of friendly fire. I discovered how many countries still had troops stationed in Iraq as a part of the coalition. There were still some thirty or so nations with soldiers fighting for the freedom and safety of the Iraqi people. Our British instructor pointed out that one of the former Soviet Union eastern bloc countries only had four soldiers in Iraq. We all chuckled, then really laughed and cheered when he reminded us that the four coalition soldiers from this eastern bloc country equaled four times as many as the French.

While sitting through the briefs and presentations, it was easy to become angry at the terrorists. The phrase that continuously came to my mind was "Kill 'em all." Obviously, that is not a good answer, but that was the simple, humanistic, and proud American reflexive answer, at least in my head. What my ER docs and I had to realize was that we would be leading our medics and young nurses, many of whom were sterile to death and disfiguration, into the bowels of destruction. For fifteen months, we would see what devastation the worst of mankind could produce, and we had to keep in mind that we as American soldiers must also treat not only the victims but the culprits as well. They must be treated equally with dignity, compassion, and care. It would be emotionally challenging to deal with the carnage we were about to endure, but we had to be ready, and we had to remain steadfast. We would be the rocks our medics and nurses would rely on, the pillars of strength they were to lean on for explanation. We would be affected by what we were about to endure, but we felt that we must not let it show. There would always be a time to talk about the horrors we planned to deal with daily, but not in front of our teams of medics and nurses. I thought that we as doctors and leaders must find another time for ourselves.

In retrospect, I could not have been more wrong in my thinking. The medics and nurses serving in the EMT with us were our equals, all doing one job as important as another. We leaned on each other, and we quickly became a family.

Our first sergeant, 1st Sgt. Leonard, seemed to be a good leader with his hands full trying to corral all three hundred or so heading to Baghdad, attempting to keep us all in the right place, at the right time, and in the right uniform. He was doing an outstanding job in my opinion, and we were impressed with him. However, inevitably when you collect that many people together, some are going to complain. First Sgt. Leonard was racking in my tent, his bed just across from mine. He would tell my friend Pat Hickey and me each night about some of the officers complaining to him because they were staying in tents with lower ranking officers or enlisted personnel. Others were apparently unhappy about the uniform policies, or upset about their projected room assignments in Baghdad. Therefore, due to many of these stupid complaints, Pat and I took it upon ourselves to make lists of our grudges and give them to 1st Sgt. Leonard, in an effort to keep the mood light:

1) The basketball court should have a dome. It's hot here, and we don't want to get sunburned while playing.
2) Why are Kentucky Fried Chicken and Taco Bell not colocated? It would make it much easier if we could order from the same menu like back home.
3) What about installing moving sidewalks all over camp? It would be much easier than walking.
4) Could we get sherpas—the people who live around Mt. Himalaya and help climbers carry their gear up the mountain—to help us?
5) Could we get rickshaws and drivers to carry us from place to place in a cart?
6) In the dining facility, the Baskin-Robbins advertised having thirty-one flavors, yet only has four. Where are the other twenty-seven for us to choose from? Are we animals here?
7) We should be given our own Sharpies, at the army's expense, to

defend its honor from the Marine Corps in the Porta Johns.

8) Could we get Pergo flooring in the tents instead of the plywood?

We were having a good time coming up with stupid complaints just to give the first sergeant a hard time and to harass those who were actually complaining about senseless issues.

I had a four-year commitment to serve as an emergency physician in the U.S. Army. My military medical residency did not count for time, so my four-year payback began when I graduated medical residency and joined the Second Cavalry Regiment at Fort Polk, Louisiana. My four-year commitment was set to terminate on June 30, 2008, and I had orders to get out of the army as I deployed. However, after the stop-loss implementation order for personnel selected from army hospitals, I anticipated I would be with our unit throughout the fifteen-month deployment. I was not excited about the prospects of an extra nine months of active duty, but several of the soldiers deploying with the CSH were in similar situations.

We had been at Camp Buehring, Kuwait, close to a week, and it still did not seem like such a bad place. I think it was all a matter of attitude, because I began seeing some of my colleagues getting angry and frustrated with the sand, heat, boredom, and the stupid little things that can drive one crazy. As medical professionals, and despite being in the army, we normally did not have to go to formation, have accountability checks, and have the small aspects of our lives structured by demanding noncommissioned officers, or NCOs. However, we were not at the hospital anymore, and we had to fall in with the real army and do things their way. Sometimes that meant getting up at 6:00 AM for formation, being released, and then discovering later that another accountability formation would be called at 8:00 AM, right about the time we would get back to sleep. We were not doing much, just a training item or two each day, leaving most of our day unstructured. We made feeble attempts to get on the Internet and contact our families, sometimes with success, but usually without. We would call home, play games, and watch movies, but mostly we socialized as we bided our time. I was concerned with the frustration shown by some of my friends, as they had a long way to go and many more issues to face before their tour of duty would be completed. Most of us stayed flexible and decided to go with flow. We would be stuck overseas for fifteen months, and I honestly believed our attitudes would make the difference between a tolerable time and misery.

The next day, we were in formation at 3:30 AM with our battle rattle, and loaded up on buses at four to head to the range. We lined up twenty-five across and were given thirty rounds of ammunition to expend in our M16s. We were able to shoot them on burst, with each trigger pull dispensing three rounds rather than the usual one. It was the first time I had been able to fire a weapon on fully automatic. Still, I wanted to fire the fully automatic squad automatic weapon, or SAW, but I did not get the opportunity. While traveling from the range, I saw camels for the first time. They were funny looking creatures; I hoped, at some point, to get a better look so I could take some pictures. I was able to take a quick photograph of a herd of what I *think* were sheep and one of their shepherds and his donkey sitting nearby. I am not sure what they were doing, as there was no grass, water, or shade within miles, but who knows.

I think the two most specific things I remember about Camp Buehring are the generators and the Porta Johns. The generators ran twenty-four hours a day, seven days a week. They produced emissions that reminded me of their constant presence each time I walked nearby. Their noise could be noticed anywhere, but the whine of the generators all night lulled me to sleep. I was afraid I would not be able to rest once I got to Baghdad without the white noise produced from these massive machines.

The Porta Johns, while usually pretty clean and respectable, smelled terrible. Not surprising, but any time I walked downwind of one of the pods of six toilets, the smell would just about knock me down. Of course, we all laughed about it and said it "cleansed our palate and opened our sinuses" anytime we would find ourselves nearby. What else could we say?

One of my goals for deployment was to play basketball frequently, like I did prior to entering medical school. I was never a star player by any stretch of the imagination, but usually I could out-hustle and out-rebound my opponents and frustrate them. I enjoyed playing intramural basketball in college, in church, and in city leagues. But that was twelve years and a few pounds prior. One night at Camp Beurhing, I stepped onto the court with five young enlisted guys, rolled up my sleeves, and tried to show some confidence, remembering that if I was intimidated at the start I had already lost.

Sometimes when playing basketball, you are on and sometimes you are not. This night, I was on. It was awesome. I could not miss a shot, even if I tried. I was getting most of the rebounds, scoring most of the points, and even making crazy behind-the-head passes. My team dominated each game, even when I was matched up with guys who were telling me how good they were a couple of years ago in high school or college. I even overheard them calling me "White Jordan" and saying "that little guy can ball." What a confidence builder to assist me with my new goal! I told Pat Hickey about it, and he said I was at the top; I was now ready to go to Baghdad and should not play ball in Kuwait again as it could only go downhill! I agreed, as I was confident that the next time I played with these guys I would likely get dunked on and injured. I knew I would never get that lucky again, so I had to throw just one last shot their way by telling them I was a trauma doc at Ibn Sina. I am sure that rubbed salt in their wounds, getting thumped by an officer ten years their elder!

The following day, the majority of us received our second or third anthrax immunizations and then went to a slide show put on by 1st Sgt. Leonard about the time he spent at Ibn Sina two years prior on his previous deployment. These were the usual pictures of mutilated bodies, many barely hanging on to life in the EMT. He offered the slide show for everyone, regardless of rank. It was a good idea, although he did not seem to get much reaction. I was sitting with a group of fellow officers, and no one was willing to admit the anxiousness we all felt about the upcoming trauma. First Sgt. Leonard spoke about his concerns, not for those who would break down and have issues while we were downrange but rather for those who "do great" the entire deployment and then return to the U.S. only to have their lives fall apart three to six months later. I was concerned I might be in that group, as I felt I could not afford to show any of my subordinates that the carnage was getting to me. I felt that they *must* know I was solid and ready, no matter the event. Who knew? Maybe it would not be an issue at all. I was learning from observation of the others around me how important attitude was; I noticed when talking to certain people how the conversation would seem to turn to negativity and discontentment each time. These people would be there fifteen months, just like me. I was determined to make my fifteen months and the time of those around me positive rather than negative.

Pat Hickey and I eventually decided to start taking pictures of the Chuck Norris jokes in the Porta Johns. We told the first sergeant that we would be "the official Eighty-sixth CSH historians" and began documenting our adventure. Some of the quotes I photographed for the records are below:

1) Chuck Norris' wife asked him, "How much wood could a wood-chuck chuck if a woodchuck could chuck wood?" so he roundhouse kicked her in the face.
2) Superman sleeps in Chuck Norris pajamas.
3) Chuck Norris is so fast he ran around the world and dropped-kicked himself in the back of the head.
4) When Chuck Norris crosses the street, the cars look both ways.
5) Chuck Norris lost his virginity before his dad did.
6) Chuck Norris can slam revolving doors.
7) Chuck Norris went to Burger King, ordered a Big Mac and got it.
8) Chuck Norris built the log cabin he was born in.
9) Chuck Norris turns water into wine by kicking the piss out of AA members.

Two days before we headed over the berm into Iraq, we had a phenomenal day of training for our mission. The officers and noncommissioned officers in charge of all the sections attended a class on IEDs and counter-sniper training. It was informative and extremely interesting. We learned many techniques the bad guys utilized to try to kill coalition soldiers, as well as several ways to detect, prevent, or counteract them. Some were very simple, and others were complex. The sniper training was multifaceted as a recently retired army sniper, with many kills to his credit in the Iraq War, briefed us with his techniques to avoid becoming a victim of an enemy sniper's rifle.

We also learned how we as medical personnel could help prevent future attacks by watching injury patterns and other aspects of insurgent attacks. The class was a real eye opener, and I discovered an additional role in the war to play that I did not realize.

They educated us about many of the region's complicated issues, including the role of Iran and the country's quest to influence Iraq and have a real stake in the embattled country. The situations we discussed related back to the Byzantine, Ottoman, Persian, and Assyrian empires and still influence the events occurring in the region today. Many of the differences are based on what occurred in the book of Genesis when Abraham took his son Isaac to the mountain to sacrifice him. We all know that God provided a ram to be sacrificed instead and that the nation of Israel was born from Isaac. A fundamental aspect of the Islamic religion is the belief that Abraham's son Ishmael was the one who was almost sacrificed rather than Isaac.

At that time, many of the instructors felt that we were beginning to turn the corner in Iraq. Attacks on both coalition and Iraqi forces had decreased over the two months prior to our deployment. Vehicle-borne IEDs, or VBIEDS, were not working well against our troops, so the insurgents had begun resorting to attacking civilians and Iraqi forces almost exclusively with those devices of terror, attempting to derail the progress of the surge. The types of weapon systems that had been successful against our troops in the past were now being counteracted and defeated at an amazing rate. However, due to these accomplishments, the terrorists were resorting to more and more inhumane attacks, such as using people with Down's Syndrome as suicide bombers with remote detonation devices. They also would kill and decapitate men, and then plant bombs in the abdomens of the corpses to kill those who came to care for the bodies. I question to this day, "Do these people have no soul? No remorse?" They obviously placed a much lower value on human life than we in the Western world, and the results of their misguided thinking are catastrophic.

Later in the afternoon, we climbed into a Humvee rollover trainer and were rolled over upside down and practiced escaping. Of course, being more adventurous than those around me, I requested to go in the last group, as they were rolled over with the lights off in the room versus the earlier groups. All the other groups rolled once, but they flipped our vehicle over five times! It was fun, and we all escaped to the instructor's delight. I was thrown around quite a bit, as the others did not hold me down in the gunner's hatch like they were instructed. I guess it made it more eventful for me, but it was essentially everyone for themselves so I could not complain.

We then relaxed and played volleyball with the medics. It was the best day of training I had since I left my loving family. I heard from my wife Laura that our smaller dog, Emmee Lou, was following her around and missing me quite a bit. It was obvious because she used to always ignore Laura and only pay attention to me. Laura also sent me a funny picture of Avery and Houston on the couch, both looking at the camera. I loved it and laughed each time I glanced at it as the background on my laptop. I had one day left to pack my gear at Camp Buehring and over the berm we would go.

———

While the officers and senior enlisted began to pack our stuff and prepare to travel, most of our medics went to guard duty training. They participated in a live-fire, multiple-scenario range where they engaged and reacted to different situations they would face while pulling guard duty. Many of the guards at Ibn Sina Hospital were foreign nationals working for security contractors, and our own intrinsic medics would reinforce them. I hated the thought of losing some of our crew to guard duty as it would make the tour more painful for our medics, but it was a chore that obviously had to be done and should be shared by the entire hospital, including our EMT.

Our guys did a fantastic job painting our mural at Camp Buerhing. It looked great and will serve as a proud marker of our tour for years to come. During this last full day in Kuwait, October 31, 2007, I relaxed and reviewed trauma procedures and policies for the hospital, as I felt it would not be long before my hands were bloody. My colleagues and I were ready to do our part to save lives and make a difference in the war. It did not take long for us to get our chance.

That night, the USO at Camp Buehring held a Halloween party with games including football toss, darts, water bottle fights, and others. They also served treats and showed scary movies outside on the wall of the steel building. They gave points for each event and had a prize table available where you could trade in your points for treats. Utilizing the football toss and the darts, I was able to obtain thirty-one points and got a nice T-shirt out of the deal.

I had never thought twice about the USO until I arrived in Kuwait. They provided Internet, phone cards, movies, books, video games, cell phones to call home, and many other items of entertainment for us during our stay at Camp Buehring, all free of charge. The USO was a bright spot for many of us in the middle of the Kuwaiti desert. The USO also brought celebrities to the Middle East for concerts and interaction with the troops. I had always noticed the USO in airports everywhere I have flown, but I never thought twice about talking to them. My attitude on that changed tremendously during those ten days.

Our senior NCO in the EMT, Sgt. 1st Class Lamneck, was taken from us and relegated to stay behind in Kuwait for a few months at Camp Buehring as a liaison. What a terrible job! He was replaced by Sfc. Richard (pronounced Reechard), a Cajun raised in South Louisiana. His accent and dialect revealed his place of origin upon his first words to us. He seemed to be a good leader, and although I was concerned that he had little ER experience, his primary job in the EMT would be as an administrator and organizer of our fifteen medics.

Later that night, I was informed that our second most senior medic, S.Sgt. Longnecker, would be taken away from us as well. What were they doing to us? He had a year of deployment under his belt, and we had planned to tap into that. Now we had exactly one medic and two nurses with any trauma experience. Our "green" EMT became a lot "greener" the night before we were to head into north.

I spoke with Lt. Col. Sue Raymond about these issues and let her know I was not comfortable with the decision to pull our NCOs. Once we had arrived in Baghdad, I planned to take my concerns up the chain of command. She seemed to appreciate my concerns, but I doubted it at the time. She had a background in the ICU, and for whatever reason, the ICU and ER staffs back home usually did not see eye to eye. I also spoke with her about my plan to expand the role of our nurses in the EMT by allowing them to intubate patients, perform chest tubes, and suture lacerations, with our supervision of course, freeing up the one ER physician on duty and allowing them to keep up with the patient load. She did not feel that was part of a nurse's job description. While I agreed with her in principle, I pointed out that many of our nurses wanted to be flight nurses and they must be skilled in airway management. Our nurses were also young, they wanted to learn just like our medics, and this would be the time to teach them. Time would tell on the issue, and in time I was eventually crushed on it by our command. It was the first of many disagreements I would have with them over the next fifteen months.

Our CSH was loaded with lieutenant colonel nurses! We were pretty sure at the time that the command had created administrative jobs for them, because their rank essentially precluded them from patient care. That sounds crazy, but that is typical for the Army Nurse Corps. I could not figure out what they would be doing, but as long as they did not get in our way in the EMT, it was no concern of mine. Later, I would even have more than one of them tell me they did not really have a job throughout our tour and had no idea as to why they were even there.

With our bags packed, we planned to travel to an air base in Kuwait, load onto C-130s with all of our gear, and fly into Baghdad International Airport, or BIAP. From there we planned to carry our gear to a helicopter and then be transported into the International Zone, or Green Zone, later that night. I was advised not to sit over the wheel wells on a C-130 as there would be no room, but I likely would have to file in line with everyone else and see where I ended up. I was lucky on the flight to Kuwait to get some room to myself, so I felt I could not complain if I did not have a great ride into Baghdad. I heard we would do a "combat landing" into BIAP, where we would circle down quickly and drop out of the sky. Word was also that there were no windows and the air would not be great in the back of a C-130. We might even get barf bags, and several people would likely puke. I made a special trip to the PX and bought some Dramamine to help out. Who needed Six Flags theme park when I had the U.S. Air Force?

I said good-bye to Camp Buehring. It was an experience, and I would remember the snoring tent mates, air raid sirens, heat, sand, Chuck Norris jokes, and the constant smell of the human refuse. But it was time to move on to our future rendezvous with destiny in the war zone, and while I did not feel our team's skill level was up to par with our mission, we would rely on our attitude and work ethic to make up the difference.

It was Thursday, and that meant Laura received flowers that day. She was doing great, and that made my job infinitely easier. I still was laughing out loud at the picture she sent me of Avery sitting beside my dog Houston, with it warming my heart every day.

———

Finally, on November 1, our day arrived. We began to mentally prepare ourselves to move from the safety of Kuwait into the perils of Baghdad, the most dangerous city in the world. If only it would have been that easy! We were organized into new platoons, and the mood became much more serious. While those of us in the EMT kept joking around and trying to keep the mood light, our platoon sergeant and new platoon leader were very uptight about our upcoming movement across the border into Iraq. Our platoon was the first to go, and we were to be flown into Iraq as the initial chalk of the Eighty-sixth CSH. Once our trucks and busses arrived, we donned our body armor, helmets, and other gear and began loading. With all fifty-six of us having at least one rucksack, one large duffel bag, and a carry-on, it took a while for us to finish the loading job. I was happy just to be doing something, as the past four weeks of having to be away from my family, only to find myself sitting around all day and night, were getting old! I helped load the truck with the rest of the crew, and once that chore was completed, my first thought was to find the Porta John prior to hopping on one of the busses. However, it was too late for that, as we were put into yet another formation, given one loaded magazine for our M16s each, and crammed onto the busses with our gear. Needless to say, with everyone carrying an extra forty to fifty pounds of body armor, backpacks, and other items, we did not fit into the buses well, but fit we did. We were taken to an air base in Kuwait and placed into another tent, apparently because the air force decided that we had not waited long enough yet.

Just after arriving in the newest holding tent, they asked for twenty volunteers to help load the bags onto pallets to prepare them for the flight. Not wanting to sit and wait, I jumped at the chance and loaded another bus to be taken to our luggage. We rode in a large circle, only to arrive one hundred yards from where we were sitting in the tent! I think I could have walked that far, but I guess the air force rides wherever it goes instead than walking. I had always heard their physical fitness tests were much easier than ours after all! Four of us jumped into the back of the large cargo truck and began unloading the bags, while the rest stood to receive and load the pallets.

I soon grabbed the rucksack of Lt. Col. Kim, our internal medicine physician. By this point, she was one of our favorite people, as she did not exactly want to pull her load much of the time it seemed. She was not on our flight and was to go later, meaning the poor soul she forced to carry her gear back at Camp Buehring must had placed it in the wrong pile. I later discovered she was told her bags were to be placed in a different group, but she demanded they be placed in with ours. When I discovered the bags at the air base, I received several suggestions to put her gear in the pile heading to Mosul rather than Baghdad so she would not receive it. Others wanted me to push it aside and then call the bomb squad and call it a suspicious package. We all would have enjoyed watching the ordinance guys blow her rucksack up, but we knew the right thing to do was to forgive her laziness and load the equipment on the pallets for her, so load it we did.

Once the pallets were loaded, I was given a wonderful compliment. A young enlisted specialist, called an E-4, in his early twenties, approached me and said he had never seen a major work like that, helping move baggage or volunteering for physical work. Most labor details in the army consist of the lower enlisted doing the majority of the lifting. That meant a lot to me, as I have always attempted to demonstrate that I am not some stuck-up doctor who is holier than thou. It actually reminded me of my days in the cavalry regiment when I got along better with most of the infantry and cavalry officers than I did many of the physicians at the hospital. I guess it means that being a physician is what I do, but not who I am. The compliment from the specialist really made my day.

We next returned to the tent and waited to be called to the flight line. After about forty-five minutes and a quick meal ready to eat, or MRE, a guy entered our tent, barked some instructions, and called my name first. I went to the first bus and loaded, followed by the rest of the group. We then drove about twenty minutes to the airfield. In the darkness of the desert nighttime, it was difficult to figure out where we were going, but there were air force planes all around us. Once the driver located the plane he wanted, he stopped the busses and we began to dismount.

The pilot and first officer of the C-130 were both sitting and relaxing on the lowered tail ramp of the plane, so our operations officer Cpt. Depalma, Jason Cohen, and I went to talk to them. They told us the plane was broken and was under a quick repair. They were based out of Germany and seemed like good guys who enjoyed their jobs. They told us we would be ready to fly soon, and we would not be waiting much longer.

Soon afterward, we began to walk up the cargo ramp into the bowels of the C-130. Jason Cohen and I worked our way to the front to avoid sitting over the wheel wells. The cargo bay was split lengthways down the center, with two sets of cargo netting seats facing each other, one set of seats on the left and one on the right. We all crammed in, and despite not being on the wheel wells, we found our legs were interlocked with the person across from us, as there was about a foot and a half of space between the seats. With our body armor, it was tough to locate the seat belts, but we did eventually. We next watched our luggage pallets being loaded behind us into the cargo bay by forklift. After twenty or so long, hot minutes in the stifling cargo area, the pilot began cranking up the four large prop engines, one at a time, and the plane began to lumber across the tarmac. Air began to flow in the cargo bay, and I then decided that despite not being able to move my legs, turn my head from side to side, or relieve the back pain I seemed to get when wearing body armor, I at least would not die of heatstroke that night.

Flying on a C-130 is not as glamorous as Hollywood seems to portray it. I cannot recall how many movies I have watched with ten or so soldiers spread out all over the cargo area, relaxing on their flight. Not so in the real world! As I mentioned, there are fifty-six seats and usually fifty-six passengers. Our big joke was suggesting that, for everyone to fit, each person had to put their right leg behind their head, and then take the knee of the person across from them in their crotch for everyone to fit on board. It was definitely not as sexy as I had seen in the movies!

The flight lasted a long hour and a half. During the flight, Jason and I could not help but notice the young air force crewman, as he could not have been older than twenty-five years old, sitting in his jump seat behind us. While several high-ranking army officers and NCOs were crammed into his plane, he was kicked back in his lounge seat reading a magazine. That was a major part of his job during his four-month air force deployment. Once again, we agreed that we should have joined the air force! I had taken Dramamine at the beginning of the flight to counteract any motion sickness from the combat landing, and it must have worked because I had no issues. We swerved, dropped, ducked, and dove down onto the runway at the Baghdad International Airport, arriving around 10 PM. We were dying to get off the plane, but we had to wait for the forklifts to unload the luggage pallets first. Eventually the pallets were moved, and we began filing off into the Baghdad night.

Baghdad International Airport was a surreal experience. Quickly we were led off of the plane, with all four engines still running, as another fifty-six soldiers from some other unit were waiting to board immediately. They were likely heading home, and the air force was in a rush to get them there. We were led in single file, zigzagging at right angles across the flight line, with helicopters taxiing all around. The black night combined with the aircraft lights and deafening noises all around us made this busy scene an unbelievable experience. We were now in a combat zone, and the speed of operations and attitude of movement proved it to any doubters. We lumbered past the thunderous Blackhawk and Chinook helicopters, passing many more soldiers preparing to fly, and were escorted into a small meeting room. Everything was hurried. I felt as if my bladder was about to explode, but there was no time to go.

Our ID cards were collected, and we were rapidly pushed outside to a staging area with our bags and about two hundred other soldiers between us and two Chinook helicopters that had just landed. Continuing to power their large dual rotors, the Chinooks made it difficult for any of us to hear anything above their thunder. A crew chief came over and instructed us to grab one bag off the pallet and load the birds. He kept yelling, "Quickly, quickly, let's go!" My first thought was to wonder if he knew everyone had three bags; taking one and loading the birds obviously would not get the job done. I grabbed two large bags and followed the person in front of me. I could not see well in the darkness, and I could not hear myself think due to the rotor noise, so I relied on hand signals as my group piled up the cargo ramps of the massive transport helicopters. We loaded down each side, careful not to hit the large-caliber machine gun hanging off the back. Once on board, we passed our bags down the center toward the front until they all were loaded, and then we sat down and waited to lift back into the sky. Our entire BIAP experience did not last more than thirty minutes as we were expedited in and out in a hurry.

The crew chief then loaded onto the back of the Chinook and brought the ramp up about 30 degrees to a horizontal position, strapping himself in. He manned the machine gun mounted in the back of the bird, and we lifted off into the night sky. The second Chinook of our tandem flew behind us, and its blacked-out silhouette against the moonlit sky was a remarkable sight that would have made an amazing picture. To prevent being shot out of the sky in hostile territory, aircraft are blacked out, flying with no lights. I thought about getting my camera out for the picture, but realized that I could not risk the flash going off. Army aircraft fly at night with no lights for safety and to assist the pilot's night vision devices, and I was sure a camera flash would not be a great idea.

The flight lasted about ten minutes, and we landed in the middle of the Crossed Sabers, Saddam Hussein's old parade ground that has been broadcast throughout the world. I thought it was funny. It was the ultimate way to show up Saddam by turning his prize military parade ground into a landing zone for U.S. helicopters. We dragged our bags across the length of the monument and loaded busses that transported us to what would be our new home for the next fifteen months, Ibn Sina Hospital.

Into the Combat Zone

November 2, 2007

We spent our first night unloading our gear and moving into our new rooms. Jason and I met the next morning for breakfast and quickly ran into Maj. Rob Hennessy, an ER doc from the Third Infantry Division rotating through Baghdad ER to keep his trauma skills current every four to six weeks. He was a residency-trained ER doc serving as a flight surgeon at Camp Victory, part of the BIAP complex. His aid station was apparently overloaded with providers, as they only cared for a few patients each day. He told us they had a total of sixteen physicians and physician assistants working there, with four of them being emergency trained guys. He and a couple of the emergency medicine–trained guys would come to Baghdad ER regularly throughout their tours to try to get back into the world they had trained seven years for, the world of emergency medicine. When they arrived to help, it also provided much-needed relief for the guys currently working in the ER, and I looked forward to that.

Rob gave Jason and I a quick tour of the hospital's footprint, also called our forward operating base, or FOB. He then escorted us across the street to another FOB, where we had our IDs checked before being allowed to enter. We crossed through the main door between fifteen-foot-high t-barriers that consisted of reinforced concrete approximately two to three feet thick with razor wire on top. These barriers lined every roadway and stretched in every direction. It was an amazing sight as every building in this area of Baghdad was walled off from the street to prevent unauthorized access and to keep potential car bombs a safe distance away.

This FOB was called the GRD Compound, and Rob pointed out the gym and a few other features, and then escorted us through a different exit onto another street. Immediately after stepping outside the protection of the blast walls and onto the sidewalk, Jason and I received another reminder that we were in a combat zone. At one end of the street we heard a sharp, quick, piercing siren coming from a full-sized Chevy pickup, likely a 2500 series three-quarter ton. The truck flew down the street toward us as people scattered from the road, running for safety. Security guards standing at the entrances to several nearby FOBs stepped back to be sure to give the vehicle a wide birth. The windows were tinted very dark, which was surely illegal in the United States. In the back of the truck stood four Iraqi Army soldiers with large-caliber machine guns in hand and bandoleers of bullets hanging across their chests. Weapons pointed in every direction, and these guys looked ready for action. Some had facemasks on to conceal their identity, while others did not. Their red berets contrasted against their solid green uniforms, giving us our first glimpse of the Iraqi Army.

The truck was followed by two more, then two Iraqi Humvees flew past us with gunners in the turrets. The Rhino systems on the Humvees were engaged to prevent against an explosively formed penetrator, or EFP, and they looked incredibly menacing to someone standing on the sidewalk. After the Humvees passed, three jet-black Chevy Suburbans with small red and blue flashing lights and mirrored dark windows sped by, followed by two more up-armored Humvees and then three more Chevy pickups filled with heavily armed soldiers.

The street cleared as the high-speed convoy approached, and Jason and

I were both startled. I had seen movies growing up where war-torn veterans were not fazed by anything, while rookie soldiers such as myself were scared to death as the bullets began to fly, and that was how Jason and I felt. Rob Hennessey had been in Iraq seven months by that time. He barely even looked up at the convoy, while Jason and I were honestly thinking, "Are these guys going to shoot us? Surely not." But who could we trust in this environment? As fast as the vehicles approached, they were gone, and things were back to "normal" with the foreign national security guards holding their AK-47 or M4 rifles all around us. It was an interesting introduction to the streets around our new home.

The rest of the day we toured the area and became familiar with our FOB. We also became familiar with our dining facility, since that would be our kitchen for the next fifteen months. The rest of our hospital was to show up that night, twenty-four hours after our chalk as they had been stranded at BIAP and left to sleep all day on the concrete while waiting for a ride to the hospital in the International Zone. It made us feel lucky to have been able to get from BIAP to the International Zone so easily! The bags for the rest of our remaining chalks arrived several hours before they did, so we sorted through the gear and pulled out the EMT personnel's stuff to make their arrival a bit smoother.

We then went to the chapel, where several of the physicians present since July were participating in their weekly Friday night movie night. The movie for the night was *Battlestar Gallactica*. It was a good chance for me to get to meet some of the other docs I would be working with. I still could not figure out why all of these guys only had to do six-month rotations, as there were pathologists, radiologists, surgeons, OB/GYNs and several others. But complaining would provide no relief; I planned to drive on with the fifteen-month mission I had been given and that was all there was to it.

The next day, I reported early for my first shift in the Baghdad ER. I was to shadow Dr. Steve Taylor, another emergency medicine physician who had been at Ibn Sina the past fifteen months. He called himself the "old man" of the CSH since most of the physicians he worked with came and left during his tenure. The pace had been very slow over the past few months, likely due to the troop surge and Sunni Awakening movement among other factors. Most of the crew from the Twenty-eighth CSH stated that several months prior, Muqtada al Sadr, an outspoken anti-American Shiite cleric, declared a cease-fire for his Mahdi Militia, as many of his fighters had broken off into splinter groups and began doing their own operations. He informed the coalition led by the Americans that his group would not attack our forces for six months as the Mahdi Militia attempted to reorganize.

The mortar-fire had also decreased, as the hospital had not been hit by indirect fire in several months. Earlier in the summer, a nurse was killed by a mortar that landed close to her while she was crossing the street. The cease-fire was set to expire on the December 14, 2007, so we figured we did not have long to wait to discover if it truly had an effect on patient census.

When I arrived in the ER, Dr. Toi Stubbs was just finishing the night shift when an Iraqi man was flown in with a mortar wound to his left leg, causing his knee to be dislocated posteriorly, or toward the back. The patient's pulses were intact, and the knee was relocated by Dr. Stubbs just before he was taken to the operating room for a surgical repair of his leg. It was the first trauma I had witnessed in Baghdad ER, but it would not be my last of the day.

An hour or so later, we received report that an American soldier with a double amputation was coming in by Blackhawk. Dr. Taylor was now on duty, and he was to care for her as I would observe the trauma to see their team in action. When the patient arrived, much to our surprise we discovered a young female with burns to her face and soot seemingly seeping from her nose. She was able to speak clearly, despite the burns and the racket created by the nonrebreathing oxygen mask placed on her face by the flight medics. She felt she had trouble swallowing, meaning to me she would need to be intubated emergently in the ER and placed on a ventilator to protect her airway from internal swelling. However, these burns were the least of her worries.

She had tourniquets on each arm above the elbow, with nothing left below on either side, except for a long forearm bone, the radius, on the left, sticking out about ten inches with no tissue or muscle around it. What was left of her left forearm, with only the bone remaining, looked like the skeletons we had just seen days before at the Halloween carnival in Kuwait. The bandages placed by the prehospital medics were unwrapped, and she did not have extensive bleeding from either extremity. Her wounds were rebandaged by Dr. Taylor's team, and her resuscitation continued. Dr. Taylor placed a large IV, referred to as a central line, into her right groin, and a "code red" consisting of four units of red blood cells and two units of plasma were given through a Belmont rapid infuser. These infusers could pump blood in faster than the nurses and medics could spike and hang the new bags, with all six units going in within six minutes. Multiple surgeons arrived on the scene from other parts of the hospital, and she was rushed to the CT scanner to evaluate for other injuries. She was then transported to the operating room to complete her amputations. As she was wheeled out of the trauma room, several of us saw her wedding ring laying on the gurney, placed just beside her head. I prayed for that poor girl, her husband, and her family several times that day. She is a hero, and unfortunately she will have the scars to prove it for the rest of her life.

Soon thereafter, a middle-aged Iraqi man with three gunshot wounds to his abdomen arrived with a heart rate of 160 beats per minute and a blood pressure in the eighties, very abnormal vital signs for an adult. These represented significant injury due to loss of blood. I ran this trauma—the first of several hundred major resuscitations I would lead over the next fifteen months—as we checked him over and stabilized him. His heart rate decreased mildly with pain medication, and at that time we discovered his rapid rate was from more than simple blood loss, but rather an irregular heart rhythm called atrial fibrillation. We presumed this was also the cause of his low blood pressure. My usual course of action for patients with uncontrolled atrial fibrillation is to give a medication called diltiazim to slow the rate. However, we could not give this as his low blood pressure would get even lower. Giving him blood, we sent him off to the CT scanner and away to the operating room for exploratory surgery of his abdomen. Better heart rate control could be implemented once we knew he was not bleeding internally.

Later, several Iraqi men in suits and ties came into the ER, escorted by Col. Rowe and his counterpart from the Twenty-eighth CSH. The gentlemen walked by me, and I knew they were VIPs, but I did not know whom. I then glanced into one of our exam rooms and saw the patient. He looked familiar to me from television, and as he left, it dawned on me that he was the current prime minister of Iraq, Al-Malaki. It would be my first of many meetings with diplomats and generals during my time there.

Throughout my first shift, I cared for patients with lacerations, hand infections, broken ankles, a high-speed rollover motor vehicle accident with a fractured pelvis, and many more. It was a slow shift by the Twenty-eighth CSH standards, but it was plenty fast for me. I was amazed at the speed and gracefulness of the trauma team from the Twenty-eighth CSH. I could only hope that our crew would become that high speed, and basing our upcoming experience on my first shift, I expected over the next few months we would get our chance.

At the end of the shift, several of us went to the rooftop of the hospital to smoke cigars and reflect on our first day. We arrived on the rooftop around 8:00 PM, and throughout the night, all we could hear was the constant whoop-whoop-whoop of helicopters racing throughout the dark sky over Baghdad. We witnessed several flares fired by American artillery to our south as they turned darkness into daylight. Once again, it sank in to all of us we were in a combat zone, and this would be our new home for the next fifteen months. What a surreal experience it was to sit, relaxed on top of a building, with combat missions ongoing all around us. It was the first of many cigar nights we would have at Ibn Sina, and we anticipated that these respites would prove to be a great place to talk the stresses of our day away and dwell on thoughts other than the American hero who will never be able to wear her wedding ring again.

We worked alongside our counterparts from the Twenty-eighth CSH as they prepared to hand operations to us for about seven days. While we had several penetrating traumas from gun shot wounds, mortar blasts, and bomb explosions during our first two days, our third day consisted mainly of blunt trauma. We had multiple patients with femur fractures that required surgical repair. Most of the injuries were sustained from motor vehicle crashes, but one resulted from a large shipping container falling and landing on an American contractor, snapping his leg above the knee.

I also had a pleasant, nineteen-year-old Arabic-speaking Indonesian female take a two- or three-story tumble off the roof of her apartment building. Serving in Iraq as a contractor, she was knocked unconscious for thirty minutes before being discovered by an Iraqi police officer without a scratch on her! She was admitted to the hospital and watched overnight, but no injuries were discovered. I would say God was watching over her for sure, as she escaped a thirty-foot-plus fall uninjured.

Later that day, I had a suspected insurgent transferred to our facility in cardiogenic shock, a condition usually caused by a heart attack. The heart fails to squeeze properly, and patients suffer essentially from a lack of blood flow to the body. This man was very ill, with blood pressures in the seventies, and we started him on drips of vasoconstrictors designed to help his heart function and improve the "squeeze," keeping the blood flow to his brain intact. He was admitted by our cardiologist, but his prognosis was very poor, and he passed away rather quickly. I guess it is good he did not get the chance to kill any more Americans or Iraqi civilians, but we still did everything we could to keep him alive, a pattern that would repeat itself often when dealing with the bad guys.

The next shift was much slower. I cared for three patients, with only one of them being "sick." He was a high-ranking Iraqi Army officer with a history of a three-vessel heart bypass two months previously; his chest pain returned and prompted him to come see us. I was able to relieve his pain with medication, and he was sent to our ICU for further care. However, that was not the most interesting part of his visit.

One of the most fascinating aspects of his care were the words spoken to me when I told him what we would do to help him. When I said that we would take his pain away, he took my arm and said, "I trust you" in broken

English. That was the last thing I expected to hear from this former high-ranking Iraqi officer, as I *never* hear those words in the United States. Back home, when a patient comes into the emergency department, it generally implies they trust us and will allow us to care for them. However, overseas, local Iraqis, even some high-ranking officers, are either informed that they cannot trust us or simply do not want to believe they can. What a powerful and meaningful phrase this man said to me!

After my shift, I went outside and sat in one of the John Deere Gators that our medics used to transport patients from helicopters on our landing zone. Afterward, I walked out to the street to see a couple of soldiers lazily tossing a ball back and forth, only to hear the loud siren of the CRAM indirect fire attack system squealing overhead, indicating that mortars or rockets were coming our direction within seconds. Immediately, the guys from the Twenty-eighth CSH disappeared and scrambled to safety, knowing all to well from the past fifteen months what those sirens represented. I ran into a concrete blast bunker and waited to hear and feel the impact from the mortars landing somewhere around us, but no blasts found their way to me. Evidently it was a false alarm, so no harm, no foul, I guess. But observing the reaction of those Twenty-eighth CSH soldiers reminded me that things could change in a moment's notice.

I also noted that the Twenty-eighth had learned to have fun as well. Frequently, when patients had minor shrapnel wounds that did not require a trip to the operating room for repair, they would wash out the wounds in the ER prior to discharging them. These procedures could be very painful, and since the patients were awake and alert, they had to be given a sedating medicine to keep the procedure from hurting too much. Ketamine, a derivative of the street drug PCP, is a favorite emergency medicine sedating agent for children in the U.S., and its use worldwide in both adults and children is very common. It dissociates the patient from their pain and senses, and it allows the medical personnel to perform painful procedures without the patient feeling or remembering it.

Ketamine also causes a real "trip" as well, and patients say all kinds of crazy things when it has been administered. About midway into their tour, the Twenty-eighth CSH began to take advantage of this aspect of the drug, with their medics creating a life-sized purple alligator costume. They would occasionally nonchalantly walk by a patient who was high on ketamine. If the patient began commenting and "hallucinating" about seeing a purple life-sized alligator standing on its feet, the others would just deny it as the alligator came closer to the bedside, sometimes even talking to the patient. Apparently, they got some pretty good laughs out of it, and once the patients came off their trips, they laughed about it as well. I was sure it was pretty funny, and I looked forward to discovering what kind of crazy things we would do at two in the morning when the command was not around!

About four days after we began working side by side with the Twenty-eighth CSH, they took a step back, and our medics, nurses, and physicians assumed control of the EMT. Like gladiators entering the arena, we boldly stepped in, not knowing what fate awaited us. Would we be up to the task? Would we even be tested that day, while the Twenty-eighth guys sat back and said nothing? We discovered the answers to those questions early.

We received a call from our tactical operations center, or TOC, that we had an unstable patient with a serious head injury on his way into our EMT; he was about ten minutes away by air. Assembling our team of nurses and medics, we set up the trauma room, preparing for our first serious casualty of the tour that would be our own. Soon enough, a thin Arabic man arrived with a breathing mask with high-flow oxygen and a blood-soaked bandage wrapped around his forehead.

We transferred him to our gurney in bed one of the trauma room and the team quickly began attaching monitor leads and cutting off clothes to expose the patient and assess his injuries. The medic on the left side placed the patient on the monitor in quick form, while the medic on the right arm had difficulty establishing an intravenous line and was replaced by a nurse with more experience. The patient had a Glascow Coma Scale rating of seven, unfortunately meaning that the gunshot wound he had received to his right eye was devastating and his brain function most likely would not be recoverable utilizing the Iraqi health care system. The entire right side of his face and forehead were one mangled mesh of meat and bone, with no eye anywhere to be found. After having no luck on the intravenous line, we quickly placed an intraosseous line into the tibia, or shinbone of his right lower leg, and gave him sedation and paralytic medications in order for me to place an endotracheal tube down his throat and help him breathe.

After I intubated the patient, his heart quit beating and he lost his pulse. We performed cardiopulmonary resuscitation with chest compressions and specific drugs to restart his heart. We got him back, and pushed him over to the computed tomography scanner, or CT, to evaluate his head trauma. The CT scan demonstrated that he had bone fragments blown into his brain, excessive swelling and bleeding in his skull, and a copious amount of air around his brain. A quick call to the army neurosurgeon at the Balad air force hospital confirmed our initial thoughts. His wounds were nonoperable and there was nothing we could do would save him.

After a talk with our medics and nurses explaining the situation, I ordered the withdrawal of the ventilator support and asked for sedation and pain medications to help ensure he would not suffer. There was no way to tell if he ever felt anything throughout his resuscitation, but we did not want him to suffer any more than he already had.

We placed him in the specialty room, the one reserved for VIPs, OB/GYN care, and our dying or dead patients. At that moment, one of the Twenty-eighth CSH nurses who was sitting back and observing our team said something I will never forget. The nurse walked up to the patient and observed his wounds, then said, "Rot in hell, motherf**ker." At first I was taken aback, wondering to myself, "How could he feel that way or say such a thing?" I guess that after fifteen months of treating young girls who had been tortured with gasoline poured on them and then set ablaze … after seeing patients who have had their eyelids and tongues cut out … after witnessing American soldier after American soldier die at the hands of men just like this, I could see myself at least thinking the same thing if not verbalizing it by the time *my* fifteen months were completed.

The patient had been shot in the face by American forces as he was firing rocket-propelled grenades, or RPGs, at American helicopters. He was either trying to kill or had already killed some of our forces, and the right thing to do was to shoot him. However, after he was "neutralized" by our soldiers, they rushed care to him and even placed him onto a helicopter and flew him into the CSH urgently in an attempt to save his life. Great effort, risk, and cost were taken to save the life of a man who wanted Americans to die. It still amazes me to think that many in the world, including some in our own country, view us as the bad guys.

That day, the patient with the gunshot to the head was only the beginning. Later, we received three U.S. soldiers who were injured in an IED blast. The first came in with faint vital signs, and despite the heroic efforts of our new team and surgical staff, he passed away in the ER. I intubated him, and a large IV known as a central line was placed. He was given copious quantities of blood, and his chest was cracked open as he was given open cardiac massage to no avail. This procedure is known as a thoracotomy, and it has a survival rate of only 2–3 percent in the U.S. Our staff did everything possible to save him.

I cared for the other two patients injured in the IED blast; both had fractures of their extremities and multiple shrapnel wounds. It was my first chance to try to cut off the body armor worn by our soldiers, and it was not an easy task! However, we finally got the armor removed and our team was able to keep these guys intact until they made it to the operating room for repair of their wounds and fractures. They were friends and were located beside each other in the EMT; it was enjoyable to see them harass each other and "enjoy" their treatment while they were both high on narcotics! They each talked about their upcoming Purple Hearts, and they could not believe they had been injured. They did not ask about their buddy who lay dead in the trauma room, and I was not about to tell them what happened unless they asked. After their surgeries, I am sure they sat in the hospital rethinking the events of the day and crying over their lost friend while thanking God they were still in one piece. It was a bad day for their unit and a bad day for these three soldiers in particular.

While we were working on those three patients, a man with a gunshot wound to the abdomen arrived in an unstable condition. He was intubated, given blood, and rushed to the operating room, where his life was saved.

I knew he would never be the same as he would likely have to defecate through a bag for the rest of his life, but he was still alive. Later in the day, more patients came in, but none were as serious as the ones we'd already seen. Our first day of "running the show" in Baghdad ER left two dead, one seriously wounded, and two more in surgery for shrapnel wounds and fractures. It was truly a trial by fire for our new trauma teams, but they stood tall and came through.

Later that night, we had Bible study for one hour with our hospital chaplain, Maj. Felix Sermon. He held a Sunday service in our hospital chapel throughout our time in Baghdad. I had missed church on the first Sunday as I was on shift in the ER, and I would do the same the next two weeks. However, the Bible study was a great chance to refocus on Christ and realize that, even though this place felt like a concrete jungle with walls all around, God would not give us a task we could not handle. We could not forget that!

Laura let me know that night that my daughter Avery was beginning to crawl. I was dying to get a video of her doing so, as Laura told me she was getting into everything now. My beautiful wife even said that Avery enjoyed sitting in front of our television armoire and pulling everything out of the bottom shelf; it just made her day apparently. I was sure she was becoming a handful! I knew Laura had a tough job, but she was doing great and would succeed. God reminded me frequently that I was incredibly fortunate to have her at home holding down the fort.

Over the next few days, the Eighty-sixth CSH officially took over for the Twenty-eighth. All patients were managed by our team, as the Twenty-eighth guys only sat back and watched. We received interesting causalities during that time, including multiple people with gunshot wounds, IED blasts, and motor vehicle accidents. Three of those patients stood out to me.

The first was an Iraqi gentleman in his mid-twenties serving as an English interpreter on one of the forward operating bases in the International Zone. He was shot in the leg and clubbed in the head with the butt stock of an AK-47 rifle, along with his mother-in-law, who was shot in the abdomen. Already used to graphic violence, they were the usual run of the mill Baghdad ER–type patients, but we discovered that the shooter in both of these cases was none other than the woman's son and brother-in-law to the interpreter. The shooter was a member of the local militia, and for whatever reason, he decided to take his anger out on both his mother and brother-in-law. Crazy stuff, but I guess it could happen in the U.S. as well.

The second interesting case was a man who was transferred into our facility from a town north of Baghdad. He had a traumatic injury to his hand, as if something he was holding exploded. When questioned by our interpreters, he claimed that his "cell phone charger" blew up, causing a devastating injury to his hand. Marti Roellig and I decided that story was quite fishy, and if so, I sure did not want to buy a cell phone from that company! We both suspected he was a making bombs or at the very least working with explosives, likely designed to kill our soldiers. We called our military police down and were told that, due to the incredibly stupid pictures taken at the infamous prison Abu Ghraib a few years before, unless American soldiers actually caught him in the act or he confessed to making explosives, we had to set him free *after* giving him world-class healthcare that he could not receive anywhere else in Iraq. Thanks to the care of the Eighty-sixth CSH, he would still have a few fingers left to create a bomb that may kill an American soldier sometime in the future versus losing his hand. Unbelievable!

The third interesting patient was, in fact, a mistake on my part. A gentleman from Fiji working with the United Nations presented to the ER for pneumonia. We were told that his physician only wanted a chest x-ray, and then he was to leave. The patient arrived and showed no signs of distress, his vital signs were normal, and he did not appear to be in pain. He only complained of weakness. Immediately upon his arrival, we received call that we had three inbound critically wounded U.S. soldiers hit by an IED, and they would be upon us in a few minutes. As the doctor in charge of the ER, I made the call to send the gentleman with pneumonia to the outpatient clinic for evaluation. I was then informed that upon arrival to the clinic, he was looking worse and requiring oxygen. He was sent directly to the intensive care unit for admission. He was later placed on a ventilator, as his breathing efforts were failing due to his profound muscle weakness. It was likely caused by either a neurological condition known as myasthenia gravis or by Guillain-Barre syndrome, both disorders of muscle weakness that can lead to respiratory failure and death. Several physicians and our chief nurse of the hospital came down to let me know what happened and to essentially tell me how wrong I was for sending him over to the clinic. I took all the blame and essentially came out of it looking pretty bad. I had to answer to the medical staff, members of which were wondering why I sent him out to the clinic. However, I made a decision and went with it. I felt we had a duty to keep the few precious beds that were available in our ER open for trauma, for those who were sick and dying and may not have several hours before they had to be intubated or stabilized. In the U.S., patients arrive to the ER frequently and find nowhere to go because all of the beds are full. In Baghdad ER, if a patient had four or five hours before they need to be placed on a ventilator, then they had more time than many of the other patients we saw. That was just the reality of the situation. In emergency medicine, quick decisions must be made frequently, and that is what I did this day and would continue to do In the future, whether right or wrong.

On November 11, 2007, the bad guys seemed to respect our Veteran's Day holiday. I worked a twelve-hour shift in the ER and only saw three patients. A vary rare event indeed. I even got the chance to walk down the hallway and attend church while on shift. Maybe all our guys were watching football and not going on patrol, or maybe people forgot where we were located for the day. We even joked that the war was over and no one had told us. Personally, I had stopped watching the news over the past year prior to deployment, so I really did not know where we were in all the "pull out of Iraq" talk. Honestly, I did not care. I just knew that this was a calm day on our end, and hopefully our combat guys enjoyed it.

Due to the monotony, some of our crew went outside about 4:00 PM and played hacky sack in the courtyard. Normally being one to play games, for some reason this time I decided to sit on one of the gators and watch.

We were required to wear helmets any time we drove one of the gators, and our enlisted personnel had to go through training to get to drive it, but I just could not resist the temptation and had to fire up one. Everyone gave me funny looks when I drove it across the courtyard and then backed it into the new parking spot I decided it should have. I am sure some NCO with nothing better to do would have loved to chew on me for that one since I had no helmet or formal training; too bad for them they did not catch me! I was sure that before too long I would be driving it on the landing pad, spinning donuts or drag racing it down the road, but I wanted to wait for that to be a nighttime excursion when the brass was asleep.

While our crew was playing hacky sac, some folks from the operating room decided to throw water balloons onto our guys from the outside stairs. Not taking kindly to that, 1st Lt. Sam Matta, one of our nurses, grabbed a wound irrigation gun that shoots water ten feet, and I found a super soaker water gun from the ER. He ran up the stairs and gave the OR guys a frontal attack, and I snuck around behind them, nailing them in a classic trap. One of our medics yelled, "That was textbook, a frontal assault while closing off their escape!" It was fun, and no one questioned which section won the fight.

By this time, I believe everyone in the hospital was beginning to realize that we in the ER had the most fun. Our guys worked more hours than others in the hospital, cared for almost 100 percent of the sick patients, and planned to bear the brunt of the post-traumatic stress disorder cases when the deployment came to its merciful end. But we would do stupid things like have water gun fights, hacky sac parties, shrimp boils, cookouts, play video games, watch movies, and all kinds of other fun stuff to keep our sanity throughout the tour.

The boredom of our shift in Baghdad ER the day before contrasted greatly with the next day. Like that crazy shift in residency, it was another day I will reflect upon for years to come. It began with a very ill young American female with an infected kidney stone. Jason Cohen was caring for her, and I came on shift at 7:00 AM and assisted him by placing a central line into her subclavian vein just beneath her collarbone. She was taken to the operating room and stents were placed to help her pass the stone through her system. She was a very ill patient, but she was only the beginning.

Soon afterward, a three-year-old Iraqi child was brought in with second-degree burns to 20 percent of his body. He had been burned the day prior by hot soup and taken to the local hospital, where his care consisted of wrapping the burn in a sheet. Not satisfied with the care he received, his mother carried him from the hospital and frantically waived down an American convoy as it passed by. The soldiers took both the child and his mother and transported them to us. As the burn center for all of Iraq, we had a surgical specialist, Dr. Booker King, who could assist these children and try to help them retain as much of their previous lives as possible. This would be a trend throughout our tour, and the Americans at Ibn Sina Hospital had treated several hundred Iraqi children and adults since the war began. Many of these burns, like the patient mentioned above, were not due to violent trauma, but they still required life-saving interventions. Unfortunately, many could not be saved, as it was very difficult to fight through the paperwork and bureaucracy to get one of these children transported to the U.S. for care. A deep burn to 50 percent of one's body usually was a death sentence in Iraq unless our guys could get the patient back home for care. Luckily, this particular boy only had 20 percent body-surface-area burns, and the fine surgeon Dr. King was able to do a wonderful job with him over a few weeks' time.

My next patient was a high-profile figure in the local government who presented with abdominal pain, which turned out to be appendicitis. Once I had talked to our surgeon and he was taken to the operating room, we received four American soldiers immediately. One was shot in the chest and taken immediately into our main trauma room. We worked on him quickly, and within one minute his chest was opened and attempts were made to revive his heart directly. At that point we noticed that his wounds were unrepairable, and with disgust we pronounced him dead. He was the second soldier to die in our ER since our arrival.

I immediately exited the trauma room to evaluate our other three U.S. casualties, first stopping at a warrior with a gunshot wound to the head. I have always believed in miracles, and I think he must have too as the bullet had entered his helmet, grazed his head, cutting the skin down to his skull, and then exited his helmet in the back. The bullet then ricocheted into the shoulder of his buddy, barely entering the skin. He just reached over and pulled the projectile out prior to arrival to the ER. After asking a quick one or two questions to the gentleman with the head wound and the soldier with the shoulder injury, I deemed them stable enough to wait for me to get back to them and rotated over to the last soldier, who had been shot in the hip. The bullet traveled into his pelvis and out the back, and I quickly began assessing his injuries and stability. While I was working on the soldier hit in the chest in our main trauma room, our medics and nurses were already stabilizing all three of these patients in the back, and the care and comfort they provided before I could get to them cannot be appreciated enough. The soldiers then went upstairs for further care, and within minutes we received call of more casualties arriving.

An Iraqi man of unknown age was flown in by Blackhawk. He had been previously intubated and cared for somewhere prior to coming to us. We jumped on him quickly and noted him to still be alive and have vital signs, but upon examination, we noted his brain protruding from his head, and he was essentially scalped. We had no idea how he was injured—was it by our forces, or was he blown up by an IED? Only God knew, but he was now in our ED and was unsalvageable. We determined him to be expectant, meaning there was no chance to repair his wounds. We removed him from the ventilator, and I ordered medications for comfort care. We placed him into our expectant room, and he died after about thirty minutes. No one died alone in our ER, and two of our medics stayed with him, having to observe his agonal respirations as his brainstem shut down along with what was left of his brain.

Later in the day, I cared for two gunshot wounds to the arm and a soldier with nausea and passing out unconscious. Next, a ten-year-old Iraqi boy was flown in with massive head trauma. In an eerily similar scenario to the man who had just expired, he also had vital signs yet had brain matter and massive hemorrhaging to the head and face. Once again, his wounds were deemed unrecoverable, and we brought his mother into the room to be with him while he died.

The worst part for me about many of these IED blasts was not the gruesome wounds the victims received; it was the dirt and mud. Many of these bombs were buried, so when they exploded, they blew dirt and mud with the explosive projectiles and gasses. The boy's massive injuries killed him, but he was also caked in dirt and mud. It was as if mauling and killing people were not good enough, the terrorists had to cake their victims in mud and dirt as well. It was appalling and tragic, and this was the first day I saw anger demonstrated by our caregivers. It took us about twelve days to become angry. Twelve days. I immediately recalled the nurse from the Twenty-eighth cussing the dying terrorist, and it made more sense to all of us now why he was so mad.

Sprinkled into this crazy shift was another patient with appendicitis, one with an amputated finger, and a female soldier with severe abdominal pain due to ovarian cysts. At 6:45 PM, my shift was almost complete, as Jason was scheduled to replace me at seven. We then received call of two more patients, both set to arrive in one minute. The first was a three-year-old Iraqi girl with burns to 30 percent of her body. Pat Hickey, our pediatrician, was present and assumed care for her, while the second patient was an Iraqi Army officer with an amputated leg. We pounded blood into him, placed central lines, performed CPR, and pushed life-saving drugs, all to no avail.

He would be our fourth death of the day. It was a crazy and tragic day, the first day of physician single-coverage in the ER for us, the first day I was on my own. After shift, all I wanted to do was get food and go to sleep. We all grew up this day: our entire team of nurses, medics, and myself. We grew as a unit; we gained valuable experience while witnessing incredible tragedy, and we became battle-hardened that day. I thanked God when that day was finally done.

The next shift was much nicer. Being slow, it was a stark contrast from the carnage and death of the day before. All was quiet until the end when a man was rushed through the back doors without warning with a head and chest injury due to an IED blast. We placed him in our main trauma bed, and our nurses and medics began attempting to place IVs with no success. I rotated down to his right leg to place a femoral central line, but our surgeon Dr. Heather Currier was present and beat me to it. We gave him medications to sedate and paralyze him in order to intubate him, and that is where the trouble began.

Once paralyzed, I used a laryngoscope blade to open his mouth and attempt to intubate him, but at first I was not able to see his vocal cords in order to place the tube. I repositioned him and took another look, obtaining a slight view of the cords while our nurse called out his blood oxygen level. One hundred percent is perfect, 80 percent is poor, and below 60 percent is very bad and approaching death. As she called out, "Ninety-two percent, 84 percent, 75 percent," I attempted to manipulate the endotracheal tube into his trachea, but I could not get it to bend in the correct direction. I then made a crucial mistake.

I removed the blade and we bagged the patient back up into the nineties as I went in for another try. Once again, I was able to see my target, but could not get the tube to bend appropriately, so I asked for a bougie, which is a long soft rod used to place into the trachea and then slide the breathing tube down over it. I placed it in the correct position and then took my eyes off the vocal cords as I loaded the tube on it. I slid the tube down the bougie, not realizing it had pulled out of the trachea and had passed into the esophagus. The endotracheal tube followed, and we bagged the patient aggressively, assuming the tube was in the correct spot. He then threw up, aspirating vomit into his lungs, and we were back to square one again as he had no definitive airway. I then asked for a different airway device called a LMA.

Just as I was opening the LMA package, an anesthesia provider arrived and quickly intubated the patient. I do not know how he did it so fast, but it of course was a humiliating experience for me and obviously a worse experience for the patient. Likely he would be fine, and while he did get pneumonia from aspirating the vomit into his lungs, he eventually did well. But I could not understand why I could not get the tube placed, why I could not get it to curve forward. Why was it so difficult? I had done hundreds of intubations over the years, and I had not encountered this issue since I was an intern in residency learning how to perform the procedure. I knew we were all to practice "egoless" medicine there at Ibn Sina or patients would die, but I was taught that lesson much quicker than I expected.

The next day, I transitioned to night shifts, so I attempted to sleep in and stay up all night. However, I was awakened by an explosion, followed quickly by a second blast, around 7:30 AM. The sturdy walls of the hospital did not move or shake, but the furniture and windows rattled loudly from the force of the blast. I did not know what that meant—were the explosions mortars, bombs, or rockets? I did not hear any more at the time, so I decided not to think too much of it.

Thirty minutes later, Jason called me from the ER and asked me to rush down to help out as the two explosions were from EFPs hitting a U.S. Stryker Combat Vehicle, which could hold up to eleven soldiers. We had casualties pouring in by ground, with combat vehicles rushing through our checkpoints without notice and skidding to a stop just outside the ER doors. When I arrived, one soldier was dead and two more had been significantly injured. Many surgeons and other staff were present in the ED waiting for the patients to come, and a few slowly began to arrive. We went into our mass casualty plan, expecting to see many more patients. Jason took the front to do triage along with the chief surgeon. Marti Roellig took the three beds in the trauma room, and I took the seven beds in the back. Our plan was to have patients come through triage, and then a surgeon/ER doc would manage each patient individually, and the ER doc in each room would manage any airway issues for all the patients in that area. Running the department this way would provide continuity of care. If a surgeon took a patient to the OR, there would be an ER doc present they could check out to who could continue care for their patients. Fortunately, only a few more soldiers arrived, all with minor injuries, and there was only one death from the bomb.

The bomb was over a kilometer from our building, yet our windows and furniture rattled. I had difficulty imagining how powerful these explosives must have been that the bad guys were using. Knowing I had a twelve-hour night shift to go, I rested that afternoon and mentally prepared myself for my first of many graveyard journeys in Baghdad ER.

My first night shift went well. We had several transfers from the Air Force Theater Hospital in Balad from a bus rollover accident involving Iraqi soldiers. Most of them were not injured too badly, although one poor man had a bilateral below-the-knee amputation and his jaws wired.

I did have one of those patients who make you feel wonderful about being an ER doc, however. An Iraqi security guard came in with a dislocated shoulder due to a recent fall. We communicated with him through a translator, and once our staff was prepared, I sedated him with a drug called etomidate. He was unconscious for about five minutes, during which time I relocated his shoulder. Upon awaking to find his shoulder back in the socket and corrected, he began speaking English saying "I love America" and "I want to go to America!" He was smiling from ear to ear and rubbing his shoulder, and we all got a big laugh. It reminded me of Yakov Smirnov, the comedian from the Soviet Union who became famous for his love of America. It was very rewarding to say the least.

A few days later, I had the pleasure of enjoying my first day off since our arrival to Baghdad, and I had a fantastic day. Jason Cohen, Sam Matta, and I went to the Presidential Palace/U.S. Embassy Compound in the International Zone and ate at the sandwich bar. Afterward, we nervously walked to the traffic circle past the palace. We did not dare walk too much further at the time, as we had been informed that the bad guys were looking for American soldiers to kidnap. We felt safe in a group, and of course I would never go wandering around to new places alone; that would be asking for trouble. We then went to the PX and did more exploring in our new neighborhood of the Green Zone.

That evening we sat on the roof smoking cigars and watching Blackhawk medevac helicopters fly in and out of our landing pad, with as many as four at a time touching down. It made for a tight fit when they were all squeezing onto it simultaneously. Two different times, when the birds launched, they fired automatic antimissile flares onto the building next to us, and both birds were very low to the ground when doing so, maybe only 100–150 feet up. It became monotonous over the course of time for us to see the flares shooting, but at the time it was a startling sight indeed to have the Roman candle–like fireworks shooting in my direction. On more than one occasion throughout my tour I had to sidestep the burnt flares as they drifted to ground.

The next week was quite busy. The start found me leaving the gym and walking into the front door of the hospital when an old familiar tone caught my ear. From the corner of the room, where a nineteen-inch television sat playing the Armed Forces Network, I heard the beautiful honking of Canadian Geese. I have always found the sounds of giant Canadian Geese honking to be among the most beautiful music in the world.

Mesmerized by the tones, I looked to the screen and saw a nine- or ten-year-old boy on *Good Morning America* whaling on a flute-style goose call. He was good, a much better caller than I, and he was going to town on the call. The announcers did not exactly know how to respond, as I was sure the boy had been flown into New York City because he placed first in some kind of calling contest from a town in rural America. Some of the anchors were doing the chicken dance, while others stood laughing and looking at him like he had a mental problem. Who knows, maybe it was the first time a goose call had ever been blown on Times Square!

Next the boy broke out a hen mallard call and began to blow. Having spent several years duck hunting in eastern Arkansas, with mallards being the main quarry, I was very familiar with his hail calls, soft quacks, and comebacks. The kid was a talented caller, and likely he was from a small town like so many other championship callers. But he brought a taste of home, the sound of nature's calls, all the way around to the other side of the world, and it brightened my day and brought a huge smile to my face.

Later, we went back down to Saddam's old palace and ate at the grilled sandwich bar. While sitting there amongst the many civilian members of the U.S. State Department, I said to my colleagues, "I feel kind of guilty sitting in a palace eating sandwiches while our boys and girls are still out in harm's way." It was a true reflection, a true sentiment, but those sandwiches were good, and the delicious taste kept me from feeling too guilty.

The patient I had esophageally intubated a few days prior now had pneumonia because he did indeed inhale vomit from his stomach into his lungs, an injury directly caused by my mistake. I felt terrible, but I could not lose sleep over it. My attitude was to have the mentality of a cornerback in the National Football League. Millions of people can watch him make a mistake and allow the receiver to catch a touchdown pass. His team may lose the game because of that mistake. But he has to go back out on defense again, he has to keep his nose in the game, and maybe, just maybe, he can make the game-changing interception to win the game. Maybe he can go from goat to hero, from the valley to the mountaintop, from the shadows to having the bright sunshine upon his face. I had to be that player. No matter what happened on my next shift, what harm I caused or help I gave, I had to keep coming back the next day or night and start over from scratch. I knew that I must forget about the events that had transpired in the recent past, because my team would rely on me to make the play. The next day, just like a football player, I got my chance.

We received notice that three American soldiers were coming in after being hit by an IED, and one was seriously wounded with multiple amputations. When they arrived, we quickly placed him into bed one and went to work. After only nineteen days, our teams were beginning to mold into one body, one coordinating unit, and it was beginning to show. With one medic on his left placing him on the monitor, and one on his right starting an IV, our surgeon dove into a central line successfully. I spoke with the soldier and informed him as to what our plan of action was and told him he would be okay, hoping that was not a lie. His nurse, Robyn Stafford, pushed his rapid sequence intubation medications, and I intubated him and placed him on a ventilator. We pumped blood quickly through the central line, and gave him a total of eight units of red blood cells and four units of fresh frozen plasma in the EMT. He went quickly on to CT scan and then to the operating room and was surgically stabilized.

The other soldiers were not injured as badly, although their Iraqi interpreter had a vicious injury to his right elbow, with all the bones shattered. After the critically wounded soldier left for CT, I placed a femoral central line into the interpreter, and he went on to the operating room in anticipation of waking up unfortunately to an amputated arm.

An hour or so later, a ten-year-old Iraqi boy arrived who had been hit by an IED. He was missing his right arm below the elbow, and his right leg above the knee. In one fluid motion, our team established IV access. We sedated him and I intubated him, but despite knowing that the intubation was successful, his oxygen saturation never improved. Multiple chest x-rays and tube manipulation by me proved his tube was in the right place. Despite children sometimes being more difficult to intubate due to their anterior airways, I did not falter on this patient as I had previously. The surgeon placed a central line, and we pumped two units of blood into him, without much response. We gave him other blood products including fresh frozen plasma, and while his blood pressure increased somewhat, we still were not able to measure his oxygen saturations on our monitor.

Our lab work showed us that his blood gas had a pH of 6.7. This was a terrible number, as the normal pH of the human body is around 7.35. When we drew the blood from his artery, it had the dark, nonoxygenated color of blood from a vein, once again an ominous sign. His hemoglobin and hematocrit, both measures of oxygen-carrying cell capacity, was dangerously low at 6 and 19. He needed blood and other resuscitation products in the worst way. To this point in my career I had seen very few multitrauma patients survive with a pH less than seven, but we had him intubated and rapidly receiving blood. He was rushed into the CT scanner, and up to the operating room. Our pediatrician, Pat Hickey, came to his aid in the ER while we were working on him and stayed with him throughout his course, doing anything he could to help.

A few hours later, Pat reported to me that the little boy was still alive, and his blood levels had been corrected. Overnight, after the ER resuscitation and surgery, he required a total of fourteen units of red blood cells, fourteen units of plasma, two six-packs of platelets, and other blood products. He was still sedated on a ventilator, but he was getting better and would likely survive. Thanks to the great efforts of our ER staff, surgical staff, and ICU staff, an innocent little boy received world-class care from start to finish and would live to see another day. His care and resuscitation began with us; we made the game-changing play that day to win the game.

While on shift the next day, I received three American soldiers wounded by a mortar blast that landed on their dining facility. Two had fragments to the chest and one to the abdomen. God provided a miracle that day, as all three had wounds that did not penetrate deeply, despite shrapnel hitting them in the torso. They all avoided the operating room, and it was a nice, positive start to the shift.

We also received an insurgent who had an open lower-leg fracture on both legs. He was running from our forces, and as he jumped over some sort of obstacle he landed wrong on his legs, shattering both bones in each. Once the x-rays returned, we noticed that he already had metal rods holding both of his tibias, or shinbones, together. Our orthopedic surgeons looked at the films and thought it looked like work done by an American surgeon. Likely this was another one of our "compassionate releases" who was released from one of our prisons only to attack our guys again. Just like the outgoing ER doc Steve Taylor from the Twenty-eighth CSH told me, "We do everything to save these guys, and they just go right back out and attack us again." I was sure this would not be the last time we would see repeat business from the bad guys.

We later received an eleven-year-old boy with a gunshot wound to the pelvis, entering on the left and exiting on the right. He was in very bad shape, and I quickly intubated him while the nurses gave blood. Our surgeons rushed him to the OR, but he died from his wounds upstairs. As usual, our forces did not shoot the child, but once his parents presented him to the Americans, everything was done to save him, but to no avail this time.

Later, I got into an argument with our deputy commander of nursing, Col. Steve Lomax. It was not a big deal, as I was showing frustration with the rules of the command stating our nurses and medics were not allowed to do many of the procedures they were taught to do in training. At one point, he yelled at me, "That's how it is, and quit talking about it!" He was a full-bird colonel; I was a major. In this situation, the entire, "But I'm a physician and you're a nurse" argument would not get the job done. Smartly, I said, "Yes, sir." But then we had what I thought was a very cordial conversation about the scope of practice for nurses and medics. We chose to disagree, but our conversation was appropriate. While I let him know that I did not agree with his point of view, I assured him we would not break any of the rules put into place, whether I liked with them or not. I assumed that, despite him being a colonel and me being a major, we could have a conversation that was rank independent. I guess I was wrong, because I was later informed that he pulled the nursing supervisors together and told them to "watch me," meaning to look out and see if I was allowing the nurses and medics to perform procedures they are taught but not allowed to perform there in the CSH. Obviously, he did not trust me and he was telling others about it. Awesome. As I said, I did not get to this point by breaking rules, although sometimes they must be bent to get the job done, especially when the command was clinically ignorant. But I made it a point not to discuss our conversation with others, not to "talk behind his back," and this is what I got. All I could think was, "Three weeks down and only fourteen months and one week to go!"

───────

Soon afterward, I received several letters from my sister-in-law Sheila's high school class. Some were addressed to me, others to any soldiers serving with me, and yet others were written to wounded troops. They were entertaining to read, with many talking about their plans after graduation and others making political comments about the war. After reading them, I sorted them and kept some to hand out to my medics. I gave the letters for wounded troops to our chaplain to distribute. It was amazing to see how something so small as a letter from a high school student could brighten my day so much.

I had just enjoyed the quietest shift I had worked to that point. I arrived at the ER to discover several injured British soldiers coming from a helicopter crash on the outskirts of Baghdad. Apparently, one bird with fourteen soldiers on board just dropped out of the sky due to mechanical failure, resulting in a very hard landing. Several were injured, and survivors as well as members of the accompanying aircraft were pulling out wounded men out when it caught fire and exploded. I never discovered know how many died, but I heard later the crash made the news back home. The guys were obviously shaken up when they arrived to us, and some were in pretty bad shape. However, the crash was the only obstacle I had to face that night, making it quite peaceful.

Ibn Sina Hospital was built back in the 1950s or 1960s by four Iraqi physicians who desired it to be a hospital for the people of Baghdad. It was state of the art at that time, consisting of advanced operating suites and patient care wards. When Saddam came to power, like most nice things in Iraq, he claimed the hospital as his own, disallowing the general population access. It was reserved for use only by members of his family or ruling party. In the emergency department, or EMT, he had a suite created for himself with marble floors and gold-inlayed bathrooms. It was quite elaborate for an ER, but I guess only the best for Saddam!

It was named after a Muslim physician and scholar known as Ibn Sina. While his name was much longer than that, he was known only by that accolade as he made incredible advancements in both medicine and science several hundred years ago. Apparently, he was a man who provided for the people and worked tirelessly to improve the lives of everyone around him. Of course, being a Christian I do not agree with his religion, but the contributions he made to all of mankind should not be underestimated. After learning more about his life, I think it was appropriate to name a hospital after him; I just hate that soon after it was built, it was taken away from the very populace it was created to serve.

We were scheduled to have several Democratic lawmakers come though the facility the next day. Be they Democrat or Republican, I figured some politicians would come through for good photo opportunities during Thanksgiving week. Several of these individuals were leading the "get out of Iraq" charge, including U.S. Representative John Murtha, a former Vietnam veteran. I chose to avoid the ER that day as much as possible, as I did not really care to meet with any of those individuals. I still supported our actions in Iraq, but I knew others had different opinions, and I respected that. I just wanted to avoid the issue. However, their plans changed, and they did not make the trip to see us. Senator John McCain, a Republican running for president, was scheduled to tour the ER the next day, and I did plan to come down and meet him. I had met former President Bill Clinton once and former Arkansas Governor Mike Huckabee a couple of times, and while I did not think McCain would win the 2008 election for the White House, it would have been neat to meet another presidential-type at least. However, he also had a last-minute change of plans and did not get a chance to come by.

There were many dedicated Iraqi interpreters who worked with us. One of them was an older woman who was as warm and kind as anyone I have known. I will leave her name out to protect her, as anyone working with the Coalition forces was a target for the insurgency. She had three children, all boys, and one currently lived in the United States. Another son had been working with American forces over the past year and was wounded by insurgents. He was rushed to Ibn Sina, and despite the best efforts of the Twenty-eighth CSH before us, he died of his wounds. Since that day, she had dedicated herself to our cause and continued to be a bright ray of sunshine for us all. Every day when she would see me, she would stop me and teach me a new Arabic word or phrase. I would feel very guilty because I never did get them right, and I honestly was not studying or trying. My plan was to learn Spanish while I was gone, and I did not want to mess with Arabic. I owed it to her to start listening and practicing the phrases she was trying to teach me, and I eventually got some of them down. I admired her courage and could not imagine how she dealt with the pain of entering the trauma room everyday, the room where young men and women lived, struggled, and died just like her son. I wondered at times what she would do if we gave up the war and left her? I was sure to ask her opinion on our presence in Iraq later in our tour.

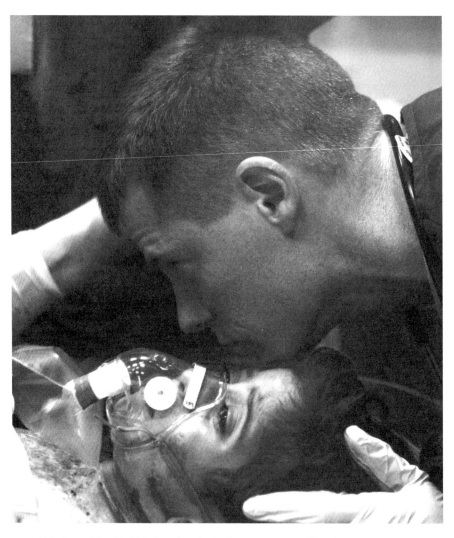

U.S. Army Maj. Todd Baker the chief of emergency staff at Ibn Sina Hospital in the Green Zone in Baghdad, Iraq, comforts four-year-old Fatima as she arrives at the emergency room with severe burns on Friday, Dec. 14, 2007.
(AP Photo/Maya Alleruzzo)

A Close Call

November 22, 2007, Thanksgiving Day

There have been two days in my life that I was literally a few feet away from severe injury or death. When I was eighteen years old and a freshman in junior college, my friend Justin Powell and I were driving in his Toyota pickup truck and stopped on a two-lane highway to turn left. Moments later, we were hit from behind by an underage driver, pushing us into the lane of oncoming traffic. While moving across the lane after being hit from behind, my passenger door was struck by a sixteen-ton railroad truck traveling about fifty miles an hour. We flipped three to four times and landed on another vehicle about sixty yards away. Unconscious and bleeding, the fire department used the Jaws of Life to remove me from what was left of the Toyota. My eventual injuries turned out to be a mere laceration to the head and a fractured pelvis. God was watching over me that November day in 1993, and he was doing the same again this Thanksgiving day.

It began innocently as several of the other physicians and I made the walk to the palace about 12:30 to pick up several helpings of Thanksgiving lunch from the Embassy Department's dining facility. We each carried two to four Styrofoam boxes down the street to the hospital, and we all had a bittersweet Thanksgiving lunch away from home. It was nice to be able to sit and relax with colleagues for a special meal, but it was also sad that I could not be with my family. I missed Laura, Avery, and my extended family greatly during that lunch, enough to make me realize that the holidays would definitely be our toughest, loneliest days in Iraq.

After the feast, I headed to the ER to find Mr. Dave Roever, a wonderful man who was wounded and burned terribly during his service in the Vietnam War. He was in his early sixties, but his face was still very scarred from the severe trauma he incurred in service of his country. He travels the world now as a motivational speaker, and just the week before he visited us, he had given a talk to thousands of people. He brought a message of gratitude and thankfulness to us that others had not mentioned before. I was touched by his presence in Baghdad on Thanksgiving Day and impressed by his undying spirit and positive attitude despite the unimaginable difficulties and horrors he has faced due to his service to our great nation.

I was not scheduled for a shift that day, and I was enjoying my day off. About 4:00 PM, Sam Matta and I headed out to throw the football. What good is Thanksgiving Day without some pigskin fun? After playing catch for about twenty minutes, most of the physicians of the hospital gathered in the motor pool area to play whiffle ball. I would estimate that approximately 80 percent of the physicians of the hospital, including the surgeons, anesthesia providers, ER docs, and several nurses, were gathered in a friendly competition outside and having a great time.

About twenty minutes into our game, we noticed black smoke rising up in the yard just behind our landing pad. I remember asking some of the others about it, and a few of the onlookers began walking down that direction to investigate. They disappeared around a building to check it out, and I thought nothing of it.

A few minutes later, I was standing around home plate when the first mortar hit. We heard the whistling nose of the round coming down, followed by a loud BOOM one second later. There was no time to react prior to the first round touching down, as we heard no warning and it was on us before we could realize what was happening. Scrambling, we dropped whatever we had, whether ball, bat, cell phone, or other. Some of the gang ran to the left and into a bunker that was about twenty yards away. Others made the forty-yard jaunt into the hospital, and I ran to my right into another bunker that was about twenty-five yards from where we began.

Our duck-and-cover shelters consisted of rebar-reinforced concrete that stood about five feet tall. They had sides and a roof approximately twelve inches thick, and they were open on each end. About two feet from each open end, there was another five- to six-foot-tall concrete t-barrier that allowed people to dive inside, yet still provided protection against the open sides of the bunker. It was a good thing they were there.

Two mortars hit a small distance from our compound before I reached my bunker. Thank God neither was close, and we all had a chance to run to cover! Sgt. Ramirez, one of our facilities guys, jumped into the same bunker, and we both squatted against the walls, with he on one side and me on the other. A third round hit, much louder and closer than the first two. Seconds later, a fourth mortar landed, this time in our compound about twenty feet from my bunker. Rocks and debris came around the side barrier into our bunker after the impact.

I had about two to three seconds until the next impact, and noticing the makeup of our bunker, I decided the other wall was safer so I quickly relocated to it. Back to back with Sgt. Ramirez, we crouched down and held our ears from the deafening impact. The next round landed just behind us, about ten feet away. We could feel the impact of the projectile, as dust, smoke, and sulfur filled the air. We both yelled, "That was close!" and then BOOM, another round landed twenty-five feet on the other side of us. The rounds walked down the road toward our landing zone, with three rounds landing within twenty-five feet of our bunker. Two more shells rained down into our compound, and one injured one of our orthopedic surgeons as he was taking shelter in a bunker by the LZ.

After the barrage ceased, I faced away from Sgt. Ramirez, too stunned to move. I yelled, "Are you okay?" I received no answer for two long seconds that stretched into eternity. I remembered the close impacts and the dust and rocks that had been sprayed into our bunker. The smoke with its sulfur-like aroma permeated our bunker. But I did not think any shrapnel had made it inside. But not hearing a response, I just knew I would turn around to find him injured or dead! Finally, he answered back and was thankfully untouched.

After the attack ended, and before the all clear was given, I jumped out of my bunker and quickly scanned for casualties. Seeing none, I sprinted about one hundred feet to the ER to find several people who looked just as shell-shocked as me. We quickly set up our teams to brace for the wounded personnel we were sure would inundate us. Jason manned the back room, Marti took the trauma room, and I handled triage and front room duty. Slowly, the injured began to trickle in, and overall, we treated five or six patients, with none of them wounded badly.

Reports of the attack were on CNN news within thirty minutes, and nervous families began to call. Our phones were blacked out for security reasons, and no one was able to telephone out for a while. Overall, it was a scary and humbling experience. All along, I had fully expected to be mortared while in Baghdad; it would be a part of my life. However, I did not plan to be caught outside in a bunker with rounds landing ten feet away! I figured we would be hit again during our tour, but I did not plan to get caught outside again.

The next day, I picked up pieces of shrapnel from all over our complex. Several pieces I picked up were lying beside the sidewalls of my bunker. There was no doubt the concrete of that bunker saved Sgt. Ramirez and myself from injury and perhaps even saved our lives. It reminded me of the time I was almost killed at eighteen years old; it was not time for God to call me home yet. Little did I know those mortars were small fries compared to the rockets that would hit us in the future.

One of the negative aspects of emergency medicine is that we do not often get follow up on our patients. At times, I have received great feedback, like the patient with an allergic reaction who I intubated before her airway could close a few years ago in Louisiana. I visited her the next day, and as I walked into her ICU room, she stated, "There's the man, that's my hero!" I will never forget that experience, but unfortunately that is the exception rather than the norm with my profession. Usually, we stabilize our patients and then transfer their care to the doctors and surgeons who will meet and care for both the patient and their families, leaving us in the background. A patient arrived two days later who would return to us and complete the loop that so often is left incomplete.

She arrived as a gunshot wound to the head. On the same aircraft, there was a three-year-old little girl with a gunshot wound to the abdomen. Placing both patients in the trauma bay, I immediately jumped over to the middle-aged woman shot in the head while Jason took charge of the little girl's care, as he happened to be in the ER when they arrived. My team of nurses and medics quickly cut though the lady's bandages and removed all of her clothing, and found that she was shot through the left temple, with an exit wound just in front of the right ear. She turned out to be an attempted execution that did not kill her ... yet. Most of the penetrating head injures we had seen to that point had all been nonsurvivable, with brain matter hanging out or with other life-incompatible issues.

Having no intravenous access or any other way to intubate or treat her, I jumped to her right groin while our nurses and medics attempted to access her arms. We could not pick up vital signs on the monitor, but she was moving around and had a weak pulse, so that would have to be sufficient to determine proof of life. While attempting to place a large central line into her femoral vein, I could hear the screams of the little girl in the bed just to my right as she was stuck with needles, probed, and examined. My patient was resisting, still able to move her arms and legs, although she could not speak and was not thinking sensibly. I asked a medic to hold down her leg as I successfully placed the catheter and sewed it down to her skin.

Once the monitor was working, I noted her heart rate to be very high and her blood pressure to be very low; it was obvious she needed blood immediately. I asked for and promptly received a "code red," consisting of four units of packed red blood cells and two units of fresh frozen plasma through the central line in her groin. Our nurses then pushed a combination of drugs to both sedate and paralyze her in order for me to place the endotracheal tube. Once paralyzed, I used a laryngoscope to place the tube through her vocal cords and into her trachea. During this process, I could hear the child in the bed next to ours still crying and screaming even louder as our nurses, medics, and Dr. Cohen diligently worked on her. I did my best to block that out and focus on the mission at hand. I could not worry about the little girl—she was in good hands, and if she distracted me, then my priority, my patient, could die.

With blood on board and now on a ventilator, my patient's vital signs began to stabilize, so we rushed her to the CT scanner and discovered that the bullet had taken out her left eye and passed through the back of her nasal cavity. She had resultant air inside her skull around her brain, and we were worried it could build up pressure and cause her brain to herniate, or squeeze out the hole in the bottom of the skull and kill her.

I called the ER at the air force hospital in Balad thirty minutes by air north of us, which had both an ophthalmologist and a neurosurgeon on staff. The ER doc in Balad accepted the patient, and we rushed to set her up to fly. I placed an arterial line into the artery in her wrist in order to give our nurses a better blood pressure reading while in the air. During this time, the little girl Jason was working on was rushed to the operating room to have her abdomen opened and her bowels explored and repaired. Later that night, the surgeons returned to inform us that she did well and, while having repercussions from her abdominal surgery, the little girl was stabilizing and would be okay. The lady, however, we never expected to hear from again.

However, much to our surprise, we did hear from her. The next night we received our nightly transfers from Balad. They would send Iraqi patients to us who were to be discharged to the Iraqi health care system. Unbelievably, she arrived on that bird and was back into our ER, still alive and having been cleared by both neurosurgery and ophthalmology! She had undergone a surgical enucleation (removal) of her left eye, and was on antibiotics for her sinus issues. The neurosurgeons felt the air in her skull would be absorbed back into her brain, and she was released to go home. While in the ER, I tried to talk to her and let her know how proud we were to see her doing so well, and she told me she had a headache. She held and drank a bottle of water, and she spoke and gestured clearly throughout her stay with us. She was still somewhat confused and did not remember us, but we did not mind at all.

We did not often have follow-up on our patients, and to be honest, many times we did not want to know. It was just a way that we dealt with the trauma. We would do our jobs and move on, trying not to worry about what would happen to our patients once they left the ER and moved upstairs. But this was different. This was a save—this was a great save—and I was proud and honored to be the leader of the team that gave her a chance to live, by the grace of God. Today, once again, we won the game.

———

I performed two transvaginal ultrasounds on U.S. soldiers who recently found out they were pregnant. I had been trained to do those and enjoyed very much the thrill of showing a prospective mother the ultrasound pictures of a healthy child. When performing the scans, I always turn the screen toward her, especially if there is a heartbeat to demonstrate, so she can see it real time for herself. Occasionally, I will have a mother act disappointed she is pregnant; it is usually pretty obvious who is excited and who is regretful. When the time calls for it, I will tell her what a miracle a child is and how excited she should be.

One of the ultrasounds I performed did not go well, and I had to inform the soldier she was about to miscarry. I always talked quietly and offered the patient anything I could, from a phone call home to a chaplain, or even just a warm meal. The general public, including many in the medical community itself, just do not understand the devastation that a miscarriage can bring. I fully understand that God is in control, and things do not just happen randomly, but it is still a terrible thing to go through and cannot be disregarded.

The next day, we heard that a player for the Washington Redskins had been shot in the leg and died subsequently from his wounds. Working in Iraq, at the premier trauma hospital in the world in my opinion, that was unacceptable. We treated those injuries every day, and our soldiers in the field were trained so well on tourniquet use that they threw them on quickly and saved lives. In the U.S., tourniquets are not in widespread use because most trauma is blunt rather than penetrating, with many more car wrecks than gunshot wounds presenting for care everyday. Ambulances can usually get patients to the hospital quickly, so tourniquet use is not routinely required. In Iraq and Afghanistan, countless soldiers have been saved after being shot solely due to tourniquet use.

Thinking of this problem, I came up with a great idea I called the "gangbanger tourniquet," or GBT. Many gunshot wounds resulting in death in the U.S. are at the hands of gangbangers, and this idea would provide a tourniquet they could wear on their head rather than the traditional bandana or skullcap. It could even come in designer colors, red for one gang, green for another, and so on. When in a shootout, the gang member could quickly take the tourniquet off his head and throw it on his wounded arm or leg. Everyone in the ER liked it and thought it was a great idea. Maybe I should market it and see if it sells one day. The slogan for our product could be, "When the shit goes down, it'll keep you off the ground."

Before we moved too far into December and it got too cold for me, I found myself sitting on top of Jones Hall, the dormitory connected to our hospital, and relishing the beautiful sunset out to the west of the city. Looking panoramically, I could see the stalled work on the Al-Rahman Mosque, which had been under construction for several years and then halted by the U.S. invasion in March 2003. Smoke was billowing from somewhere in the distance to our west, likely the result of a bomb or some sort of sectarian violence. Distant sounds of gunfire could be heard between the constant music of the orbiting helicopters and the F-16 fighter jets flying overhead. There was a large layer of smog I had not witnessed before. Not being from a large city, I was not used to smog, but I eventually learned to cope with it. I am not sure why it was present this day; there had been no change in the weather.

The F-16 fighter jets were flying over constantly, more than I had seen in my first month in Iraq. Likely they were taking part in some mission north or west of the city, where there had been some fighting recently. I could see two Apache helicopters slowly orbiting the eastern aspects of the city, likely keeping watch over Sadr City, one of Baghdad's most volatile neighborhoods. Blue colored Huey helicopters were constantly launching from Washington landing zone, escorting their American Blackwater security contractors out into the danger of the red zone, or Baghdad proper. In the distance, I could see the constant flame from the large oil refinery south of town, as well as hear the Adhan Muslim call to prayer from the mosque to my east.

There I sat, in the middle of a war zone with jets, helicopters, and gunfire all around me. But it was a peaceful time, a very serene moment. I do not know why I was so relaxed. I had actually missed my wife, kid, dogs, and home much more this day than any day recently. However, right then, watching the sunset, I was at peace. I remember thanking God that I had the rooftop to go to for serenity when I was free.

Intelligence reports later informed us that the mortar barrage on Thanksgiving Day was only the beginning, as the cease-fire from the Madhi Militia, JAM, or whatever they called it, was now officially over. The militias apparently had received shipments of TNT and other explosives and planned to attack school children. Did these criminals have no shame? Unfortunately, I already knew the answer to that question without asking. But whatever they did, we would be there, waiting on the mortars to come and the patients to arrive. Overall, causalities were down nationwide, and the Sunni Awakening movement was really taking shape. As many as six thousand Sunni Muslims had sided with the U.S. against Al Qaeda in Iraq over the recent few months. One Iraqi tribal leader was quoted at that time, "Do I love my neighbor in Hawija? That question no longer matters. I must work to help him, because his safety helps me." That attitude was fine with me. I did not care if the Sunnis disliked the Shia or vice versa; if they would just work together Iraq, America, and the entire free world, would benefit. I think we were finally beginning to see that happen in this war-torn country.

The next week, several of us were enjoying sitting on the roof watching the helicopters shoot flares over the city, when we began to hear an alarm wail nearby. We looked at each other, with none of us realizing it was the CRAM system. We stared like idiots when the voice in the sky screamed, "Incoming, incoming, incoming" in its loud voice, warning us of approaching mortars or rockets. In unison, we all jumped to our feet and made a break for the door to the top of the stairwell, with me running straight into Jason Cohen and knocking his glasses off. We sprinted down the stairs and waited, only to find it was a false alarm.

That was twice now that we had to jump up and run from mortars. Both times I ran square into someone going the opposite direction. Everyone decided it was best to avoid me when rounds were incoming, and I did not blame them!

Each week, the physician staff held a morbidity and mortality conference (M&M) to discuss cases with poor outcomes. In the U.S., these sessions all too often turn into a 20/20 hindsight, second-guessing, and finger-pointing event where everyone jumps on the person who made the mistake or simply was unlucky enough to care for a patient who suffered a bad outcome, despite their efforts. M&M in Baghdad was no different, as one of our ER docs had recently suffered a bad outcome. Anesthesia and surgery were called and came to the ED to help, but it was blamed on the ER doc, even though the "experts" were present at bedside when the problem occurred. But that was okay, we were the ER and were used to being in the fish bowl and being second-guessed by everyone around us, who always seemed to know better after the fact.

After being informed that all ER docs are idiots from some of the surgical staff, I went down to begin my twelve-hour shift and began a class teaching our medics basic x-ray interpretation. During this time, Cpt. Solberg, one of our nurses, ran to us shouting, "Four gunshot wounds!" as Stryker combat vehicles had just skidded to a stop at our back door without notice. We sprang into action, running to the back door to find a group of soldiers being dragged in by their buddies, who were telling us the victim's Stryker had just been hit by an EFP. We quickly learned that EFPs, or explosively formed penetrators, were a devastating, puncturing type of IED with a 2,500-degree copper projectile. The first soldier brought in was unfortunately killed, and we tried to place him in our specialty room while his poor buddies yelled, "He's not dead, do something, DO SOMETHING!" The shell-shocked soldiers were grabbing our nurses and medics by the shirts and trying to pull them over to help their dead buddy, while our guys were attempting to help the other wounded troops. The next soldier in was walking wounded and placed in the back.

The third patient brought in was a young American warrior who had both of his legs amputated above the knees with tourniquets in place. We threw him into bed one and went to work. We cut clothes quickly, and our medic Spc. Desillier nailed a large bore intravenous line into a vein in his right arm. As we pounded blood into him, I leaned down and told the awake, terrified kid, "You're going to be okay, we're going to take great care of you." He asked me if we were putting him to sleep, and I said, "Yes, you hang in there." Our nurses quickly sedated him and I intubated him. The surgeon on call placed a quick central line, and we gave him six more units of blood. I jumped down to evaluate what was left of his right leg. His shell-shocked buddies brought in his right boot, with foot and lower leg still attached, separate from his body. His left leg was connected by soft tissue only, with the boot hanging off the end of the bed and his foot still inside. Blood was oozing out all over the bed and splashing on the floor, soaking the trauma room in a sea of crimson. The right leg had two tourniquets on and was still bleeding. I placed a third tourniquet, and the bleeding subsided for the most part. We wrapped his wounds, and he went to the OR for surgical repair.

We received word later that he did well after receiving several units of blood and surgical repair. Sam Matta and I went to his unit outside and told them their medic had done no less than save his life. Without those tourniquets, there was a 100 percent chance that he would have died. The twenty-year-old medic who worked on him should stand proud, and we told his unit to let his commanders know what he did.

Several of the other soldiers involved in the EFP were seen in the back, and I moved to them when the patient with the amputations went to the OR. All of them had a dazed and confused look on their faces—their minds were trying to process the death of one friend and the double-amputation of another. What can you say to those guys? Our chaplain, Maj. Felix Sermon, arrived promptly at the ER and talked to all of them, but once again, trying to comfort them was a daunting task. We treated their wounds and released them all back to their units to be with their battle buddies.

While trying to decompress from the morning's events, my anger at the bad guys grew more and more. I just could not understand how some bastard could sleep at night knowing he had killed and maimed other human beings. This was war, and I understand there is no honor in trying to kill your enemy, but it sure made me want to go out and blow up the bad guys myself.

Later in the shift, a young, unresponsive Iraqi man covered in mud was brought in. I placed a quick endotracheal tube while CPR was being performed, and we worked on him several minutes. Blood was spewing from his mouth and nose, and I had no idea what happened to him. A quick ultrasound of his heart demonstrated no cardiac motion; he was dead.

His father was in front of the hospital, and we cleaned the mud off the face of his dead son. We brought the poor man into the room to see his child. The elderly father teared up, kissed the body on the forehead, and then walked out of the room saying, "That is destiny" in Arabic. The father was incredibly grateful to us for trying to save his son, and then he loaded on the helicopter that brought him in and he was gone. That was it. I was amazed at the lack of emotion that the father demonstrated. He obviously cared for his son, but it just reaffirmed to me how this culture viewed life and death so differently than we do in the Western world. Life seemed to be so much more precious to those of us in our Western culture than it was to the people in the Middle East. Maybe it is because we are not used to death like they are; hopefully we will never be.

———

Later, we received our first tour of the Green Zone when Mike, a physician assistant from one of the U.S. compounds, came to the CSH and picked us up in his up-armored Suburban. He drove us to the Crossed Sabers, the Tomb of the Unknown Solider, the Fourteenth of July Bridge, and other interesting places in the IZ. We took several pictures and had a great time during our tour, with me sneaking in shots wearing my University of Arkansas Razorback hat with my army uniform and body armor beneath. Other than these "touristy" destinations, the rest of the IZ was filled with concrete and razor wire. The intimidating t-walls with razor wire resting on top lined both sides of every street, converting most of the roads into narrow alleyways with high sides. Huge speed bumps attempted to curtail speeding, but the busses and armored convoys did a much better job. Iraqis, Americans, and drivers from all nationalities cruised around from place to place, waiting in long lines each time they drove certain streets or tried to enter parking lots. Foreign national security contractors lined the entrances, looking each vehicle or pedestrian over with a fine-toothed comb before allowing them inside a compound. Trash lined the streets and sidewalks everywhere. The Iraqi government was doing construction on some of the traffic circles, building fountains, statues, and other elements designed to please the eye. We affectionately called the International Zone the "prettiest shit-hole in Iraq" with all of the improvements adjacent to run-down buildings or piles of trash.

The next day, after completing my workout at our spot known as the "prison gym," I walked into the ER to find everyone rushing around to accommodate a general coming down the hallway with a minor complaint. It was Sunday afternoon, and the outpatient clinic was closed, so people with minor issues were seen in our ED unless we were busy. A quick glance down the hallway revealed the commander of coalition forces in Iraq, Gen. David Petraeus, walking to our counter with his entourage. Our most junior nurse, Lt. Heather Cataldi, was assigned to the back treatment room for this shift, and she nervously went to the back with him. When all was said and done, we had a large group photo and he gave Lt. Cataldi his general's coin for her care. He then went upstairs to give a wounded soldier a Purple Heart.

We later walked a half-mile to the PX and got some fast food for the first time since eating at a Subway trailer in Kuwait. We settled on Burger King, and while waiting in line, I noticed a middle-aged American contractor wearing a trout fishing vest. I asked him if I was correct in that assumption, and he told me about fishing in Colorado and about his son in Jonesboro, Arkansas. I told him it was a small world, as I was from Arkansas and I exclaimed proudly, "I'm a Razorback." He turned out to be a former Southern Baptist minister working in the Baghdad area, and I informed him of my roots at Ouachita Baptist University. We had a discussion about the chances of former Arkansas Gov. Mike Huckabee getting the nod for president of the U.S. in the 2008 election, and he gave me his business card and I went off with my group. It was great to meet someone from back home, and I figured the more friends you have, the better you will be in life.

———

Later that night, we took care of an American soldier hit by an IED. He had shrapnel wounds to his extremities and was taken to the operating room for washouts of his lacerations, but overall he had no major injuries. The unique thing about this soldier was his attitude and personality. There was no lack of cursing as we moved and manipulated him during his stay in our ER, and he let us know for sure when we did anything that caused pain. His Southern accent reminded me of home, and his colorful language was actually quite funny.

The most humorous aspect of this particular soldier's stay was the fact that, between his cursing, he kept saying, "They got me! I can't believe those bastards got me!" He kept repeating it over and over, and by the time we had pumped him full of enough pain meds to make him loopy, he became more and more vociferous, "Those bastards! They got me! I can't believe they got me!" He kept saying it over and over all the way to the OR. I assume he has no permanent injuries from the blast, but he made our night with his bright and colorful personality.

The next day, around 5:00 PM, while returning from the gym and preparing to go on night shift, I heard a loud explosion and everyone outside, including myself, scrambled into the building to seek cover. We were all still slightly paranoid from the mortars on Thanksgiving! It turned out to be a large bus-borne explosion in the Red Zone that killed twenty-five people and wounded scores more. Most of these traumas went to the local Iraqi hospitals, where the Iraqi physicians would do the best they could to care for as many as possible. They simply were overwhelmed and did not have a U.S.-style triage system. When mass casualty events occurred, they did everything they could for the first patients that arrived, sometimes utilizing all their resources on a few patients who likely would not survive. The victims arriving afterward, sometimes even with survivable injuries, would just have to do without. We did the opposite. When our resources were pinched, we triaged them into categories, trying to save as many as possible rather than the first few to get to us. It did create many hard decisions; ordering your team to stop caring for someone was an incredibly painful decision to make. It went against everything we had been taught as physicians. But we had to save as many as possible, and that meant that gravely wounded people had to be let go sometimes to in order to give others a chance to live. That was never an easy decision, and some of those decisions still haunt my soul.

A few hours later, victims began trickling into us, one with an open fracture of his leg, another with shrapnel blown into her abdomen, and another with shrapnel to the spine and resultant paralysis below the arms. I was not sure what the animals behind the attack were trying to accomplish, but they did create the pain and suffering they were seeking.

We had issues with our anesthesia providers that night, griping to our nurses as they rolled patients to the operating room about not having something done or complaining about patients not receiving blood or other treatments. They even went so far as to say, "The ER doesn't know what they are doing or have a clue about giving blood." As I had mentioned before, in the ER we are always second-guessed with 20/20 vision in hindsight. I have come to accept that in my life, but I was done being shoved around. We knew we would take hits being the new kids on the block in the hospital, with all the surgeons and anesthesiologists having been there three months prior to our arrival, but I decided that night it would be no more.

I wanted to charge up to the OR and tackle the jerk who gave my nurses a hard time, but obviously that would not be the right answer. I had a long list of complaints I was storing up for our department chiefs' meeting the next week, especially after listening to certain individuals blatantly lie at our most recent morbidity and mortality conference. I planned to put it all out on the table and see what happened. I have never been a great arguer, and I think that I would be a terrible lawyer. But I had to stick up for Marti and Jason, as they were the two ER docs with me for the long haul, working or available 24/7, and they should not have to deal with the second-guessing of a bunch of six-month rotators. I knew I might be crushed, but I planned to fight for my crew in the process.

Our hospital morning report meeting and our weekly department chiefs' meeting began at 7:30 AM each day. Morning report was easy, but then I hit a snag at the chiefs' meeting where the medical directors of the other departments ganged up on me. Lt. Col. Kim, now the chief of the outpatient clinic, brought up the point that the ER was sending too many people over to the outpatient clinic, and I argued with her. The chief trauma surgeon then agreed with her and I countered, but then the other chiefs spoke up and agreed with those guys. I knew that if one or two people had a different opinion than I, they could still be wrong; if all of them did, I likely was taking the incorrect position. I gave up my argument and conceded their point, but then I took them to task with several issues I wanted to address. As I have mentioned, I am not a good debater, but I got my points across, and they all agreed to comply. It was a huge win for the emergency department, as we took our hits until we had our feet under ourselves, and then we were fighting back.

I immediately trekked down to our department and discussed the meeting with Deb Chappel, our head nurse. My plans were to then head to the gym and on to the weekly market bazaar across the street to buy my family rugs for Christmas, but those plans were quickly cut short.

The first two helicopters dropped from the sky without much warning, carrying four injured Iraqi soldiers who were engaged in a firefight around FOB Falcon. A grenade had erupted nearby, and these guys were all caught in the shrapnel's path. Marti, Jason, and I always pitched in to help each other out, regardless as to who was actually on shift at the time. Marti was on, so she took the first, most serious victim, and I took the next. Her patient was screaming in pain, and we learned through the translator that he felt his right leg, with an open knee joint due to the blast, was on fire and causing excruciating pain. He also had a nasty head injury and would need to be transferred to the air force hospital in Balad for neurosurgical care.

While Marti was evaluating her patient, I jumped to my guy to find shrapnel wounds to his lower abdomen and pelvis. Despite his immense pain, he was alert and doing okay, so I ordered antibiotics, pain medications, and a tetanus shot. I performed a quick ultrasound exam looking for bleeding in the abdomen, called a FAST, and then he went to the back treatment area to wait in line for our CT scanner.

As Marti completed the workup on her patient, two more arrived with open head injuries, and we each took one. Her patient was awake and moving, but had a small amount of brain matter exposed. My soldier was awake as well, but he immediately began vomiting profusely upon arrival, an ominous sign of a potentially serious head injury. Standing at the head of his bed, the nurse and I turned him to his right side in an attempt to keep him from aspirating the vomit. Once he was done, our medic sank an IV and I performed a rapid sequence intubation without problems. Marti was doing the exact same thing two beds over with her head injured patient, almost as if our actions were synchronized. Once intubated, I sent my patient to CT scan to see what damage the projectile that entered just above his right eyebrow had caused inside his skull.

Immediately after my patient was rolled outside to the scanner, we received two more, both with chest pain. One was unresponsive and not answering commands. We worked on them and attempted to revive the unresponsive patient, and we quickly discovered he was faking his altered mental state in order to be seen quicker. Patients do that in the U.S. very frequently, and this gentleman's antics were not unusual to us. Despite the people with open skull fractures and shrapnel to their abdomens in the ER at that time, this guy just *had* to be seen right then. His narcissistic personality would not allow us to stop and take care of the sicker patients first. We confronted him, and then dispositioned him quickly as we began to receive an eighteen-year-old Iraqi girl with a gunshot wound to the chest.

Marti began working on her, and I called the hospital in Balad to begin coordinating our transfers. I spoke with a medic in the Balad ER on the phone. As I was asking her for a physician to talk to, she told me they were busy as they were expecting four casualties to arrive. She then paused, listened to someone else tell her something and then quickly said, "We have a real-world mass-cal, we can't take any patients and I've got to go!" There we were, stuck with three head-injured patients. One was having a herniation of his brainstem through the hole in the bottom of his skull, and there was nothing we could do about it other than send him to the ICU and maybe drill a hole in his skull to try to relieve some of the pressure, a stop-gap procedure at best.

We coordinated with our surgeon on call and admitted all of our patients. Marti's first patient, despite ridiculous amounts of narcotic pain meds, continued to scream in pain throughout his ED stay. He may have been having some sort of neuropathic pain due to his head injury, or maybe he was used to narcotics and had tolerance to the medications. The head-injured patients were eventually sent to the Iraqi health care system, and I am sure they had poor outcomes. It was unfortunate that we could not send these guys to definitive, American standard-of-care surgeons in Balad, but thanks to a suicide bomber killing people in Dialya province to our north, we were not able to help these people as we wished.

Once we had emptied the department somewhat, I snuck out to buy the Middle Eastern rugs for the Christmas gifts I wanted to send home. We later met at 5:30 PM in front of the hospital for a special treat. Our great PA friend from the State Department who gave us a tour a few days earlier took us down to his complex for dinner. We needed his special pass to get in, and we all had to wear special identification badges saying "Escort Required" in large letters.

We then ate the best meal we had since the steakhouse at Fort Campbell several months prior. Steak, shrimp, chicken, real baked potatoes ... you name it. It was awesome. After supper, we were treated to Ben and Jerry's ice cream and then given loads of candy bars and cookies to take back to our nurses and medics.

The compound we were visiting used to belong to one of Saddam's sons. Apparently, he would take women there and rape them before having them killed. But with the negative connotations of his atrocities gone, I felt like we were in the Caribbean! We were given a tour through the huge gym with its brand-new equipment, with a television for every treadmill, and an unbelievable array of weights, both nautilus and free. We then went to the full-service bar, complete with a big screen television and large pool table.

The crown jewel to me was the outdoor patio area, complete with nice ceiling fans and beautiful wicker furniture. The patio overlooked the crystal blue, heated swimming pool, along with the plethora of lounge chairs and gazebos. We all realized that we were in the wrong part of the U.S. government—to think we could have had it this good if we were not in the military! It was a great time, and I felt very fortunate to have been able to participate.

The next day, I sat at my table typing with a huge plume of black smoke accompanied by flames shooting several stories into the sky to our south. The fire appeared to be in the direction of the large oil refinery just to the south of Baghdad proper, and I was not sure if it was the refinery or something else. I attempted to search on the Internet, but I kept losing my connection with the rudimentary system at Ibn Sina. I later learned that mortars had hit the refinery and set parts of it ablaze.

We had noticed the pace was picking up just a bit over the previous week. During the prior forty-eight hours, I had cared for every one from blown-up elderly women to a one-year-old child with large burns, with several terrorized patients in between. I had also been exposed to primary tuberculosis from a guard from Peru, the first of several cases of active TB to be treated during our tour. I had been working days, but I was transitioning to night shifts and was afforded the chance to sleep in late that day, something I had been looking forward to for a while. However, the terrorists had different ideas and began lobbing mortars at civilians around 6:00 AM. The explosions across the river in the Red Zone woke us all. Realizing there was no danger at the moment, I drifted back to sleep only to be awakened by Jason calling to tell me ten patients were arriving in the ER and I needed to get down there *stat*. So much for resting before my night shift!

I scrambled to get dressed in my PT uniform, as it was the fastest "authorized" uniform I could find, and ran downstairs to find the first of three patients arriving from multiple blast explosions. Overall, we only received six Iraqi soldiers, with only one being critically ill. We cared for those guys, and once everything calmed down, I went upstairs to the roof to witness firsthand the smoke plume that others were telling me about. By the time I returned downstairs, a soldier with an amputation and more Americans with gunshot wounds were arriving, although by now Jason had everything under control.

I spoke with one of our interpreters soon afterward, and she informed me that mortars had been lobbed into the far side of the four-square-mile Green Zone the day before, and things were beginning to pick up outside the wire. I hoped these last few days had just been a small escalation, one tribal leader being angry at another or something simple like that, but it was naive to think that way.

The unfortunate ten-year-old boy who was hit by an IED while walking the family cow to get water a few weeks ago, the one with multiple amputations and injuries as he arrived to us within moments of death, was still alive after his right arm and leg were amputated. He spent several days in our ICU until he was finally released. He came back with his mother for follow-up, and I spoke to them when I recognized whom they were. She told me, "God allowed him to come here, he belongs to this hospital." She was so incredibly grateful for the care that he had received that she essentially willed his life to us. What an incredible sign of gratitude! Unfortunately, however, she had a home remedy of rubbing acetaminophen, or Tylenol, that had been ground into a powder on his amputated extremities to help with the pain, which was a very bad idea. He was readmitted and taken back to the operating room where his wounds were cleaned and revised. In retrospect, he was a child maimed and willed to die by the bad guys, but through the incredible efforts of the Eighty-sixth CSH he not only would live, but he would eventually be fitted with prosthetic limbs and have a chance for a meaningful life.

We were relieved by the day crew around 7:00 AM, and several of us high tailed it to the front entrance of the hospital where a Special Forces medic named Drew picked several of us up in a worn-out van. It was great ride, complete with rusted holes in the floorboard, a transmission that refused to go into third gear, and a broken back door. We drove around the Green Zone and eventually arrived at the range, where a couple of his buddies were waiting for us. They brought several different types of weapons for us to fire, and after a brief introduction process, we prepared to shoot up the place.

Suddenly, a large explosion shook everything around us, and the six of us from the hospital all flinched, while the Special Forces guys, having been in the line of fire for a good while, just casually looked over to the area that had just endured yet another vehicle-borne IED attack. A black cloud of smoke rose from over the horizon where another suicide bomber had just ended his time on earth. Whether he receives his seventy-two virgins in heaven is up to you as the reader to decide, but those who know me have no doubts of my opinion on the subject. This marked the third day in a row that a car bomb or some other type of explosion greeted us in the morning.

We began firing the weapons, and I shot everything from AK-47s to MP-5s to my new favorite weapon, the Heckler & Kock UMP. It was a .45 caliber fully automatic machine gun made of composite material. It was very compact, lightweight, and with an amazing feel. The AK-47 was also fun to shoot; emptying a thirty-round clip on fully automatic was a rush! It was well worth missing some sleep to escape the hospital and have the opportunity to go to the range. We had to keep our command out of the loop, however, as they would freak out if they knew we were going to the range unauthorized. However, it was a great way for our guys in the ER to get out of the hospital and take a breather for a few hours. The ranges were great respites for our guys, and I would support my guys going throughout our tour as long as they did not advertise it to anyone!

As we were policing our brass, I saw a group of seven ducks flying in the distance, which helped me realize the Tigris River was just behind us. Immediately afterward, I witnessed another thirty or so getting up off the water and flying by, and being a waterfowl hunter, I could not help but be curious as to where they were going. I asked the Special Forces guys if I could duck hunt over there, and they jokingly said "just head across the bridge to the red zone and go down to the water …" Needless to say, I did not plan to be duck hunting while in Iraq, but I was working hard on a chance to go fishing.

The guys told us that things were about to escalate, and that Al Qaeda was preparing for an offensive after being on the run for so long from the troop surge. They told us to plan to have an eventful Christmas and New Year's Day, as the bad guys did not like for us to celebrate our holidays unhindered. I wish they would have told us that on Thanksgiving Day *before* the mortars, and I would have stayed inside.

On shift that night, we treated a poor three-year-old Iraqi girl who had second and third-degree burns to her face, abdomen, back, and legs. Patients with burns to the face can have swelling and scarring to their internal airways and vocal cords, so we obtained IV access quickly, gave her morphine, and then quickly prepared to intubate her. When I looked into her throat with the laryngoscope blade, she did not have burns or soot in her airway, so I had no difficulty passing the tube. I guessed her body surface area burned to be approximately 35 percent, and those fears were confirmed by our burn specialist Dr. Booker King. He took her to the operating room to work on her, but unfortunately she would have a very poor prognosis. She would most likely die from her severe burns at some point over the next few days to weeks, succumbing most likely to organ failure or infection. However, the resuscitation went very smoothly, and we did the best we could do for. We had to let God do the rest.

There was another resuscitation being performed upstairs in the ICU at the same time I was working on the little girl. The day before, I had cared for an elderly Iraqi woman suffering from end-stage liver disease and hepatic encephalopathy, or confusion due to her liver failure. She required a liver transplant and was in very bad shape, with her jaundiced skin glowing a bright yellow hue. She was admitted to the ICU, where she was given lactulose, a stimulant laxative designed to reduce the toxic ammonia levels floating in her bloodstream and causing her altered mental state. The main side effect of lactulose is horrible smelling diarrhea, bad enough to clear the room even from a small event. The effect is much worse when the patient codes from a cardiac arrest and defecates all over their bed. The closest care-giver to her at the time was Pat Hickey, our pediatrician who should have been in the ER helping us with the child. Instead, he was on the lady's bed performing one-handed chest compressions while covering his nose and mouth with the other, saying repeatedly to himself, "Don't puke on the patient. Don't puke on the patient." These thoughts were followed closely by, "This is why I did pediatrics." They got the patient's heartbeat back, and after a day or so the stench of lactulose-enunodated feces finally cleared the air in the ICU.

———

I went to see our little burned girl in the ICU the next night, breaking my personal policy of not following up on patients, which I created because I did not want to know what happened to them once they left the ER. I could not concern myself with the final outcome, whether they lived or died. I could only do my job to the best of my abilities and move on from there, and it was too hard sometimes to discover the outcome.

I regretted my decision after walking to her bedside in the ICU. Her entire face, all with third-degree burns, was massively swollen. Her lips, now pink from the charring, were about four to six times their normal size, along with her cheeks, eyelids, and neck. I did not bother to look at the rest of her, hearing that the surgeons had performed escharotomies on her extremities, cutting them all to prevent the pressure inside her arms and legs from being too high and cutting off the blood flow. Unfortunately, with my previous fears confirmed, I knew she would die soon, if not in days, then surely within weeks. If she did survive, by a miracle from God, she would need years of surgery and skin grafting to her face to try to retain a somewhat normal appearance, but we would have to get her out of Iraq for that to happen. Pat Hickey, our pediatrician, told me he was beginning to contact some nongovernmental organizations that might be able to assist us to get her to Jordan, the U.S., or some other country that could help.

That day on the front cover of *Stars and Stripes*, the military-based newspaper we received daily, was a huge photograph and article about our little boy with the amputations. It told of how he was watering his cow and got blown up by the IED, and then heard a U.S. foot patrol several meters away. He called to them and crawled their direction, trying to say, "Mister, mister, please help me" in a weakened voice. Our forces found him and then quickly found two other IEDs waiting to kill them. The article spoke of how the "U.S. hospital in the Green Zone" saved his life and how thankful he and his mother were to the Americans.

Stealing a lesson on leadership from Maj. Rob Blankenship MD, one of my emergency medicine mentors, I took the newspaper with the article and picture on the front page and showed it to a medic pulling guard duty out front, someone unknown to me from some other section in our hospital. I showed her the picture of the little boy, told her that I had intubated him and directed his resuscitation when he arrived to us, and that our trauma teams and surgeons had not only saved him but given him a chance at a meaningful life directly because she was willing to stand there outside on guard duty and keep us safe. Because of her, this little boy was alive. Her eyes lit up and she replied, "Thank you." I had no idea if she appreciated that gesture or not, but it felt good to me to convey my thoughts.

I was not on shift that day, but I found myself downstairs in the ER when a U.S. soldier hit by an IED was carried in on a litter. He was wearing his body armor, but one fragment was able to penetrate the weak space near his underarm and get into his chest, collapsing his lung. He had a large exit hole in his back, which we discovered when we rolled him over. Marti was the ER doc on duty, and being the physician off duty, it was my job to stand back and offer assistance if required. She asked me to place a central venous line into his groin, and I did so quickly without incident.

Upon his return from the CT scanner, Marti set him up to be evacuated to Balad because he had a piece of shrapnel in his skull and needed neuro-surgical care. His unit arrived, along with their commander and sergeant major. They wanted to give him a Purple Heart prior to his departure on the helicopter, but we were in such a rush to package him for transport there was no time to waste. I could tell the commander was very moved by everything going on around him, and I eased up to him and said, "Sir, just do it while they are working. The bird is on the pad, and we can't stop." Ten people were working on the patient, wrapping blankets around him and taping equipment down to his litter. Blood and trash covered the trauma room floor, and the lieutenant colonel was too nervous to step in, trying to keep himself out of the way. I stepped forward and escorted him to an open spot, and he then cautiously pinned the flimsy piece of ribbon and metal to his soldier's rigid neck collar. I was deeply touched by his actions. I knew it was just a piece of metal and ribbon, and a replacement could be bought at any military post in the free world. But this commander wanted to be the one to present this soldier, *his soldier*, a well-deserved Purple Heart. He stepped up to the plate despite the chaotic movements around him and the craziness of the trauma room. That was another example to me of the amazing leadership demonstrated by our forces.

An hour later, we had a very young looking U.S. soldier arrive with a partial amputation of his right leg due to a land mine. Apparently, it took a while for him to be rescued by his unit because they had to sweep each step toward him for additional mines since they may have been in a minefield. He was awake and in excruciating pain. We placed lines into him quickly, giving him pain medications and blood, and Marti and I went to cutting his tourniquets down in an attempt to evaluate what was left of his leg.

He had great sensation to his leg, despite the section above the knee being split open from knee to groin, and then with bare tibia hanging out the bottom. His lower leg was splayed open as if someone had taken a fillet knife and just sliced down from knee to ankle, slicing all of the musculature away from the bone. Miraculously, his nerves seemed intact in his leg and foot, and despite its purple appearance, it showed great capillary refill and blood flow. Marti and I, when first removing his tourniquets, pulled clumps of blood-soaked dirt out of his leg, and I cannot imagine how much dirt was removed in the operating room.

While being fully awake, he lifted his head and looked down at what was left of his mangled leg, and said, "That's not good." He then paused and nervously questioned, "Is my dick still there?" We gave him an assuring yes, and it was quickly followed by, "What about my balls? What about my balls?" We told him all was okay in his groin, and I think he was satisfied. Our nurses took turns holding his hand, as it gave him great comfort. Our staff tried to leave him alone while in the CT scanner to avoid radiating themselves. However, the soldier was not comfortable, and our radiology NCOIC, 1st Sgt. Tim Gallagher, put on a lead vest and stood beside him the entire time, holding his hand. What a job well done! I was very impressed with 1st Sgt. Gallagher's compassion, and he demonstrated it time and time again throughout our tour. I was incredibly proud of our team for the professionalism they demonstrated, all the while giving this American boy fantastic trauma care. Do not get me wrong, we still had to improve—we had yet to get up to the level of the Twenty-eighth CSH when they had been there over a year, but I was proud of our guys nonetheless.

The next day I cared for two U.S. soldiers who were gathering near their vehicle when it was struck by a rocket flying in over the t-walls of their FOB. They both had shrapnel wounds to the legs, and while they were admitted to the hospital, they would turn out fine. An army Humvee ambulance, or FLA, then rushed into our back gate with a ten-year-old boy with a blast injury to his abdomen, surprising us. He was combative, typical for many traumatized patients, so we sedated and intubated him to control the situation before he went upstairs to the operating room for surgical exploration of his wounds.

Moments later, a thirty-something-year-old Iraqi woman came to our front gate and asked to be seen. She had blood oozing down the right side of her face. She told the guard at the front gate that "The Americans shot me," and she was rushed back to our ER from the front of the hospital. We began stripping her clothes off to evaluate her injuries, and she began to claw and scream at us because we were removing her clothing and exposing her, typical for many of the Iraqi women for whom we cared. It seemed that, even on their deathbed, they would rather die than have their wounds exposed and treated. When I began to cut the burka off her head, exposing her hair, she began crying louder and thrashing violently. I felt for her, but we had no choice if we were to help her, so we continued cutting. She had an injury to her right forehead with exposed brain matter hanging out about two centimeters. I could not believe she was fully awake, alert, and able to walk with her brain hanging out of her head! While cutting off her burka, a metal object fell to the bed from her hair. I picked it up and noted it to be the bullet she was shot with. It was a full metal jacket, only slightly deformed projectile that obviously was not a 5.56 mm NATO, 9 mm, or .45 caliber round that the U.S. forces use. Our guys did not injure her, but it was a moot point at that moment. We intubated her, placed an ultrasound-guided arterial line, and flew her by helicopter to the air force hospital in Balad where a neurosurgeon was waiting to operate.

A short time later, an older man was brought to us with a gunshot wound to the right lower leg resulting in an open fracture of his tibia and fibula, with the resultant foot hanging on floppily. He had no pulses to be found in his foot, and it seemed that both of his major arteries to his foot had been disrupted. He went to the OR for repair, but it did not look like they would be able to save his leg due to the damage, according to our surgeons. We did not get much history as to how he was injured, but the flight medic said something about he was injured by a "warning shot." According to our rules of engagement, our forces had to escalate their steps slowly before they actually shot at someone, unless they were in imminent danger. Maybe this was a bullet that ricocheted off the street or something like that, who knew.

We had an imbedded AP photographer with us for a week or so during December 2007, taking hundreds of photos of the CSH in action. She published several to the Internet on Yahoo, and one came out of me leaning down and trying to sooth a three-year-old Iraqi girl with deep burns to her entire chest and abdomen. The little girl was terrified, and while our nurses and medics were sticking her arms with IVs, there was not much for me to do as the physician other than order medications and direct. The best I could do was to comfort her and try to alleviate some of her fears of the "mean" foreign people trying to stick her with needles. The photo turned out wonderfully and actually appeared in several newspapers back in the U.S. the following week.

I was later notified that the Iraqi woman we cared for who had been shot in the head, with some brain matter hanging out, did well. She made it through her surgery and was acting and talking normally. Due to the location of her lesion in the right frontal lobe, she likely would have some lasting personality issues since that is the area of the brain where personality is derived from. But it was great news to hear she was doing well.

Intelligence experts told us the pace would likely be picking up in the near future, due to a combination of a large-scale operation by our forces and fact that the JAM militia was starting to heat up again. They had warned us to expect indirect fire the day before, but the munitions never came. Maybe they were waiting for just the right opportunity to hit us, but any day they did not was a good day for me.

Later that day, we unfortunately received two soldiers who were trapped underwater in a Humvee after it had flipped over into a canal. I was not sure if there was an IED involved or not. Many of the bad guys had learned they could not penetrate our armored vehicles with simple IEDs unless they had an EFP. Therefore, often they would place an IED on a side of the road with water opposite it, hoping to blow the vehicle into the water and trap the soldiers inside. The doors on the up-armored Humvees can weigh up to three hundred pounds each. Could you imagine being upside down from a blast, strapped in, wearing a bulky sixty- or seventy-pound body armor vest and trying to open a three hundred–pound door underwater? What a nightmare that must be! I can only imagine the terror going through their minds during that process. One of the two soldiers who came in did well; the other did not. I do not know how many died at the scene, as we usually did not get that information. This gave me yet another reason to respect our troops in the field and the dangers they faced daily!

The night prior, we had an American soldier commit suicide by shooting himself in the right chest. He was transported to us by an outlying aid station after the ER doc assigned to that unit did a masterful job giving him blood, placing a chest tube to drain the lung, a central line to give fluids and blood, and intubation prior to transfer to us. However, the soldier needed surgery immediately and had to be flown to us, costing precious minutes in the air, where very little could be done for him other than to hold on. When he arrived to us, we pounded him with twelve more units of blood, placed more chest tubes and central lines, and performed a thoracotomy, delivering the heart out of his chest to repair any damage discovered, but it was too late. He had essentially bled out into his abdomen and chest en route. There was nothing that the physician who initially treated him, the flight medics, or us in the ER could have done unfortunately.

The little girl who suffered massive burns to her chest and face, the one I made the "mistake" of visiting in the ICU, eventually died. We were hoping to get her to the U.S. or Jordan for further care, but it just was not meant to be. She put up an amazing fight for life throughout her stay, but there was nothing else our burn surgeon and ICU team could do.

At this time, the 2008 presidential election was beginning to heat up, and on the Armed Forces Television Network I saw a very funny commercial. Former Arkansas Gov. Mike Huckabee had teamed up with none other than action star Chuck Norris for a television commercial for his campaign. In it, Chuck Norris was shown saying that Huckabee will do this or that good thing for America, and then it flashed to Huckabee giving Chuck Norris quotes, some of which we had read on the Porta Johns in Kuwait! The two I remember were "Chuck Norris doesn't have a chin under his beard, it's another fist" and "Chuck Norris doesn't do push ups, he pushes the world down." We all got a big laugh out of it after our Kuwait experience.

The weather continued to be wonderful, and while I had lost my voice while fighting a cold, the calendar kept moving and the clock kept ticking. Christmas was approaching, and we were all ready to be done with 2007 so we could at least say, "We are coming home next year."

All along we had been told we were deploying for fifteen months, but whether we admitted it or not, we all held out hope that it would be twelve months and we would be home for the next Christmas. I had been hearing from everyone I knew that would be the case, but that day, Gen. Casey came on a visit from the United States. I was not sure exactly where he was on the food chain, but I knew he was on the news quite often and he had four stars. He was asked if we might be cut short to twelve months and basically he said that it did not look good for us, but by the next group, the deployments would be back down to twelve.

I guess our shortage of emergency physicians helped out the Tenth Combat Support Hospital, which was set to replace us in January 2009. Our commander told us they would get extra ER docs to fill the slack caused by splitting the unit between two sites, and they would also get twelve months instead of our fifteen. Good for them, but that stunk for us! Later, we would discover that our replacements would only deploy for six months. Even better.

Days later, an Iraqi woman presented to our front gate in active labor. She had just left the Iraqi hospital where she was told it would be another week before she delivered. By the time we got her into our OB/Specialty room, she was eight centimeters dilated and pushing. In the U.S., sometimes that means I have to deliver the baby because the OB may not make it to the hospital on time if they are that dilated, but in Baghdad, I was fortunate enough to be able to call one of our OB/GYNs to take care of it. Dr. Allison Lattu arrived and prepared her for a trip to the operating room that was to be set up for delivery. Laboring patients were routinely taken to the OR; if a caesarian section was required, it could be done right there rather than being stuck in the ER. After ten to fifteen minutes, the OR was ready, and I saw the crew pushing the patient down the hallway to deliver the child.

Ten minutes later, I was involved with a U.S. soldier who had been shot in both feet when I saw our pregnant patient's bed come screaming around the corner of the long hallway from the elevators, with her still on board! Our nurses were yelling, "We're gonna have a baby right now! The elevator is broken again!" We threw her back into the specialty room, and about ten minutes later, I heard the reassuring cry of a healthy baby boy. I had been told that we would deliver about one child per month, as some of the Iraqi women though that a child born in the U.S.-run hospital would earn U.S. citizenship rights. Much to their chagrin, they did not get that desire fulfilled, but they did get the best medical care in Iraq, even when the elevators were not operating.

The next day, we had an unfortunate American soldier who had been hit by either an IED or EFP, and he arrived with his right foot split open and severed, with just the skin hanging on. I hate to say it, but that was his good side, as he only lost his foot at the ankle on his right. On the left, his boot was still on, but his tibia, or shinbone, was hanging straight out the bottom of his boot about six inches. The blast had disrupted his knee somehow, blown off his foot, and then pushed his tibia down through the bottom of his boot after ripping all the flesh from it. It was a gruesome picture, and he was taken straight to the operating room for a just-below-the-knee amputation, or BKA. While I was caring for the other soldiers injured in the blast, one of them informed me that it would be his buddy's third Purple Heart since arriving in Iraq, and unfortunately, it would handicap him for life.

Having come within a few feet of being hit by the mortars on Thanksgiving Day, I could only imagine what it was like for these guys who got slightly injured by an IED or gunshot, only to be returned to duty to go back in harm's way. That had to be such a psychological wall to climb, being back out on the street just a few days after your friend was killed or maimed, and you were within a few feet of death yourself. These guys had to ask themselves, "How many times will I get lucky?"

That week we created great looking Eighty-sixth CSH "Baghdad ER" T-shirts. However, true to form, the command sergeant major was upset that he did not "approve" them for wear. We gave one to Gen. Casey during his visit, and just to irritate our command sergeant major, our Sfc. John Richard said to the general, "On behalf of the commander, command sergeant major, and the EMT staff," when presenting the shirt to him. The general was very pleased and exclaimed, "This is great. I'm going to wear it for PT [physical training] tomorrow." To me, if the chief of staff of the army had authorized the shirt to be worn with the PT uniform, that meant I could wear it as well. That went over like a lead balloon with the command of the hospital, but after only a few months we in the ER did not really care about keeping people happy anymore, only about saving lives.

Christmas Day

December 25, 2007

The days leading up to Christmas were action-packed. I cared for several people who died, popped wheelies on John Deere Gators, and even went fishing. One of the patients I had to watch die was a man Jason cared for who had burns to over 80 percent of his body. When entering the room, the unavoidable smell of burnt, charred flesh permeated all barriers. The poor Iraqi solider was still alive, as he had been a victim of a large car bomb just outside one of the local checkpoints. The medics on the ground had performed a cricothyrotomy by cutting a hole in his neck and placing a breathing tube, and then they sent him to us. His face and head were burned to the second and third degree, and his facial features were unrecognizable. Unfortunately, there was nothing that could be done to help the young man, and he was placed on a morphine drip and was expected to die quickly. The morphine was to keep him out of pain and to keep him sedated so he did not suffer any more than he already had.

Later that night, a local contractor who had injured his leg came to the front gate seeking medical care, since he had fallen from a truck. Not wanting him to have to wait to go to the clinic the next day, we placed him in the treatment room as we were concerned about a femur fracture. Usually a simple fall from a truck should not break someone's leg, but I had seen stranger things.

The radiographs confirmed that the small, thirty-something-year-old Ugandan who spoke limited English had a midshaft femur fracture. After telling the patient and his escort the bad news, I left to call our orthopedic surgeon on call. As I returned to the room, I noticed his escort had disappeared. Asking the patient where his "friend" went, he said he did not know and had no way to get in touch with him. That fact, along with his fishy story about falling only two feet from a truck, proved to me that something was not right with the mechanism of injury that was presented to us. I am sure there was much more to the story that we never discovered, but that "friend" did not want to found anywhere around this guy. We never saw his companion again, but the man was seen by our orthopedist and prepped to go to the operating room for surgical repair. He likely fell from a moving truck onto the asphalt, and his coworker did not want his company to know exactly what happened.

I went back into the room a few minutes later, and he was very solemn and quiet. I asked if he was okay or in pain, and he paused to reflect, then whispered, "Okay." The nurse working with him, 1st Lt. Ann Gockley, went in and talked to him a few moments later and noticed the same thing, that he would only say "Okay" when engaged. He was very downtrodden, and we worried something else was wrong. Ann spent more time in the room, and then came out with a look of relief on her face. She said that he told her, "People who can't walk or have only one leg can't get a job in my country. I won't be able to feed my family." He was convinced that he would never walk again due to his fracture. She reassured him, and then I returned to do the same.

"Our surgeon will fix you, and you will walk again," I told him. His eyes lit up like a child on Christmas morning. "I will walk? I will be okay?" Ann and I gave him more reassurance, and by the time he left the EMT for the operating room, he was in much better shape, knowing that his world was not going to collapse. In the U.S., we take our incredible medical care for granted, but to this poor gentleman from Uganda, a broken leg could have been a death sentence or at least a harbinger of nightmares to come for both he and his family.

The following night shift found me walking downstairs into a busy situation at 7:00 PM. We had a few patients present, and my boss Col. Rowe told me he had received a call from another American infantry officer about four Iraqi soldiers who were burned in the same car bomb that killed our patient the day before. Apparently this officer authorized members of the Iraqi Army to go to the local hospital that was caring for the soldiers, pull them out, and send them straight to the CSH. Col. Rowe instructed me to go out to the Iraqi ambulances when these patients arrived and triage them; if they were sick we needed to take them, but if they only had minor injuries, I was to turn them away since we could not give them any better treatment than they were previously receiving. If we kept them, we would just have to send them back out to the Iraqi health care system the next day.

The call for the patients' arrival came about an hour later, and two of our medics put on their protective headgear, jumped on one of our John Deere Gators and rushed to the front gate to meet the ambulances. At that point, we were not sure if the patients coming were the correct ones, but a quick phone call from our medics asking for my presence confirmed these were the guys we were expecting.

Spc. Cotton, another EMT medic, and I ran outside to triage the patients, and she asked if I wanted to take the Gator versus walking. I quickly gave her a yes and we both jumped in, not taking the time to go back and grab our helmets. I drove the Gator down by the LZ and out to the front gate, where people were yelling and Iraqi soldiers inundated the scene. By the time we arrived, our medics had already loaded two of the patients onto the back of their Gator, and a quick glance at their charred faces let me know they were sick enough to keep. I ran to the back of the ambulance and helped an Iraqi soldier pull out the third and fourth patients from the litter racks. All four had severe facial burns and were wrapped in blankets to keep them warm. There was no question about turning them away, as all four of these soldiers were in critical condition.

The first Gator sped away toward the ER, and I jumped into the driver's seat of the second with our two patients and Spc. Cotton on the very back holding onto the litter straps to keep from falling off. As I began backing the Gator up, all the Iraqi soldiers were yelling "Go, go, go!" along with the one American soldier present, as they were all in a huge rush to get their friends to the definitive medical care they sought at our CSH. I threw the Gator in forward and began heading up the road toward the ER, slowing down for the speed bumps. One speed bump I went over too slowly, and as the front end went over it, the weight of the two patients combined with Spc. Cotton proved too much and the front tires jumped off the ground, popping a wheelie. Having done this on ATVs, I realized I was going too slow and gave it some gas, kicking the back tires onto the speed bump and bringing the front end back down to the ground with a thud. One of the poor patients yelled in pain when the Gator dropped back to its six wheels, but I was more worried about making sure Spc. Cotton was still with the rest of us on the vehicle and that I had not spilled her off the back—but she was still on board.

We rushed to the back door of the ER and brought our patients inside. Once inside the well-lit trauma room, we realized that three of the soldiers had burns to over 70–80 percent of their bodies, and it broke our hearts to know they would all die soon. One unfortunate man's eyes were burned shut; another was gasping for air but unconscious. The third was the most heartbreaking, as he was fully awake, alert, and oriented, knowing everything going on around him. I am sure he was thinking to himself, "Thank God I've made it to the American hospital, I'm going to be okay now." I did not have the heart to tell him that all we could do was put him upstairs and let him die. There was nothing we could do.

The fourth gentleman had less severe burns, and our burn surgeon Booker King felt he could save him. His hands were wrapped in plastic bags, with white, pus-like flesh dripping off his fingertips from the full-thickness burns he had received to his hands combined with the growing infection.

We gave him pain meds and prepped him for the operating room.

The other three patients were placed upstairs and given pain medications to keep them comfortable. After being placed in the room together, two died rather quickly, but one—the one who was alert when he arrived—through the translator said, "Thank you. Thank you. Thank you. I have been in so much pain until I arrived here. Thank you for taking away my pain." He died not too long after saying those words. At least we were able to help take away the pain as these guys passed from this world, even if we only saved one. The patient in the OR lost both of his hands, but at least he had a chance to live.

I was off shift on Christmas Eve, and while walking through the ER, Marti asked me to help out with a badly injured patient from a motor vehicle accident. The patient arrived and appeared to have a bad head injury at first glance, and I went to work placing a central line into her femoral vein in her groin. American contractors ran American-style ambulance services on posts in the Middle East, and the Green Zone was no exception. The paramedics told us that the other two people in her vehicle were dead at the scene, and she was the only survivor. She was given blood and resuscitated for over two hours by our team in the trauma room. Several times her heart stopped and she began to code. We would revive her only to have her become unstable and code again. Once she was stable for a short amount of time, we rushed her into the CT scanner to investigate her head injury. At that point our suspicions were confirmed: her head injury was too massive to sustain life. That is why she kept coding repeatedly, no matter what measures were taken. We shot her scan to the neurosurgeons in Balad and they concurred that our efforts were futile. She died shortly thereafter.

An hour or two later, I received a call from a local U.S. officer I had met who did some fishing in the International Zone. I had expressed my desire to go with him, and he invited me for a quick trip close to dark. He picked me up outside the entrance to our hospital, and after a quick drive through the IZ, we were on the Fourteenth of July Bridge, leading into the Red Zone. It was prohibited for us at the CSH to go there, so we all jumped out on the bridge and shot some quick pictures, knowing we would likely never return. We then went down a border road and took several shots of the Hotel Babel, a tall historic building in the Red Zone on the other side of the Tigris River. From our vantage point, we could see kids playing in the parking lot, just across the river in the Red Zone. I wondered what it was like to live over there with the frequent gunfire and threat of death all around.

We then parked and began walking to the fishing spot. Stepping into a dense grove of palm trees made me feel like we were in the jungles of Vietnam! As I walked through the trees, something jumped in front of me and charged my direction, coming right for me. At the last moment, the stray cat veered off course, right before it jumped into me. When I told everyone my story later, I embellished it by saying, "While walking through the Vietnam jungles to go fishing, a small tiger jumped onto the trail and almost attacked me." I thought "tiger" sounded much better than "stray cat."

Once we arrived to our fishing hole, we dug out the bacon stolen from the dining facility and went to work. We only had a few minutes of daylight left, and Steve quickly put it to good use by catching two small asps. They were a long and slender fish that resembled a small tarpon. I struck out in our twenty minutes of fishing, but I was thrilled now that I had somewhere to escape to if I could land a vehicle. The Peruvian guards nearby kept us good company throughout our short expedition, and the Christmas Eve fireworks across the river in the Red Zone were entertaining. The sound of constant gunfire across the Tigris River was a different sort of background noise than anything I had encountered on a fishing trip!

Driving back almost got us killed. Steve drove very erratically and fast in order to "keep from getting blown up" he said. We were passing cars on the right, passing on the left, and I think we pulled a *Dukes of Hazzard* stunt and even jumped one car somewhere along the way. We sped around a curve and quickly found ourselves well within the one hundred meter distance that U.S. Army vehicles always kept between themselves and local cars for safety from vehicular-borne suicide bombs, or VBIEDs. The soldiers in the Stryker in front of us quickly lazed the windshield of our unmarked Ford

Explorer, aiming lasers at us to warn us they were close to shooting if we did not back away. Needless to say, we slammed our sport utility vehicle to a quick stop and waited for the convoy of Strykers to pass by. I am still not sure if I wet my pants or not that night, but it definitely scared the daylights out of me!

After a Christmas Eve meal in the dining facility, several of us from the EMT went to our Christmas Eve service. It was great, and I was thrilled to be off shift and able to attend. During the service, I got choked up somewhat because I wanted to be with my family—I wanted to be with Laura and Avery. I hated to miss Avery's first Christmas; she was eight months old at the time.

We then went to the rooftop to smoke cigars and enjoy Christmas Eve. About ten of us sat and relaxed, despite the cold weather with temperatures in the thirties. A campfire would have been great, but that would be tough to do on top of the dorm we lived in. We spent a couple of hours talking and laughing, and it was a great way to spend Christmas Eve while deployed. I went downstairs to the ER about 11:45 PM to wait until midnight and wish everyone a Merry Christmas, but a bad guy decided to engage our soldiers somewhere out there and ended up getting himself shot and received a trip to our trauma room right about that time. After helping out with his care, I wished everyone a good night and went to bed.

I slept Christmas morning, resting up for my next swing of shifts beginning the next day. Once awake, I ran downstairs to grab my weapon and head over to the dining facility, but a guy with both legs amputated was to arrive within a minute so I stuck around to help Marti. Several procedures and units of blood later I looked at the clock in the trauma room to notice that at noon on Christmas Day 2007 I had my hand in a man's chest massaging his heart. I hoped I would not be doing the same for Christmas the next year.

Afterward, I went upstairs to my room and began opening the packages I had been sent over the past couple of weeks from family and friends back home. I had not opened any of them as I wanted to wait for Christmas Day. I went all the way through them, having a great time, when I finally got to the last one. It was from Laura, and when I opened it I noticed a note written and placed on top that said a few things on it. Most significantly it said, "I'm proud of you." Three months of tears erupted, and I finally lost it. I missed my family and life so much, but to have my wife, my rock, let me know that she approved of what I was doing and to know she was proud of me absolutely meant more than anything. Of course I had no choice, but I felt like I had abandoned her and my young daughter to fend for themselves. It was the best Christmas present I could have ever asked for at the moment.

The next two days were very busy, and our hospital began to fill. As a combat support hospital, our goal was to always have plenty of open bed space in order to be ready for a large influx of patients at any time. The ER was rocking and rolling, and we were seeing double the number of patients that we had been caring for each shift. I had been on the day shift, and by the end each day I was exhausted, just like a busy shift back home. Many of our patients were of the medical variety, with several heart attacks, abdominal pains, and usual medical cases we see daily in the United States. Our trauma numbers were not high, although we had had our obligatory gunshot wounds and IED explosions to local Iraqis each day. Our American trauma numbers at the end of December were steady and low, and that thrilled each of us, despite the rise in our overall patient census.

Politicians at home were continuing to argue and banter about pulling out of Iraq immediately, ending the war, and bringing our troops home. At what price? At this time, both U.S. and Iraqi forces were being maimed and killed on a daily basis for the safety and sovereignty of Iraq. The majority of these casualties, by far, were Iraqi—they were poor men trying to free their country and get it to its feet to govern itself. If we abandoned those guys and pulled out during that timeframe, the sacrifices of our men and women in uniform, as well as their coalition partners, would be wasted. Our enemies were on the run; despite what Sen. Harry Reid said on the floor of Congress about the war being lost, the tide was turning to our favor.

I feared that if the newly elected president came into office a year later in 2008 and followed some of the Congressional cowards' leads, my children would be forced to come back and fight here once again. According to me, now was the time to get this job done right, not pull out!

Prime Minister Al Malachi returned, along with a high-level cabinet minister. We cared for them and then sent them home. Dena George continued to operate as our "VIP Doctor," and I enjoyed teasing her about someone important having a bad outcome. If something bad happened to the prime minister after he was treated and released from the American hospital, it would have international incident written all over it!

That day, I opened a Christmas package from Steve and Dorene Bryant, the parents of my best friend Steve during my teenage years. There were still like parent figures to me today. Being a third grade teacher in Texas, Dorene had been talking to her class about me since I left for Fort Campbell several months prior. The box had several things in it, most importantly a stack of homemade Christmas cards from each of her third-grade students. Below are excerpts from some of their humorous, candid, and sometimes brutally honest writing:

1) "Keep fighting for the USA all the way. Keep doing your thing. Hay Todd I have a question, Are you strong or are you Army strong?" — Luke (Even though I've never met him, Luke's mom says he insists on praying for me at every meal)
2) "Thank you for saving the soldiers that got hurt. Also thank you for saving us from the bad soldiers and not letting them come over here." —McKenzie
3) "I hope you have a Merry Christmas. PS: Third grade is awesome." —Matt
4) "Thank you for being a soldier in war to give freedom. You are saving people right this minute in this USA. Yes, yes you are." —Sophia
5) "Thanks you for what you are doing for us, so I hope you win. PS: Go Americans." —Matthew

6) "Hi, my name is Nate. I hope your okay. Your baby is very cute ... Thank you for even saving people that aren't on the USA team ... Are the meals good?" —Nate

7) "I'm glad you are okay when the bomb went off ten feet away from you. Thank you for helping the hurt men in war. Do you like your job? Where do you sleep? What do you eat? You're a brave doctor. How are you doing? Do you stay on a ship? Do you sleep in bunk beds? Have you ever been shot at before?" —Jordan

8) "I'm glad you've decided to be used in military use. I'm also glad that those bombs didn't harm you. I think you have to be brave to be in the military, even for a doctor." —Joel

9) "What does the place look like?" —Nicolas

10) "You are so asom [sic] even though we have not met face to face. But I wish we could meet face to face. Good luck over there in the USA. The USA means United States of America ... Hope we win!" —Avery

11) "How are you doing in Iraq? Do you like drawing robots? I do. Keep warm." —Patrick

12) "Ms. Bryant misses you so, so much. She wishes that you are okay." —Ashlee

Are kids not the best? They are so honest, sincere, and yet inquisitive all at the same time. These Christmas cards absolutely made my day. I read them to our staff and my roommates, and everyone enjoyed hearing from the bright future of America.

A few days after Christmas, about midnight, we had an American serviceman en route to us with the worst headache of his life. This is a very common emergency medicine complaint, one that we see every day back in the U.S., and we are always concerned about a bleed in the brain or some other life-threatening condition. Most of the time, the patients turn out to only have a simple headache or migraine, which can be debilitating but not life-threatening. If the patient's history does not exclude the bad possibilities, we perform a CT scan of the brain, followed by a spinal tap to be 100 percent sure there is no bleed, tumor, or other pathology.

While on his way to us, the flight medics called to say he was deteriorating and becoming combative, and we began thinking that maybe this was not just a simple headache after all. Upon arrival, he was noted to be agitated and would not follow commands or respond to verbal stimuli. He was obviously in an altered state of mind, and we noted his heart rate to be very low, a potential ominous sign of increased pressure inside his head. Once he was placed onto bed one of our trauma room, he would not be still in any other position other than lying on his stomach. Each time we would turn him over and try to put an IV in, he would fight us until he maneuvered himself back onto his belly, resting at that point. Our medics simply placed an IV with him lying in that manner, and our nurses pushed the sedation medication etomidate. He was sedated within seconds, and we flipped him over onto his back and paralyzed him so I could intubate. Once intubated, we him into the CT scanner.

Then came the bad news. The unfortunate twenty-something kid had a huge tumor in his brain. It had obviously been present for a while, but it had finally eroded into some aspect of his brain that caused an abrupt deterioration of his condition. Continuing to keep him sedated, I placed an arterial line to monitor his pressure closer, and called the Air Force Theater Hospital in Balad to transfer him to a neurosurgeon's care. We gave him steroids to shrink the tumor, followed by mannitol to help decrease the pressure.

After flying him to Balad, I received a call from the neurosurgical team letting me know that he had a very poor prognosis. Our team did a great job caring for him, and there was nothing else we could have done to help. Hopefully, he had a miraculous recovery and did great. Only God knows.

Later that afternoon, I watched a beautiful sunset over the Tigris River while sitting on the bank fishing. It was great to get away from the CSH. Maj. Steve Parrish, my tour guide from the U.S. Embassy, caught a small two- or three-pound carp, and I saw an Iraqi family fishing over across the canal catch a small asp, but once again I struck out. But that was not the point. I rarely heard any gunfire, and I was able to get out and simply spend some time outside. I watched flocks of cormorants fly by against the backdrop of the Hotel Babel and the Red Zone. Large herons swung through the air with their characteristic low-pitched call. Sunlight reflecting off the canal was beautiful to my west, and for a few moments, I was in the country again, with beautiful fields and trees around me, at least in my mind. There were no traumas, no amputations, and no dead soldiers. There was only the simple picture of me with a fishing pole watching the sunset. Who cares if I caught a fish?

Turning the Corner

January 2008

On January 1, we finally turned the corner. Laura and I could finally say to each other, "I'll see you later this year." It was now 2008, and I was scheduled to go home for leave in August. We could look forward to being together again after the deployment ended in January 2009. It sure beat saying we would not be done with this deployment for two more years, which is how it seemed with me arriving in 2007 and not returning until 2009.

The New Year started with a bang. While I was resting for my day shift on New Year's morning, the night crew apparently had a celebration of their own. There were reports of nonalcoholic beer funnels being made in the ICU, and apparently there was some aggressive beer shot-gunning going on in the emergency department at midnight as well. I was glad it was slow enough for the night crews to celebrate the turning of the calendar.

However, early New Years Day, the bad guys decided they were tired of the fun and games and used an IED to send eleven patients our way about 10:00 AM. Arriving by helicopter, we triaged them rapidly as they were rushed through the doors and started sticking people in the hallways to make room for the carnage. After checking two children who were wounded, I went to the back to witness patients and staff filling every bed we had available. Scanning to my right, I could see Dr. John Oh, one of our surgeons, with a patient in bed four; Dr. Stacy Koff, our urologist, with a lightly injured patient in bed five; and my famous ER colleague Marti with patients in beds six and seven. I went around the corner to beds eight through ten and saw two nonseverely injured people in two of them and a 350-pound Iraqi woman with blown up legs in the third. Our family medicine doctor, Dena George, was beginning to tackle her care, an enormous task indeed. Larger people are much harder to care for; they are harder to move around on the bed, have less oxygen reserve than smaller people due to the weight of their chest, and are much harder to get intravenous access.

I noticed we had some extra medics from our administrative sections who came to help, and they were placed on this bed with Dena. They were doing the best they could, but they just were not used to trauma and they had the wide-eyed look, of "Oh crap, what do I do?" Dr. George quickly began attempting a femoral central line, and I worked with the medics to quickly assess the patient. Due to the patient's size, Dena could not start the line successfully, and the medics were struggling to get her care started. We noted her to have a heart rate around one hundred, and a blood pressure around one hundred, but we did not have a proper blood pressure cuff for someone that large, making the reading potentially inaccurate. She was conscious, but slow to respond and breathing on her own. I used ultrasound to guide my central line placement while Dena removed the tourniquets from her devastatingly injured legs. Once I had access obtained, we gave her blood and sent her to the operating room for repair.

I commended Dena for tackling a very tough patient in our ED during the mass casualty, especially with no nurse and only inexperienced medics from other sections of the hospital available. I was thankful that we did not have to intubate her immediately, as she very well could have died during the process with our inexperienced crew and her size. But she made it up to the OR, and despite several people losing their legs, no one died during the process, so it was a success and a busy start to the New Year. Later that night, Sfc. John Richard made us some chicken and sausage gumbo. It was different from the shrimp and crawfish gumbo I had in the past, but it was great escape from the dining facility. We all enjoyed it and looked forward to trying it again sometime.

The next day, an Iraqi police truck whipped up to our back door carrying a man with two gunshot wounds to the head. Apparently, he was the driver for an Iraqi general. Someone apparently had driven up to the car, pulled a weapon, and shot at the general twice—only to miss and hit his driver in the face and head. We worked on him aggressively, but once the CT scan results came back showing us that he had multiple bullet fragments in his brain, a severely fractured skull, and an essentially nonfunctioning cerebrum, we realized there was not much hope. After a quick call to the neurosurgeons in Balad, we put him into an expectant care mode and made him comfortable for his approaching death. He did not expire in the ER, so after an hour or so, I sent him upstairs to the ICU to die. As usual, I pulled all of our medics into the room and did a question-and-answer session with them, making sure they all understood why we had withdrawn care from this gentlemen. I think that was helpful for them to remember that it was not because we did not care or quit trying; we all just had to realize when there is nothing that we can do to save someone. Our poor medics had to sit in the room with the patient and wait for him or her to die, a task I did not envy. I cannot say enough when describing our incredible medics!

Just before I was to get off shift that night, I had an American soldier come in from an IED blast, along with one of his fellow companions who was with him in the vehicle. Both soldiers checked out okay, and they were to just be admitted for monitoring when the NCO began to get emotional. Second Lt. Marc Brinsley, his nurse, let me know what was going on, so we began thinking that maybe there was more to this story than we realized. I went back in to talk to the soldier, and instead of just the two of them in the vehicle, he told us there were four. Two of them were in the ED, and he said a third was not hurt.

The fourth, however, was his medic and was wounded severely and trapped in the vehicle while it caught fire. The soldier said he escaped quickly and ran to the aid of the wounded medic. He attempted to pull the medic free by the arm, but then noticed that the medic's arm was "just hamburger," having sustained a serious injury in the blast. Attempting to get closer to help, through the smoke, flames, and heat, he stepped in only to have his own ammunition on his body armor begin to explode due to the heat. Of course, he had to step back immediately and remove the gear to protect himself and everyone around him. By the time he got back to his medic "it was too late."

Could you imagine living though that? We saw death and destruction daily, but we did not know these people personally. Even though we witnessed dead, dying, and wounded American soldiers routinely, we did not know them, did not go to their funerals, talk to their families, or see their children mourn the loss of their father or mother. It crushed every one of us to see our American brothers and sisters suffer, but how much more it would hurt if we knew them personally! These soldiers, these men, are the true heroes of our generation, and I fear to this day that post-traumatic stress disorder will devastate their lives and tear many of their families apart, just as it did with the Vietnam War veterans. I can sure see how that could possibly occur.

I have always been a huge fan of the popular television sitcom Seinfeld. My family provided me with all nine seasons of the show, and every day that I could, I watched one thirty-minute episode, still occasionally finding ones that I had not seen previously. One of the more popular episodes was the "Soup Nazi," where the angry owner of a soup kitchen in Manhattan would take away the customer's rights to his highly prized soup by yelling "No soup for you!" It is a very funny line with which many people are familiar.

While caring for a lightly injured insurgent who had harmed some of our troops recently, we tried to give him some ibuprophen for his minor pain when he chastised us for having "pills too large to swallow." It was all we had, and he had no intravenous line for liquid medications, so it was these pills or nothing. He angrily refused the medication, and I got a kick out of saying in Arabic, "Mako shurba ilk!" which of course translated to "No soup for you!"

The next night shift was slow, and our nurses put up a large nylon American flag in the entryway to the emergency department. It covered the ceiling lights, providing an amazing background effect as the glow shined through the stars and stripes. We figured it would be a wonderful comfort to our soldiers as they came in wounded on stretchers. They could not miss it when laying on their backs as they were carried into the facility. We were all very proud of it, and we expected the sergeant major to complain about it since he did not approve it before it was hung, but we decided it was our department and we were keeping it.

For the first time the next day, four of us checked out a sport utility vehicle from the CSH and drove around the International Zone. We were all nervous about making a wrong turn here or there, or maybe getting caught in the wrong traffic lined up to get into some high-security area or something similar, but it went well. We drove over to Forward Operating Base Prosperity and ate lunch there at a small place called the Baghdad Restaurant. I had some sort of beef pie that was not very tasty, but once again, it was great to get out and play around on my day off. I also discovered more potential fishing spots as well. Later in our tour, once we were comfortable with the IZ, driving around was not a big event, but it was nice to have an uneventful first trip on our own.

Our patient load dropped over the next few days, likely due to the freezing January weather outside. It was getting down into the twenties at night, not exactly what I expected when preparing to come to Baghdad. The days were still beautiful and sunny, making me wonder if it would ever rain. It was no surprise as to why there were date palm trees all around; I think they got as much sun there as they do anywhere else on earth. I guess if you added a beach or two and then took away the trash, concrete t-walls, bunkers, and up-armored Humvees, this would have been just like any other tropical paradise.

Although the patient census was lower, I had still seen several very remarkable cases. One evening a convoy of Humvees was hit by a large IED, and I walked into the trauma room to see Marti working on a soldier that was missing the bottom third of his face. The soldier was sitting up in bed holding a suction catheter in his mouth to suck the blood from his airway, and he was obviously in bad shape. Anesthesia was called to the ER, and he was intubated with a Glidescope System, a special intubating camera used for difficult airways. Bill Knight, a member of the corporation that manufactures them, loaned it to me to use in Baghdad. The intubation went smoothly, and he was taken to the OR for repair. He most likely would have a decent outcome, as surgeons can usually put together facial structures surprisingly well.

I cared for a couple of other soldiers wounded in the blast, one with an amazing injury I have never seen and likely never will again. He was in charge of the scene at the blast site, and this NCO refused to allow himself to be evacuated until everyone else was at the hospital and the scene was secure. These actions demonstrated true leadership, and I was very impressed by what he did, especially with his injury. He had the soft chin-strap from his helmet impaled directly into his cheek! The entry wound was just big enough for the strap, almost as if someone placed it there surgically. It was amazing, and the CT scans were even more impressive. I left the strap in place, as we have all been trained to *never* remove an impaled object until the patient is in the operating room. If the object is sitting against an artery or other vessel, the bleeding could be immense and the results catastrophic.

It was an amazing sight to see these war-torn, tough, gritty men crying together in our emergency department, but of course, I would never blame them. One of their colleagues never made it to us as the bomb killed him instantly. The unit's medic was obviously shaken, and he kept repeating to us over and over again what he had done to control the bleeding and stabilize his guys. He was upset at himself because he had treated a young Iraqi boy with severe burns the day before, and he had not resupplied his bag yet for this mission, although it did not make any difference in this case. I made a point to tell him in front of his peers that he had done everything right, a true statement in my opinion. Day in and day out, I witnessed America's medics, many with only their high school education and minimal medical training, do amazing jobs treating our soldiers at the point of injury, and they should be commended for the astounding job they do.

Two nights prior, I had two American servicemen in the back treatment room, beds side by side, both with abdominal pain. Neither had great stories for appendicitis, but I was concerned enough about both of them to obtain a CT scan to look for an inflamed appendix. Once the CT results were obtained, for the first time ever I walked into a treatment room with two patients and made an announcement, "If you are a patient in this room, you have appendicitis. A surgeon will come evaluate you, and you will be taken to the operating room for surgery. Afterward, you likely will be sent to Germany or Qatar for recovery prior to returning back to your unit. Does anyone have any questions?" With the privacy laws and overcrowding of emergency departments back home, I would never be able to make such a statement in an open room to two patients at once. Both patients and all the ER staff laughed at my announcement.

The next week, it snowed in Baghdad briefly. One of our translators said it was the first snow there in six or seven years. Someone else told me it had not snowed in over one hundred years in Baghdad, and Laura told me the news back home said it had been the 1960s since the last snow in central Iraq. It only lasted a few minutes, but the flakes were large, and they were just as beautiful as I remember back home. I was not fooled into going back in my mind and daydreaming of the Rockies of Colorado, Denali in Alaska, or even Mt. Rainier in Washington, but I did go outside and enjoy the large flakes while they lasted. I was hoping this was a sign, maybe a predictor of good things to come to this war-torn region of the world. Who knew if it meant anything, but it was a peaceful and wonderful, welcomed sight nonetheless.

I received a package from my mother in the mail containing all the ingredients to make beans and cornbread, one of my favorite recipes both growing up as a child and still to this day. She included an old iron skillet from a garage sale for making cornbread from scratch, and I had a fantastic time cooking up the loaves and serving everyone. Most of the EMT crew shied away for whatever reason, but those of us who tried it had a great meal. I retired for the evening with two full loaves of cornbread on the counter, and when I returned the next morning, most of it was gone as the night shift was not so picky.

Later, while walking back to the CSH from the palace after a meal, we walked by a company of Iraqi soldiers and several new Iraqi MRAPs, the up-armored personnel carriers that were new to the military and were designed to survive IED blasts better than the Humvees. They were massive vehicles, with cabs almost as high as the passenger compartments on tractor-trailers back home. The lead vehicle was personalized with gold antennae-like bars sticking up from the front bumper, along with another bar topped by a large feather in the center of the grill. The passenger door was open, and as we walked by, I could see curtains hanging from the top of the windshield, as well as a carpet-lined dash board inside the cab. We got a laugh out of it, as it seemed they liked to dress up their vehicles in the same way kids do back home! The Iraqis were all playing soccer with some American soldiers on the side of the road, having a great time. It was a welcome sight for me; I enjoyed seeing the Iraqi soldiers happy and playful rather than the trauma-tized state in which I usually encountered them.

Our weekly intelligence brief told us that a weapons cache was just discovered close to us in the Green Zone, about a quarter mile down the road. It contained three antitank mines, three EFPs, and over thirty 60 mm mortars. Who knows how they snuck those items into the Green Zone, but obviously they were intending to use them in the IZ. There were plenty of high-value targets running around, so maybe they were waiting for the right chance. I thanked God they were found before they got an opportunity to attack the Iraqi Parliament, the U.S. Embassy, or even us.

A few days later, we got to do the dog and pony show for the new Surgeon General of the Army, Lt. Gen. Shoomacker. He was accompanied by three U.S. Congressmen representing Pennsylvania, Minnesota, and Arizona, but

I honestly do not remember their names. They arrived to the ER in grand fashion, and our head nurse Deb Chappel was introduced first. She immediately received a coin from the surgeon general, an age-old army tradition. I was introduced as the chief of the department next, and I only received a handshake in lieu of a coin. Next came Sfc. Richard, who received a coin. He continued to go down the line, sporadically handing out his coins to various people at random. I guess I was just unlucky this time; but it was a theme, as I did not get many coins throughout the tour. Deb received several, as she would always give the VIP tours each time someone important came through. We then took the visitors into the trauma room to show them around, and they disappeared into the hospital a few minutes later.

About an hour later, the crew came back down in preparation to exit the hospital, stopping by to take pictures in the ER. While posing for pictures with the VIPs, the phone rang and told us a man with a gunshot wound to the chest was coming. I took the pleasure to tell everyone loudly and quickly to "Get out, everybody clear, traumas coming in!" It felt good to be able to tell these guys to exit and be able to take my ED back over from the command and all the brass! It was always nice to be able to meet important generals, senators, and politicians, but having to entertain them so often did get old. I loved opportunities that enabled me to regain control over my territory. To their credit, not one general or VIP ever complained when we limited their access or kicked them out.

Every day and night, local Iraqi citizens living close to us in the Green Zone would walk up to our front gate and ask to be seen at our hospital. Since 2003, Ibn Sina had been very busy taking care of its own critical patients, and noncritical Iraqi civilians were traditionally instructed to seek medical care at one of many local Iraqi hospitals in the Baghdad area. The hospital had been utilized strictly for American soldiers, contractors, government employees, coalition nation contractors and soldiers, and Iraqi soldiers and government officials. The sheer volume of trauma routinely seen in the facility, along with its relatively small size, necessitated these decisions. Local Iraqis who walked up to the gate had always been triaged by the nurses from the ER, and if it was deemed they might die or lose a limb, they were brought into the facility for care. If they could wait to go to another Iraqi hospital, they were turned away. It sounds terrible to not let the local population use the facility, but we had to remember the hospital was only allowed for people with specific approval from Saddam Hussein prior to our invasion in 2003; it was only for his Baathist Party cronies. America had opened the facility to thousands of Iraqis who had been seen there since 2003. While we did have restricted access, it was still vastly improved from the previous government, and it was eventually given to the Iraqis after our departure.

A sixty-year-old Iraqi man came to the front gate for triage by our nurses one day. The unfortunate individual had been shot in the jaw about one or two hours prior and was presenting to us for care. His teeth were in bad shape and required surgical repair; his mouth was filled with blood-soaked gauze. Did we accept or reject him? He was stable and not about to die, so I had to make the tough decision to send him away to go to a hospital in the Red Zone. We were hopping busy at the time, and he was maintaining his own airway and not bleeding to death, so medically it was the correct decision. Ethically however, I felt terrible. What about the Hippocratic Oath? As a physician it is my job to help people, especially when they have been shot! I wrestled with the decision the rest of the day and night, but it had to be made. We simply did not have the resources to care for people from the local Iraqi population that would be able to survive by going somewhere else. Since our arrival in November, we had already been dangerously close to capacity; what would we do if we had twenty blown up American soldiers come in? What if we were full of Iraqis and there were no beds for our soldiers? Our guys could not go out to the hospitals in the Red Zone; we were the hospital for them. They were our primary mission; they were the reason for our presence. Even when it made me question my oath as a physician, I had to remember my mission at all times.

Sitting later that day upon the rooftop of Jones Hall, I continued to hear loud explosions in the distance, southeast of our position. Apache attack helicopters continued their patrol over the skies as usual, but I had not seen any of them swoop out of the sky and fire upon a position, or even fire from altitude like we had witnessed before. I was to go on shift in a couple of hours, so if we were involved in the melee going on in the Red Zone, I expected to see some of the aftereffects that evening.

Around 7:00 PM we heard two explosions resulting from mortars fired into the IZ. They did not land too close to us, and after our lockdown, we only had two local nationals come in for treatment, one with a broken ankle and the other with shrapnel to the face. Both Iraqi men had minor injuries and, after much convincing from me, were discharged home to expect a full recovery.

Many local Iraqis came to us for treatment, but then seemed to argue with our plans. One of the gentlemen I treated from the mortar attacks had a scratch on his eye known as a corneal abrasion. He insisted that we put a patch over his eye, and I continuously tried to inform him that was not the proper treatment; it would actually retard his healing. He would have none of it, and I discharged him with a piece of gauze and said, "After you leave, you can tape this over your eye, but I'm not doing it." He left angrily, and who knows what he did from there. Later in the shift, I evaluated a nine-year-old girl for appendicitis. When her CT scan came back negative, through the interpreter I informed the mother that her daughter would be fine and did not require surgery. She was angry and demanded to know why we would not operate on her child. Eventually, she left in a bad mood as well, but what could I do other than try to explain it again and again?

A drunk American soldier was flown into us the next night. The American military was not allowed to partake of alcohol in Iraq, and to make matters worse for him, he was done with his fifteen-month tour and set to leave the country in four days. However, due to his impatience to drink, he likely sobered up to his Article 15 punishment and a reduced rank and loss of pay. Four days! Could he not have waited? His blood alcohol level was twice the legal limit back home, and he was unconscious. I broke a smelling salt under his nose, which quickly brought him up in the bed after the ammonia penetrated his nasal cavities. After several moments of gagging and coughing, he settled back down and passed out again. Due to his reaction and potent gag response, I did not have to intubate him like we do some drunks back home, so he was admitted to the ICU to let his liver do the work and burn off the alcohol. I am sure he was a real happy camper by the time he finished the punishment process several months later!

— —

Pulling the sheets over the head of a deceased patient was always hard to do, but when that patient was a young child, it was that much tougher. A beautiful eighteen-month-old baby girl was rushed into us by an outlying American unit that had been flagged down by her parents. The Iraqi couple had two previous children, both of whom had died for unknown reasons at less than a year old. This little girl was their only child left.

At arrival, she was unresponsive and unconscious. We placed a line into her right tibia to give medications, and I intubated her. We noted her to have fever, so we quickly gave her antibiotics and began resuscitating her. She then lost her pulse, and we began doing chest compressions and CPR. Her blood sugar was only twenty-five, a likely complication of her infection, and we treated that and worked on her for close to an hour, bringing in her parents to witness our efforts. Everything we tried failed, she was so sick from the infection in her bloodstream, called sepsis, that there was no bringing her back.

Her parents began wailing and beating themselves about the back and chest. I had heard of these reactions before, but never witnessed it. Their cries resonated throughout the ER, and our nurses and medics began to join her parents with their own tears. It was always tough to watch someone die, but always more difficult when it was a small child, especially if you had a child at home of your own. We wrapped her body, and her parents took her home, planning to bury her before sundown in accordance to their traditions. What a horrible thing for those poor people to endure! This death had nothing to do with the war in Iraq, it had nothing to do with trauma, but it was still one of the more difficult ones we had faced in this journey to that point.

The next day was much better. Around 9:00 AM, Maj. Joe Theiman, our hospital executive officer, Col. John Rowe, and I boarded a Blackhawk helicopter for a flight over to BIAP and the Victory Base Complex. It was my first trip out of the International Zone, and I was very excited and anxious for the escape.

When loading the bird, I was quick to get a seat in the back facing forward, and I accomplished my goal of being close to a window to see out and take pictures. I think I embarrassed my companions somewhat with my picture-taking, but I was not sure how many daylight trips over Baghdad I would get, so I took advantage.

Baghdad from the air consisted mostly of tan buildings of similar construction, with most all the houses being multifamily in nature. Clotheslines stretched on the backsides of half the living quarters. I could see a few cars on the streets, and children playing in the alleyways and small open areas behind the townhome-like structures. Once we got closer to BIAP, I could see the famous Water Palace, where Saddam would take business clients to one of his many resorts. Numerous palaces were built all along multiple large manmade lakes, with beautiful rotundas, palm-covered terraces, and amazing architecture. During his regime, he cut no corners to ensure his comfort!

After landing at BIAP, Maj. Stewart McCarver, an ER doc who rotated over to the CSH to help us out periodically, picked us up and gave us a tour of the area, with stops at several of the troop medical clinics that routinely sent patients to us. I was able to meet with some of the providers and get a feel for what they encountered every day. We drove by hundreds of Humvees, Strykers, cargo trucks, and tanks. After lunch, we went to a meeting with our higher headquarters. Afterward, a trip to the huge post exchange resulted in me buying frozen steaks and chicken that we could not obtain in the IZ, stuffing them into a backpack I brought along for just that purpose.

It was fantastic to see how the other half lived. In the IZ, I would usually go days without seeing an actual military vehicle; Ford and Chevrolet SUVs were the contractor's and state department's ride of choice. We were fortunate enough to live in hard buildings, with flushable toilets, even if we had to put the toilet paper in the trashcan because we could not flush it. The guys at BIAP were not as fortunate. We could go to the embassy in the IZ for fun; I was not sure exactly what they did for entertainment at BIAP.

The dirt and sand reminded me of Kuwait. It was wide open, the type of open area I thought I wanted to deploy to. I did not like being enclosed in the center of the big city, but I learned that day the open areas in Iraq were not exactly like the ones back home! Sure, there was a palm tree here or there, but it was a vast, barren wasteland of desert and dirt, and I could not imagine how hot it would be a few months later in the summertime! I finally realized that in Iraq, a lack of concrete did not mean grass; it meant dirt and mud. The vehicles were all covered in dirt, sand, and mud, and the place had an amazing feel of dreariness, even on a beautiful sunny day. Those of us in the Eighty-sixth CSH had no idea how fortunate we were to be living in a hard structure, with very little dirt and mud in the IZ.

Once our tour was over, we scurried over to the helicopter landing zone and got checked in for our flight back to the IZ. It was dark by this point, and it amazed me watching the Blackhawks operate in a lightless environment. We flew on Iron Horse Air, the service operated by the Fourth Infantry Division. Our flight consisted of military personnel, contractors, and civilian government employees. Everyone had their own required body armor and helmet, but the similarities ended there. The civilians were in blue jeans and khakis, with nice suitcases. I wondered how they would cram everything on board!

Four Blackhawks landed on the pad, and our crew chief walked over to get those of us standing in line to go to the IZ. We followed him onto the pad and walked through the deafening racket created by the twin jet engines of the first two birds, making sure to keep directly behind our guide. He walked at right angles to the helicopters, keeping a safe distance from the tail rotors, and then turned sharply to his right to lead us all down the center between the four aircraft. There was no light other than the safety lights shown by the birds. The landing zone was not lit, and it amazed me that no one had been killed by walking into a rotor blade at night. I was sure to stay in line with the crew chief, as I did not want to stumble into a helicopter blade I could not see.

Once on board the Blackhawk, our crew chiefs settled us in and then turned off all the interior lights, blacking out the bird. We launched and flew over Baghdad, and this time I was in front and able to see the flight crew work. The two crew chiefs sat in their assigned seats, facing sideways, with one behind each pilot. They both brought the machine guns mounted on each side to bear and aggressively searched the ground below for hostile actions. At one point, the aircraft automatically shot out two of its flares, indicating we were possibly targeted. The two gunners aggressively turned and prepared to fire on the ground if they noticed any threats coming our way, but nothing happened, meaning as usual that the flares picked up a false reading. That was fine with me.

We safely and uneventfully landed in the IZ, and the big day was over. It was great to be able to get out of the CSH and the IZ for the day, but my eyes were opened as to how well we really had it there. I always loved to fly, and I was fortunate to go several times during my tour, but it was interesting to add the whole "I hope no one tries to shoot us down" dynamic to air travel. I am glad I never have to worry about that back home.

That night, while checking email, I opened a message from the emergency medicine consultant to the surgeon general with the subject heading of "Good news!" Evidently the memo did go through, and ER docs were officially to begin doing six-month deployments rather than the twelve or fifteen months we had been doing. The catch, however, was that it would begin with the next unit to deploy, the 115th Field Hospital out of Fort Polk, Louisiana. They were set to deploy in a the spring of 2008 and then go home next fall while we were still there, as we would not get replaced and still do the full fifteen months. Our shortages in the upcoming summer would have been alleviated if we were included, but I guess the final answer from the army was simply to "Suck it up."

We had just recovered from the little Iraqi girl's death two days prior, as the patients continued to flow in and we accepted several more in the following days, from infected contractors in septic shock, to lacerations and head injuries. I was running from bed to bed rapidly while attempting to keep up, and here is a sampling of some of the patients I cared for:

A British contractor injured the extensor tendon to his middle finger left hand on a saw. This tendon is responsible for lifting the finger when trying to straighten out the hand. It was exposed due to the cut on the back of the hand, and looked to be about 80 percent ruptured, with the remaining 20 percent holding it together. As the ER doc, it was my responsibility to test for strength in the digits, and while stressing the tendon by pushing down on the gentleman's finger, we all heard a crunch. Everyone, including the patient, quickly looked at me, and I looked down to see the tendon completely ruptured. I felt like an idiot for making his injury worse, but he required repair of the tendon anyway, so I did not cause him any extra harm, although I did have to explain my way out of that one!

While working on another British patient with a ruptured appendicitis, I was called quickly to the trauma room to find a twenty-something-year-old Iraqi woman who had multiple blast injuries. Due to the patient influx throughout my shift, I had no surgeons or ER docs available to help me work on her, so I was on my own. While our medics and nurses were attempting to place her on the monitor, I quickly had to decide between intubating her first or placing a central venous line to give her blood. Back in the U.S., airway always comes before everything else, so she should be intubated initially. However, with the massive penetrating injuries we saw in Baghdad, often patients required blood first, so it was not quite as cut and dry.

Quickly scanning her over, I noticed she had a nearly amputated left arm and right hand, and likely 60 percent of her small and large bowels were eviscerated, or hanging out of her open abdominal wound. The smell of bowel permeated the trauma room, and as she lay before me, obtunded and nearly lifeless, I could not help but be reminded of the smell of a deer's abdominal cavity as it is being gutted and cleaned. I noticed her to have shallow and insufficient respirations, and I chose to intubate her first. Her arms and legs were so damaged that our nurses and medics had no where to place an IV, so they would have to wait for me to finish placing the endotracheal tube before I could place the central line.

I asked Mark Brinsley to prep her left chest for a subclavian central line that I would place just beneath her clavicle, and I placed the endotracheal tube and rotated straight over to put in the line. At that time our team notified me that her systolic blood pressure was sixty, and she was desperately in need of blood and could die at any moment. Subclavian lines sometimes have complications; it is sometimes hard to find the vessel, and occasionally they do not feed well enough to place the catheter over the wire. Not this time. I nailed the vessel within seconds, and in less than a minute after I started, she was receiving life-saving packed red blood cells. After the first six units, her blood pressure crept up, and we pounded her with six more units and wrapped her exposed bowels in wet dressings, packaged her, and rushed her to the operating room with a systolic blood pressure of eighty. The surgeon on call arrived at the last minute for me to tell them what her injuries were, what we had done for her, and to rush to meet her in the operating room. I was told later that she did fantastically after leaving the ER; she was still alive and slowly recovering the next day. Her left arm amputation had been completed, and her abdomen was left open after her bowels were replaced to prevent infection.

A few patients later, as the steady flow of trauma continued, an American soldier was brought in with CPR in progress. I intubated him, and a quick exam, conducted while working around our medic doing chest compressions, revealed a hole in the top of his head. Further exam demonstrated a puncture wound to his perineum, just behind his scrotum and extending into his abdomen. I was not sure exactly how he received these wounds, likely from an antitank mine buried in a roadway, but we worked hard to revive him with no success. It appeared he had expired prior to arrival, but in the melee of multiple patients rolling in, including some with CPR en route, we pushed hard to revive him. After pronouncing him deceased, I went to the back to help out with the other soldiers who had arrived with him from the blast.

All in all, several hundred Iraqis throughout the country died that day, many as they were celebrating Ashuraa, the annual pilgrimage to the holy city of Karbala, in order to mourn the death of an early century Islamic imam, or saint. The terrorists loved to target the civilian population on religious holidays to create as much death and destruction as possible. Their actions kept us very busy that day, but despite its results, violence overall was still down markedly in the fragile democracy.

The day finished with news of me being selected for a random urine drug screen the next morning at 5:30 AM— more army-style fun and games. However, Dena George and Pat Hickey cooked up some of the steak I had purchased at the PX during my trip to BIAP last week, and a nice steak and rice dinner capped off the events.

My next shift was much quieter. I was able to work on projects that required some time, and the bad guys must have been tired from terrorizing people the two days prior. Just as my shift ended and Marti came to take over for me, I walked into the trauma room to see a beautiful Iraqi girl, a few years on either side of twenty years old, laying in bed one. She had the largest, most beautiful eyes, and they were sick with despair. As Marti pulled the sheets back to expose her severely charred legs, my eyes locked on to hers. I had no idea how she was burned. I did not want to know. Perhaps, when I walked in the room, she thought I was the man, the man who would take away her pain and make her better. Maybe she could see herself walking again, since she was not able to do anything other than lay in extreme pain over the three weeks since her injury had occurred. Her eyes demonstrated despair and hope at the same time, as if she knew a miracle would happen despite her circumstances. I did not have it in my heart to talk to her, or even be in the same room. I was spent from the last few days, and she put me over the edge. I quickly walked out of the room and left the ER. No more despair, no more pain for me that day. However, her struggle was only beginning, and who knows where she would end up? The next day I was informed that she likely would live, but would need a complete amputation of both legs. Such a beautiful girl, such a tough fate.

However, she would still be alive, and that was more than can be said for many others, including the Iraqi policeman with burns to 70 percent of his body I cared for the next day. I knew nothing could be done for him, so I placed him on a morphine drip and admitted him upstairs to die, just like I had done for so many over the past few months.

My mood was lightened when my friend Anthony Knighton sent my Christmas present to me. It was a remote controlled General Lee, from the television show *Dukes of Hazzard*. It even had a horn that played the famous tone from the show. I wasted no time taking it outside and jumping it off curbs and doing my best to tear it up, but hey, it was the General Lee, so it was indestructible, right? It actually stood up to any challenge I could throw at it, just like the real thing on the television show. As I enjoyed driving it around outside of the ER, I got lots of funny comments and laughs. Great Christmas present!

The next few days were relatively quiet in Baghdad, and we immensely enjoyed the break in the action. Of course, we still had an amputee here, a gunshot wound there, but things had considerably dropped off since the trauma associated with the religious holiday the week prior.

While sedating an Iraqi interpreter with ketamine to reduce his dislocated shoulder, he said some very funny things. He looked at his nurse, Cpt. Robyn Stafford, and asked her how old she was. She told him she was too old for him, and he exhaled a sigh of depression, telling her, "But you are soooo sexy." During his entire twenty-minute drug-induced stupor, he continued to make passes at her, and we all enjoyed teasing about her "Iraqi admirer" just to watch her blush over the next few months.

While off shift a few days later, I was watching AFN on the TV in the physician's office in the ER as I noticed a mother and little girl walk into our orthopedic clinic. I recognized the girl as Fatima, the four-year-old who had been severely burned a month ago. She was the patient the AP photographer snapped the photo of me leaning down to comfort, the one that appeared on the Internet and in newspapers across the nation. Of course, neither the child nor mother recognized me, as they were talking to the physicians who cared for her over the course of her stay at Ibn Sina a month or so prior. But that was okay, patients seldom remember the ER doc, in Baghdad or back home, since we usually stabilize them and ship them upstairs quickly.

While the little girl's wound healing was being evaluated in the clinic, I ran up to my room and pulled up the photo on my computer. I quickly printed it and ran back downstairs, hoping to catch them prior to their departure. I was in luck and delivered the picture to the mother. Tears began to flow as she kissed the photo and began to cry. What a powerful moment it was for me! She then reached down and hugged her child about the head and kissed her. We all stood back smiling, and while none of us were crying on the outside, I think all of us were choked up inside.

The next day, while driving my remote controlled General Lee around the CSH, drawing laughter and "Just a good ol' boys" singing from the peanut gallery watching from the outside smoking section, I had a revelation. It had been four days since I had resuscitated a patient. I was antsy; I was in withdrawal. I realized that I might be addicted to this stuff, to the emotional roller coaster ride of life and death in the ER.

The rumor is that physicians graduating from medical school choose emergency medicine as a specialty because they are adrenaline junkies. I have always disagreed, stating that my choice was due to my poor attention span and undiagnosed attention deficit disorder. In medical school, I always found the operating room to be the most boring place in the hospital, hour after hour of tedious work that had to be perfect. I could not take that; if I was a surgeon, I would give up and say "It's good enough" and want to go get some lunch or take a break. However, I did not want the doldrums of clinic life either; a seven-to-five clinic schedule as a family medicine physician would drive me nuts, kind of like it did when I was a brigade surgeon from 2004 to 2006 with the Second Cavalry Regiment.

I wanted to be an ER doc because they move fast from patient to patient, can multitask, and can "handle anything that comes through the doors." Sure, an ER doc cannot amputate your leg, take out your appendix, or perform a c-section to deliver your baby. But no matter what your complaint is when you come through the ambulance or waiting room door, I can stabilize you and keep you alive until definitive care arrives. I can spend a small amount of time working on you, and then be able to walk away and move on to something else when the specialist, the one who will spend the next few hours or days working with you, gets there to assume care. I need to treat and move on—that is a big reason I wanted to be an emergency physician.

But no more runny noses. No more primary care stuff coming to the ER rather than going to the clinic where they should be. I had become used to rapidly intubating, placing central lines, arterial lines, chest tubes, and other procedures; now I was accustomed to pumping six units of blood into someone within ten minutes, only to keep them alive long enough to make it to the operating table. I was addicted. It had been four days, and I needed a resuscitation to get my adrenaline rush. Obviously, I did not wish ill on anyone, but if there was a sick or blown up person out there, I was ready and waiting.

I did not have to wait too much longer. A local national arrived with an amputated left arm above the elbow and significant head injuries. Marti intubated him while I placed a central line in his leg, allowing our nurses and medics to get life-saving blood into him. On ultrasound, I could see he needed a chest tube to drain the air from his chest due to his collapsed lung, so we inserted chest tubes on each side of his thorax. After a CT scan, we determined he should be flown to the neurosurgeons in Balad, so I placed an arterial line to better manage his blood pressure. He then left a couple of hours later, on his way to definitive care by the brain surgeons.

Now I could move on to something else. I got my rush, so I was ready for it to be quiet again for a while.

———

The next night, several of us went over to the palace and checked out the board game Risk and played for a couple of hours. It had been years since I played, and after two hours of getting to control and impose my will on all of South America and Australia, the group of us ate at the palace dining facility, followed by cigars by the poolside. What an amazing setup they had for the embassy personnel down there, and when the weather warmed, we planned to spend serious time swimming and relaxing by the water. I was sure the Department of State civilians would get tired of us using their immaculate facilities, but hey, they used our hospital, right? I guess we could send them out to the Iraqi hospitals for care if we wanted, so I would say it was a symbiotic relationship.

Upon return to the CSH, we found a poor host-nation lady in bed four of the ER with CPR in progress. After several minutes, Rob Hennesy, who was spending a few days with us from his TMC out at BIAP, and the ER crew were able to get her heart restarted. She was rushed to the operating room, where the surgeons opened her belly to find her arterial supply to most of her small intestines had clotted off, which is the intestinal equivalent to a heart attack. She coded on the operating room table and died shortly after the operation began.

The next day, I participated in my first "angel flight." An angel flight was a reverent and respectful time when the body of an American soldier was transported from our morgue to a waiting Blackhawk helicopter. As one of the bystanders, my job, along with several others, was to stand at the position of parade rest, and to salute the Gator, led by Chaplain Sermon, carrying the body to the bird. The soldier's unit sometimes would follow the Gator if they were present, and then the body would be loaded onto the aircraft with both flight crew chiefs standing on each side rendering salute. Once the body was loaded, the team would retreat back to the Gator, and the birds would take off into the sky with us saluting again. It was a very touching ceremony, reminding me that while I was down at the palace playing board games and smoking cigars, our troops were still out on patrol in harm's way. They deserved any ceremony or salute respectfully given to them and so much more.

The next day I was not on shift, but several U.S. soldiers came in after being hit by an IED filled with ball bearings. Luckily, they all had extremity wounds, thanks to the life-saving body armor they were required to wear. I was called in to help, and I dug a perfectly round, blood-tinged silver ball bearing out of one soldier's leg. Between her winces from the pain of the needle and the forceps I utilized, she was audibly thanking God for her safety.

Later in the day, a suicide bomber was able to muster enough gumption to explode his explosive-laden car just outside an American FOB about twenty miles north. He succeeded in his task of killing himself, but he failed to inflict the carnage and damage his brainwashed helpers and fellow jihadists desired. Several local Iraqi contractors were getting off work, and as they left the American compound, the suicide bomber struck. However, thanks to checkpoints and security procedures, he was not able to get as close as he wanted, and his blast did not have the desired effect, with no one being killed at the scene, although there were several injured.

When we got notice of the ten-plus patients en route, we assembled the mass casualty personnel and went to work. Rob Hennessey would take the sickest patients in the main trauma room. Jason and Marti would take the remaining beds in the treatment room, and I would stay out front and triage along with our chief trauma surgeon. The first two patients came through the door, and they both looked injured yet alive. They had no life-threatening injuries, and they were quickly dispositioned to the back treatment room. The third patient was a different story, however, as he had burns to his face and a chest injury. He was immediately placed in the trauma room with Rob. Patients four and five were walking wounded, one with an open lower leg fracture with the bleeding controlled, and the second with burns to both hands. They were placed in our hallway beds, and after triaging the others, I assumed their care.

The flight medics informed me they had another bird coming with six more, so we quickly prioritized the patients in the back and began moving them in and out to the CT scanner. Two patients with minor injuries were sent upstairs to the floor in order to open more bed space for the new arrivals.

The next wave of patients arrived, and most were also walking wounded. We sent one to the outpatient clinic, and the others were placed in the hallway. This was not a real mass casualty, as we only ended up with ten or so patients, but during these exercises, we never knew how many would truly come. We had to do our best to keep moving patients through in order to free beds for the next possible wave of patients. For a mass cal, it went very smoothly, and the trauma system we had in place continued to amaze me.

For the rest of my day off, I went to a new dining facility and ate my first gyro sandwich with lamb meat. Interesting ... not the best sandwich I had ever eaten, but a welcome change from our DFAC. The next day, I walked to the PX and picked up a grill as Mike, one of our Special Forces medics, had given us an ice chest full of thirty-two T-bone steaks and ten pounds of shrimp. We quickly hid the ice chest in one of our large freezers intended to keep bottles of water cold, located just outside the ER and within line of sight. Twenty-four hours a day, if anyone tried to get our steaks we would catch them! Thanks to Mike's generosity with food, we were able to use our grills on a regular basis throughout our tour.

Earlier, we had a middle-aged American active duty male transferred to us because of a foreign body found in his bladder. He needed urological care to have it removed, and after we obtained the CT scan, Stacey Koff took him to the OR. When cutting into his abdomen, she was amazed to find a full-length, full-size McDonald's drinking straw folded up in his bladder! Several of us tried to quiz him to discover how in the world the straw ended up there, but he continued to say he knew nothing about it. Come on, it did not get in there by itself! I have heard of people putting cocaine up the urethra of their penises to get high, but how did the straw get from his penis all the way around the curves into his bladder? I guess we will never know, but it did make a great story.

— —

Three bad guys were brought into the ER the next day by Chuck, another of the Special Forces medics who had been working with us. We went by first names with the SF guys; I did not even know the ranks of Mike, Drew, Scott, the three who worked with us the most. These three insurgents were caught by our drones carrying AK-47 assault rifles and stopping their car on a road in the middle of nowhere. They had dug a hole and were placing a large bomb inside when the C-130 assault plane opened fire. Several bursts of 40mm grenades later, these guys were in a world of hurt. They were brought in by the Special Forces team involved in the operation, and were all stabilized and saved, despite their blast wounds and other injuries.

Chuck was asked why there were only three insurgents brought in if they were hit by a weapon as powerful as the C-130 gunship, with its 40mm grenade launchers, 20mm and 105mm cannons, and other armaments. He told us that the others involved "will still be there when we get back." I do not think the bad guys, however many there were, fared too well in the assault.

They were back in action the next day as well. While on shift, I had two different groups of U.S. soldiers arrive after being hit by IEDs. Each group had one of their fellow squad mates killed by the bomb, while the rest only had minor injuries. They both said the charges were IEDs, and apparently were simultaneous, coordinated attacks. The injury pattern, with one dead and the others not hurt too badly, was consistent with an EFP and its single, 2,500-degree projectile that slices though anything. But as usual, we would never know what was the true cause.

While evaluating one of the guys, I noticed that he had small amounts of emesis, or vomit, on his chin. I asked him if he had thrown up after the injury, possibly due to a stress reaction or a head injury, but he looked me in the eye and with a slow, solemn voice said, "That was my battle buddy." His poor friend must have vomited at some point around his death, likely while this hero was working on him and trying to help. I stepped back and said, "I'm sorry, man, but we're gonna take good care of you." What else could I say at that point?

Later in the shift, an Iraqi man arrived unresponsive and in bad shape. I intubated him and noted him to likely be suffering from a major heart attack. We gave him clot busters, a drug class known as thrombolytics, and by the time he went up to the ICU, I had him on a dopamine drip to sustain his blood pressure. His heart attack caused a condition known as cardiogenic shock, which resulted when the heart is not delivering the required blood to the rest of the body. It has a miserable survival rate, as realized by the fact that he died in the ICU about two hours after we transferred him there.

Just as we were about to end our shift that night, an American colonel appeared at our front gate with an Iraqi police captain who was wounded gravely. He was apparently a high value target to the bad guys, and he had been hit by an IED about four hours earlier. He was taken to an Iraqi hospital, where he was given blood and not much else. This American colonel, likely directed by the navy admiral who came in shortly afterward, ordered a "snatch and grab" from the Iraqi hospital, as word was out that the bad guys were trying to find him and kill him in the hospital. I put a central line into his left subclavian vein, pounded him with more blood, and whisked him off to surgery, where our surgeons repaired his injuries. Score another one for the good guys!

Appendicitis was rampant in Iraq it seemed. Since our arrival, I had already seen more cases than I had since beginning my emergency medicine career after graduating medical school in 2001. We averaged about five patients with appendicitis per week, and we had six patients within one twenty-four-hour period at one point. We kept racking our brains trying to figure out the cause, but the only common link we could think of other than the pure patient demographics was the food we all ate from the contractors! I seriously doubted that had anything to do with it, but at this rate we figured that someone in our ER would go down with an appy before we got to go home. It was only a matter of time.

The next week, around one hundred people were killed and over two hundred injured in dual suicide bombings in Baghdad. I could only imagine how crazy the scenes were at the local hospitals, with their short staffs and even shorter supplies. We had a handful of patients arrive from the blasts, with one even being a local national who we all knew from his time working with us here at the hospital. He was burned and had other injuries, but overall he would recover and survive.

But here is the kicker. Apparently both of the bombers were females with Down's Syndrome. The bastard terrorists strapped bombs to the bodies of these two girls and sent them out into a crowded public market. When they had enough victims around them, the bombs were detonated by remote control. I am sure I have said it before, but there has to be a special place in hell for these people! I had heard of this occurring multiple times throughout Iraq, but this is the first time since I was there. Unbelievable.

It was February 2008, and all of the physicians in the hospital were changing over after their six-month tours, all but the five of us who were there for the long haul. There were several new faces and personalities to deal with, but it went well at first. It was nice being the experienced group; we knew how things should run, we knew what to do. I was sure the new physicians and CRNAs would figure it out quickly, just like we did three months prior. They would not have a choice but to adapt and go with the flow.

The guy who was supposedly responsible for mortaring us back on Thanksgiving Day was shot in the chest by our forces about a month prior. He came in to us in bad shape, and we had to place him on vasopressors and do all kinds of procedures and actions to keep him alive. He had been in our hospital for several weeks, teetering on death the entire time. We all knew he had no hope of living, but if he were ever able to get better and stabilize, we planned to transfer him to the CSH at Camp Cropper, where the detainees were located. However, he was still too unstable to transfer, and he ended up staying in our ICU for weeks.

He became our longest-tenured patient, as we normally tried to move people in and out quickly, both Iraqi and American, to stay open for trauma. Pat Hickey, familiar with seeing him lying lifeless in the ICU every day, with tubes in every orifice and multiple medications hanging, came up with the idea to make "Free Cropperman" t-shirts for everyone. I know it was rather disturbing humor, but we had to laugh at any chance we could get of course. Maybe someday "Cropperman" would be set free to go to jail, and our t-shirts would actually mean something!

I was covering the night shift when I received word that a Hellfire missile had been fired into a house, and we were getting the casualties within one minute. One of the patients was undergoing chest compressions and CPR. I quickly ran into the trauma room, calling the surgeon on call as I went to give her a heads up that we had business rolling in. The first patient was unresponsive, with fixed and dilated pupils. She was placed into bed one, and I quickly intubated her while our nurses felt for a pulse or signs of life. CPR was continued as I witnessed a man, bloodied and in bad shape, carried by litter into bed three, just across from me. I was informed that there were injured children in the back from the blast, and I decided to discontinue efforts on the female and focus on the patients who still had heartbeats.

While evaluating the man, our medic placed an IV into his right arm, and I noticed his left eye was swollen shut with a penetrating head injury to his left forehead. He was trying to sit up off the gurney and was combative, so we sedated and paralyzed him for intubation. He was taken to CT scan for imaging, so I moved to the back to find one of our surgeons, Dr.

Mike Gooden, working on the children. One was noted to have a penetrating abdominal injury, and Mike took her to the OR for abdominal surgery. The other child, a young boy, had serious chest injuries and was taken to the operating room by our cardiothoracic surgeon. He was found to have an injury to his aorta, the main blood vessel in the body located in the chest. After surgery, he suffered cardiac arrest and received CPR once, but he was brought back quickly and was slowly stabilizing.

When my patient returned from CT scan, we noticed his left eye that previously had been swollen shut now was proptotic, meaning that the eyeball was being pushed out of its socket, likely from bleeding behind it. I realized this would be the first and possibly only time in my career to perform a lateral canthotomy, an emergency procedure consisting of cuts to the ligaments on the outside aspect of the eye. Once the cuts are made, the eyeball then has more room to expand out of its socket, thereby preserving blood flow and future function. I used large scissors to cut on his eye, trying to remember the last time I had practiced the maneuver on a goat several years ago during residency. I doubt the procedure helped, since it looked on CT scan like the guy would lose his eye anyway, but I had to try at least.

After getting the report from the radiologist and realizing the man had shrapnel in his brain, I called the air force hospital in Balad and arranged transfer emergently for neurosurgical and ophthalmological care. After obtaining an accepting physician, I placed a central line just beneath his clavicle into his right subclavian vein for blood and medications, an arterial line in his groin to monitor his blood pressure more accurately, and then tackled the challenge of his penis injury. He had a laceration to the glans of his penis, the "head" in layman's terms, with blood coming from the tip. Men with these types of injuries may have an injury to their urethra, the tube that urine flows from when traveling from the bladder to the penis, and a catheter cannot be placed until injury has been ruled out. Therefore we performed a retrograde urethrogram, otherwise known as a RUG. During this procedure, contrast dye is injected into the tip of the penis and a quick x-ray is taken. If the dye flows in a line straight to the bladder, then there likely was not a severe urethral injury and a Foley catheter could be placed into the bladder. If the dye spreads out into the penis, then a catheter is not safe for placement, as it may cause further injury. His RUG looked good, and we placed a Foley and prepped him for flight.

Thirty minutes later, the patient was packaged and ready to go, with only one problem. His blood pressure was beginning to weaken, and the systolic was now struggling to be in the low eighties. I ordered the flight nurse to give him small amounts of a vasopressor called neosynephrine, a drug that keeps the blood pressure up so the brain and other vital organs are better perfused with blood. He then launched into the night sky on a helicopter, and I never heard what became of him. I hated it that this family was destroyed by a potentially stray missile, but I guess civilian injuries are sometimes part of the cost of freedom.

The next night, we received a nineteen-year-old-girl with a hip and head injury that said she was inside the residence when it was attacked. It seemed this was an extended family unit, as she told us she had several brothers, sisters, and aunts living in the home. We had no idea whether the patient who died was the mother, an aunt, or one of the sisters, as women have children at a young age in Third World countries, and Iraq was no different. Due to the chronic poor nutrition of the people there, it was honestly difficult to guess ages on them much of the time. We hoped the girl would be able to help us determine who was actually injured, as we did not know what to tell the one child on the floor who was awake and alert after her abdominal surgery. Did her mom die? Was it her sister or aunt? We had no idea. The only thing we knew was the house was hit by a missile, presumably fired from one of our aircraft. I did not know if it was a mistake and this was an innocent family, or if one of the patients we treated or someone dead at the scene was targeted by our forces. We will never know, but I do know that our guys did everything they could to save life and limb of everyone involved, as usual.

Later, we had a great time cooking the steaks and shrimp provided by Mike. The feeling was eerily familiar with normalcy, with a bunch of friends hanging out and grilling together. We stood around the grills, almost as if they were warm campfires keeping us company as we gazed into the flame. For about two hours, we were not in Baghdad; we were back home, wherever that was for each of us. We were just a bunch of friends having a great time together. We thought it was worth any flack the command would give us for doing so, but they never said a word.

We had a stuffed fish in the ER resembling the Walt Disney character Nemo. During the boredom of a slow shift the next day, the nurses gave Nemo devastating injuries, with burns to the fins, an amputated tail, and a plucked out eyeball. A plastic butter knife also impaled him on the side. Despite the carnage, trauma, and suffering Nemo endured, we managed to save him by sewing his wounds closed, replacing his amputated tail with more sewing, and an interesting intubation performed by myself. I assumed, since Nemo was a fish, that he required a supply of water rather than air. Therefore I placed a catheter into his mouth and attached it to a bag of sterile water, ensuring that he would inhale water rather than air with each breath.

It was decided then that Nemo was stable enough for the CT scanner, so he was taken over and a scan was performed. We never got an official radiology read, but I was sure the radiologist thought he was devastatingly injured. Our next plan was to move him to Balad and to see if we could get him evacuated all the way back to the United States. A picture of Nemo from Walter Reed Army Medical Center or somewhere like that, after being evacuated from Baghdad ER, would be an impressive sight indeed. Sure, it was a waste of time to play like this, but time is one thing we had a lot of at that time—about eleven more months to be exact.

Fresh Meat

After a couple of weeks overlapping with the new physicians, the group of twenty or so surgeons, surgical subspecialists, and anesthesia providers who came to the sandbox three months prior to our arrival for their short six-month tours went home. Several of those guys were great: Mike Gooden (surgery), Tate "Street Justice" Viewhig (oral maxillofacial surgery), John Tis (ortho), William Rice (surgery), John Oh (surgery), Clark Brixey (radiology), and Sabri Malek (anesthesia). Some of the other twenty or so providers were decent to deal with as well, but we were all thrilled to see the ten or so malignant and angry members of the group leave. When getting on the bird, we were all sure that a couple of them demanded headsets and tried to teach the pilots how to fly the helicopter, but now they were the pilot's problem and not ours! Several of us had cigars on the roof and joked that soon after they flew away into the night, we would see the CH-47 Chinook helicopters return to the CSH and spit a couple of them back off, already tired of dealing with their complaining and overall "better than you" attitudes!

Earlier, I wrote about a teenage Iraqi girl with burns encompassing her legs, up to about 40 percent of her body. Nothing could be done for her at the CSH, and some in the old group of surgeons were pressing hard to send her away to med city to die, saying we could not help her. For the most part, unfortunately, they were correct, but a miracle occurred. Thanks to God, and the hard work of Pat Hickey and Booker King, a group in the U.S. paid everything to send her to Shriner's Hospital in Boston, where she would receive the world's best burn care. She may still lose her legs, but she had a fighting chance. She still had the beautiful eyes that mesmerized me when I saw her in the trauma room, and someday she will not only survive, but she may even walk again.

I had a Peruvian gentleman with hypoxia the next night, a condition where the oxygen levels in the blood are not as high as they should be. Normal is 95–100 percent, and he was in the low eighties despite a large amount of supplemental oxygen. After a quick workup, my ultrasound of his heart revealed cardiac tamponade, a condition where fluid accumulates between the heart and the pericardium, or sac that contains the heart. It is normal for someone to have a small amount of fluid, but this gentleman had so much that the walls of his heart were caving in with each heartbeat. The immediate treatment for tamponade is to give large amounts of intravenous fluids, followed by a large needle stuck into the pericardium around the heart to drain the fluid.

Pericardiocentisis is a procedure that all emergency physicians are trained to perform, but few of us have actually done one. I called our cardiologist, Lt. Col. MJ Rorher, and she came to the ER with special equipment. With her assistance, I placed a large needle just below his left nipple, about three to four centimeters into his chest and drained off about 250 milliliters of bloody fluid. We sent the fluid for testing, and unfortunately discovered later that it was resulting from a cancer in his chest. We were afraid that tuberculosis might be the cause, as we had all been exposed several times by this point. Many of the contractors employed in the IZ were from Peru, a nation where untreated tuberculosis was still rampant. We treated multiple Peruvians for their TB, exposing all of us in the process. We expected to all be on the drug INH for nine months after we returned to the States, as it is the main medicine used to treat tuberculosis. However, despite our exposures, I do not know of anyone who has tested positive for TB from our ER.

Intelligence reports began telling us that three suicide vests had been snuck through security into the International Zone. We were being told to avoid large groups, as that could make us a good target for a would-be bomber. I did not really understand how this occurred. There were myriad checkpoints to get into the IZ, and I could understand that things occasionally got through, but how did we know about this? It seems that we would either know what was going on and catch the guys, or we would have no clue and get surprised. There was no use worrying about it, however. When they were ready to strike, we would be ready to respond in Baghdad ER.

Maj. Kathy Richardson, an ER nurse deployed with us from my home station of Fort Lewis, received two large hippity-hop balls in the mail. They were the large balls that a person sat on, with a rubber handle built into the top. Soon afterward, the hippity-hop races ensued. We had raced on multiple night shifts, and we always would post a sentry at the end of the hallway to look out for the brass. When the coast was clear, we would hop down the hallway about forty yards, touch the wall, and hop back. So far, our record was twenty-seven seconds, with several nonqualifying races secondary to people crashing into the walls or each other. The best spill I saw was Sam Matta. As the ball went forward, he spilled off the back, landing straight on his back with his arms spread. How easy we were to entertain!

While upstairs in my room one afternoon, the entire building began shaking as a helicopter took a unique approach to land on our pad, coming straight over the building. The walls shook, and I was concerned that stuff would begin falling off our shelves. I looked out the window to notice a helicopter with an Iraqi flag on the side; one I had never seen before. I raced upstairs to the roof with my camera, only to have it fly off before I could get a good shot. It turned out to be one of the few helicopters of the Iraqi Air Force, making a practice landing at our facility in an MI-17, a large Russian bird.

The next day, we had a seven-year-old Iraqi boy arrive with what appeared to be burns all over. His skin was peeling and crusted over approximately 80 percent of his body, but he had not been in an accident or fire. His father stated that he had suffered from a similar problem over the past several years, and he showed us an unrecognizable wallet-sized photo of his son before he was afflicted with the disorder. His eyes were crusted, almost to the point where he could not open them. Our nurses attempted to place an IV, but it was next to impossible as there were no veins visible or palpable due to the diffuse redness, scarring, and swelling of his tissues. He was fully awake and talking, asking us not to touch him due to the pain. Our medics gingerly placed blood pressure cuffs and monitor leads on him, and he cried in distress as his nurse Cpt. Robin Stafford attempted to place an IV in his arm without success.

Several conditions that I learned about in residency ran through my head, all things I never expected to see in my career. Could this be an over-whelming infection, such as staphylococcal scalded skin syndrome? Or was it toxic epidermal necrolysis with an unknown cause but a result of diffuse skin cell death? I called a dermatologist to come to ER for the first time ever in my career, and Maj. Scott Henning told me he would be right down. I also called Pat Hickey and our burn surgeon, Booker King, to help with his evaluation and management, as I knew they would want to take him to the OR. Booker operated on him and scrubbed and cleaned under general anesthesia. Our thought the next day was that he might have a condition I was unfamiliar with called bullous disease of childhood, where the victim periodically gets these horrible lesions all over their body. In ancient times, I am sure this would be associated with leprosy, and Scott Henning even-tually worked out a treatment plan for him that at least improved his life somewhat. Poor child, we all felt bad for him and his chronic ailment.

Our next intelligence report informed us that two guys riding tandem on a moped were driving around the International Zone and throwing gre-nades at people walking by. Apparently in Iraq, drive-by grenadings were in vogue versus the drive-by shootings we see in the United States. They were engaged by the local Iraqi police, but they were able to escape the hail of bullets from the good guys. I could just picture two idiots riding on a tiny moped, just like the movie *Dumb and Dumber*, as they lobbed grenades across the street. Only in Iraq! We were locked down on the FOB due to the threat. We decided it must have been a false alarm, as we did not receive any patients that day hit by grenades, and anyone who was hit in the IZ would have shown up on our doorstep. There was likely nothing to it, but at least it was an interesting reason to be locked down rather than just more false alarms for mortars.

Later in the week, we dealt with two distinguished visitors. The first arrived with much fanfare in the EMT, as he was Maj. Gen. Lynch, the commander of the Third Infantry Division. He flew into our helipad and presented our hospital commander with a large Third ID "Dogface Soldier" print. He gave us a speech thanking us for always being there for his soldiers, and he stated that our presence allowed the twenty-five thousand soldiers under his command to do their jobs without fear of injury. He then gave the forty or so of us present in the ER a Third ID commander's coin. It was the first and only coin I have ever received from a general, so I was sure happy to receive it. Deb Chappel usually did all the VIP tours in the ER, and she was currently winning a competition with other hospital head nurses to gather the most total stars from the general's coins they received for their tours. She always received coins for giving them, so it was nice to get one for myself for a change!

An hour or so later, the United States Attorney General Mukasey came by for a tour, along with his personal security detail, armed to the max! They had headsets, body armor, and weapons hanging everywhere; I honestly could not see how they could walk with so much garb. Deb Chappel gave him a quick tour of the ER, and then he went upstairs to see the rest of the hospital and patients. When the day was done, we could chalk up two more high profile encounters in the Eighty-sixth CSH EMT.

Diligently continuing my search to find ER docs to come in and help, I located a few more ER docs in the Baghdad vicinity. In February 2008, there were more than ten ER-trained guys working in small aid stations and clinics doing routine sick call and physicals within fifteen miles of the CSH, so I made it my personal goal to get them all over to work with us. By this point, we had six rotators who had come and helped at least a shift or two since our arrival in November. It was a symbiotic relationship: they helped us see patients and get rest, and they got to keep their emergency medical skills up and experience the craziness of Baghdad ER. My colleagues at the CSH were calling me the KBR of emergency medicine in Iraq, as I "contracted out" shifts to other army ER guys, giving Jason, Marti, and I a break when possible.

The next few days were very uplifting at the CSH. The weather became beautiful, with sunny skies and highs in the midseventies. For several days, Stewart McCarver from the 101st and Chris Crowell, a former resident physician I worked with at Madigan Army Medical Center, now with the Third Infantry Division, worked with us. Jason, Marti, and I were able to receive a very nice respite. We had a great time and were able to sit down and talk more than usual. When discussing the recent "moped grenadiers," several other funny stories about unfortunate terrorists came up. Below were my favorites:

1) Just two days prior, over eight thousand Iraqis came into the International Zone for a large summit at the Al-Rashid Hotel. They were coming to compete for bids from the U.S. government designed to stimulate the Iraqi economy and help individuals improve their lives. Intelligence reports came through indicating that the bad guys were planning to place a large car bomb just outside the hotel, as it was on the edge of the IZ and the Red Zone. The area was crawling with Iraqi Army and police in search of suspicious vehicles, but they did not have to look hard. The day before the convention, an old beat-up hooptie car came down the road with a single occupant. The car drove over a speed bump a little too fast and part of the bomb it was carrying fell off the car and landed right in front of the Iraqi soldiers! They simply stopped the car and arrested him. There were no problems during the convention.

2) Many car bombs were prepared in small villages in the desert north of Baghdad. Apparently, once a car was ready, the would-be suicide bomber loaded up and began driving toward Baghdad, likely dreaming of all the innocent men, women, and children he would kill or injure. Sadly for one of these guys, he set the timer on the bomb

wrong, and the car exploded about thirty minutes north of Baghdad in the middle of nowhere. The bomber was the only victim.

3) The year prior, a man was creating an IED to be detonated by cell phone. He purchased a shiny, brand new phone to do the trick, and he was assembling the bomb when he apparently decided that he wanted to keep the new phone for himself since it was so nice. He traded it out with his personal older one, and right after he hooked it up to the bomb, someone called him on his old cell phone and detonated the bomb! He was injured badly and subsequently caught and treated by our forces. Served him right!

4) In Mosul earlier in the year, a car full of men ran through an intersection and collided with U.S. Army Stryker Infantry Vehicle. One was injured badly, and he was taken to the CSH in Mosul, where he was treated for his injuries. The other occupants gave the victim's medical information to one of the translators working with the Americans, and the translator realized the three other men in vehicle all had different accents, indicating they were from different countries. All three were arrested at the hospital, and the car bomb they were building was found close by.

These were just a few of my favorite examples of the stupidity of some of these thugs. They only managed to get themselves killed, wounded, or caught. We all hoped the people continuing to terrorize this nation would continue to be idiots!

Another funny story I enjoyed had nothing to do with terrorists, but still has stupidity at its center. Earlier, over New Year's night, two American soldiers got themselves high and overdosed on dextromathorphan, a leading component in over-the-counter cough syrups. Both were hospitalized in our ICU, and a very high-profile command sergeant major (CSM) toured the hospital hour later. He noticed the two American soldiers in the ICU, and before anyone could stop and tell him the guys were only in the ICU because they were trying to get high, he gave each one of his CSM coins and patted them on the back for a job well done! The nurses and medics were trying to let the CSM know the truth, but no one could tell him in the heat of the moment! I would have liked to see the CSM's reaction when he realized why they were there!

Days prior, one of our nurses, 1st Lt. Kristy Bischoff, was transferring a patient to the ward from the ER. During this transport, somewhere around the elevator, the patient had what we in the medical community call a "code brown." Most laypeople understand that a "code blue" occurs when a patient dies, but not many have heard of a "code brown." One occurs when a patient poops in their bed, and as you can guess, it's a terrible, stinky mess. I have seen "code browns" clear out the ER and make life miserable for the poor nurses. If it occurred in the ER, our team would always do the right thing and clean up, but the only way Kristi realized the patient had defecated was the smell in the elevator. When the doors opened, she handed care over to the floor nurses and did her best to keep a straight face in the process as if she did not know. The floor nurses were suspicious that something was up as the pungent odor began to permeate the air, but Kristy gave a verbal report and took off back to the ER quickly before anyone could ask!

I understand that people pooping on themselves is not a funny subject, but it must be remembered that it was a normal part of what we do, what we see everyday. Medical gallows humor can be cold, crass, and ugly, but sometimes we just have to laugh about it, to laugh about life. No one was dying, and if that was the case, all was well at Baghdad ER.

I received five hundred Valentine's Day cards in a large box from a teacher at North Mesquite High School in Mesquite, Texas, the next week. Ms. Cindi Scott had challenged her students, and they answered the call and then some! It was amazing to go through them all, and on top of that, she attached a PowerPoint presentation showing pictures of the students making the cards and posing with them. In the PowerPoint presentation, Ms. Scott included a picture given to her by Dorene Bryant of my wife Laura, daughter Avery, and myself just prior to deployment. It was very touching and made my day to see it. I printed it out and placed it on the wall in my room.

One of the Valentine's cards was from an eleventh grader named Pedro and he wrote this: "Happy Valentine's to all the ladies in the army." Pedro must have been a lady's man, and all the nurses of the ER enjoyed that one especially.

Mrs. Bryant's third grade class also sent me several Valentine's, and my favorites are below exactly as written by the kids:

1) Nate: "Hang in their!"
2) Brooke: "Do you like horses or riding at all? Well if you do I do too."
3) Patrick: "How are you doing? I can't believe you don't like drawing! ... Have you ever written a story?"
4) Hunter: "I hope you don't get hert."
5) Trent: "When Mrs. Bryant tells stories about you they make me laugh."

These heartfelt writings cracked me up! I loved receiving them and enjoyed writing back and answering their questions, even if they were about horses, stories, and drawing.

The next week, the skies began turning black, meaning that helicopters could not fly due to the fine, silty sand that periodically filled the air that time of year. When I walked outside, I could barely make out the street-lights just fifty yards away, and everything was covered with a brown, dusty haze resembling fog. I felt like I needed to wear a mask wherever I went, and it surely could not be good for a person's lungs to breathe that stuff, but people lived here to a ripe old age so they must get used to it. The dust covered everything. It seeped through windows, door cracks, and air conditioner vents. It was inescapable. Weekly, I had to dust my room, removing the thick layer of fine dirt that caked my every possession.

Usually when the skies were red or black, it would be quiet in Baghdad ER. But that was not always the case, and especially not this night. In the first five hours of my shift, we used eighteen units of blood, as well as countless units in the operating rooms and intensive care unit. We had been running full-bore since I came on shift at 7:00 PM, and even though we had no birds land on our helipad, plenty of devastatingly wounded patients arrived by ground to keep us hopping.

The first was an American contractor who had been hit by mortar or rocket fire; his right shoulder appeared as if a shark had taken a huge bite out of him. When undressing the wound to see the damage, I could see and feel all the way down to the head of his humerus, and I was even able to stick my hand further, reaching into his chest cavity. He was intubated, and he had a chest tube sticking out of his right side helping to drain the blood from his lungs and keep his right lung inflated, but it was not in all the way or working properly. I ran my index finger down the length of the chest tube and felt it running between his ribs and into his thorax. Keeping my finger in the hole, I removed the tube and placed a larger one into his chest, hoping to help reinflate his lung. Once partially stabilized by twelve units of blood, we rushed him to the operating room where the orthopedic and general surgeons were waiting for him. He survived the surgery, but it was truly a grim wound.

Moments later, an Iraqi general was brought in with a large hole through his right shoulder, where fragments from a blast had blown it open. He was more stable than our first gentlemen, and we were able to get him to CT scan and later to the operating room. We quickly received word that three American soldiers had been hit, and two of them had been killed at the scene. The third was en route to us, but before he could arrive, another high-ranking Iraqi officer was brought in with fragments to his lower abdomen. He was a very large man, and IV access was difficult to obtain. I struggled, but I was able to place a central line into his subclavian vein, just below his clavicle. The needle we used for the lines were several inches long, and I had to hub the needle and depress into his skin to make the line reach the vein due to his size. His blood pressure plummeted as I was working to get access; he needed blood quickly. I finally finished the line, and we pounded him with blood and rushed him straight to the OR.

We then received the sobering news that the American soldier was not coming; he had died in route. It was a bad night to be outside. Due to the sand, you could not see, you could not breathe, and the bad guys were using our inability to fly to their advantage. Our Apache attack helicopters were disabled, and our unmanned aerial vehicles could not see the ground below. We could not use our Blackhawk birds to fly casualties into the CSH. The choking sandstorm, the first of many to come for us in the spring, was a killer in several ways.

The next day, we received a young Iraqi man who had a gunshot to the head from an attempted execution. He somehow appeared at one of the American forward operating bases, and they did a great job of getting him to us quickly, but it was too late. We worked hard on him, but his head injuries were too massive, and he had an unstable cervical spine fracture from a second shot. We were forced to make him expectant and give him morphine to make his death more comfortable. I guess they were successful after all.

The following shift was better, and the bored day crew created a wheel-chair obstacle course, requiring participants to navigate around tables, between beds, and perform tasks at several stations, including taking their own vital signs, maneuvering aid bags, and performing various other medical tasks. Each participant was timed, and I hear Kristy Bischoff was the big winner. I am sure it was fun, but not as good as the hippity-hop races.

Another enjoyable activity we discovered was ER baseball. 1st Lt. Megan Solberg used her fast-pitch softball skills to throw a four-inch tape roll past the swing of my broom handle. Whiff ... strike one. Whiff ... strike two. The third pitch was a charm for me as I nailed a line drive right back at her about twelve feet away, hitting her in the abdomen and dropping her to her knees. I dropped as well, but my fall was due to laughter, and everyone else in the ER joined me. She turned out to be okay, but she endured a large bruise to her belly. Needless to say, that ended our ER baseball game. Who knew it could be dangerous? It was not like we were playing with needles!

Two nights later, at 1:00 AM, I found myself standing by the helipad with thirty to forty others, waiting on an angel flight to arrive. With quiet reverence, we all stood on the flight line waiting for the Blackhawks to come take the body of another fallen American hero, another soldier who gave the ultimate sacrifice. After attending a few angel flights, I had quit going; I just could not stomach it anymore. I usually was involved in the death of the soldier before the flight, and I did not want to endure any more sadness. I feel guilty to this day for not attending every flight that I could have, but I just could not do it. It was my way of moving on to the next patient, typing the death summary, turning it into Maj. Wade, our patient admin officer, and moving on. I could not dwell on it, but I do feel badly still.

This angel flight resulted from an IED hitting a U.S. vehicle, and as the patients rolled into the ER, I took the two in the back while the most criti-cal came to bed one of the trauma bay. Our crews worked on him for over an hour, performing CPR, getting a pulse, losing it, and starting over again numerous times. They cracked his chest open in an attempt to massage his heart and keep any blood from bleeding into his abdomen, all to no avail. He was taken to the operating room, with Marti performing cardiac massage directly on his heart, but it was not to be. He was pronounced dead in the OR, and then the bombshell dropped. One of our nurses, 1st Lt. Ann Gockley, was friends with the soldier; she knew him from four years of ROTC together. She was a rock throughout the code, working on him and keeping her composure, doing everything she could to save him.

We knew it would happen; we all had been waiting to see someone we were familiar with arrive in the trauma room, and this night our fears came true. Our prayers went out to this fallen hero, his family, his band of broth-ers left behind in Iraq, and to Ann, his old friend who fought through the emotions to try to bring him back from death. The cost of war hit home that night in Baghdad ER.

The next day I awoke to mortars landing around 6:30 AM. The day before, radial Shiite cleric Muqtada Al-Sadr had told his vast Mahdi Militia to con-tinue their cease-fire for another six months, a very welcome announcement to all coalition forces and the CSH as well. Once they started attacking more, we knew our casualty numbers would increase. I think he had backed himself into a corner with these cease-fires, because when he called them off, violence would obviously increase, and the Iraqi people would have no doubt as to why. How could he afford *not* to continue the cease-fire? I was sure we would be quick to point the finger at him whenever violence increased, and we would make sure the Iraqi people knew who was responsible for their lack of safety, and that is exactly what we did eventually. I think this mortar barrage was the result of a few disgruntled Al-Sadr followers who wanted the cease-fire to end, and they decided to express their view of Americans by sending a few rounds downrange toward us. It was not a big deal, however, because very few Mahdi Militia members would choose not to follow their leader's instructions. It made me feel optimistic about peace over the next six months, but soon I discovered how wrong I was.

Violence picked up over the next week, and we cared for a few brave American heroes, some who lost their lives to the terrorists. A young man came in with both of his legs amputated by an IED, and our crew worked on him feverishly in the trauma room by opening his chest and clamping his aorta in efforts to slow the massive bleeding. He was intubated and given five code reds, thirty units of blood in all, once again to no avail. After he was pronounced dead, my favorite interpreter, the one who was like a mother to all of us, broke down and cried, bringing tears to everyone's eyes. As I hugged and comforted her, she told me this was exactly how her son died a year ago in that same bed. She vowed that day to always be there to help the soldiers, both American and Iraqi alike, but she would not speak to the bad guys who came through our doors; she could not bring herself to do it. I led her into the trauma room, where she took the soldier's hand and kissed the back of it. She held it for a few moments, and then she had to let go as we were preparing the room for another person with a gunshot wound to the chest soon to arrive.

She was like our mother in Iraq; she always brightened our day and brought a smile to everyone's face. She even "knighted" me and called me Sir Baker, and she did a rolling-out-the-red-carpet hand gesture every day when she first saw me. How could we say that the Iraqis were doing *nothing* for their country, when they were there helping us each day, with many being killed and dismembered in the process?

The next day, we were picked up by the head of Triple Canopy, one of the largest private security contracting groups in Iraq, to get a driving tour of the new U.S. Embassy compound in the International Zone. It was nearly complete, but it would not open for several more months. It was amazing; I had no idea how big and spectacular it would be! There was a large school for children, apartments for two thousand State Department employees, fire stations, indoor and outdoor basketball courts, softball fields, and many other assets. It was designed to be fully self-sufficient; employees could stay and not leave the compound for their entire tour if desired. All the buildings were blast proof, and it would be a great asset for the long-term U.S. presence that we all knew would be in Iraq.

After the embassy tour, we arrived back to the CSH to several Iraqi Army soldiers arriving with gunshot wounds. I took one who had a gunshot to the chest, but was amazingly talking and fully awake, alert, and doing fine. A quick ultrasound revealed no collapsed lungs, and a chest x-ray followed by CT scan demonstrated that the bullet went directly into his chest, through his sternum (breastbone), and stopped just before it entered his heart. Are you kidding me? We no doubt had a winner of the "luckiest man in Iraq" award! He went to the operating room to have the bullet removed, and he did just fine. I was amazed by something new every day.

——

The next week, a German magazine interviewed me. Two reporters asked me myriad questions about my job and experiences at Ibn Sina. It was interesting to talk to them, but part of me could not help but want to ask them why they were interested in us since their country would have no part in helping when the war began. I did not mention it, and overall the interview went very well, with topics ranging from care in the trauma room to how my family related to my experiences back home. I got he impression they wanted to ask me if my family supported my mission or not, but they never broached the subject. I quickly let them know how important I felt my job was each time they began to ask those kinds of questions.

Speaking of family, Laura had just informed me that I had just missed my daughter's first step. On one hand, it broke my heart to be missing her first crawling and now her first step, but I was so thankful that she was advancing on or ahead of schedule. I had been gone from home for five months and was almost halfway to my R&R leave time. I could not wait to get to play and watch my beautiful daughter go throughout her day. I knew I would never take those experiences for granted again.

I so longed for the day when I got see my Laura and Avery again! I was amazed as to how much I missed my dogs as well. We had two beagles, one very large and one very small. The larger of the two, Houston, weighed sixty-two pounds. He was not pure beagle, as he had received some bigger hound in his bloodline somewhere, and despite all the diet food and exercise, he could still outrun, outmaneuver, and outlast us at whatever activity we did, so we quit worrying about his weight. Our smaller dog Emmee was purebred and a quaint sixteen pounds. Laura told me that while I was gone, Avery and Houston got along great and played together most days, with Avery trying to lay down beside him on his dog bed every so often. Houston would stare out the window at the driveway during the daytime, as if waiting on me to drive up at any moment.

One of the biggest things I looked forward to was lying on my back and having Houston come sit beside me. I know it sounds weird, but anytime I would lay down on my back, he would come to my right side and sit down beside my waist facing me. He then would put his right "elbow" on my stomach, and his right front paw would come to rest on my chest every time. He would then lay down on the floor beside me with his front leg on my stomach and chest, and come to rest his face about eight inches above mine. He would then stare at me, daring me to move. I know it is strange, but anyone who owns or has owned a loving dog understands the bond that we owners have with him or her. The only dog interaction I got in Iraq was trying to avoid all the strays roaming around the International Zone. Rabies was rampant amongst the wild dogs. Obviously, I did not pet those dogs, but I could not wait to get home to see mine.

As army emergency physicians, many of us are placed into combat units upon graduation from residency, as I was. Those jobs are usually all administration or minor cough and cold sick-call type posts, so when serving in those positions, many of us try to work in local civilian emergency departments on the weekends to keep our emergency medical skills up, as well as earn extra pay. In February 2008, I received notice that I had had a medical malpractice claim filed against me from an encounter on one of those moonlighting weekends a couple of years prior. I spoke with the attorney representing me, and she told me that 1) the patient suing me turned out to be okay (praise God—I don't want anyone hurt by my carelessness or fatigue) and 2) the case had already been dropped by other malpractice prosecutors, so she felt it was likely a negligent suit, meaning there was not much to the case and it would likely be thrown out as a waste of time. Of course, I was very thankful that the patient was okay, but this sure added more stress to a deployment! I had malpractice insurance, but it capped at $100,000. If a jury awarded the plaintiff more than that, I could be coming home from war to file bankruptcy. I had to wait on documents to arrive from the U.S., and then prepare a statement in my defense for the medical review panel a few weeks later. What an extra burden this turned out to be during the next year in Iraq! Many physicians lose sleep, become severely depressed, or quit medicine altogether due to these suits, even when they are deemed negligent. All I could do was write my statement explaining why I cared for the patient the way I did, and then wait several months for the next step in the slow and painful process.

Now at the five-month mark, I was halfway to my R&R leave. I was able to set up my leave in August 2008, about ten months after I drove away from Laura and Avery way back on September 30, 2007, in Searcy, Arkansas. After spending R&R with my family, I would have just four months left to go! It was also the 33 percent mark; we were twenty-two weeks into our deployment and had forty-four to go, making us one third of the way through! I tried not to check our progress too often, as it only depressed me to see how much further we had yet to endure, but five months down was nothing to laugh at. I therefore made it an unofficial rule to check our progress on the first of each month and no more, so I would not dwell on how slowly the calendar was moving. We had a computer program called the Wheel of Pain that created a pie chart, slowing uncovering a tropical island hidden by a sea of desert. Each day, more and more island was shown.

Each month, a 5K run was held in the IZ, sponsored by the U.S. Embassy. I have never been a strong runner, so it was a great feat for me not only to run and finish, but also to finish ahead of so many others. I will not mention my time, as I am sure it was still terrible for thirty-two-year-old skinny guy, but I was proud. I also weighed in and saw I had gained another 2.5 pounds, making my total weight gain five pounds since beginning my rigid weight gain and calorie intake program. It felt good to be going in the right direction for a change!

A few days prior, I had two Iraqi kids, both close to ten years old, arrive after being hit by an IED. They presumably were just like most of the other blown up kids we saw, out playing or working somewhere when they tripped an IED intended for American or Iraqi soldiers. Who knows, their father or relative may have even set the device. While working on one of the children, I noticed he had a right-sided hemothorax, meaning his right lung was full of blood. I placed a chest tube in between his fourth and fifth ribs, on his side just beneath his arm. I was stunned when half a liter of blood poured out and around the tube as I punctured his side. Blood splattered all over my scrubs and shoes while I inserted the tube into his chest and hooked it up to suction. After I sutured the tube into place, he was rushed to the operating room, where our surgeons worked on him. His brother did not fare as well after receiving heavy loads of shrapnel to his abdomen.

The carnage of the week did not stop there, however, as the next day I received an Iraqi man with a gunshot wound to his epigastrium, the area just inferior to the sternum, or breastbone. We placed a right-sided tube into his chest and hit him with blood, then sent him on a rushed trip to the OR immediately after. Our surgeons packed what was left of his liver and did the best they could to repair the devastation to his inferior vena cava, but after 150 units of blood products ranging from red blood cells to platelets to cryoprecipitate, he finally died in the ICU. He was flown in by our helicopters, and after the intense resuscitation, the unit responsible for shooting him called and told us he was a bad guy. His partner in crime apparently accompanied him to the CSH, and after wandering all over the building, he was promptly arrested by our MPs! I wished that call had come earlier so we could have taken the guy into custody before he got to see the whole place, but at least he did not walk out the front door and get away, especially if he had done anything to hurt our guys.

We also had a thirteen-year-old-kid come in who was blue and cyanotic, meaning he was not getting sufficient oxygen to his body. His mother brought him in, and after getting a quick history, Rob Hennessey, who was back over and helping out for a couple of shifts, realized he had a horrible congenital cardiac problem from birth. His aorta, the large vessel coming from the heart that carries blood to the body, was transpositioned with his pulmonary artery. This is a known condition called transposition of the great vessels, and it is not compatible with life after the first week unless certain medications are given. The only feature keeping this poor child alive was a ventricular septal defect, a hole in his heart that mixed the preoxygenated blood with the oxygen-rich blood, pushing out at least some oxygen to his body. He had lived this way, unable to walk or tolerate activity like most kids, and he had little hope of recovery. Unfortunately, we could do nothing for him other than set him up with the special cardiac hospital there in Baghdad. I had no idea if they could help him; I did not even know if surgery could help by that point. In the U.S., these children are aggressively treated from birth and obviously fare much better than this poor child, but hopefully they could do something, although we were not optimistic.

The next shift was very busy, and trying to keep up as the only doctor covering the ER was a chore. Here are the conditions of the patients I treated this day:

1) Fifty-two-year-old active duty airman with pancreatitis, admitted to the hospital.

2) Twenty-one-year-old active duty soldier with a crushed and fractured pelvis and left lower leg from a large piece of metal falling on him.

3) Twenty-four-year-old Iraqi police officer hit by a VBIED with shrapnel to the abdomen, face, and chest. He also had devastating

injuries to both legs, and spent several hours in the operating room, including a left leg amputation. He required twelve units of blood in the ER.

4) Twenty-three-year-old Iraqi police officer hit by the same bomb with facial injuries and finger amputations.

5) Twenty-nine-year-old Iraqi police officer in the same bombing with shrapnel wounds all over his body resulting in a significant bleed into his pelvis, as well as ball bearings to his chest.

6) Thirty-four-year-old Iraqi police officer, once again from the same event, with shrapnel to the neck resulting in a carotid artery injury requiring surgical repair.

7) Fifty-two-year-old man with chest pain who had to be admitted to the intensive care unit.

8) Forty-two-year-old Iraqi woman with a large cut on her finger requiring stitches. Sgt. Matt Mitchell, one of our medics, did a great job sewing her.

9) Fifty-four-year-old Iraqi man with an open abdominal wound due to an IED. When taken to the operating room, a tumor was found and removed on his small intestine. He later turned out to have cancer in his abdomen.

10) Thirty-six-year-old American contractor with diverticulitis, which is an infection of the colon.

11) Sixty-year-old Scottish contractor with bronchitis and chest pain.

12) Fifty-three-year-old Iraqi man with chest pain requiring admission to the intensive care unit.

13) Thirty-nine-year-old Iraqi man who shot himself in the left thigh, transecting the main artery to the leg and requiring surgical repair.

14) Thirty-six-year-old American reporter with a dog bites to the arm.

15) Nineteen-year-old American soldier with epidydimitis, or an inflammation of part of the testicle.

I describe these patients to give an overall synopsis of the types of patients we routinely saw at Baghdad ER. They were not all due to trauma and violence, but were definitely different from our typical ER patients back home!

I had an interesting meeting with our new trauma czar, or general surgeon in charge of trauma, the next day. He seemed to have good intentions, but unfortunately, he was not used to working with emergency physicians. Since the arrival of our new surgical and anesthesia providers, we had several negative interactions in the trauma room. As ER docs, we had been there for four months; we had seen and treated a tremendous amount of carnage. These new surgeons had all deployed before, but most were in locations that were not busy. During the course of their previous six-month deployments, they cared for a gunshot wound or blown up victim once or twice a month, totaling seven to fifteen patients in the entire six-month period. Since November, we had seen that many in a day or two!

Most of the new guys were easy to work with and seemed to be good people. However, for the previous five months, we three ER docs had been through more trauma situations than we could count, and we were familiar working with the nurses and medics we had come to know over the past five months. Since the arrival of the new crew, a couple of them attempted to run the room, barking orders and trying to take over, much to our chagrin. During the first few weeks with the new group, we had several run-ins with them, and traumas were getting to be situations where we had too many people barking orders and not enough ancillary staff to follow them. Our poor nurses and medics sometimes could not reach the patient to help due to all of the surgeons getting in the way!

It finally boiled over when we had to start kicking people out of the trauma room, so the two lead surgeons and the three ER docs got together and talked about it. Lt. Col. Mike Myer, a cardiothoracic surgeon and experienced voice of reason, came to an agreement with us that we would run the trauma with the surgeon, if available, at the foot of the bed, taking in data to help guide their decisions as to what they want to do with the patient once they left the ER. Do they send them to CT scan, the ICU, or straight to the operating room? Our new trauma czar, unhappy with our presence in the room and our unwillingness to back down, then told us, "Well, if I get mad and start yelling in there, don't be surprised if I jump in because I'm really fast at putting in central lines." We could not believe he said that—of course he should be fast, that was his job. We did not have to remind him, but he discovered that we were fast too.

I mention the above issue, because a week later in a meeting with this same individual, he said to me, "I can't stand someone else being in charge in the trauma room; I get so angry, it messes with my mojo." Are you kidding me? He wanted me to acknowledge his frustration, but to his disappointment I only said, "OK," implying essentially, "Well too bad, I'm going to do what's best for the patient rather than your ego." When discussing this with Dena George, her mild, soft-spoken manner disappeared when she said, "Well, did you tell the great surgeon to zip up his pants and be a man?" It was priceless, especially to be coming from her! As ER docs, our crazy idea was to work with the trauma teams that we were familiar with, use the volume of experience we had gained over the past few months, and utilize our surgeons simultaneously to create the best environment to save patient's lives. Did we not owe our patients that much? We felt we should throw away our egos and give our patients the maximum chance to live. If that pissed off one of our surgical colleagues, he or she could just be angry and have their "mojo" bruised until they went home in six months. Then our nurses, medics, and ER docs, still in Iraq, would train another group of surgeons and begin the fight all over again.

I wrote earlier about an Iraqi soldier who came in after being hit by a Humvee. He suffered a closed head injury, and we stabilized him and flew him to the neurosurgeons in Balad. Apparently, he had surgery, and then was flown back to us for discharge. They said he was able to care for himself and doing well, but unfortunately he was altered when he arrived back to us to be transferred to Medical City. He was stable, but he was pleasantly confused, typical of many head-injured patients. The decision was made to return him to Balad, but until transportation could be arranged, he was asked to sit down on a gurney in the hallway, to which he complied. A few minutes later, he was sacked out on the stretcher and motionless to the point of concern for those of us just walking into the EMT who did not know the story. Next, we looked up to find him wandering down the hallway, going into the nursing supervisor's office, before he was turned around and asked to sit back down. Five minutes later, he was asleep again, and then back up and wandering the hallways. Back home when this occurs, we always have security or a tech sit with the patient; there we did not have the staff for that, so everyone just had to keep an eye on him. He was smiling and totally harmless, it was just funny to see our charge nurse Sam Matta have to chase him down somewhere in the hospital every thirty minutes and round him back up.

At the end of my senior year of residency, several us played a funny trick on my classmate, Dr. Laurie Pemberton, and another resident, Dr. Troy Coon. My wife put on an Oscar-worthy performance by loading into an ambulance and allowing one of our civilian paramedics to place an IV in her and give a report to Dr. Pemberton of a young lady who had done something so bad she was too embarrassed to say what it was.

When the patient arrived at 3:00 AM to the Darnall Community Hospital, Fort Hood, Texas, Dr. Pemberton assigned her to a bed in the back and went to meet the patient as she arrived on the gurney. Much to her surprise, Laurie and Troy looked over to see my wife Laura screaming wildly with a pillowcase over her head to avoid being recognized. The pink fuzzy slippers on Laura's feet actually belonged to Laurie, since we were in transition and staying with her during the last week of our time in at Fort Hood. Laurie kept asking her to remove the pillowcase and tell her what was wrong, while Troy did his best to keep a straight face and support Laurie as she attempted to care for this difficult patient. Hiding in the background were Jake Roberts and myself. Every overture to remove the pillowcase from Laurie resulted in my wife going ballistic and refusing to cooperate. Finally, after several minutes of frustration from her two physicians, Laura pulled off the pillowcase and surprised Laurie and Troy, after which Laurie yelled, "I knew those were my slippers!"

I tell this story because later that week I unexpectedly encountered Sabrina Baker, the paramedic who helped us pull the prank back in 2004. We sat down to catch up, and of course, the prank was brought up and we had a good laugh. Baker was working in Baghdad for a contracting company as a medical liaison. What a small world, to be running into people I had not seen in years in Baghdad, Iraq, of all places.

Also relating to my past as an Eagle Scout, the Boy Scouts of America had reached across the world and set up an operation in Iraq. Members from the Baghdad Area Council visited us and handed out popcorn and treats—the exact kind as I used to sell as a kid. When speaking to the local leader of the group, he told me the Boy Scouts had been active in Iraq since 1915! That was not long after they were established by Lord Byron Scott in the U.S. in the early twentieth century. He told me Saddam had changed the Scouts into a paramilitary group, loyal to him, and have given them military uniforms, essentially forming them into part of his army. Looking around at the young faces in the ER, I could not help but wonder if some of these kids were listed in Saddam's suicide brigade of his esteemed Republican Guard. Who knew? The council met in the International Zone regularly, and after telling the leader that I was a former Eagle Scout, he invited me to come to their meetings and participate. I wanted to, but I knew that I would not be able to do too much as I was too often on shift and could not regularly leave the hospital. But what a great and uplifting thing it was to see the smiles on the kid's faces, and watching them participate in something as wholesome as the Boy Scouts in Iraq was fantastic. How could Saddam have wanted to turn those happy faces into suicide machines for his protection?

Later in the week, I was awakened from sleep by a strange vibration of my bed, my room, and the entire building. This time it was not a Russian-made Iraqi helicopter flying directly over, but most likely American tanks and their steel treads churning by on the asphalt outside. I had large windows in my room, but I could not look out to see as we had them barricaded by our furniture and very thick "blast" curtains to help keep the mortar and rocket fragments on the outside rather than inside with us. I then fell back asleep, but dreamed that over the intercom came the words "Tank! Tank! Tank!" which apparently meant in my dream that an enemy tank was right outside the building and preparing to lob rounds inside. What a strange delusion! However, I was thankful that I did not have to worry about that ever being a reality.

It had been six weeks since I helped care for the ten-year-old boy who was part of the accidental missile attack. Four weeks later he came in, and we discovered he had an aortic pseudoaneurysm, a condition caused by the attack. His aorta had developed a dangerous "out pouching" in the lining, and it could rupture and bleed into his chest, killing him. I remembered caring for several members of his family that night as they were brought in after the incident, and this boy was rushed to the operating room, where our surgeons opened his chest and repaired the damage to his aorta. He had an excellent postoperative course, but he then developed the pseudoaneurysm after the surgery and presented back to me this day with a chief complaint of vomiting blood. Once his pathology was discovered, our cardiothoracic surgeon Dr. Mike Myer began working with Pat Hickey to get him flown to the U.S., where his injury could be repaired.

When I spoke to the boy's uncle, one of the last members of his family left from the attack, he reached out his hand to me, taking my right hand, then put his left hand behind my neck and pulled me into him. It actually startled me quite a bit; I was not sure if it was a gesture of appreciation or of anger, since the U.S. had accidently killed most everyone in his family. After pulling me into him, he smiled and hugged me. It was a touching moment for me; despite the destruction, he was still willing to work with us and held us in high esteem. I did not want to let him down!

Over the next several days, Pat and Mike worked the diplomatic paperwork shuffle diligently, while the young boy hung out on the wards of the hospital, playful and looking like he did not have a care in the world. He quickly befriended all the nurses and medics on the ward and followed them around, and he became a welcome sight for all of us during his stay. It took several days to get approval from the U.S. government to allow the child to go to UCLA Medical Center in California for repair. Once everything was arranged, a bittersweet CSH wished him well and sent him away on a helicopter, with his trip to begin on our landing zone and end up in Los Angeles, California.

Days later, we received the tragic news that the boy died onboard the plane just an hour away from UCLA. His aorta ruptured into his chest and he bled to death, with the helpless crew of the plane there to do nothing but watch him die. It was suggested that the vessel would likely rupture within a few days of discovery, and after all the paperwork, phone calls, and high-level approvals required, he died on the tenth day, thirty thousand feet over the western U.S. It was a blow to everyone who worked so hard to save him, but as usual, we had to pick up the pieces and move on. Hopefully, his uncle did not lose faith in our cause.

Later, a Stryker army vehicle was hit by an EFP, and the wounded were rushed into our facility, with no time for warning. I was busy putting in an invasive line into an Iraqi gentlemen's radial artery at the time. He was suffering from heart failure and cardiogenic shock. By the time I made it into the trauma room, our team had put an IV in the soldier in bed one and had his clothes stripped off to expose his injuries. But when they put the oxygen mask on him, right as I walked in, he flipped out from his head injury. He was screaming, "Let me sit up!" among several other things, and flailing around the bed, making it a dangerous situation for himself and my crew. Our team could not hold him down, and I yelled, "We'll just intubate him sitting up ... Push the drugs!" as he was coming up off the bed. Sam Matta quickly pushed etomidate, a sedative drug, and he collapsed onto the bed into the arms of our medics. We then paralyzed him and pulled his limp body to the head of the bed, where I intubated him quickly, and after receiving the CT scan results we prepped and flew him to Balad for neurosurgical care.

On a routine shift back home, I see young women having miscarriages routinely. They are unfortunately extremely common, occurring in almost 40 percent of all pregnancies. They also occurred in Iraq. I cared for a contractor who was six weeks pregnant having her first miscarriage. Usually, I perform a pelvic exam and an ultrasound and then send the patient home to follow up with her OB/GYN, since she is frequently stable and in no danger. The reassurance from me is often the best medicine for these unfortunate women, and it gives me great satisfaction when I can show them a healthy baby on the ultrasound to alleviate their fears. This patient, unfortunately, was a much different case. When performing the pelvic exam, I pulled clot after clot of blood from her vagina, and more hemorrhaging followed immediately afterward. Preparing to give her blood due to the amount of loss she was enduring, I had to call our OB/GYN to take her to the operating room for a dilation and curettage, or D&C. It was just another example to me that even the normal, routine cases there in Baghdad were not normal and routine!

Early March was the beginning of a very hard time for our troops in the Baghdad area. When leaving the gym after a workout, I heard sirens blaring from three Humvees as they barreled down the narrow roadway beside the landing zone, bringing casualties. Sweaty in my PT uniform, I ran to the third Humvee to assess the victims inside while nurses and medics poured from the ER entrance and sprinted to the first two vehicles. The wounded soldier in my vehicle was bloodied everywhere, with large dressings to his face and head. I noticed within a few seconds that he was breathing and alert, so I knew we had time to get to him later. I ran to the second vehicle and assisted Cpt. Pat Smith, one of our nurses, as he was unloading a soldier from the backseat of the Humvee. The soldier was strapped to a spine board. Pat pulled on the end of the board while I climbed inside the vehicle and helped dislodge it from the console. The board had to be tilted 30 degrees toward the front of the vehicle to dislodge it, and the soldier strapped to the board loosely began to slide onto the floor of the vehicle. I grabbed his belt and jacket top, soaking my hands in his blood, but accomplishing my goal of holding the patient on the board while Cpt. Smith pulled the soldier and the board over me.

Once we had him out of the vehicle, both Pat and I realized from the way his body lay on the board, with the left arm hanging lifelessly, that he was likely dead. However, neither of us was about to abort our rush into the waiting arms of the trauma room just because we felt it was too late. What message would that send to his buddies? Those poor guys were covered in blood, vomit, and sweat and were all going through the realization and disbelief of what just happened to them! Placing the patient on bed one, where Jason, the ER doc on duty was waiting, I told him that it did not look good, but I was not going to quit in front of the patient's crew of brothers without trying. I then jumped over to bed three, where the victim from the first Humvee was placed, while Jason and his team began CPR and did their best to revive the soldier we brought him, but all with no results. When going over the body after the chaos had cleared a little while later, we noticed him to have thirty or so ball bearing wounds all over the parts of his body not protected by his armor. We could roll some of them under our fingers, just deep to the skin, and some even hung partly out, with the shiny metal surfaces reflecting the room light back to us. Ball bearings. We were discovering them more and more frequently in our victims, as that seemed to be one of the new weapons of choice for the bad guys.

Just after delivering the first soldier to Jason's team in bed one, I went to bed three to find that the squad's Iraqi interpreter had traumatic wounds to the left side of his face and a decreased mental status. I listened to his breath sounds and noticed the right lung to have diminished air movement when compared with the left, so despite his screams of pain, I quickly stuck a needle into his chest, a few inches above the nipple to relieve the potentially life-threatening collapsed lung. After Sgt. Sion Ledbetter expertly placed an IV into his arm, I intubated him and we sent him to the CT scanner, where a ball bearing was found at the base of his brain. He died two hours later.

Less than an hour later, CNN news reported a suicide bomber had ran into a crowd of American soldiers and detonated his vest of ball bearings. The destructive force killed four American soldiers at the scene, and eventually the death toll was expanded to include five soldiers, their Iraqi interpreter, and I believe two Iraqi civilians.

The next day, a roadside bomb north of us killed three U.S. soldiers, and we also had two GIs come in with extremity wounds due to an IED hitting their vehicle, where another soldier died at the scene. Later in the day, we received two soldiers with massive 50–70 percent burns to their bodies from a rocket attack a couple of hours to our south. Nine dead Americans in three days. The price of our freedom and the freedom of the Iraqi people—the freedom of the entire Middle East—had just increased by nine. I understood why the EMT personnel of previous CSHs to occupy Baghdad ER would have goals of "no dead American soldiers today." We had been somewhat spoiled because the violence has dipped to its lowest point in years due to the surge and other factors. We hoped the new violence did not represent a trend, but our worst fears came true over the next few weeks thanks to Muqtada Al Sadr, the radical Shiite cleric.

—

Our new goal was to have no dead Americans each day. That would make any day great. A suspicious vehicle was found nearby, and everyone was locked down wherever they were while the explosive ordinance detachment (EOD) investigated. Some were stuck in duck-and-cover bunkers for hours, others at the dining facility, and others who knows where. But I was one of the lucky ones. A few of us had just checked out an SUV and driven over to another FOB in the International Zone to go fishing. With bacon stolen from the dining facility, Burger King French fries, and a can of SPAM, we went after anything we could catch.

We sat in lawn chairs for two hours, each of us getting small hits but no one connecting on anything, when finally, just before we were to start packing up, I hooked one. The small, four-and-half-foot travel-sized rod and reel with six-pound test line gave me everything they could, but I was hooked into a ten-pound carp that had different plans. As I fought the fish, four Iraqi soldiers cheered me on excitedly, continuously asking with hand gestures and smiles if they could have the fish to eat. They kept rubbing their stomachs and putting their hands to their mouths, whooping and hollering, drawing a small crowd to the fight. The fish gave me slack as I reeled in, and then took off again every time I would get him to the surface. Finally, he came to the top within a few feet of me before jerking his head and breaking the line. He won that day. But Anthony Knighton sent me fifteen-pound line the next week, so after respooling my reels with the stronger line, I went back after them a time or two. Whether I landed a fish or not did not matter; it was a great way to relax and not worry about anything in the world for a while. I have always been an avid outdoorsman, but this day especially I thought, "Thank God for fishing!" It was fulfilling to be able to escape the CSH and get a break from the trauma and politics for a couple of hours, even if I did not catch anything.

Reality set in the next day. Four wounded soldiers came in, three of them with significant lower extremity amputations. Multiple-array explosively formed projectiles, or EFPs, had hit their vehicle from all sides. These tank-penetrating rounds blew through their truck from multiple directions; it was an elaborate setup that took time, planning, and funding to accomplish.

The soldier who was hit the hardest had bilateral amputations of both thighs. Tourniquets were applied to each side, but he was still suffering from massive blood loss and his pulse disappeared about one minute after he was placed on the trauma bed. CPR was initiated, and he was shocked twice with a return of spontaneous circulation and good pulses. He was given blood, along with several medications, and rushed to the OR, where he survived his surgery. He was taken to the ICU to recover in critical condition but still alive.

The second soldier had what looked like a shark bite taken out of the back of his upper legs. All the muscle and tissue was ripped off the bone, leaving what was left of the front of his thighs. All of his posterior leg muscles were gone, and it took several pneumatic blood pressure cuff–type tourniquets to stop the bleeding. When rolled over for his back and rectal exam, he yelled "I hate you guys! F***kers!" as Stewart McCarver's finger went into his rectum to evaluate the injuries. He was intubated and given blood and also rushed to the operating room. When talking to Dr. Bill Ralston, one of our orthopedists a few hours later, he said that the soldier would likely require the rest of his legs to be amputated because he would never be able to bend his knees again; there was simply no muscle left. It would be the patient's decision as to whether he kept his legs in a nonfunctioning state or if he would elect to amputate them and have prosthetics placed. What a tough decision this soldier, this hero, would have to face in the near future.

The third soldier came to the back treatment room. We placed him in bed seven, and Deb Chappel and I went to work. We required medics to help expose him, place him on the monitor, and get IV access, but they were all busy in the front room. I grabbed a patient admin clerk who was collecting information, gave her trauma shears, and told her to start cutting off clothes while Deb worked on an IV in his right arm. His left leg was amputated, and he had a high tourniquet placed around his thigh. Another new medic came to the back to place the fourth patient in a nearby bed, and looking across the room, I could tell the fourth patient was still breathing and sitting upright through his bloodied face. I grabbed the new rotating medic, not knowing his name yet, and pushed him over to my patient and told him to get the monitor on and get our airway items ready for us to intubate if needed.

The soldier was fading in and out of consciousness, and initial vital signs indicated a heart rate of 140 beats per minute, and a blood pressure of 75/53, both indicators of massive blood loss. I rotated to the soldier's left groin and felt guilty because I did not take the time to give him anesthetic medication prior to placing the large-bore IV into his femoral vein, but every second counted. We hit him with twelve units of blood products quickly, and I sedated and intubated him to relieve his screaming from the pain and to protect his airway.

When he left to go to the operating room, the entire trauma room and the back treatment areas were covered in blood. Crimson streaks a foot wide were splattered all over, and when Pat Hickey wandered in about that time, he said the smell of blood emanating from the ER was nauseating. In total, we went through thirty-six units of blood and plasma on the three patients within twenty minutes. All survived their OR time, and all made it to Germany alive. They ended up missing various extremities, but they all three survived, a feat that would not have been possible anywhere else in my opinion. Two of them, maybe all of them, would have died in many U.S. hospitals, as they are just not set up for trauma like we were at Baghdad ER.

The battalion commander for the four troops came into the ER after they were taken to the operating room, and I took him outside and explained the injuries to his soldiers, his men, one by one. With the description of each wound, he would wince and lower his head, looking away as if to keep me from seeing the pain in his eyes. It was all over his face; he could not hide it. After briefing him, our chaplain Felix Sermon took the lieutenant colonel upstairs to see the one soldier still awake to talk to. That was enough trauma for us, but later in the day, a sniper shot another one of our heroes through the temple. He died on our table.

Getting a day off the next day, I went back to FOB Prosperity and caught my first Iraqi fish, a three-pound carp from one of Saddam's old ponds. I had a fantastic time relaxing in a lawn chair and getting a hook wet, and I planned to do it again as much as possible in the future. Afterward, we were lucky enough to be treated to a fantastic meal. One of the private security contracting groups from the IZ took several of us to their compound, Saddam's old zoo, to enjoy freshly grilled lamp chops. I had never eaten them before, and they were absolutely amazing! Grilled potatoes and lamb chops made for an incredible meal I will not forget. We watched the Peruvian guards in their off-duty time playing soccer in Saddam's old alligator pit, a sixty-yard-long structure recessed in the ground to keep the beasts inside. Rumor had it he would push people down into the pit to watch them die, but it was not surprising as he would also fish with dynamite while forcing scuba divers in the water to pick up the fish ... if they survived the blast themselves.

Later, in March 2008, I received the call from my older brother Carl just as I was getting off the night shift about 7:00 AM telling me that my paternal grandmother had just passed away. It was something that we had been expecting for a while, but it still cut me deeply. She was in her nineties and had suffered from a stroke a year or so prior that had complicated her situation, requiring full-time caretakers to live at home with her. Her husband, my grandfather, died when I was less than ten years old after suffering from Parkinson's disease for the last twenty years of his life. I do not remember much about him, other than the trembling hands, weak voice, and big smile that would come across his face whenever we arrived at their home. Grandmother, however, outlived him by twenty years, and until a couple of years before, when she lost the ability to write, signed her name as "Mrs. W.W. Baker." She loved him so, and it made me feel good to know they were now together again with God after twenty years.

I could not go home to her funeral. I understood that. My family understood that. I was certain that grandmother understood that. But it still killed me. I knew that five years from then, all I would remember about her death was the fact that I did not show up for her funeral. It was like missing the birth of your child due to deployment. There is not a choice, you cannot go home in two days for the event, and everyone understands, but the bottom line is that you missed it. This feeling stunk, and it crushed me to realize I would not be able to pay my last respects, to honor her by stopping what I was doing and be by her side. Once again, I knew that my absence did not matter to her in the least, and my family understood, but the fact was that I missed her funeral. Ten or twenty years later, I will still have missed her funeral. I could not help it, but I have learned to live with that fact. After I returned home, I was able to visit her grave and pay my last respects.

However, despite my bad news, I still had to work, and the patients kept coming. We did have a very entertaining patient, one who made us all chuckle and brightened the day for each of us. He was an American soldier who was shot in the right leg. He came to us with a tourniquet on and in terrible pain. After quickly assessing him, we loosened the tourniquet to find that his bleeding was not bad, and his pain subsided once the blood flow returned to his leg. I leaned over to him and told him he was going to be okay, and his demeanor completely changed. He went from being in extreme agony to elation, from misery to jubilation and excitement. He began looking around the room, saying, "So this is Baghdad ER?" and telling the story of how he was wounded. He asked me to get his camera out of a pocket in his body armor and take pictures of him in the trauma room. We had no other patients at the time, so I had no issues with his request.

When I started taking shots, his personality really came out. As I begin to take the first picture and looked through the camera to frame it up, I noticed that his genitals were uncovered, as we always completely exposed our patients to discover unknown injuries. I pulled the sheet down to cover up "his boys" and then began to take pictures. He sat up in bed and began to pose, one shot with a serious face and then another with hand gestures and his tongue hanging out. He requested that all of us pose around the bed with him and get a group picture. We had a great time and a good laugh, and he told us how much he appreciated our presence in Baghdad several times. I wish all trauma patients were that entertaining!

Later in the week, Laura called me from home in a panic as the hot water heater in our home had burst open and was flooding the master bedroom closet and bathroom. Apparently it was running out the garage and down into the street, and she stood in ankle deep water while attempting to turn off every valve she could reach. She finally went across the street to the neighbor's house, and he came over and shut off the valves leading to the tank. Thank God he was home and she had the presence of mind to go find help! A $1,000 insurance deductible later, the carpet was replaced, the bathroom floor repaired, and we prayed there was not any structural damage from the flooding. There was nothing I could do for her but listen, but she did a fantastic job dealing with it so calmly and effectively!

The news also became much worse in Baghdad at the same time, as early in my next shift we received an American soldier burned beyond all recognition. He was placed in our trauma bay. The front of his body armor had been incinerated off him. His legs and arms were frozen in a contracted position, with both his elbows and knees bent and frozen at about 40 degrees of flexation. His face was charred black and singed, and he had a purplish hue from some unknown chemical to the right side of his head and spread onto the back of his charred armor. I assumed he was likely dead upon arrival, but a quick cardiac check by ultrasound by Marti Roellig confirmed a beating heart. I attempted to pry the soldier's dry, charred lips apart to intubate him, but the burns to his face and neck were so severe and his skin was so tight from the thermal trauma that I could not open his mouth.

He arrived to us with an intraosseous IV line punched into his sternum, and Kristy Bischoff pushed sedating and paralytic medications through it as other members of our team were attempting to place large IVs through the charred, dry skin. I opened his mouth much more forcibly the second time and suctioned out the vomit from the back of his throat. Either due to the relaxation of the medications, or the increased aggressiveness of my mouth-opening maneuver, I was able to insert the laryngoscope blade. However, due to his contracture, I could not see the vocal cords as I usually try to do, so I inserted the endotracheal tube based off the few landmarks I could see. The tube passed into the right place, and he was successfully intubated.

Our leads would not stick to his blackened, charred skin, so our medics taped them to his chest, occasionally picking up cardiac activity through the burn, reporting to us a heart rate in the 100s to 140s. With no hope of an IV placement by a medic or nurse due to the immense scarring to his arms and legs, the only option was to place a central line to give further medications or blood. At one point, we had four physicians sticking him with needles in rushed attempts to gain access. Once obtained, he was given six units of blood products; at the time, it was just a guess to decide if he required them or not. While attempting to run the resuscitation, I did not know what his blood pressure was as we could not feel a pulse or obtain a rhythm through his burned skin. It was so stiff and contracted that our blood pressure cuffs would not work; they could not squeeze down onto his arms or legs. The only way to obtain his heart rate at times was to have someone stop what we were doing and focus on obtaining a carotid pulse through the burn in his neck.

The trauma room began to smell of charred, burnt flesh. Marti performed a FAST ultrasound exam and noted him to have blood in his abdomen from internal hemorrhage from the blast. His chest x-ray came back looking good, so the decision was made to take him to the OR, if he survived that far, for full escharotomies, where the surgeons would cut the skin all over his body to relieve the pressure caused by the burn and open his abdomen to investigate the bleeding. Our nurses and medics wheeled his gurney upstairs, and about five minutes later his commander and first sergeant arrived at the EMT.

I took them down the hallway so we could talk in private, and then I began to tell them about their soldier and his resuscitation. While talking to them, one of my medics pulled me away and informed me that the soldier had just been pronounced dead in the OR. I went back to tell his unit, and they let me know there were two other soldiers in the Humvee, as well as two Iraqi interpreters. The other four individuals were unable to be removed from the vehicle, as their bodies had essentially been incinerated. It was a horrible start to my shift, and unfortunately was a harbinger of things to come. That day, I had a few more blown up people throughout my twelve-hour shift, as well as one man with an open skull fracture, another shot in the leg, and a man having a heart attack. I had no other deaths on my watch that day, but everything was about to change.

The crew of Baghdad ER

Easter 2008

It's Raining Lead

BOOM! A few seconds later, our building was shaken by another blast. It was 5:55 AM on Easter Sunday, and the insurgents were giving us a wake-up call by firing rockets at us. I was just climbing out of the shower, preparing to go on shift at seven after stopping by Chaplain Sermon's outdoor Easter sunrise service at 6:30. I quickly got dressed, and headed down to the ER to check the damage. A Nepalese security guard came in about 6:35 with a large cut to his leg from shrapnel, but that was the only injury we received from the twenty-two rockets that landed in the International Zone that morning, as they all landed in uninhabited areas.

An hour later, we were given a one-minute heads-up that a Blackhawk headed to the neurosurgeons in Balad was diverting to us because their patient, a U.S. soldier with a massive open head injury, was becoming unstable and the flight medic did not think he would survive the extra thirty minutes to Balad. Once in the trauma room, I quickly noticed him to be unresponsive and intubated him, followed by venous and arterial line placements by me and Marti, who had come downstairs to help. We gave him six units of blood, antiseizure medications, antibiotics, and an extra high-salt saline solution to decrease the pressure in his skull. The nurse chosen to fly him sprinted upstairs to prep for flight, and we packaged him and got him back into the air, this time with more stable vital signs, as fast as possible for the rest of his trip to Balad.

After the early morning action, the day became quieter until around 5:00 PM, when explosions rocked the building once again. Some of our medics, sitting outside on the Gator at the time of the blasts, sprinted inside as we received calls telling us that multiple casualties were on their way in from the latest round of rocket attacks into the International Zone. After hearing that we had up to fifteen patients coming, we put our mini-mascal plan into place and began stationing physicians, nurses, and medics around the ER to take patients. Dr. Mike Myer, our cardiothoracic surgeon, and I went to the front and began triaging patients as they arrived. Most were walking wounded, other than one poor gentleman who took a nearby hit and suffered an open skull fracture. We cleaned up the other patients, flew the patient with the open skull fracture to the neurosurgical team at Balad, and began to wonder when the third round of rockets was coming.

We only had to wait a couple of hours to find out. BOOM! BOOM! The building shook by two hits nearby, and we all looked at each other, thinking, "Here we go again." I was off shift by this point, so I rushed to the ER and joined the crew of the night shift preparing for the next wave of victims. A few moments later, two local Iraqis were brought in, one with significant flank trauma and another with superficial injuries. While our team was working on them, I once again waited in the front for more casualties to arrive from the rockets, but none came.

However, a patient came in twenty minutes later who will haunt me forever. Jason, the ER doc on shift, was in the back working on the victims hit by the rocket fire, so when the burned solider from an IED blast came in, I was waiting for him in the trauma room. We had prepared by calling down our burn surgeon, Dr. King, and Marti joined us to assist with the resuscitation. When the patient was brought into the trauma room, it was a replay of the incredibly burned soldier I treated just two days before.

Once he was placed in bed one, I immediately leaned down to his face, inches from mine, and looked into his eyes. I will never forget him looking straight back at me. His eyelids were missing; he had no hair, eyebrows, or eyelashes left. His skin was black and brown from the flame and heat, and the rest of his body was covered in third and fourth degree burns. His fingers were blackened, shriveled, and mostly amputated from the heat. But his wedding ring was somehow still in place. It was carefully removed, and while the other physicians worked feverishly to get central access on his groin, our medics tried their best to stick a vein in his arms, going right through the charred skin. I never pulled away from his face. I held a bag-valve oxygen mask over his nose and mouth, and each time he would take a breath, I would help him. I suctioned out his mouth to try to remove anything that could be impeding his airway.

His eyes burned into me; they burned into my soul. He was fully conscious; he knew everything that was going on. What could I do? What could I say? I asked him if he had any allergies, to which he weakly shook his head no. He could not speak due to the extensive burns to his mouth and airway. I explained to him that after we got an IV placed, I would put him to sleep and relieve his pain. I said, "Just hang in there, they are putting IVs into your groin and your arms. You are doing great. We're going to take care of you." I would assist a breath for him. "Do you need me to suction you again?" He nodded yes. "Hang in there, you are doing so well. You are doing great. I'm going to take away your pain, buddy. I won't leave you." His eyes continued to stare into mine; he had no ability to blink. I just kept looking into his eyes, keeping my face close to his, and I kept trying to comfort him. "We're going to take care of you, you're going to be okay." He stared back at me, saying with his eyes, "I trust you to take care of me. Don't let me down." It was one of the hardest moments of my life. I have never connected with a patient like I did this hero. I did not know his name, but it did not matter. I was not about to pull away from his face; I would never leave his side. I decided I would never abandon him in this time of need.

Three physicians and multiple nurses and medics were attempting to gain IV access through his burned skin, and I could have tried an IV in his subclavian vein just below his clavicle, but once again, standing at the head of the bed, with his eyes locked on mine, I would not leave him. If he died right there, I was determined that he would not die alone. I was with him, and at the moment, that was the only thing I could control. His beautiful, white, and untraumatized eyes were locked on mine, and I continued to help him get air and tell him how I would take the pain away momentarily. Jason successfully placed a central line, and I told the soldier, "We are going to take five deep breaths together." He nodded. I wanted to get his lungs as full of oxygen as possible, in anticipation of a difficult, swollen, burned, and charred airway. "One." He took a huge breath, and I squeezed the bag pushing oxygen into his chest. "Two." The same. He followed all of my directions until the sedating medication was pushed at "Four." By the time he took the fifth deep breath, he was unconscious from the medication. We paralyzed him, and I quickly went into his mouth with the laryngoscope blade. His airway was swollen and beefy red, but by the grace of God I was able to visualize his cords and get him intubated successfully.

We continued the aggressive resuscitation, giving him fluids, and rushed him to the operating room, where Booker King performed escharotomies all over his body to allow his skin to expand for the swelling to come from the burn. When he left the ER, I went into our office and did my best to choke back the tears. I went outside for some fresh air, not caring if more rockets came right at the moment or not. Knowing full well that the last thing this soldier may ever see was the look on my face, I did my best to keep it together. All of our docs, medics, and nurses could tell I was exasperated; this soldier had touched me. As he was resuscitated in the ICU after his surgery, I broke my rule about not following up patients and went upstairs several times to check on him.

Booker and Kevin Chung, our new intensive care physician who also specialized in burn management, had already notified the burn team at Brooke Army Medical Center in San Antonio, TX, and they were en route to Germany to meet the soldier once he arrived there. I left the ICU for the last time about 1:30 AM and cried on the phone to my wife back home as the patient was wheeled past me on his way out to the helicopter, wrapped in a hypothermia blanket and covered by monitors, ventilators, and other equipment.

After coming within feet of being hit by mortars, I wrote earlier that I would never forget Thanksgiving 2007. After the rockets this day, and the patient who touched my heart in a way it had never been touched, I will never forget Easter 2008 as well. I prayed for this hero of America, his wife, and his parents. God bless them all.

Two days later, we were greeted again by another round of rockets slamming into the buildings nearby. Thankfully, there were not too many people injured by the attacks, but it made the third day in a row that we had been hit since the action began Easter Sunday. Just before I came on shift at 7:00 PM, rockets came in while I was outside on the phone with Laura. For the first time, I had to tell her in real time that the barrages were coming, and thankfully she took it well once I was safely inside the building!

Multiple patients with gunshot wounds and blast injuries began pouring in, with Bradley fighting vehicles and the new MRAP trucks bringing them in by ground since the Blackhawks could not fly due to the fine sand limiting visibility to several hundred feet. Apparently the Madhi Militia had received permission from Muqtada Al-Sadr to begin hitting our forces again, and his militias had now been seen out on the streets of Baghdad for the first time in six months. We were told that traps had been set up in Sadr City, a local slum of Baghdad, waiting for our soldiers to rush in to catch the guys firing rockets into the Green Zone. They would be greeted with multiple IEDs and EFPs that were lined up in the potential entry and exit routes.

That night, members of the Mahdi Militia in both southwestern Baghdad and Sadr City overran multiple Iraqi National Police stations, and the casualties rolled in for several hours. One Iraqi police officer had a gunshot wound to the neck, transecting his trachea, hitting his backbone, and then ending in his chest. Jason took him in our trauma room, and we directed another seriously injured man in there as well. Triaging multiple incoming patients one by one as they came toward the ER, I made my way to the U.S. combat vehicles to speak to the American soldiers bringing in the casualties. They told me the firefight was ongoing and the Iraqi forces were attempting to retake the police stations, and there were likely more wounded people to come. The American first sergeant of the unit told us the National Police were "fighting valiantly beside my boys," and he went from patient to patient to thank them for their support for his soldiers and their country, contrary to the media reports of mass Iraqi desertions when the fighting began.

Our command informed us the next day that we would be hit hard over the next few days, and we eventually were relegated to wearing body armor and helmets to go to the dining facility. Everyone living in trailers with nonballistic or nonconcrete roofs was moved into the main hospital building, and they slept in every nook and cranny that could be found. CBS news began reporting that a major battle was going on in the southern city of Basra, the fighting had spread now to Baghdad, and the next few days would likely be very busy for us.

The few days after the attacks began on Easter Sunday were anything but quiet. They liked to hit us early in the morning, as our night shifts would end, with more rocket barrages into the Green Zone. Just after one attack, two Americans were brought in who were hit severely. One had an open femur fracture and multiple penetrating abdominal wounds from a rocket that landed near the room in which he was sleeping. While I was working on him, a U.S. soldier was brought in after being hit by shrapnel, resulting in wounds all down his left side and head. He was talking, but acting in an agitated manner, so I intubated to protect him after Robyn Stafford pushed the medications for sedation. I performed an ultrasound of his chest and noted his left lung to be collapsed and full of blood, so Booker King threw in a left-sided chest tube, and out rushed 750cc of blood. I placed a central line into his femoral vein, and we gave him two code reds, or twelve units of blood products. Booker then took him upstairs to the operating room and cracked his chest, repairing a bleeding vessel that was exanguinating into his lung. I took the opportunity to go to sleep for a few hours afterward and get some rest.

However, just four hours later, the rockets were back, and I found myself back down in the ER caring for more rocket injuries from the Green Zone, as well as more Americans and Iraqi soldiers alike from the fighting occurring all over Baghdad with the Madhi Militia. An American soldier had just been pronounced dead upon my arrival, and about thirty minutes later, we found ourselves doing unsuccessful CPR on another warrior with a gunshot wound to the neck. Throughout the day, intelligence reports kept coming, preparing us to be hit by more rockets and for us to expect many more casualties from all the fighting. All day, we diligently worked on injured warriors and found a chance to grab a meal from our dining facility around 6:00 PM.

Wearing all of our body armor to make the two hundred–foot journey to the DFAC, we trudged over for our first hot meal in a couple of days. While enjoying a square piece of fried fish, explosions suddenly rocked the building, and we were once again locked down inside. After a brief rest, where we were not allowed to go anywhere, we were released and made our way to the ER to treat a two-year-old Iraqi girl with burns to 51 percent of her body and more battle injuries from the firefights.

All day and all night, over the week beginning with Easter, I felt as if I was on speed, running from one injury to the next, intubating someone here, putting in a line there, and giving blood somewhere else. "Shifts" disappeared, and we essentially kept all three ER docs working together pretty much all day. We all felt an incredible sense of purpose, and while I hoped to never see a violently traumatized patient again, I truly did enjoy the moment. How many people will ever get the opportunity to care for America's heroes in this manner? Sure, all the rocket fire was worrisome, and we knew we could not stand a direct hit, but we knew that we must ignore it and go about our duties, being there for those who kept us safe. The news was predicting this would go on for several days, and that one they did hit right on the head. Thankfully, Cpt. Steve Beckwith, an ER doc serving with the Thirty-first CSH at Camp Bucca, Iraq, literally came out of the blue to help us. Flying as a medical attendant with a detainee from southern Iraq who was transferred to us, he somehow convinced his commander to let him stay and work with us a while. He served as a fourth ER doc for us during that time, and he helped us keep two to three docs covering the ER at all times.

———

After my forth or fifth sixteen-hour shift in a row, I headed to my room to crash about 2:00 am, and was able to sleep through the night without incident for the first time in six days. Later in the morning, the daily rocket barrages began to fall around us again, and some landed near us, awakening me. Turning over in my rack and feeling the epinephrine surging from my adrenal glands, my mind was spurred to a wakeful state rapidly as the rocket blasts landed closer and closer. However, this time, instead of springing to my feet, putting on my PT uniform and rushing down to the EMT, the week's worth of rocket barrages and massive trauma had jaded me, and I moved at a somewhat less excited pace. Our ER docs and surgeons had been working around the clock for six days now, all stopping to catch a nap whenever possible. The last night was great, as I was able to get several hours of sleep and recharge for the long days ahead. But the barrage of rockets coming in now would mean more casualties, so I had to get moving once again.

The next day and into the night, we were hit by several additional volleys of rockets. Most of the 150 or so rockets launched into the International Zone during the week had landed near the U.S. Embassy, and that is where we were receiving the majority of our patients from, with several dead and many more with various types of injuries. Most of those killed or seriously injured had been in hooches or trailers with no hardened roof on top of them, and others were in bunkers that received direct hits. Our hospital commander continued to order all personnel assigned to the hospital living in trailers on our FOB to stay inside the hardened structure of the hospital, so we worked around the makeshift cots and beds. Some of our guys began "hot bunking," with two people sleeping in the same bed on different shifts in order to stay inside the building.

At one point in the day, I found myself putting on my body armor and helmet before climbing aboard one of our John Deere Gators to drive to the front of the hospital where a patient had been shot through the arm and was waiting for triage. He was not a soldier, Iraqi, American, or other, so if his injuries were not life- or limb-threatening, I was to send him to an Iraqi hospital. We had not been hit by indirect fire in two hours, so my medic Sgt. Wesner and I hoped that we would not be attacked by rocket fire while we were outside, but we both knew the next barrage was coming at some point. Pulling the Gator up to Haifa Street, I noticed several Iraqi army soldiers gathered around a young man in his twenties, lying in a large pool of blood. Flies hovered and buzzed about him, as if waiting patiently for him to die while simultaneously jockeying for position to ingest the pools of blood staining the sidewalk.

He was alert and conscious, so I leaned down and examined the large pressure dressing that had been placed on his upper arm. A makeshift tourniquet had been tied above the wound, just past the armpit, and it was doing a great job of compressing the artery enough to stop any bleeding. Until I untied it to examine him that is, as I released a rhythmic pumping and squirting of blood from the transected artery that bled in tune with his heartbeat. I asked Sgt. Wesner for a CAT tourniquet from his aid bag, and we applied the device and cinched it down extremely tight on the man's arm. The bleeding slowed, but did not stop, so we then placed a large pressure-dressing on his wound and quelled the bright red flow. Instructing Sgt. Wesner to turn the Gator around and position it to transport the man into the ER, I helped him to his feet. He was wearing only what was left of a loose-fitting shirt that was already too large for him before it had been cut down and a pair of white underwear that had been stained red all over from his bleeding.

I climbed on the back of the flatbed Gator with the patient and positioned myself on my knees with my chest against him to allow him to lean into me and cushion the ride over the speed bumps. He generously reached out with his uninjured arm and held onto our medical bag as I held him on the back of the Gator. Upon arrival to the ER, Jason assumed care, and within the hour the man found himself in our operating room undergoing a vascular surgical repair of his transected artery. Later, while Deb Chappel was briefing our command about the days events, she told them that I had gone out front to triage and care for this individual, and the response she received was not "thanks," or "good job," but rather, "Why in the world did you let one of our docs go outside to do that while we are getting hit by rockets and mortars?" Funny, but all of us had gone into business mode, taking care of blown up patients. That was my second trip out to get patients while we were receiving frequent indirect fire, and it would not be my last. It was all part of the job, as we were all one team in the EMT, even if the command did not understand that. Our medics and nurses were just as important as me, and they went outside every day.

Later that evening, the rockets began landing closer and closer to our FOB, forcing our hospital commander to order everyone indoors to don their body armor, helmets, and eye protection in case we sustained a direct hit. We were caring for three soldiers who had sustained minor injuries from IED attacks and two bad guys who were brought in for care prior to being sent to jail. We loaded up in our body armor and moved all of our patients into the hallway and away from the windows. It was a true traffic jam of hospital beds, and we were in bad shape to accept more casualties since we could not use our treatment room due to the large windows exposing patients to possible shrapnel. Could you imagine being one of the soldiers at the hospital due to a roadside bomb and sitting beside two bad guys who had been attacking your fellow brothers? They demonstrated great restraint, and I was impressed with their professionalism.

Boom. Boom! BOOM!! Three rockets suddenly impacted on our FOB, and we all feared the third actually hit our building somewhere due to the concussion and noise. Two impacted on the landing zone outside, and the third struck about twelve meters outside our door. Immediately, all nonessential personnel were ordered out of the EMT and into the heart of the building for safety, and we made immediate preparations for more injuries, perhaps coming from our own. The anxiety and fear were palpable; everyone was doing the best they could to do their jobs and care for our patients, even while wearing combat gear. If needed, we could not get to our treatment room due to the hallway jam, so I had to make a decision as to how we would prepare for more action. It may have not been the most ethical decision I have ever made, but I ordered the two bad guys to be moved into the treatment room, despite the windows making it more dangerous, and we put the wounded Americans into our specialty room without access from outside blasts. Thankfully, no more rockets landed on our FOB that night, and I did not have to worry about explaining my decision to the command as to why I put the bad guys by the windows and in harm's way, but I would make the same decision again if I had to.

After the barrages, we took a quick look outside to see the damage. A rocket had been fired from the direction of Sadr City, and with its low trajectory, it skipped a few feet across the top of our operating rooms that were full with several cases going at the time secondary to the trauma of the last week. It landed in the open area just outside of the ER, about twenty-five paces, or twelve meters away from our entrance. The rocket detonated, but the blast was directed downward and away from the ER, digging about a ten- to twelve-inch deep hole in the asphalt before jumping and blasting through a concrete wall a few feet away. A three-foot-by-three-foot section of the wall was blown out, and what was left of the rocket then skipped into a few trees before disappearing off our FOB and speeding away to some unknown destination. Praise God its blast force projected away from the hospital and ER! Who knew what the damage would have been caused to those of us in the ER working at the time if it had detonated in our direction.

The chaos died down, and the next day, our intelligence reports began to tell us that the guys who had been shelling us were planning an attempt into the IZ. Penetrating the IZ defenses would be a huge victory for the terrorists, and at one point, multiple armed guards were positioned around the hospital, and several of us even began discussing rudimentary plans as to how we would defend the EMT if our security was breached. We also had to quickly create plans for an alternate ER and OR in case the next rocket connected and destroyed either place. Contingency plans were established as to how we would supply the new facility with medical gear and personnel and how long it would take to accomplish the task. We had not slept or eaten much in days, but we all knew it would take much more than that to break our spirits and prevent us for caring for our fellow men and women in uniform! We were informed that more rockets were coming, and they feared the 107 mm rockets were about to replaced by bigger 122 mm and 240 mm rockets, all supposedly from Iran, our "friendly" neighbor to the east.

Nine days into the daily rocket assault on the Green Zone, I slid into the late swing shift in the ER. Everyone was on edge, and even though the patient flow had slowed somewhat, many people were not sleeping or eating well due to the anxiety and knowledge the next rocket may be a 107 mm, 122 mm, or large 240 mm that took out one of us. At one point, an x-ray machine was moved upstairs on the second floor, making a loud bang and causing Col. Sue Raymond, the chief nurse, to begin screaming, "Incoming, incoming, get down!" Every slammed door, every slammed lid on the Dumpsters outside, everything made our hearts skip a beat and made us jump. Maybe it was the beginning of PTSD or some other fun thing like that. With my regular workouts, calorie shakes, and eating regimen, I was proud to have gained five pounds of muscle over the past three months, but a reweigh earlier in the day demonstrated that I had lost four pounds in nine days due to not being able to get to the dining facility and working constantly. Not good for a skinny guy like me, but at least I had nine more months in Baghdad to get it back and then some.

The four ER docs were each working most of the day everyday, but we had been assigning times of the day when two physicians would be the primary docs, allowing the others to rest up some. As the patient load would pick up daily, docs three and four would jump in and get moving. After midnight one night, we began to hear a series of loud, thunderous explosions occurring over a few hours, and we all assumed that the joint Iraqi-American assault on Sadr City was underway. Working until about 2:00 AM before heading to my room to sleep, I ran to the top of the hospital to see if I could see the direction from which the explosions were coming.

We were prohibited all week from going outside for any reason other than official duty or to get food, and anytime we were outside we had to be in U3 posture with our body armor, helmet, and eyewear. I took a chance and disregarded the rules and snuck upstairs in my scrubs to get a quick peek of Baghdad from the roof. To my surprise, nothing was happening to my northeast, in the direction of Sadr City. The flares lighting the nighttime sky and the palpable explosions were coming from the south. Who knew what exactly was going on down there, but I would imagine the explosions were due to artillery or air force bombs on Madhi Army positions.

Earlier that day, the news reported that Al-Sadr ordered his fighters off the streets, and they were to disengage the Iraqi and American forces. His announcement caused us all to gain a faint hope that those orders would quell the rocket fire into the IZ, but I think we all knew better. Individuals strictly loyal to Al-Sadr would likely put their weapons away and blend into the local populace, but those who wanted to keep fighting would not lay down their arms. I also doubted our commanders in the field would let up with any plans we had to take out these guys, as evidenced by the likely American aerial assault to our south we were listening to.

Hitting my rack about 2:30 AM, I tried to sleep in the next morning, since I would be moving to the overnight shift that evening. Knowing they would call if they needed me downstairs in the ER, I took the opportunity to get caught up on rest from the past week. However, as usual, the explosions caused by rocket fire landing nearby served as my alarm clock and startled me to a wakeful state of mind. The first explosion was not very loud, likely meaning a hit down at the palace or somewhere else in the IZ, but the second explosion rocked our entire building. The windows shook, the walls cracked, and I was convinced that our building had been hit. Springing to my feet to get dressed, I knew the only thing between me and the window of my room facing Sadr City, the launch site of most of these relatively horizontally flying rockets, was a thin curtain blocking the sunlight, so I bailed and headed downstairs to the ER. Everyone was gathered in the hallways of the hospital, all wearing their body armor indoors as had just been directed by our commander. I put on my armor when I arrived at the ER, and I was told the projectile we had just been hit by was headed straight for Carl Hall, the dormitory used by our enlisted soldiers just a couple of hundred feet from my building.

The rocket apparently was designed to burst in the air, similar to some of the mortars that hit us back on Thanksgiving Day, and praise God for that miscalculation by the bad guys. No one was injured in the blast, but if it had been a normal projectile, as most of them were, its course would likely have buried into some of our soldier's rooms in Carl Hall. Who knows what the damage would have been, but it would have been significant. We had now had four rockets land on our small FOB in the past three days, and by the grace of God we had dodged two *major* close hits with no injuries.

The next day, I cared for a soldier who had been in a Humvee struck by an EFP. While listening to his story, I was amazed at his courage and the number of attacks the bad guys attempted. During this one road trip, his vehicle had been shot at by small arms fire, rocket-propelled grenades, indirect fire, and three IEDs, the last of which took out their vehicle. Unbelievable. He was going to be okay, but he was to lose his right big toe, and when we told him of his fate, his laughed and told his buddy in the bed next to him, "I guess the next time I surf I'll have to hang nine rather than hang ten!" with a big smile. How could you not be amazed by his resilience and attitude? Everyday I was amazed by our soldiers' fortitude and resistance.

I also had the misfortune of caring for a little ten-month-old Iraqi girl who was malnourished and plagued by paralysis from the waist down due to spina bifida and a life-threatening lung infection. She had beautiful, huge brown eyes, and as she lay on the bed with her ribs protruding and rapid breathing due to her poor lungs, she would engage us and melt all our hearts. Each time I left the room to check on something or someone else, I would return to her. As I got closer, her eyes locked on mine, and she tracked me everywhere I went. She had dark curly hair, just like my eleven-month-old daughter Avery back home, and it crushed me knowing that, in the morning, we would have to send her to an Iraqi hospital to die. We did not have the resources to care for her; we were a combat hospital. Pat Hickey and I just looked at each other and did not say anything. We both knew what her outcome would be; we both knew what fate awaited her. I prayed she would die quickly so those beautiful eyes would not have to suffer much longer.

The night before, I cared for a sixty-something-year-old woman our soldiers had shot in the leg with a .50 caliber machine gun. We assumed she was an unfortunate bystander who was hit in crossfire, but as we were working on her, our command notified us that she was a suspected insurgent. We were told that some of our soldiers rolled into an area and caught several people breaking curfew and setting up an IED. They engaged the group of people and noted someone on a roof rolling up the detonation wire to keep our soldiers from recovering it. Our guys shot that individual, and she turned out to be our insurgent grandma! The story spread all over the hospital, and I was hearing from people that she was also holding a detonator in her hand as she was shot, and then we were told she was not a bad guy after all. Oh well, it sure made for an interesting story for a while.

We began to run very low on blood due to the massive amounts we were using. A whole blood drive was initiated, and I began using blood taken from one individual, checked quickly for HIV and hepatitis, which was then given to another person for the first time in my career, with the insurgent grandmother being the first. Americans from all over the surrounding FOBs responded to the call for blood donors, and the numbers of volunteers was staggering. Everyone around us banded together to help our soldiers in the fight, as well as our fellow people who had been injured or killed in the IZ by the rocket fire. We had the misfortune of having several soldiers and marines die that week at Ibn Sina, but it was never from a lack of blood thanks to the response from those around us.

———

We did not get hit by any indirect fire the next day, although it was reported that a few rounds sailed over us. Over the previous ten days, the IZ had been hit over 150 times by rockets, accounting for 40 percent of the total number of hits sustained in all of 2007. However, the fighting in and around Baghdad began to decrease considerably, and our patient census reflected that fact. An email was sent to all military personnel in the IZ that night that lifted the full body armor restrictions, and people began driving around the IZ again, resuming their normal duties. We could now go outside the building without putting on all that garb. Pat Hickey and I quickly took advantage of the new uniform policy, and we both went to the smoking area outside the ER for a cigar.

About ten minutes into our cigar break, the CRAM incoming alert sirens were activated, and we both sprang to our feet and sprinted toward the ER. I think we could have set an Olympic record with the speed at which we sprinted toward the doors of relative safety—the doors of the hospital. We had to make a right turn as we came around a corner on our way, and as I passed it, I grabbed a pole on my right and felt like a gymnast as I swung my body 90 degrees and landed facing the building and sprinting inside with Pat just as the first round struck just on the other side of our landing zone, a hundred or so yards away. We then heard more rounds striking around us, and we both looked at each other, smiled, and each lifted up his cigar as if to say, "I didn't drop it!" despite our frantic sprints. I guess someone must have sent the emails stating we were out of our body armor on to Al-Sadr, and he decided to take advantage. Pat Hickey even joked that someone forwarded the message to MuqutadaAl-Sadr@yahoo.com or some other crazy email address. Either way, it was another close call for the members of the Eighty-sixth CSH. At this rate, we were going to run out of luck, and I feared someone was going to get hit by one of these rounds, but we had to wait to find out.

A few days later, I decided either I was stupid or I just had not learned my lesson yet. Despite getting caught outside by the rockets and mortars a couple of nights ago, several of us were up on the roof smoking cigars at about the same time when my wife called. While enjoying a great conversation on the phone with her, and happy because I had kept my family in the dark about what had been going on so they would not worry about me, I was pained to hear the CRAM incoming alert sirens erupt. I ran for the door, waiting for a break in the line of my colleagues pouring inside the building, forgetting to hang up the phone. She got to hear a few rounds landing around us, and although none of them were too close, they were loud enough for her hear. My answer of "Thunder" when she asked, "What was that? Were you guys being hit?" did not convince her, and she now knew we were being fired at, although I was able to avoid telling her exactly how close the hits had been recently and that we had not had injuries yet simply by an act of God in my opinion.

Fingers and toes. Ten of each, twenty to be exact. Since Easter on March 23, when the rocket attacks began, that was my point of focus. I still had all of my fingers and all of my toes. By definition that meant that my arms, legs, and most likely head were still attached, so life had to be good. The increasing volume of rocket fire into the Green Zone, along with American and Iraqi casualties resulting from probes into the Madhi Army stronghold of Sadr City, had caused me to reassess what it took to make me happy. As I was thinking about this concept, we had several American soldiers in the building with us who could not say they had all of their fingers and toes anymore. If not being a part of that group did not make me feel fortunate, I do not know what would. I was now beginning to have dreams of people missing their hands, feet, and extremities, including some of our personnel there at the CSH. Those were the first dreams I had of carnage and trauma, and they continue to this day. It is all part of the normal, stressful process of war.

We received a rush of patients the day prior when a rocket attack into the International Zone hit a gymnasium just up the road from us. Being outside and hearing the CRAM incoming sirens wail, I was amazed at the speed with which the casualties began to arrive. We went from an empty ER to a mascal within five minutes. Two soldiers expired from their head injuries, and we filled every bed in our ER with others who were wounded in the attack. I positioned myself out front and triaged patients as they came through, pouring out of SUVs just like a dog busts out of his kennel when the door is opened. Nontactical SUVs began filling up our parking area, each with a share of wounded and dazed Americans who had been in the building when it sustained a direct hit. Buddies carried and dragged their colleagues to our door, and I stopped each at the door, helping our crew direct them onto stretchers, wheelchairs, or into the hallway if they could walk. Our other ER docs and teams sprang into action and began working immediately on some of the wounded who were in bad shape.

Within five minutes, we received radio notice of seven more urgent patients en route to us from a smaller FOB in Baghdad that had received a coordinated rocket attack at the same time we did. We had nowhere to put them. Running to the treatment room, we began immediately selecting patients who were stable, at least for the time being. We pulled several of them off their beds and put them onto litters and rickshaws and rushed them upstairs to the wards, leaving the hospital beds downstairs in the ER to receive the next wave of patients. I went into the room where our chaplain Felix Sermon was performing last rights, and once he was done, we placed the patients who were killed onto litters on the floor and stole their beds to use for arriving casualties. I felt terrible for ordering the deceased heroes to be pulled from the gurneys they were on, but what could I do? We needed beds for the living at the moment.

During this turnover time, some of the patients from the initial blast were rushed upstairs to the OR, while walking wounded who were too severely injured to be sent to our outpatient clinic stacked the hallways. They were crowded in by all of the sergeants major, colonels, and generals who came to the ER to see what was going on with their soldiers. At one point, I was forced to yell over everyone in the ER, saying, "I don't mean to be rude, but if you don't work in the EMT, get out now!" I got a couple of funny looks from army general officers with stars on their chest, as they were not used to being yelled at by a major, but at the time I did not care. It was our ER, and we would not let a bunch of generals—even those with great intentions—take over our facility.

As patients were rolling upstairs, a helicopter delivered an African-American gentleman being carried on a stretcher covered by a blanket. Standing at the ER entrance to direct traffic, I assumed a rocket had hit him and I leaned down, pulled out his earplugs and said, "Where are you hurt?" Not answering me, he just looked away. With the stress of the moment, the refusal to cooperate on the part of this patient infuriated me. We see patients regress when traumatized on a regular basis; sometimes they will not answer questions or they will be belligerent. But I did not have time for that kind of behavior at the moment, with a still mostly full ER and multiple blown up Americans arriving. I jumped down and got in the soldier's face, about ten inches away, and yelled "WHERE ARE YOU HURT?" while ripping away at his blanket to find injuries. He just stared back at me. At that time, Jason Cohen came out of the trauma room and told me he was not a patient from the blasts, he was a Ugandan with blood in his urine who turned out to have tuberculosis. No wonder he would not answer my questions! I felt badly for yelling at a guy who did not speak English for a few minutes, but the new influx of patients took away any chance I had to be worried about being rude to someone who did not understand what I was saying to him in the first place.

As the other patients arrived, our system performed beautifully. Mike Myer and I triaged them out front, and everyone went to work on the new group of mangled humanity. Most of them were okay, but one unfortunately did not survive from his devastating head injury. Overall, we lost three American heroes that day due to the rocket attacks, and thirty-one were wounded. Since Easter, I had been concerned that the bad guys would get lucky at some point and hit us, our ER, or some other soft target in the International Zone with their Iranian-made rockets. My concerns came finally came true, and I feared we would have several more explosions to endure before it was over.

Due to the indirect fire threat, I had lost my place of tranquility, my spot to get away from the carnage of Baghdad ER and reflect. I did try to go up there, but when I sat there with the others as stupid as me, my ears were constantly peeled for any whistling sound, CRAM sirens, or any other clues of rockets or mortars coming toward us. Each of us now felt as if he or she was placing their lives on the line each time we would go outdoors, even if it was just to walk over to the DFAC for chow.

Al-Malaki, the prime minister of Iraq, who we saw several times for nonemergency complaints, had just publicly told Muqtada Al-Sadr to stand down his army or they would be destroyed. Al-Sadr told his guys that if the Iraqi government or U.S. forces entered Sadr City, the 2.5 million-Shiite-strong slum northeast of Baghdad proper, to "defend themselves at all costs." That meant they would use the IEDs and EFPs that had been placed to booby-trap any forces entering the slums. Rockets were fired at the International Zone daily from Sadr City, but our guys could not get to the launch sites by ground because of all the bombs and traps set up for them. The Mahdi Army had utilized the six-month cease-fire to set traps and prepare for an invasion of ground troops, and they had plans to cut off escape routes for the wounded and trap our soldiers in once they invaded the district. However, our guys were going to have to go. I knew it would happen. And the casualties would be great, both to our American soldiers and their Iraqi Army companions. We expected it any time now, and I feared we would be looking at another Mogadishu *Blackhawk Down* scenario all over again. We were informed this was the most dangerous time in the International Zone since the war began, and unfortunately it would take a lot of American and Iraqi blood to make it safer by going into Sadr City.

A few nights later in the ER, still waiting for the invasion of Sadr City to begin, Jason and I put on our body armor and had a swordfight, pummeling each other about the head and chest with yellow whiffle ball bats. We stood toe to toe in front of the nurses' station and went after each other. At times I attempted to grab his bat with my left hand and pound him with the bat in my right, but I never could get a good grasp of the barrel of his bat. We each landed several shots to the head, sides, and chest. I guess we needed a fencing judge to determine who landed the most blows, but I think I won because my bat had several more dents in it than his did. I later gave everyone a description of each dent in my bat and told them, "This was from his skull, this was from his spleen" and so on. We were sure the command would freak, but they were all asleep at one in the morning anyway! Next, we planned to add the hippity-hop balls to our endeavor and joust each other. Already wearing our body armor, a call came for a pickup from Blackhawks arriving, so we jumped on the Gator and did the job. The medics appreciated us moving over to their arena, and everyone got a big laugh out of us being funny, so it was great to lighten the mood somewhat in an otherwise tense time.

—

After nineteen consecutive days of rocket fire into the International Zone, the projectiles claimed seven lives and wounded fifty or so. During this time, Gen. David Petraeus, the Coalition commander, and Ambassador Ryan Crocker were testifying to Congress and answering questions regarding the future of America's involvement in Iraq. This date was also the fifth anniversary of the fall of Baghdad to the rumbling armor of the Third Infantry Division, a moment in history most adult Americans will remember due to the immense media coverage of U.S. tanks and tracked vehicles pulling down statues of Saddam. We were locked down over the previous forty-eight hours, as intelligence reports had indicated a spike in the indirect fire during these two days that were crucial to our future in Iraq, but to this point only a few small rockets impacted the IZ, resulting in no casualties.

Unfortunately, we did have three American soldiers die in the EMT on this day, one with a gunshot wound to the head, another with a blast injury to the head, and the third with a blast injury to the chest that some how snuck past his body armor. We worked on all of these men, desperately trying to get back a pulse that we knew would not return. Blood, trash, and needles were strewn all over the ER. We all knew the outcome, but we never once gave up on any of our guys until it was not humanly possible to bring them back. We always gave every soldier our all, despite the odds. We owed them that for their sacrifice. Their families deserved to know that everything humanly possible was done to save their loved ones. Our save rate in Baghdad was much higher than rates back in the U.S. for similar injuries. We were a trauma machine, routinely saving Americans and Iraqis alike with double lower-extremity amputations and other devastating injuries. I guess we could not save them all, however, but it was not from a lack of effort.

The next shift, we had a soldier come in after being hit by an IED, and once we had him stripped naked, everyone could not help but notice the large penis ring, apparently called a Prince Albert. After ultrasounding his abdomen in an attempt to discover internal bleeding, I found myself down on his right side and closest to the jewelry in question. We all knew it had to come out since he was going to surgery, and while looking at it and trying to figure out what steps I had to take to remove it, I was pushed aside by his nurse Megan Solberg. She jumped right in and took it out in about two seconds, smoothly and without having to think about it! She reminded me of a cowboy in a rodeo roping and hog-tying a calf for the timer, with speed and a fluid motion that made us all break out in laughter. We harassed her ever since, although she never did admit to having any prior knowledge on the subject.

Another soldier hit by shrapnel arrived, and as we were working on him, our x-ray tech asked him to take a deep breath for his chest x-ray. One of our rotating medics accidentally stuck his hand in the way, ruining the shot. The medic quickly apologized, and the soldier lying on the bed said, "Hey man, that's *MY* x-ray!" We all laughed, and then we rolled him to evaluate his back for injuries, causing an increased amount of pain to his open femur fracture. Still amused by his funny comments, he made us laugh even more when he told us "Jesus is going to get you for what you do!" since we had caused him more pain. Being a Christian myself, I got a big laugh out of that. He did great, and his sense of humor kept us in good sprits for the night.

It was April 2008, and we finally experienced the second thunderstorm Baghdad had endured since our arrival in November. The first was very short and occurred during the middle of the night, so only those on the night shift were awake for it. This storm occurred in the middle of the day, and each rumble of thunder sent people's heart rates through the roof. Often, the indirect fire would plunge from the sky and begin exploding prior to the alert of the CRAM systems, so each crack of thunder had to be differentiated from the blast of a rocket.

During the storm, a soldier came into our trauma room after being hit by an EFP. He had a large bandage on his head from the field, dressed across his eyes, and an open right femur fracture. We placed him into bed one, and I landed at the head of the bed, leaning over him. He was moaning incomprehensible words and not moving his arms or legs. While our nurses and medics worked on IV access, Marti Roellig and Abby Raez, a visiting ER doc from Balad, probed his femoral veins for large-bore central line access. Unwrapping the bandages covering his eyes, I found a large amount of destruction to his entire face above his nose. After attempts to curb the massive bleeding, a quick survey showed that the soldier had no eyes, and his sinuses and forehead were blown out, along with part of the front of his brain.

Not wanting to see any more of his brain and trying to save his life, I replaced his dressing and rotated out of the way for Dr. Raez to intubate him. Marti's central line was true, and we quickly pumped six units of blood products into him. We gave him several different medications to prevent seizures, infection, and other complications, and then we called the neurosurgeons in Balad to alert them for his transfer. Our surgeon on call, Dr. Reagan Quan, used special clot-producing gel packs in the front of his head where the frontal lobes of his brain and eyes used to be prior to the 2500-degree shrapnel tearing through them. Blood continued to pour out of his head, and we could not stop the bleeding. Giving him multiple units of red blood cells, plasma, platelets, and cryoprecipitate, we could not stop the hemorrhage. We placed him on a litter for transport and listened as the Blackhawk arrived on the helipad to rush him to neurosurgical care in Balad.

Just as we packaged him on a litter for transport, he lost his pulse and his heart stopped beating. We immediately began CPR, pushing epinephrine and other drugs in through IVs to keep him alive. More blood was rushed into him, and more life-saving drugs were pushed. His heart would begin to beat on its own at times, and he would regain a pulse, but minutes later, he would lose it. We worked on him for over two hours, and finally I had to call an ad hoc ethics committee meeting, asking everyone in the room if they objected to us making him expectant and giving him comfort measures to die. What else could we do? We all realized there was nothing we could do to save this soldier; God was calling him home. We discontinued the medications and ventilator, and he died within minutes.

We were all exasperated. Such a terrible injury, but such a heroic effort. Even if we had been able to save him, he would never have been able to get out of a bed again, and he still would most likely die. The human body was just not designed for all of the trauma these warriors sustained. But it crushed us; it crushed me. I was tired of seeing soldiers die. We were all tired of it. After explaining everything to the soldier's unit and battle buddy, we all went into the specialty room with the body and prayed with Felix Sermon as he performed the last rights for the deceased among the tears of those around him.

Laura called an hour or so later, and we unfortunately got into a minor argument over something, I did not remember exactly what. I spent the next few hours in a bad mood, and I found myself later standing alone on top of the EMT in the dark and snapping a salute to the Angel Flight Blackhawk that was carrying our dead soldier away. A tear rolled down my cheek, and at the time I was not sure if I was upset because another American hero died or because Laura and I did not see eye to eye earlier. Either way, it was a terrible feeling I did not want to have again. Being so unfortunately used to death, it was the rare event when a patient got to us, but I had let my guard down once again and cried as another angel flew away into the night air.

To lighten the tone, I'll spend the next few sentences tattling on one of our surgeons. When performing ATLS, or advanced trauma life support, part of the standard exam is the rectal. The provider inserts a finger into the rectum of the patient, determining strength of the sphincter and to look for gross blood in the rectum. In any patient with a neurologic injury, abdominal, or back injury, the exam can be justified, despite most studies showing that the rectal exam does not change anything regarding the patient's management. However, in patients with isolated leg or arm injuries, the rectal exam has no part in the management of the patient. If you sprained your ankle, would you want someone sticking a finger up your ass? I did not perform rectal exams on patients without a sure indication for one, but one of our surgeons was very rectal happy, I would say.

Often, when we had multiple patients in the treatment room with shrapnel injuries to the arms and legs, this particular surgeon would come in, ask what was going on with the patients, and then nonchalantly walk over to each of them and stick a finger up their butt! Sometimes, he would not even speak to them as he lifted up their leg and penetrated their rectum. We all joked about him having his pistol holster on one hip and a holster for gloves and KY jelly on the other so he could do his drive-by rectals. At one point, he stuck a soldier after walking up and not informing him first, to which the soldier shrieked, "What the hell are you doing, man?" We all liked to sit up on the roof at night and joke about his affinity for the rectum.

A four-year-old Iraqi boy arrived on my next shift with burns to 10 percent of his body surface area from pulling hot water down onto his chest and neck. Despite sedation in the EMT, his cries from the scrubbing of his wounds penetrated the hallways of the hospital, but he was fine afterward. Several hours later, we all were told we had to go upstairs to the ward he was admitted to, as he had been running up and down the hallway playing with some cars that were given to him by the nursing staff. It was so wonderful to have a "healthy" kid running around playing with toys, reminding us of our children and families back home that we all so longed to return home to. He was discharged in a day or two, and presumably he went home and did great.

Jason Cohen and me in our smoking robes

Rockets for my Birthday

For my thirty-third birthday, I was treated to more rocket fire from the Shiite militias, marking the twenty-third straight day of indirect fire into the International Zone. By this point, it did not bother us as much; we all knew where the bunkers were and were accustomed to running for cover when the warning sirens blared. Most of the fire over the past several days had landed a quarter- to a half-mile away down toward the palace, so we did not feel too many effects from it other than the injured civilians who took out their ankles while running to duck-and-cover bunkers. However, for my birthday, the rockets were fired at us from the south rather than the usual direction of Sadr City. One landed in our motor pool area, just twenty feet away from the gym where I lifted weights every other day. We had several soldiers inside working out at the time, and the rocket pulled bricks away from and scarred the wall of one of our residential two story houses, missing it by mere feet. The explosion threw shrapnel all around, but once again, by a miracle, no one was injured. Several local Iraqi contractors were working in the area, and they basically decided enough was enough and packed up their gear and left, saying they would not return. They were tired of coming to the hospital to work every day, only to be attacked during their labors. We miraculously dodged another major bullet with this impact.

Later in the day, when I went to the ER to check my email, I was asked to come to the nurses' station for a phone call. Walking up to the large desk,

I visualized the large chocolate-covered cake with burning candles sitting just on top of the "Baghdad ER" sign, but I did not notice some of our medics waiting for me in ambush. As I walked past them, they sprang out from their hiding spots and emptied four cans of silly string on me, covering me from head to toe. Sgt. Tom Clise and Sgt. Decia Gilliam put the cans mere inches from my face as they were emptied on me. Several pictures were taken, and everyone got a kick out of getting to harass me without repercussion. I was and still am truly honored to have the opportunity to work alongside these nurses and medics. They were the unsung heroes of the Eighty-sixth CSH and Baghdad ER.

I continued to lie to my friends and family about the indirect fire threat because I did not see the use in making them worry. The news stopped reporting about the daily rocket fire into the International Zone after a few days, which was fine with us. The IZ was hit on my birthday by four different volleys, although only one group landed on our FOB.

Days later, we discovered there was a madman (or woman) on the loose at Ibn Sina Hospital. It had come to my attention, through an email I harassed out of Marti, that someone had twice defecated in the shower on the third floor of our dorm, the *women's* floor. Everyone agreed that was disgusting, unsanitary, stupid, and unexplainable. However, we got a laugh out of it, blindly accusing our coworkers who lived on that floor of being the Phantom Pooper of the Eighty-sixth CSH. It made no sense why someone would do such a crazy and gross act, but man, did I enjoy it. The rumor was that one of our local Iraqi women, part of the housecleaning staff, had witnessed a certain individual enter the shower and then leave a turd on the drain when she was done with her combo bath/defecation routine. We were all speculating and joking as to who the guilty party might be. Was it one of the CSH's older residents who went crazy at night, losing control of her bowels? Maybe it was someone who everyone thought was weird or strange, or maybe, just maybe, the Mad Pooper was someone who was well liked and normal according to everyone else. Maybe she just pooped in the shower, thinking to herself "Is that so wrong?" That was all I know about the situation, but evidently our psychiatrist had one more patient to squeeze into her schedule.

While performing a lumbar puncture, also known as a spinal tap, on an American soldier the day before, I kept having trouble getting the needle into the right spot. When performing this procedure, the patient sits upright on the side of the bed, leaning over a tray and arching their lower back to the physician. I then placed a needle into the lower back, between the spinous processes of the vertebrae, into the dural sac below the spinal cord to draw off fluid to test for meningitis, bleeding in the brain, or other abnormalities. Usually a 2.5- or 3.5-inch needle is sufficient to do the task, and I began the procedure with a 2.5-inch sharp. I pushed the entire needle all the way into the soldier's back, to his winces of discomfort and pain, and hubbed it all the way, denting the skin with no production of the cerebrospinal fluid I was seeking. I then switched needles, and tried a 3.5-inch one, thinking, "Surely this will do the trick." Wrong. After hubbing the longer needle, I gave him a break and journeyed to the back storage room to find the magnum-sized, five-inch harpoon for which I was looking. My knowledge of anatomy and familiarity with the procedure kept me from worrying about putting the needle in too deep, as the only thing I could do was hit bone as long as I paid attention. But doubt always creeps into one's mind, and I halfway expected to draw urine from a punctured kidney when I finally obtained the clear CSF. He ended up not having meningitis, but he did have a story to tell about his experience in Baghdad ER.

Later that shift, my compassion fatigue finally caught up. We had four Iraqi Army patients flown into us from the CSH in Balad, all for transfer to the local Iraqi hospital since we could not provide long-term care. As they were all off loaded into our treatment room, the scene became a depressing landscape of death and destruction, with two of the soldiers with weeping and horrid facial burns, another soldier with a tracheostomy and head injury, and the fourth with a major head injury making him comatose. As our nurses and medics tried to begin the evaluation process to ensure they were all medically stable to be placed onto a U.S. Army ambulance and transported away, my favorite translator Ann looked at me with tearful eyes and said, "They are all going to die aren't they?" I just looked down and said, "Yes, Ann they are all going to die, we just don't know how long it will take." The brief conversation crushed my spirits, but we pressed on and loaded them onto the ambulance to go to Medical City to await their certain death. They all had been wounded while fighting the bad guys, and the bad guys would win this battle.

While I was still depressed and angry after dealing with the previous patients, five American contractors were brought into the ER by the local ambulance service from a motor vehicle accident. Frustrated with death and tired of dealing with people at the moment, as they came by on stretchers I questioned each of them, asking, "Were you wearing a seatbelt? Why not!?" I was very angry and forceful with my tone, and later I was frankly embarrassed by it. To this day, I take pride in always being understanding and compassionate with my patients, but six months of Baghdad ER had finally caught up to me. I had not been outside much due to the daily rocket attacks, my exercise had slacked, and I began sleeping during the day and laying awake at night in a sleepless state—just as I was warned would happen about the six-month mark by the ER docs we replaced with the Twenty-eighth CSH. It had finally caught up to me, and I erupted on these patients. Later, I regained my composure and treated all five of them, but it was an eye-opener for me.

That night, we sat upon the roof of Jones Hall smoking cigars. The night prior, about the same time, the CRAMs sounded as four more rockets hit the IZ. There would be no rockets fired by the bad guys that night. We enjoyed watching U.S. missiles, fired either from Apache helicopters or unmanned aerial drones, lighting up the night. We watched six missiles, resembling shooting stars soaring across the night sky, go down to earth, followed immediately by a flash of light at the impact site and a boom several seconds later. During the barrage, flares from artillery lit up the sky to our southwest, but our attention was focused to the northeast, where the fire from our forces brought about the chant "USA … USA … USA." Maybe this was it, maybe our guys were cleaning some of the mess in Sadr City and lighting up the bad guys from the sky. Moments later, a huge flash of light, ten times the size of the others, turned night into day for a split second, and a thunderous explosion was palpated. We assumed that must have been an air force fighter dropping a huge bomb on Sadr City, and we all enjoyed the show.

The next day was my daughter Avery's first birthday. Laura had gone all-out and prepared a party fit for a queen, or at least fit for my little princess. She had balloons, streamers, and all kinds of party decorations all over the house. I was so excited for her big day, but of course I was heartbroken I would miss it. However, all of Laura's family and my mother would be there to cheer Avery on, so I was thrilled they would have such a great time together—and even more thrilled they would be there for Laura and Avery.

A few days later, around 7:00 pm, loud gunfire erupted at checkpoint two, the entrance into the International Zone located closest to us. The bouts of automatic gunfire lasted for a couple of minutes, and the barrage of bullets sounded very close to our location since the checkpoint was only three hundred or so meters away. Repeated questions to our tactical operations center yielded no results, so we had to wait to hear what the skirmish was about. We continued to be told every day that operations in Sadr City were about to heat up again, as Iraqi Security Forces backed up by their U.S. allies were attempting to slowly squeeze the Mahdi Army fighters back from the positions they had been firing rockets into the IZ from. Rockets did not hit the International Zone this day, making it the first day in thirty-one days that we did not receive incoming fire. We hoped the trend would continue, but none of us were looking forward to the casualties that would no doubt come from the increased fighting in Sadr City, fighting that we had been waiting two weeks for and knew was approaching.

We did have a visit from one of Sadaam's cronies, however. Chemical Ali made his appearance when he was transferred from his maximum-security cell to us for medical treatment, where Jason Cohen cared for him and admitted him to our facility. The Iraqi Baathist party member and Saddam's first cousin was made famous by his use of chemical weapons, when he gassed thousands of Kurdish people in northern Iraq in the 1980s. One particular chemical weapons attack in 1988, known as the Al Anfal campaign, killed four thousand Kurds alone. Overall, during his reign of genocide, over 180,000 Kurds were killed and 1.5 million displaced, according to Wikipedia. Hearing rumors of his presence in the ICU, one of our radiologists, Dr. Tony Allen, and I decided that we needed to go take a look at the monster ourselves.

Chemical Ali's presence in the CSH was supposed to be a tightly guarded secret, but word that he was with us appeared on CNN a day after he was admitted. Tony and I walked upstairs to the ICU and asked one of the nurses where he was, and she pointed us in the direction. Walking in the room, we witnessed an Iraqi man in security garb with a blown up right thigh. He was young in appearance and had a large external fixator on his thigh to help stabilize his femur fracture. A military police officer was sitting at the base of his bed, next to a large portable dividing screen that was covering the identity of a second patient behind it, also obviously under guard from the MP.

A medic who was unfamiliar to me walked from behind the divider and, not recognizing us, asked what we needed and if he could help us. He positioned himself just at the end of the divider, stopping our only access to get around it and get a look at Ali. I am sure people had been trying to sneak in and get looks at him all day, and we had to think fast to get an excuse to get past the medic and MP posted behind the divider. Quickly, I asked them if the patient behind the divider was the gentleman I worked on a few days earlier, the man whose name I still did not know, and they looked confused. I jumped on that opportunity, and with Tony closely in tow, we stepped behind the curtain and got a good look at Chemical Ali sleeping soundly. I piped up to the guard, "Nope, that's not my guy, he must be gone." Chemical Ali looked just like the pictures on television, and as we walked away from our successful mission, we joked about how we could get a picture of us posing with him. Since it is against the Geneva Convention to take pictures of prisoners in a hospital setting, we both settled with just seeing the man, but it was fun to get to cook up an excuse to the MP and push our way past.

Later that night, we received an American soldier of unknown age who suffered a gunshot wound to the left chest. He came from somewhere close, as the Blackhawk that went to pick him up lifted off from our pad, picked him up, and returned within seven minutes. We placed him in bed one, and continued the CPR initiated by the flight medics. Marti was the ER physician on staff at the time, so she ran the situation while I blindly stuck his pulseless groin for his femoral vein, attempting to place a central venous line to push blood through. My blind sticks were true, and I was fortunate to place the line quickly and push blood through it. Simultaneously, Mike Myer performed a thoracotomy by cutting his chest open on the left side, spreading the ribs with a medieval device called a rib spreader, and delivered his heart in an attempt to repair any holes. One of our nurses, Maj. Katherine Frost, inserted a peripheral IV quickly, and we had blood pouring into both her line and mine simultaneously. In the course of twelve minutes, we had the soldier's heartbeat back, sixteen units of blood given, a central and peripheral IV placed, and he was intubated and en route to the operating room.

About thirty minutes later, several of us went upstairs to the operating room to see the progress. In the OR, he received over thirty units of blood products, and Mike had "clam shelled" his chest by cutting across the sternum and exposing the right side as well as the previously exposed left where the heart was located. They also opened his abdomen to evaluate for sources of bleeding, but found no major sites. One of his vertebrae had a two-finger-wide hole blown in it with massive bleeding the surgeons could not stop. After several rounds of intracardiac epinephrine and other shocks directly to the heart, Mike finally called the code and pronounced him dead. It was a valiant effort to save an American life on behalf of both the ER and the OR staff, but unfortunately it was not to be. We could only wait for next time and watch another angel fly away into the night.

The next week was crazy. As usual, we had incredible highs and desperate lows, with both humorous and emotionally devastating events occurring at the same time. Such was life at Ibn Sina Hospital; it was life in Baghdad ER. Pat Hickey, my good friend and our esteemed pediatrician, had now departed Iraq, having completed his six-month tour. Since he was a pediatric infectious disease specialist versus a general pediatrician, he, like the more than 90 percent of physicians serving there at the CSH, only deployed for six months at a time, and his replacement was already there and working. Pat and I had became very close throughout our tour, as he was my cigar-smoking rooftop buddy, as well as someone I could always run to the PX with or just sit down and vent my frustrations to. He was my chief steak and lobster cook, so I knew I would be forced to step up to the plate and take over those duties myself. Mike, one of our Special Forces medics, had just brought us a lot more steak, lobster, and shrimp to grill. He had stashed the food in our large water cooler, so I would get my chance quickly before it was discovered.

The next day, an American soldier arrived with a gunshot wound to his left shoulder, with the bullet exiting and then going through the right side of his mandible, or jaw. Compared to the injuries we routinely cared for, that by itself was not a big deal, but his story was. This soldier told me he was an army sniper. He was right-handed and was shot by an enemy sniper though his left shoulder, meaning he was in firing position when he was hit. That was a big deal. Any time one of our guys loses a "chess match" with another sniper, it's a red flag. Our snipers are the best in the world, and the fact that one of ours was beaten could be an ominous sign that effective fighters had arrived to engage us in Sadr City. About once a month, we were getting American soldiers in with a gunshot wound though the chest, with the bullet sneaking over the body armor just beneath the armpit. The snipers making those shots were very good because that was such a small window to put a bullet through. However, this was the first time we had witnessed one of our own snipers taken out by another.

We were still laughing about the shower-pooping incident, and some new information eventually came to light. A third deposit was found sitting on top of some newspapers in the trash can in the same bathroom around the time the other deposits were discovered in the shower. Was this a coincidence? I think not. Several of us began a betting pool as to whom the infamous Mystery Pooper was. I was still sticking with my pooping-at-night theory, since that simply made the most sense to me. As the long day ends, confusion can set in with some older people, and they might not realize what they are doing. That had to be the answer, but we never did discover who the culprit was.

In the ER later that day, I cared for a soldier with an all-American type of injury: a bad burn to the chest and face due to a flash fire while grilling on his FOB. He was awake and alert when he arrived to the ER, and I talked to him and told him the plan of care while one of our medics, Sgt. Jonathan Desillier, placed an IV into his arm, and Deb Chappel collected her drugs for me to intubate him. While asking him questions, he was appropriate in response and demeanor, but he was clearly shaken and scared when we told him we would put him to sleep, clean up his burns, and that he would next wake up in the burn center in San Antonio, Texas. Immediately after being informed of our plan, he realized the serious nature of his wounds and reverted into what I called "boot camp mode." Just like a young enlistee in basic training, when asked a question he tried his best to comply and shouted out the answer.

I asked, "Do you have any allergies?"

"No, sir!"

"Do you have any medical problems or take medications?"

"No, sir!"

"What is your Social Security number?"

He shouted his Social as loud as possible.

We all continued to prepare to put him to sleep, everyone understanding why he was acting in this manner and no one blaming him. Our burn surgeon Booker King asked Deb what his Social was, but the soldier overhead, yelling his number out again loudly. At this point we all laughed, including the soldier, and then he went into a several-day slumber.

The next week I had two incredible patient encounters, one with a great outcome and one not so great. An Iraqi police officer was flown to us minutes after sustaining a gunshot wound to his left chest, just above and medial to his nipple. We placed him on bed one of our trauma room, and after listening to his lungs and noticing decreased breath sounds from his left side, I ripped off the large dressing that was covering the entrance wound on his chest. Immediately, squirts of blood shot up about two inches, right out of the bullet wound, with each beat of his heart! His heart had an open communication with the bullet hole, and each beat would squeeze blood out the wound under pressure, shooting it into the air. His blood pressure was in the seventies and his heart rate well above 130, showing to us that he was bleeding to death. As Mike Myer quickly cut into his chest to place a chest tube to drain blood and re-expand the lung, I intubated him and placed him on a ventilator. Mike's chest tube quickly filled with blood, draining several hundred milliliters of blood from his thorax. Our medics placed an IV into his right arm, and we pounded blood into him with our rapid infusers. Within five minutes of arrival, we prepped him to rush to the operating room to have his chest opened for repair. But we did not make it that far.

Just after we packaged him to transport upstairs, he began to lose his vital signs. His heart rate tumbled down into the thirties, and his blood pressure dropped to the fifties. Mike and I looked at each other and without speaking; we both realized that his only chance for survival was to open his chest now. This man was the twentieth patient who had received a thoracotomy in the EMT since our arrival in November, and to this point all had died. The survival rate in the U.S. routinely runs around 1–2 percent.

Mike cut into his left chest, and I placed a central line into his right femoral vein. We hooked a second rapid infuser into the central line, and soon afterward, the patient had received a total of eighteen units of blood products. Upon cutting into his chest, Mike noticed that he had a bullet hole in one of the ventricles of his heart. Mike placed his thumb into the hole to stop the bleeding, and soon the blood products began to refill his vessels, sending his heart rate back to a normal speed and his blood pressure back up to acceptable levels. We then packaged him for the operating room, and he was taken upstairs to receive a successful operation.

This patient became the first successful thoractomy for the Eighty-sixth

CSH, and we were thrilled. Our save was mentioned at morning report the next day, and we were on cloud nine. It was so exciting to have played an integral role in the successful resuscitation of someone shot directly through the heart; that was why we were there away from our families and loved ones, that was why we did what we did.

A few hours after the successful thoracotomy, a call came over the radio asking for a physician to meet a medevac bird on the pad. Jason Cohen was free and rushed outside, as we could hear the beating rotors of the Blackhawks as the call came through. I finished up whatever I was working on and followed Jason out about a minute behind. Getting close to the pad, I witnessed a soldier being bagged with a mask and his face covered in blood. I ran back into the ER and told everyone to get the trauma room ready for a critically wounded soldier.

Receiving him into bed one, I noticed that his head was wrapped in a battle dressing, and blood was soaking out all around it. I immediately attempted to open his mouth and place a laryngoscope blade in the back of his throat to try to intubate him, but blood obscured my view. That was not my only problem, however. He had suffered a LeFort III fracture, a type that essentially meant that his face was totally disconnected from the rest of his skull. Whenever I would lift his chin from inside his mouth with the laryngoscope, his face would slide off his head to one side or the other, obscuring my view. I suctioned the blood from his throat, only to have it quickly return and cover his vocal cords or the cartilages behind them, which were my targets for successful tube placement.

Continuing to suction his airway, I finally was able to clear the way to locate his cords. I did my usual routine of pulling out my suction device and asking for Sgt. Gary Scott, serving as my airway medic, to hand me the endotracheal tube. He handed me the tube, but when the suction was removed, the soldier's face fell to the left, off his head once again, and I lost my view. Grabbing his cheek with my right hand, I pulled his face back over his skull and regained my view. Our surgeon at the time arrived and began asking for equipment to perform a cricothyroidotomy, a procedure entailing cutting of the neck to get into the trachea and placing an airway tube, and I was trying to prevent that if possible. After I regained my view, I asked Sgt. Scott to place the tube himself into the mouth of the soldier while I kept my left hand on the laryngoscope blade and my right hand on the patient's right cheek, holding his face in place. Once Sgt. Scott put the tube into his mouth, I guided it down into his trachea with my right hand index and middle fingers, and pushed it through the bloody bubbles of air coming out of his lungs. It was likely the most difficult airway I had ever taken; the hardest intubation I had ever done, but with Sgt. Scott's help I got it successfully.

After his airway was secured and we were breathing for him, I began removing the dressing from his head, only to find the left side of his face, his left eye, and left forehead missing. The blast had caused incredible facial and cranial injuries, and we hurriedly called the neurosurgeons in Balad and began preparing him to fly. After the central venous lines, arterial lines, Foley catheters, and several medications were administered, we packaged and flew him. Regretfully, he died in the ER at Balad before he ever made it to the operating room. It was a valiant effort on everyone's part, but once again it was time for the Lord to call a soldier home. I hope and pray his family understands how hard we all worked to try to get him and every other wounded hero home to them alive.

After a two-day respite from rocket fire, they came back with a vengeance. Rockets fired from the Sadr City area began slamming down into our vicinity several times a day. To this point, we had been hit mostly by 107 mm rockets, although the big 240 mm, fifteen-foot-long versions also began to fly toward the IZ.

After a long day of barrage after barrage, several of us found ourselves on the third floor of the hospital watching *Seinfeld*. As we were sitting down to watch, we heard a rather loud explosion just across the street, followed by a tremendous BOOM! behind the hospital. One of our general surgeons rotating from Mosul, Dr. Jen Gurney-Weber, came sprinting into the room and collapsed under the weight of her armor, saying that the windows in her house outside had been blown out by the blast. Not knowing where the next round may strike, she had barricaded herself on the floor of her house under chairs and any other objects she could find to stop the flying shrapnel. The most pronounced detonation resulted from a 240 mm rocket slamming into the compound just behind us, igniting a fuel tank and causing a massive fire with flames shooting thirty feet into the air. The force of the explosion sent shrapnel flying all over the houses on the back of our FOB and busted out the windows of some of the houses our personnel resided in. The windows of our kitchen in the EMT were hit by flying debris as well. At that time, some of our staff were evacuated from their smaller houses outside the hospital due to the raging fire and the threat of it spreading onto our compound. Date palm trees were torched from the inferno, and a nearby ammunition dump began to cook off rounds from the extreme heat.

Being the geniuses that we were, several of us ran upstairs and took pictures and video footage of the fire from the rooftop, even catching some of the explosions on camera. Once the command discovered our actions, they came upstairs and pulled everyone off the roof. Coming downstairs, we were greeted by Deb Chappel, who told us about the piece of shrapnel that flew through her window and hit the back wall of her room. Her window was one story directly above mine.

The next day, the rockets began to rain down on other locations, and we received several patients who were injured, including one with a severe head injury. He had to be flown to the air force hospital in Balad, and Kathy Richardson, one of our nurses, was up to fly the crucially wounded patient. Not having been to Balad yet myself, I put on my flight suit and went along for the ride.

In the patient care area of a medevac Blackhawk, there is only room for the flight medic and one attendant to care for the patient. I was in a seat in the very back and could not see Kathy, the patient, or anyone else for that matter. I decided to make the flight a picture-and video-taking opportunity, since I did not know when I would be able to return to Balad again. I took fifty or so pictures from the windows of the bird as we flew over the slums of Baghdad, speeding low and fast over trash-filled, open-roofed ghettos, filled with intermittent soccer fields of dust loaded with children playing as if nothing was wrong and there was not a war going on all around them.

Leaving Baghdad, we began to fly over endless beautiful agricultural fields, with straight-rowed crops, irrigation channels, and occasional herds of sheep or cattle. The animals, especially the cattle, were thin, and not of the robust and grossly overweight shape we were used to back home. Interspersed throughout the fields were people working the land and the small hooches they called home. Many small farming villages of fifty or so homes dotted the landscape, and it was there that I could envision the effect of a group like Al-Qaeda as they came in and devastated the town with their brutal, murderous tactics.

After twenty minutes of mostly agricultural fields, we came upon a metropolitan center of houses and buildings, followed by row after row of American military vehicles. Our bird began to descend into a landing zone, and I could see the ballistic roof of the hospital out my window. We had made it to Balad, and I was about to get to see the air force hospital I heard so much about.

Six people met us at the helicopter, and we jumped off and chased the patient, carrying our bags with us. As we approached the ER, we walked into a tunnel with fifteen-foot ceilings and forty to fifty litter stands in place, ready and waiting for multiple casualties. The ceiling of the fifty-foot-long tunnel leading from the landing zone to the ER was a giant American flag, positioned so that soldiers being transported on litters could see it as they were wheeled through. Entering the ER, a team of about twenty people stood by waiting for the patient, comprised of ER docs, surgeons, nurses, medics, pharmacists, and respiratory techs, among others. It truly reminded me of a major medical center back home, with the huge, well-lit ER and its wide-open bays capable of handling many patients at once. Everyone was cheerful and happy, likely not only because of their incredible facilities but because of the short, four-month deployments as well!

After handing the patient off to the robust trauma team, Kathy and I then returned to the bird, noticing the name "Hero's Highway" hanging above the entrance to the tunnel. The words were visible to the wounded soldiers heading to Germany as they passed through the channel exiting the facility. An air force personnel was standing by with an ice chest full of cold water for us as we exited to get on the helicopter. Launching into the sky from Balad, we began to head south and flew for about half of our trip until we suddenly banked to the east and came about 270 degrees. I could see the flight medic pull out his M4 assault rifle and position himself in the window of the bird in a firing position. Not being hooked into the headset, neither Kathy nor I knew what was occurring and just kept looking out the window. We knew the M4 was only for defense of the bird, but we had no idea as to what the medic was preparing to defend us against!

We banked side to side again and cooked off flares, likely due to the Blackhawk sensing a nonexistent threat from a possible surface-to-air missile. A few minutes later, we approached a small village and found ourselves landing on a small pad with Stryker vehicles all around as the flight medic put up his weapon. Staying on the bird, we watched as soldiers loaded a man who had suffered a gunshot wound to the leg onto the trailing helicopter. We launched quickly and began to fly away into the afternoon sky, with Kathy and I trying to decipher if we were headed to Baghdad or back to Balad to deliver the patient. We noticed the sun to be on the right side of the bird, meaning we were heading south and back to our facility.

I had a great flight and loved the chance to escape from the hospital, even if I never really left the helicopter. It was nice to get to see some of the Iraqi countryside, and it was much more beautiful than I imagined. I could think of how much fun it would be to drive all over the backcountry, or even to drive an all-terrain vehicle across the fields and levees. Obviously, that would not be safe, but it did remind me of my old hunting grounds back home.

We were hit several times the next day by rockets and still miraculously sustained no major injuries. We were informed about noon that five 330 mm missiles were to be fired at our facility at 1:00 PM. Knowing that a 240 mm rocket could destroy a building with a direct hit, we could not conceive what the larger 330s could do. Knowing that the safest place in the hospital to survive a large missile attack was *not* in the EMT due to its single-story roof, we quickly began hurrying our patients to the outdoor CT scanner in order to get them back indoors and into the main hospital prior to the rounds coming in. We had four U.S. soldiers in the EMT at that time, all in due to an attack on their Stryker by a rocket-propelled grenade in Sadr City.

First Lt. Heather Brown, one of our nurses, was hurriedly pushing a soldier's bed to the outdoor CT scanner when the CRAM incoming alert sirens began to wail. We all took cover in the trauma room, since it was the only place in the EMT with a taller roof to help absorb the impact. Heather, now halfway up the outdoor ramp with the patient, immediately reversed direction and tried to pull the patient back into the ER from the exposed ramp outside. Maj. Joe Theiman happened to be outside at the time, and he began pushing the patient's bed back toward the ER while Heather was on the other end pulling. When the automatic doors opened, she quickly tried to maneuver the bed through the doorway, trying to the beat the rockets that we expected to impact at any moment. However, she overcompensated the angle and the corner of the patient's bed slammed into the doorway, knocking the door off its rails and bringing down a twelve-foot long section of lightweight metal onto the patient's bed! The bed rails on either side of the recumbent soldier stopped the fall, and he was not injured. However, they were now stuck in the doorway outside due to the size of the metal piece lying on the bed, with sirens blaring and expected impact any second.

Sgt. Scott and I sprinted from the trauma room to the doorway and picked up the metal piece, lifting it into the air and enabling their escape. Heather then pushed the soldier the rest of the way inside and into the trauma room to safety, with Scott, Theiman, and myself bailing in after. At that time, no rockets landed immediately around us; it must have been a false alarm. But when the immediate threat had ceased, we all breathed a sigh of relief and got a big laugh at our "mortar magnet" Heather, who seemed to always get caught outside when the indirect fire began.

Picking up my mail that evening, I was thrilled to receive several pictures from Laura showing me Avery's first birthday party. She was huge! Her hair had grown so much since I had seen her last, and it looked like everyone had a fantastic time at the party. I was excited that she was growing so well and progressing, but also sad to be missing it. But it had been eight months, and I knew that in just three more, I would get to return home for a few days. That thought kept me going.

That week, we also won a major victory, pushing the commanding medical brigade above us to supply modern bedside ultrasounds to all the combat support hospitals throughout Iraq. We had been fighting for this since our arrival, and all of us throughout the hospital relied heavily on the SonoSite Micromaxx® portable ultrasound machine so graciously loaned to us by Ron Dickson at the SonoSite corporation. Lives were saved with the use of this amazing diagnostic tool, and it was absurd to me that all army hospitals in country had not been equipped with them. But after six months of paperwork and fighting, it looked like the quality of emergency care provided by the army in Iraq would rise, catching up to the air force in some ways at least, as they had much more modern ultrasound equipment in Balad all along.

Having one of our rotating ER docs on the way in for a few shifts, I was able to get a trip arranged for Jason Cohen, Dena George, and myself to fly to the Victory Base Complex at Baghdad International Airport a few days later. Stewart McCarver greeted us as we arrived at BIAP, and we took advantage of a day away from the CSH. Since there was always danger in travel, it took a lot of explaining to the command to allow us to leave, and we had to bill it as a "go recruit more ER docs for this summer" mission to get it approved. While there, we did "recruit" Stewart to come work with us even more often, so I guess we fulfilled our official mission with the trip.

Departing from Washington LZ in the International Zone, we rode on the *Superman*, a Blackhawk operated by the Third Armored Cavalry Regiment. Its sister ship, the *Battlin' Bitch*, flew close behind, and we got a great view of the city from the air. Arriving at BIAP, I was amazed to see a perfectly painted Arkansas Razorback logo on the flight line! I do not know when someone worked there who was from Arkansas, but I took a picture of it, thinking it was likely from an Arkansas National Guard aviation unit.

Arriving at BIAP, Stewart loaded us into his four-door pickup truck and took us to Flintstone Palace, a half-acre or so concrete establishment on the edge of one of Saddam's large lakes built for his grandchildren to play. The structure was built in the shape of rocks, and numerous passageways throughout led me from one end to the other, with all the rounded walls and ceilings covered by American graffiti. I was not sure if any spaces or walls had been left untarnished from "S.Sgt. X loves Jenny" or "Pfc. Y was here in 2005." It was actually sad to see such a beautiful structure marred by the American's "artwork," but I guess kids will be kids. Walking onto several ledges overlooking the water, the enormous Victory Over America Palace stood in the middle of the large lake symbolizing Iraq's apparent victory over the United States during Desert Storm in the 1990s. I was not sure exactly how Saddam thought he won that war, but evidently he was convinced that Iraq defeated us on the battlefields of Kuwait. I guess he was not so lucky the second time around.

We then went to the Al Faw Palace, where the Tongan Marines served as guards. Having never met anyone from Tonga, or even knowing where it was, we had a fun conversation with them as we entered the palace. We climbed the huge, marbled stairway of the structure to the third floor to find a colossal back veranda overlooking yet another of Saddam's large lakes. Several pallets were stacked up to the ledge, accompanied by a putting green and golf tees. Twenty or so golf clubs rested between the framework of one of the pallets, and we took turns acting like we were hitting golf balls into the water. It was a beautiful view; I would not have minded working in that palace for sure! We then went downstairs and each took turns getting our pictures made in Saddam's huge throne chair, wide enough for three people to easily fit.

My favorite part of the Al Faw palace was a bulletin board inundated with Chuck Norris quotes on sticky notes. I guess Mr. Norris not only was well known at Camp Buehring, Kuwait, but also in Baghdad. Below are some of my favorites that I had not seen before:

1)   Sharks are in the water because Chuck Norris is on land.
2)   Chuck Norris has a nightlight not because he is afraid of the dark, but the dark is afraid of Chuck Norris.
3)   Chuck Norris saved 100 percent when he switched to Geico®, and it only took him one minute.

4) Chuck Norris doesn't need a bomb suit, the bomb needs a Chuck Norris suit.

5) If Chuck Norris is running late, then time had better slow itself down if it knew what was good for it.

6) There is no such thing as a tornado. Chuck Norris just hates trailer parks.

7) Chuck Norris was born in the mountains in a log cabin that he built with is own two hands.

8) The *Titanic* never hit an iceberg. It ran into Chuck Norris doing his daily laps around the ocean.

9) Chuck Norris CAN believe it's not butter!

10) Some people pee their name in the snow. Chuck Norris pees his name in the concrete.

11) CNN is actually the Chuck Norris network with twenty-four-hour coverage of ass-kicking in real time.

12) Chuck Norris clogs the toilet when he pees.

13) And my favorite: Chuck Norris once looked at an IED. Three seconds later the triggerman exploded.

Flying over Baghdad and surrounding countryside a couple of weeks prior and witnessing the immense poverty of the Iraqi people provided a distinct contrast to the enormous riches and exuberance of Saddam's palaces and lifestyle. This man was deranged, stealing from and killing his own people to add to his wealth.

At the end of the day, once the afternoon heat had cooled, we stopped by yet another lake and sat on the tailgate of Stewart's truck shooting the breeze. Jason was so happy that he even commented, "Today was such a great day, and I didn't even have to talk to anyone I hate." The scene reminded me of warm summer days back home fishing or just being outside in the evening. I loved being outside, and with the rocket fire of the last five weeks keeping us indoors more often than not, this was just what I needed. Flying back to Washington LZ that night, I was amazed to find another perfectly painted Arkansas Razorback logo on the tarmac there. It was the perfect ending to the perfect trip.

Upon arriving at the CSH that evening, the reality of our lives jumped right back as two young Iraqi women, one six months pregnant, were placed in the trauma room with 80 percent burns to their bodies. Someone had placed a bomb on their car, and it detonated with them inside. The pregnant patient's baby had already died in her womb, and she was comatose due to her injuries. The other patient was awake and patiently laid in the bed while our crew attempted IV access anywhere they could find it to give her morphine. Marti had to place a central line, and she was then moved upstairs to await her impending death from her burns. Overall, it was nice to have a day without being hit by rockets, but death was waiting for us when we got back just the same.

The next evening, we decided to have a cookout to eat some of the steak and lobster Mike had provided. Little did we know it would turn into a combat-cooking trip. While several of us were standing around the grill filled with steaks and lobster tails, we heard the Australian compound next door to us announce, "Lockdown, lockdown, lockdown." Not hearing the CRAM incoming alert, we all assumed it was a test or erroneous announcement. However, about two seconds later, an explosion several hundred meters away changed our opinion. We began to run toward the ER entrance of the hospital, only to hear the whistling of another rocket flying by. It was very loud and much closer, and we all ducked down, expecting an impact near our position, but we never heard a sound. The wheezing and chugging of the motor spiraling the projectile past us was a distinct sound I will never forget. The rocket was likely a dud and did not explode upon impact, thank God. We all then made it inside to await more indirect fire. After holding for several minutes, we realized that our CRAM did not detect the rockets, and we were officially never locked down indoors on our compound. We quickly returned outside and rescued the steaks off the grill before they burned! They tasted great, and thanks to another miracle, we had a fantastic combat cooking experience.

Earlier that day, we had dealt with copious head trauma. I received one American soldier at the beginning of my shift with penetrating shrapnel wounds to his right temple, just behind his eye. He was comatose and barely reacting to the painful IV sticks of our medics, so I intubated him quickly and then rotated down to put a central line in his groin. Our surgeon on call arrived and went to the head of the bed to begin working on the soldier's rapidly bleeding temporal artery. While I was placing the large-bore IV line, he tied off some of the bleeding vessels with suture and began to wrap the patient's head in a pressure dressing to help curb some of the hemorrhage. Another surgeon arrived in the trauma room, and I asked them to call the neurosurgeons in Balad and receive an accepting physician for this soldier. We pumped sixteen units of blood into him and gave him five or six other medications to reduce his brain swelling and stop his bleeding. He was packaged on a litter and rushed to waiting Blackhawks to fly him. We found out later that he lived to make it to the operating room in Balad, but the damage was just too great there and he expired on the table.

Not three hours later, another American soldier was rushed into us with a blast injury shearing off the entire right side of his face. His right eye was missing, and his right cheekbones were nowhere to be found. He wore thin-rimmed glasses, and the heat and force of the blast were so immense that his glasses were shifted to the right side of his head and melted into what was left of his forehead. I attempted to remove them, but they were embedded just like a fishhook gets imbedded into a finger. I moved on to perform all of the usual critical life-saving interventions, including intubation, central line, arterial line, blood products, medicines, and more, and we also arranged for him to fly to Balad for neurosurgical and ophthalmological care. He was stable when we loaded him on the Blackhawk, and I never heard if he survived.

A few days prior, we had a small mass casualty incident when a suicide bomber decided to detonate his belt at a wedding ceremony. Eighteen Iraqis were flown to us, some with critical injuries. Two died upon arrival, and several others ended up in the operating room. Finding myself in my usual mass cal position of triaging patients outside, I walked over to two individuals on the back of our gator, who had just been driven over from the helicopters. One had a penetrating abdominal injury, and as he looked up at me, I patted him on the chest and said, "Zien," the Iraqi term for "good," trying to imply to him that we would take care of him. The individual beside him had minor leg injuries and was in much better shape. However, when he saw me pay attention to the sicker patient, he began to wail the common moan we routinely heard from Iraqi men.

As he began to yell out to get my attention, without thinking I stuck my finger in his face and yelled "No!" at the top of my lungs. Neither I nor anyone else had time at the moment to deal with his histrionic antics. A startled look covered his face, and his wailing immediately ceased. He was then taken to the back and given care for his non–life threatening injuries. For whatever reason, Iraqis, men especially, would scream out in pain and make fools of themselves to get attention, even when receiving something as small as an IV stick. I guess they thought we would give them more of our time and ignore those around them who were too sick to cry out; I do not think they ever realized that we would care for those too sick to wail first.

Days later, smoking robes and martini glasses arrived for us. Jason Cohen and I received them from Laura in the mail after requesting the attire to emulate our predecessors from the television show *MASH*. Every few nights, we began putting on our robes and pouring either Dr. Pepper or nonalcoholic beer into our martini glasses and heading to the rooftop to smoke a cigar and relax in the officer's club. Once again, I was sure we would get busted at some point by the command, but did we care? When the latest 240 mm rocket hit and several houses were evacuated, some people ran outside in civilian attire, *nonauthorized* civilian attire I might add. Jason and I were not the only ones at the CSH bending the rules to keep morale up!

We were still being informed that American forces would invade Sadr City soon to stop the daily rocket fire upon the International Zone. Not having exact dates, and having been told the same thing for several weeks, we were all in an "I'll believe it when I see it" mode. When we did start receiving heavy casualties again, we guessed we would realize what was occurring. They told us the day before that our local forward surgical team, or FST, would potentially be pulling out to the BIAP area prior to the incursion. A FST team is a mobile surgical team capable of doing life-saving surgery in poor environments. We had the 102nd FST attached to us throughout most of our tour. Intelligence was stating that the Mahdi Army guys were planning to launch an all-out assault of rocket and missile fire upon the IZ as a retaliation of an American strike, so there was a chance the hospital would be hit, incapacitated, or even somewhat destroyed since we had been one of their favorite targets over the past two months. If we took heavy losses, the FST team would then be safe at BIAP and would pick up our mission if required. We were ready to get this show on the road; if all we had to worry about was rocket fire, then we were ready to be there for our soldiers as they continued to heroically fight for our freedom. They were the ones we worried about at the moment, as we knew they would meet heavy resistance whenever it was they went in.

Rocket fire began to drop off somewhat over the next week. I am not sure why it took so long for the bad guys to figure it out, but they began to wait for the skies to turn sandy, decreasing visibility and turning red. At that point, we knew the rockets would start flying our direction. The indirect fire had slowed down to only one or two volleys per day, except on sandy, low-visibility days. On these days, they knew that our Apache helicopters and Predator unmanned aerial drones could not see them setting up rockets as well, and they took advantage. It was early May, and as usual for a sandy day, we received four or five volleys of rocket fire, with the munitions landing all around us. Our FOB was spared usually, but the nearby traffic circle a few hundred yards up the road took a 107 mm round though the center, closing down the intersection for a good while. The entire rocket did not detonate however, instead burying itself into the street with the tail end sticking a few feet into the air. It would have made for a great picture, but the explosive ordinance detachment was all over it, and we could not get close until it was destroyed. As over the previous few weeks, many times we would hear the explosions without ever being warned by the CRAM systems, as they would often fail to sound before the initial impact. Even the big 240 mm rockets, the ones that could destroy our single-story ER with one well-placed shot, were often not detected. The boom of the initial impact was usually our first warning of incoming fire.

Later that night, several U.S. soldiers arrived after being hit by rocket-propelled grenades, or RPGs. They were sitting on the rooftop of one of their buildings, as we did almost every night when not on shift, when RPGs began flying in from multiple directions in a coordinated attack. They returned fire, but took several casualties in the process. One soldier had both of his eyes and much of his face destroyed, and after we stabilized him, he had to sit in our ICU and wait for the skies to clear so he could be flown to Balad and then on to Germany for definitive care.

During that patient bolus, I made my way to bed ten to find a soldier who had jumped out of a Humvee and suffered a subtalar dislocation of his ankle. It is a common injury resulting in the entire foot dislocating itself off the tibia, or lower leg. Subtalar dislocations are seen often in baseball players when they slide into a base and dislocate their ankle, causing their foot to point in the wrong direction. I had not reduced this type of dislocation recently, so I enjoyed getting to care for him by sedating and relocating his foot to face the right direction. He did well, but he would have to be evacuated home due to his unstable ankle.

The day prior, a bad guy arrived with abdominal pain. I suspected nephrolithiasis, or kidney stones, and while he was waiting for a CT scan, he tried to give us a urine sample. While having one arm strapped to the bed along with his opposite leg for security, he pulled off his bright orange jumpsuit and sat upright naked in the bed, with his penis in a urine bottle, and tried his best to push out some urine along with the rock sitting inside his urethra. His grunts and moans resonated throughout the ED, and even though he was an insurgent possibly responsible for deaths, American deaths at that, I felt bad for the guy. I ordered copious amounts of morphine for him, but it was up to him to pass it on his own! A couple of hours and a lot of morphine later, he produced bloody urine and a small stone. Another patient cured! We then returned him to the military police to take him back to jail to await his fate.

Thinking back over the tour so far, I had been shelled by rockets or mortars when outdoors playing whiffle ball, walking to eat dinner, cooking steaks on a grill, and doing just about every other activity since my arrival in Baghdad. Now I can add combat basketball to the list. Several of us played a pick-up game, marking my first time since Kuwait that I had a chance to play. About halfway through our game, a 240 mm rocket slammed into a nearby FOB without CRAM warning, sending us all scrambling indoors to safety. What is a good game of ball without a little danger and excitement?

That week, more insubordination began working its way through the ranks. In celebration of national nurse's week, a picture of our beloved sergeant major was altered to show him in a nurse's outfit, complete with white skirt and nurse's hat. The perpetrator even put the rank he was so proud of on his chest, along with his army badges, or chest candy, as we liked to call it. We dodged a narrow bullet when we were able to talk some of the people who got a hold of it from replacing his command photo at the front of the hospital with the new picture.

Occasionally, I was able to webcam with Laura, and while Avery was at her Mommy's Day Out, I did get to see my two beloved beagles, along with my precious wife. Being May, we had less than one hundred days until we would get to see each other again. It was great to see her; I was so proud of the way she had picked up the reins and kept our lives moving without a hitch back home. However, the entire time we were on camera, I nervously hoped for no rockets to come in! The building usually shook with each impact, even when the rockets were not that close, and at the time she still did not know that we were being shelled daily. I planned to keep it that way, as she had enough to worry about.

GEN Petraeus and me, Courtesy of US Army

Happy Mother's Day

Mother's Day started with a bang. Hoping for a quiet Sunday shift, walking into the EMT I was greeted with the news of a child of unknown age coming in with an upper extremity amputation with an unknown estimated time of arrival. I quickly grabbed my breakfast and began to scarf it down when a call came in informing us that the one child with the amputation had somehow turned into three blown up kids—and they were landing on our pad now. I quickly called Mike Myer to let him know I had multiple blown up kids coming, ate one spoonful of my breakfast cereal, and went straight to the trauma room to take in the casualties.

Our orthopedist on call was Mark Aierstok, a great physician and even better friend. He was running laps with Mike when I called, and they both arrived at the ER about the same time as the patients. The youngest child, a little boy about eighteen months old, was placed in front of me in bed one, and I noticed that he had some type of pacifier in his mouth and a severely wounded left arm below the elbow. I rapidly assessed him while our nurses and medics worked on IV access, and the second child was placed into bed two. She had a large chunk taken out of her right arm as well, but it was not mostly amputated like her little brother. The third patient was then brought into bed three, and looking from across the room, I knew she required intervention the quickest.

I rotated over to bed three to find a teenage girl with a large facial laceration and eyes that would not open due to the crusted dirt and blood matting them together. She would only answer with guttural sounds in response to our translator's questions, and she did not respond much to the IV sticks our medics were performing on her. Once a peripheral IV was established, Marti Roellig pressed hard to land a central line and I intubated her after she was given sedatives and paralyzing medications. After putting the girl in bed three down, the nurses in bed one called me back over to the smallest child, who was putting up quite a fight while receiving multiple needle sticks. Mark was doing his best to evaluate the partially amputated left arm, and knowing the child would be going to surgery from the EMT, I elected to sedate him and intubate him as well to help control the situation. It is always hard when patients fight and rip out IV lines, but they cannot do that when they are comatose. After I intubated him and put him on a ventilator, I looked back over to bed three and noticed that my teenage girl was about to be pushed out to CT scan.

My official unwritten rule was that no patient leaves the ER without me seeing their chest x-ray first, knowing that a missed pneumothorax, or collapsed lung, could kill them on the CT table. As she was being wheeled out the door of the trauma room, I got my first chance to see her chest x-ray, and lo and behold, there it was! A large pneumothorax was present on the right side of her chest, and it was beginning to squeeze her heart and push it to the left side. This condition can rapidly lead to death, so I quickly stopped her transfer and sent her back to the trauma room to place a chest tube, with half a liter of blood erupting. While I was placing the tube, our radiologist Tony Allen came scampering into the ER and, seeing me placing the chest tube, said, "Well I guess I don't need to tell you she has a tension pneumothorax." We put eight units of blood and plasma into her, and she was rushed to CT scan and then surgery to clean her wounds and continue her stabilization.

The rest of my Mother's Day shift was relatively uneventful. I only had a few routine medical cases, things like kidney stones, finger amputations, and a patient with seizures. But at 6:30 PM, just before I was to get off work to go to the DFAC, an American soldier arrived with amputations to both of his lower legs. His left leg was amputated at the ankle, and his right was amputated about midfoot. He was alert and awake and doing great given the circumstances. After evaluating his injuries and stabilizing him, I began to talk to him while he was waiting on the OR to be ready. He was a graduate of Auburn University and a big Tiger football fan. I told him I was an Arkansas Razorback, and we had a good college football conversation. Every time the talk would die down, he would look down at his missing feet and begin to sadden, and who would blame him? As he left the ER to go to surgery, I put my hand on his shoulder and told him, "I'll see you at a game in a couple of years. Keep your chin up, you're gonna do fine." He agreed and said that would be great to meet at a game someday.

After Mike Myer and Mark Aierstok completed his surgery, upon awakening from anesthesia he was informed that Mark was a Tennessee Volunteer fan, and the soldier went right back into talking college football again, saying, "A Razorback in the ER and a Volunteer in the OR. I can't believe that. " Then he would spurt out, "I can't believe I got treated at Baghdad ER. Cool!" I guarantee his positive thinking will make him successful in life. We always see stories about patients with amputations going on to do amazing things with their lives, and he will be no different. Who knows, maybe he will accept my offer and meet me an Arkansas-Auburn football game someday.

The news began to report a new cease-fire between Al-Sadr's Mahdi Army and the Iraqi government and Coalition forces. They would now allow Iraqi troops into Sadr City without attacking, as long as the U.S. forces did not go in as well. Twenty-four hours after the announcement, the rocket fire ceased. Was this the turning point, the beginning of a more peaceful period in Baghdad? More importantly, would this mean our troops would not have to go into Sadr City to stop the rocket fire into the Green Zone after all? We had to wait to find out, but I was cautiously optimistic.

To conclude national nurse's week, the CSH held a litter-decorating contest between all the sections. The EMT, ICUs, and wards all prepared and decorated a regular army litter and set it up on a rickshaw. Several days of preparation from each area of the hospital were put into each litter, but the brainchild of the EMT's medics won the competition hands down.

Just before the start of the judging, I looked at the litters of the other sections. The ICU's litter was decked out with palm trees, hula skirts, sand, and other stuff to simulate a beach. Another section's was set up as an American soldier super-hero, and a few others were on display as well. The EMT's litter was not present yet, but the noise of a boom box in the background playing the old 1990's hit by the Ghetto Boys, "Damn It Feels Good to Be A Gangsta," began to resonate from down the alley. Along with the others standing beside me, I turned my attention to the end of the gravel alley for the source of the noise, and an amazing procession appeared at the end of the street heading our direction.

Leading the way was Sfc. John Richard dressed in his ACU army pants and "Baghdad ER" T-shirt complemented with a huge "bling-bling" aluminum foil chain around his neck and a purple, feathered pimp hat on his head. Dark sunglasses, funky teeth, and a wooden cane completed his outfit, and he strutted in front of his procession of medics and the litter to the music. On each corner of the litter, our medics Sgt. Ron Estep, Sgt. Justin Ubert, Sgt. Jonathan Desillier, and Maj. Kathy Frost strutted in step with Sfc. Richard, all dressed similarly.

The litter they were escorting was a thing of beauty. Our team had cut large cardboard boxes into the shape of a H2 Hummer and painted it jet black. Using aluminum foil to create a chrome effect, each piece mounted to the vehicle was an exact replica of the real thing, from the taillight covers to the front grill to the hood latches. Each wheel had black spinners that actually spun on contacts mounted to them, and sticking out of the sunroof was a three-foot-tall blow-up doll taped into a position so it looked like she was driving it. The hidden boom box inside served as the truck's radio, and the back license plate read "Baghdad ER" in stark red letters contrasting against the white plate. Everyone was amazed at the presentation. It was fantastic work, and the EMT won the competition easily.

To add another funny story, I learned that one of my favorite people at the CSH had worn through all of his clean underwear about this time. When one of our surgeons was preparing to leave us after his six-month rotation, he ran out of clean underwear about two days prior to his departure. Like many of us, he did not have time to find laundry detergent and wash clothes, so we went to our local "CSH Mart" of clothes and toiletries donated by people back home. Not finding any new underwear in his size, he was forced to make a critical, some would say life-changing, decision: "Do I go commando, wearing no underwear, or wear the ladies' underwear that are here in my size?" He made his decision and flew out of Iraq an experienced trauma surgeon. He was now one of the best and most experienced physicians in the world. He was also the only one I knew who wore lady's underwear ...

After getting off the night shift two nights prior, Marti Roellig, Kristy Bischoff, Pat Smith, and I joined a few members of the Danish Ambassador's personal security team to go to the range. Rasmus, their team's medic, volunteered in the EMT during his free time, and he gave us the invitation. We loaded in their up-armored Toyota Land Cruisers, complete with gun ports in each window, camera systems on all four sides, and armament to include several automatic weapons and AT4 rocket launchers. It was the first trip off the FOB in several weeks for us, and we could not help but notice the increased presence of the Iraqi Army in the International Zone. At each traffic intersection sat an Iraqi Army Humvee decked out with some sort of automatic weapon and a gunner. We also passed a convoy of Iraqi Army vehicles, a rare sight in the IZ for a while. I was not sure why they were around everywhere, possibly it was due to the increased Iraqi Army presence in and around Sadr City for the last few weeks.

Upon our arrival at the range, we joined several other members of the security team and had a great time shooting pistols, M4 assault rifles, and fully automatic AK-47s. My favorite weapon was a M4 assault rifle decked out with a bull barrel for increased accuracy, an optical scope like a big game rifle, and a bipod for increased stability. After shooting for a few hours, we climbed above the range and watched the security team do a couple of demonstrations for us. Using a diamond formation to escort a simulated VIP, they advanced down the range until they were "engaged" by the enemy, simulated by a flash-bang stun grenade. Upon contact, the front three soldiers began slinging bullets downrange with their automatic weapons while the VIP was chased out the back of the formation by the trail member. Each of the first three guys then took turns retreating while the others continued fire. In all, they likely fired two hundred to three hundred rounds in about thirty seconds. It was impressive, and it reminded me there was usually more to the range than just shooting guns.

It had now been several days since we had been hit by a rocket. The new cease-fire between Al-Sadr and the Iraqi government must have been holding. I know our forces made some type of incursion into the ghetto itself, but we never discovered how far they went. One soldier we were treating openly questioned the incursion, asking, "Why are we having to go through this fighting to keep rockets from being shot at you guys?" I did not blame him at all for questioning it. But they were not going in to keep *us* safe. We were soldiers; we could be replaced. They had to go in for the U.S. Embassy and the civilians down the street. They had already suffered a few deaths from the constant rocket fire over the past several weeks landing on the Embassy grounds, and I do not think they would have tolerated too many more State Department casualties. Thanks to the cease-fire agreement, we continued to hope and pray that our forces would not have to go too far into Sadr City after all.

—•—

It was the middle of May, and the temperature in the sun now was approaching 120 degrees Fahrenheit. To be honest, it was not any warmer to me than a hot day back home in Arkansas, with the temperature hovering around one hundred and humidity approaching the century mark as well. But there, just like home, the evening temperatures were wonderful. Sure, it was still warm outside, but at twilight the sun was shaded by the horizon, and the air felt great on my skin when contrasted to just a few hours prior. That was always my favorite time of a warm summer day back home, and nothing about that had changed since our arrival in the Middle East. I was sure our thousands of guys running around outside all day would strongly disagree with me and complain about the heat, and who would blame them? They were out working in it, while we sat back in our nice air-conditioned hospital working indoors. So, yes, it was hot, but you would not hear me complaining.

Back home in Arkansas, Laura told me the dog days of summer were approaching rapidly. She called me a few nights prior and let me listen to our beautiful thirteen-month-old daughter snooze away in her high chair. I could hear her breathing loudly when the phone was put to her face, and about every fourth or fifth breath, a little snoring sound would escape. She would then awaken to a state of half-arousal and apparently make repetitive hand motions, attempting to shove more food into her mouth. After a few tries, she would drift off and pass out again, only to repeat the process. Laura also told me that Houston, our older beagle, continued to stare out the front window of the house at the driveway, as he had done since I left home. She told me he was waiting for me to come home, and the sheer thought of that melted my heart and brought a tear to my eye every time I thought about it. Things were still moving back home; the world was still spinning. But these stories reminded me that a small part of the earth in the little town of Searcy, Arkansas, was standing still and anxiously awaiting my return from war.

About this time, the negativity around the CSH had increased to an all-time high. The new work hours requiring nurses and medics to work a dangerous schedule of seventy-two clinical hours per week had dampened morale tremendously. As we had done several times in the past, every one of us was willing to work all day every day anytime the mission called for it, but when there was a chance for down time, our staff needed to be able to recharge and prepare for the next wave. As physicians, we had worked crazy numbers of hours for years throughout our medical school and residency training, but we knew what we were getting into when we started. Our nurses and medics did not volunteer for that, and we felt it was downright unsafe for our patients. Numerous studies were presented to the command about the dangers of increasing nursing "on the floor" hours, but so far it had been to no avail. Several other rules we considered boneheaded had been implemented, and we were all frustrated since they seemed to make no sense to us and we received no explanation for them. But some of our nurses decided to do something about it.

Megan Solberg, Heather Brown, Kristy Bischoff, Kathy Richardson, and a few others devised a plan to fix the negativity: hexes and voodoo dolls. They researched hexes for positivity on the Internet and began attempting to collect the ingredients required to put a spell on the place. The tough thing would be finding things like graveyard dirt, hair from certain individuals, and other hard-to-obtain items. The hexes were meant to provide some positive energy around here, but I was not so sure about the voodoo dolls. I would think they were designed for more sinister reasons, but as long as they were not doing a voodoo doll of me! Being a Christian, obviously I did not believe in the voodoo hexes and stayed away from it. But they were just playing around for fun, trying to make something positive out of a negative, and for that I commend them.

I cared for a forty-year-old contractor that week from Bangladesh who was flown to us with chest pain. His electrocardiogram rhythm strips from the medical clinic that sent him to us demonstrated significant ST-segment elevation, meaning he was currently having a massive heart attack. We placed him in a bed, and as our medics began to put in IVs and hook up the monitor leads, I quickly began to obtain a history from him. He was alert and aware of the situation, but about thirty seconds into my interview, he stopped responding, went limp, and began to shake all over. A quick glance at the monitor confirmed my suspicions: his heart had gone into ventricular fibrillation right before us! This rhythm occurs just before people die, and he was trying his best to die right then.

As we began CPR, I yelled for a medic to bring over our crash cart, thinking we needed to shock his heart back into motion immediately. Knowing it would be thirty seconds or so before we could send two hundred Joules of electricity though his chest, I remembered that one other response might get his heart rhythm back quicker. Never having done a precordial thump before, I took two steps to the bedside and punched him as hard as possible right in the chest. A couple of our medics stopped momentarily and looked at me as if I was crazy, but then quickly returned to their duties as I assessed the verdict of my procedure. It did not work unfortunately, but by that time the pads were ready and we shocked him.

His body lurched forward on the bed in one quick motion from the jolt, and his heart reset into a bradycardic rhythm with a heartbeat at about twenty-five beats per minute. I ordered atropine, a medicine that speeds up the heart, and also gave him a medicine that would help prevent the heart from going back into the deadly rhythm. He responded well and woke up, and within ten minutes we gave him the clot buster drug to break the clot causing his heart attack. Within thirty minutes, he was en route to the ICU with our cardiologist Dr. Brian Hemann. He was later was sent out for definitive care outside of Iraq.

An American soldier with a thumb injury was lying in the bed next to all of this, and he was alarmed as well to see me punch a patient in the chest, followed by us shocking him right before his eyes! He had a front row seat to the action, and I would imagine he began telling stories to his friends back at the unit since he left us. We saved lives working in Baghdad ER on a regular basis, but it was always a great feeling every time. I will never got tired of that!

The next night, I had a crazy dream. I had returned from the war on my leave, going to the house I grew up in, located in Texarkana, Texas. However, my neighbors from Washington State, the ones Laura and I loved so much, lived in the area. I was excited to see them, but sad because I did not live beside them any more. Later in the day, while inside one of their homes, rockets and mortars began landing in the distance. One of my neighbors told me they got shelled routinely there and asked if we ever caught any indirect fire here in Iraq. While trying to answer, the rounds fell closer and closer, to the point where they were deafening and landing just outside our window. I could see the explosions sending shrapnel every-where, and at that point I woke up.

Telling Marti about my dream, she questioned if that was a form of PTSD. I was not worried about it until then, but she made me concerned

I was beginning to show signs of the stress! I knew we all would reflect it in one way or another, but the hundreds of rockets fired at us over during the past two months really did not bother me too much, except when I was trying to sleep though the explosions all around. But I began to question it as well; what effect did they have on me? The dreams have continued somewhat after I returned home, but I assume that is normal for those of us returning from war.

—

Days later, several U.S. Marines got hit by an EFP in the Anbar province area. They were evacuated to TQ Surgical, a navy-operated level II facility capable of performing life-saving damage control surgery. After undergoing surgical stabilization there, two of them were sent our direction later that night, one with an amputated leg and the other with major abdominal trauma. Both had been worked on by the TQ Surgical team, and they were flown to us for further care and evacuation to Germany.

When they arrived, we were informed that CPR was in progress on the marine with the abdominal injuries. We rapidly placed him in bed one of our trauma bay and I threw the ultrasound probe on his chest, quickly noting that he did not have a heartbeat and was in cardiac arrest. We had no idea how long he had been in that situation, as he had significant injuries from the blast earlier in the day. I ordered epinephrine and atropine, both cardiac life-support drugs, and we continued CPR, determined to give him the best chance to survive that we could. After the medications and chest compressions, we stopped to look at his heart on ultrasound and to check for a pulse. Moments went by with nothing, and then I saw his heart move! Our nurse confirmed a pulse in his left groin that coincided with each beat of the heart on the ultrasound, and before we knew it, his pulse was up to one hundred beats per minute and his blood pressure was coming back. We pumped several units of blood into him, and the surgeon on call, Dr. Regan Quan, rushed him to the operating room, where he survived another operation.

Unfortunately, most patients who undergo CPR to be revived have anoxic brain injury, caused by the death of brain cells stemming from the lack of oxygen. I had no idea if this marine would ever wake up again. But we got him back. We did our job. Moments after he went to the OR, we all were high-fiving each other and were excited for another save.

Speaking of saves, we received word that the soldier who had touched me, the one who suffered third- and forth-degree burns to over 95 percent of his body, was still alive! We were receiving updates from the burn center in San Antonio about his status periodically. He sustained multiple amputations due to his injuries, but he was still fighting. I will never forget looking into his eyes, speaking to him and trying comfort him as he attempted to get words out of his burned mouth and throat. I will also never forget deciding that I would let him die in front of me rather than leave his side and try to help my colleagues get an IV on him. I was determined that he would not die alone, not on my watch.

A nurse who works in the burn center in San Antonio asked him if he was glad we saved his life. Was he happy to be alive? She said he told her he did not remember anything about the first two months of his care, nothing about the multiple surgeries, amputations, and procedures. But he told her he was glad to be alive. That was all I needed to hear to validate the task we were accomplishing. I did not know why God chose to save his live that day, but it was obvious the Lord was not done with him yet. Hopefully, he realized that. Someday, I hoped to have the guts to go visit him if he was still alive by the time I left the Middle East. I do not even know his name, but he will always hold a place in my heart for the rest of my life.

I had another interesting case that week, as a soldier was evacuated to us emergently with a decreased level of consciousness and a rectal temperature of 103 degrees. We were told the person who found him said he had liquid paper around his lips and that he may have overdosed on the substance. I quickly intubated him to help protect both his airway and our team as he was agitated and thrashing about while our team attempted to hold him down to work on him. At that point, once he was in a medically induced coma, I was able to properly evaluate him and begin to put the picture together.

I did not see any corrective fluid in his mouth or throat, but his skin was warm, dry, and flushed. His pupils were very dilated and did not squeeze down and constrict to light in the normal manner. Putting it all together, he fit the perfect picture of a person with an anticholinergic toxidrome, the kind manifested when someone overdoses on certain types of common medications. Other than his pupilary abnormalities, he also fit the bill for a having suffered a heat stroke. However, not knowing the story at the scene, I was unable to determine the exact cause of his condition. He went into liver and kidney failure, and it is quite possible that he may have died once evacuated out of Iraq. Later, I was told he was filling sandbags in the midday heat, and that pushed me to think that he likely suffered a heat-stroke. I hoped he would recover from his injuries, but it did not look good at the time. Temperatures were now well over 100 degrees outside during the midday heat, and it pained me to see a soldier suffer from a heat injury like that. However, with it only being early May, I was sure there would be many more to come before it cooled off several months later.

Soon afterward, we developed a new tradition at Baghdad ER. An Iraqi man suffered a serious head injury, and after I intubated him and prepared him to fly to our neurosurgeons in Balad, his head was wrapped in a pressure dressing that left only the breathing tube coming from his mouth uncovered, per our usual routine. Just as he was about to be loaded on the helicopter, Sgt. Ron Estep took a Hannah Montana sticker and put it on the gauze dressing on the side of his head. That itself was not too humorous, but we then began putting the stickers on many of the patients we sent. You could call it our signature stamp, telling others that the patient was treated in Baghdad ER! We figured it was only a matter of time before people started asking about it, but they actually never did. We thought that maybe these stickers from Bagdad ER would end up all over Iraq, maybe even the world. I do not know why we went with Hannah Montana, but who was I to change the new tradition?

About that time, we passed the halfway mark. We now had seven and a half months down, and the same to go. It felt so good to finally be on the downhill side of deployment! I had been preparing for this fifteen-month interruption in my life for years, and now we were over 50 percent done! All but one of my classmates from residency had ended their time in the army by that point, and I was happy for them to be moving on with their lives. But I would be lying if I did not say how much it pained me to have such a long way to go!

Drs. Bill Ralston, Mark Aierstok, and Steve Svoboda, three of our orthopedic surgeons on six-month tours, had jobs that were either feast or famine. Any time we were busy in the ER, they were crushed by the number of extremity traumas they had to take to the operating room. But due to the cease-fire, things had begun to slow down, and they began to receive a well-deserved break. Since they came through the quick deployment unit in the U.S. that gets individuals ready to go within days—called CRC—they all were lucky enough to receive 9 mm pistols to carry rather than the M16s we were stuck dragging around. However, for some reason, they did not receive much ammunition. Collectively, they apparently shared one clip of ammo between the three of them, and they rotated it to the person who was leaving the FOB each day. We had all been poking fun at them since learning they were sharing ammo with each other in a war zone! Luckily, none of the three ever needed the clip.

On a recovery day for me after working a string of night shifts, Scott Henning, Tony Allen, and I took the chance to get over to FOB Prosperity in the IZ to do some fishing. We tried to check out a vehicle from our guys at the CSH, but by this point they had imposed a two-hour time limit, as well as a lengthy explanation requirement to check out a SUV to drive around the IZ. Therefore, the physician's assistant from FOB Prosperity who worked with us each week, 1st Lt. James Lorentz, sent over an army front line ambulance, or FLA, to pick us up and carry us over to Prosperity. They dropped us at the aid station, and then loaded us in an up-armored Humvee and drove us over to the fishing ponds. We tried our best to hang a lunker for three hours, with the only result being a small, ugly eel-like catfish caught by Tony. James then came by in the Humvee and carted us to the dining facility. It was exquisite, like eating at a fine restaurant compared to ours! After a great meal, James then took us for a quick tour of FOB

Prosperity.

We went into the big palace that had been transitioned into a command center and walked around in a big circle until we entered a huge, unbelievable gymnasium. Any piece of exercise equipment I could think of was laid out before my eyes, and everyone working out was wearing civilian clothes! Apparently, even though these soldiers were members of a fighting brigade combat team, they were allowed to wear civilian clothes to the gym to work out. We all joked that they must not be as hard-core army as our sergeant major, who made us medical guys at the CSH wear army PT clothes to sleep in, much less to go out in public.

James then introduced us to his battalion commander and sergeant major, and we were invited to come back and smoke cigars with them on their smoking deck outside overlooking the IZ. We went upstairs to look at a mural that Saddam had put into the palace when it was built. It consisted of the outlines of mothers crying and reaching into a fire to pull out their dismembered children, while a big bomb was coming down from the sky toward them. The bomb had the three big letters, "USA," etched into it, in an effort to demonstrate America killing Iraqi children. It never ceased to amaze me to see how the Saddam propaganda machine worked to manipulate the poor, uninformed masses.

We then went into the outdoor area of FOB Prosperity. Sand volleyball courts, patio tables, outdoor music, games, smoothie stands, and colorful lighting gave the area a festive atmosphere, and it was hard not to relax in such a wonderful, vacation-like place! I bought a smoothie, and we stayed a short time at Club Prosperity, but we were brought back to earth when Scott said, "I guess it's time for us to get back to the war now." We got a good laugh from the statement, and the FLA took us back home to the CSH. What a great day and a great chance to get outside. My next step was to pack my rucksack, put on my gear, and head north to Mosul, where I would be swapping places with Rob Nolan for a month.

Since the cease-fire had been agreed to by Al-Sadr's Madhi Army and the Iraqi government forces in early May, our volume continually dropped. The rockets stopped flying our direction, and so did the patients. Sure, we still received trauma every now and then, but the hospital was empty, and the EMT census had waned considerably. Each day, the *Stars and Stripes* newspaper posted articles saying that the cease-fire was tenuous and could end at any time, but its effects were obvious. Through May 29, 2008, we had 122 people die in our hospital since we took over, with thirty-five of those being American military personnel. A new edition of the *Army Times* weekly was found in the EMT, and as usual, our crew went through all of the pictures of the deceased and circled those we had treated and shared their stories. Personally, I could not bring myself to do that; I did not think I could handle it. The only way I could cope was to remember that what was done was done, and I needed to be ready when or if the cease-fire disintegrated.

Our command began attempting to rotate our intrinsic EMT medics, the ones we trained and worked with for eight months, out of the EMT and replace them with a non–trauma trained staff. As chief of the EMT, I was furious and fought this change tooth and nail. We all relied on our medics to know what we were thinking and to be competent members of our trauma team. It was too late to start training new personnel, and it would put our patients' lives at risk when we already had a fully trained and competent staff. After fighting for weeks with the command, we finally won the battle and were able to set a minimum number of trauma-trained medics to be present on every shift. But they continuously kept making attempts to pull our medics away throughout the remained of our tour.

Just before leaving for Mosul, I was named the Iraq Theater consultant for emergency medicine by our higher headquarters. I was not really sure what that meant, but it was exciting to get the title. We also had a replacement emergency medicine physician coming from the 115th CSH at Camp Bucca, Iraq. He would be with us during some of the time we were to go on our midtour leaves, helping us greatly to keep the ER covered. Finally, after all of our worrying and efforts to keep three ER docs present at all times, we were successful. Jason, Marti, and I would be able to go on our R&R leaves back home and not have to worry about the other two getting hammered. It was a great victory and a great relief.

As our weapons were always locked in the weapons rack, when going over to an adjacent FOB for dinner one night, I could not find our shift leader with the keys to get Betsy, my trusty M16. Our Special Forces medic Mike was working with us at the time, so he kindly let me borrow his MP5 submachine gun to carry as my weapon. MP5s are essentially only carried by Special Forces soldiers, so you could imagine the looks and comments I received when people noticed a major in uniform with one. It was great, and I had fun getting to carry an exciting weapon around, even if it was only for a couple of hours.

On my day shift the next day, I treated what I think was the first case of frostbite in an American military person that ever occurred in the Iraqi summer. While I cannot say for sure if that is an accurate statement, I was shocked to have a soldier flown to us with first-degree frostbite burns blistered all around his knee. Asking him how in the world he could get frostbite when the temperature outside was approaching 120 degrees, he told me that he injured his knee, put ice all around it, and then fell asleep for seven hours, only to wake up with frostbite. I had never heard of anyone receiving frostbite from icing his or her knee, but I guess there was a first time for everything! We had him treated by our burn specialist, and he returned to duty with strict instructions on how to use ice packs in the future without hurting himself.

Mosul: Taking the Action to Northern Iraq

Beginning my pilgrimage to Mosul, my flight from Washington LZ in the International Zone over to BIAP was relatively noneventful. We flew at night, and somewhere over the Baghdad city lights, our birds began kicking out flares, with six flares spitting from the craft one after another. After the brief light show, we settled down into one of the FOBs around Baghdad and picked up more passengers. I packed relatively light for my month-long stay in Mosul, carrying only my rucksack as my luggage. Of course, combining the sixty-pound rucksack with the forty-five pounds of body armor and 210 rounds of ammo for my M16 made my job of packing light that much more imperative. Sitting on the front right seat of the passenger section on the helicopter, I held my rucksack in my hands on my lap, doing my best to keep it off the door gunner as he searched the sky and the city streets for signs of danger. It was the end of May, and the flight crews had removed all of the windows from the Blackhawks to keep the heat down. Twice the bird banked and I had to hang on tight to my rucksack as it began leaning out the window, and it did make for an interesting ride, flying low over the streets of the world's most dangerous city without even glass to protect me from bullets or shrapnel, but I was happy take the risk over the searing Iraqi heat.

After landing at BIAP, I looked back at the bird to notice that I had been

carried by the *Battlin' Bitch* once again, the same Blackhawk that carried
Deena, Jason, and I a month or so ago. Lugging my gear and rucksack to
the bus stop, I sat down and waited for the bus to pick me up and take me
down to FOB Stryker, where I would crash for a few hours waiting on my
flight. It was 10:30 at night, and I had to be back at the airport at 6:00 AM
to catch my plane to Mosul, but the hard chairs of the terminal were unin-
viting. I chose to head down to the Stryker Stables, a temporary lodging
place to crash for transient people. After checking in and finding the large
tent with its twenty cots inside, I took a space and crashed for about four
hours, getting up at 4:30 AM and preparing to head back to the airport.

By this point, I had soaked my clothes with sweat several times over the
past twenty-four hours, as each time I put on my body armor or picked up
my rucksack, whether day or night, I was drenched within moments. With
no time to shower, I just had to remember that I was not trying to impress
anyone by smelling good or looking clean, and I chuckled about it as I
jumped back on the bus to catch my plane. The feeling of relief from dropping my huge rucksack on the luggage pallet was immense; I could not even
feel the weight of my body armor at that point. I walked over to the holding
area, and soon we were lined up to hot load onto our C-130 and head
to Mosul. Securing my ballistic eyewear to my face, earplugs in my ears,
helmet on my head, and other personal effects to my body armor, I walked
from the terminal past the spinning props of the four-engine aircraft, and as
we loaded onto the bird using the cargo ramp in the rear, the heat from the
prop wash took my breath away. Luckily, once I made it into the fuselage
of the airplane, the air was much cooler, and as our group split off to either
side, I went left. Making my way down to my jump seat, I found my seatbelt and felt thankful once again to not be carrying my rucksack.

Fighting the usual back pain I seemed to endure anytime I wore my
body armor for an extended period of time, I once again could not help but
wonder, "How in the world do our soldiers live in this stuff every day?" I did
my best to sleep or read my way through the one-hour flight to Mosul, but
that all stopped when we began losing altitude rapidly and sweeping from
side to side as a part of our combat landing. Apparently the air force frowns

on having missiles or rockets shooting down their airplanes, so as a safety measure they make all kinds of crazy evasive maneuvers while landing. I remember doing the same when flying into Baghdad back on November 1, but this landing was much more extreme. I felt myself turning green, wishing for a window to view out to help curb the airsickness, but I only could see the people sitting directly across from me in the dimly lighted cargo compartment. I had never endured airsickness before, and I knew I would be okay as long as no one else vomited. If that happened, I guarantee the dominoes would have begun to fall and we would all be covered with puke by the time we disembarked the plane, but thank God, everyone's stomachs held up.

The elements of the Eighty-sixth CSH stationed in Mosul gave me a most warm greeting. They put me into one of their containerized housing units, or CHUs, for transient personnel, and my friend Dr. Rob Nolan came to meet me just after my arrival. The CSH was located on FOB Diamondback, a large, dusty area near the airport. After settling in, I left my CHU to get a tour, and then I came back to discover that my AC unit did not work and I had no power in my room. I went to our facilities guys, and they called in a work order, asking me to stay in my unit until the contractors arrived to repair my problem. They told me it would be only thirty minutes or so of sitting in the 105 degree heat with no lights, but five hours and several pounds of sweat later I finally gave up and talked the command into giving me another unit, since obviously the repairmen were not coming anytime soon. After moving, my new CHU worked out great and I had no issues.

My first day in Mosul, I saw a grand total of five patients in twenty-four hours. A broken toe, a girl with a painful menstrual period, a well-appearing guy with abdominal pain, a wrist injury, and a guy with tooth pain were the only patients who appeared for care. Not exactly what I was used to in Baghdad, with all the blood and guts that had become part of my everyday life! I would also be covering the clinic some while I was there, but I had a slow and peaceful start.

The next day, I had my first Mosul-style explosion. The hospital was a smaller building, and it rattled and creaked more than Ibn Sina in Baghdad when a bomb exploded nearby. The blast was a decent distance away, as we determined by the cloud of black smoke rising into the distance in the city, but it still shook the facility pretty well. It had been much quieter there recently, just as it had in Baghdad, since the prior month's major operation by the Iraqi government to clear Al-Qaeda out of Mosul. I just hoped the blast was not an ominous beginning to my time there.

—▪—

My first few days in Mosul were quiet. I had seen about four to five patients a day on my twenty-four-hour shifts, although one of the nights I was up several hours caring for multiple patients as they came in for various reasons. Over the past week, the most ill patient I had seen suffered from appendicitis, and the place sure did not have the acuity level of Baghdad ER. Most of my days were spent in boredom, although it was nice to get a break. I was able to make it to the gym every day, get some reading done, and most importantly, catch up on the sleep that I had been missing over the previous eight months.

One day, I went on a tour of the Monastery of St Elijah, built between 350 and 500 AD. Located in Mosul on one of the forward operating bases, it was an old monastery that dated back to the second or third century after the death of Christ. It had been a place for study, medicine, and other educational activities for over one thousand years until 1743 when a Muslim warlord named Nadir Shah gave the 150–200 monks living inside an ultimatum: convert to Islam or die. After discussing it, they chose not to betray their God or their faith, and they remained until the Muslim leader killed them all. After World War I, the British set arbitrary boundaries all over the Middle East, creating countries from scratch with borders created on paper. Many religious and ethnic groups were split apart, and many refugees from both sides of new international borders were created. The monastery was used as a refugee center during those times, where people could go for safety and to receive medical care. Later in the twentieth century, the Iraqi government under Saddam Hussein moved in and turned it into army facility.

Moving ahead to 2003, a unit of the Iraqi Republican Guard was using the monastery as a command post, with its ideal location nestled in the hills just outside the city's main entrances. During the early operations of Iraqi Freedom, a company of armor from the American army charged over the surrounding hills and met the ill-fated Iraqi tank unit at the monastery. A battle ensued, and the Iraqis quickly lost their command post and the battle. One Iraqi tank was reportedly even blown up against the wall of the monastery, putting a large hole in the wall from the trauma.

The remains were then used as a headquarters for a unit of the 101st Airborne Division, until an army chaplain researched the site and learned about its history. The 101st Airborne Division commander, then two-star Gen. David Petraeus, ordered all personnel from the facility and it became fenced. Only military chaplains were authorized access, and they gave guided tours. On the tour, we were informed that in the near future, an archeological team from an Iraqi university would begin excavating the site, and there is no telling what could be found. If it truly was built around 200 AD, there could even be documents buried there that predate Christ! I still have not heard if anything has been found at this point, but it may eventually become as important as the site of discovery of the Dead Sea Scrolls.

Word from Baghdad was that we had just lost Cpt. Robyn Stafford and two of our medics to a tasking in Talil, a town southeast of Baghdad. Apparently, the forward surgical team located there was moving out to a destination unknown in support of an anticipated operation designed to prevent the shipment of weapons from Iran into southern Iraq and Baghdad. Of course, Iran denies to this day that it was sending weapons into Iraq, but that is not surprising. Mark Aierstock and one of our general surgeons headed out as well to join the FST team in preparation to accept casualties from the operation. We were also told that a company of Apache attack helicopters had moved from northern Iraq to support the operation, so we all kept our eyes and ears open to see how the it unfolded.

With the recent Iraqi government offenses in Basra, Sadr City, and most recently Mosul, it sure seemed to me the Iraqi authorities were getting more and more aggressive and had begun taking the fight to the bad guys. They, along with American backup, were doing a fantastic job engaging the terrorists, and we imagined that the upcoming operations in Talil would be more of the same, as turned out to be the case. With Talil being far south of Baghdad, and me being in northern Iraq at the time, it really would not affect me, but of course I was still curious to keep up with everything because my heart was with my crew closer to the action in Baghdad.

The plan for the Mosul rotation amongst the ER docs of the Eighty-sixth CSH was put in place to give each of the four of us a change of scenery, a break of some sorts. The three of us stationed in Baghdad were to receive an easier schedule, with a much-decreased patient census and a much more laid-back atmosphere. Rob Nolan, our ER doc in Mosul rotating to Baghdad, was to benefit from the chance to go to the pool down at the palace every so often and to get to experience the high excitement and pure adrenaline that had become routine to those of us in Baghdad. Serving as the only non-six-month rotating physician in Mosul, it would be good to give him a break and change of scenery as well.

Upon arriving in Mosul, I was informed that Maj. Margret Young, one of the staples of the outpatient clinic, was redeploying home and would only be around for another week or so. Therefore, before he left for Baghdad, Rob Nolan had agreed to help cover the clinic two half-days a week, while also covering in the EMT. Upon my arrival, I discovered they had added me to a third half-day of clinic time, since coverage was indeed short due to the loss of Maj. Young and the unwillingness of one of the surgeons and OB/GYN physicians onsite to help cover. After working a few afternoons there, it was actually kind of fun working in the clinic, at least until my first weekend of forty-eight-hour solo EMT coverage.

The day of coverage started innocently enough, with a few of the usual nonacutely ill, clinic-type patients routinely seen in the Mosul EMT. However, an Al-Qaeda suicide car bomber decided to drive a truck full of explosives through a U.S. security gate in the town of Kirkuk, Iraq, and detonated himself as he reached his target of an American armored truck. One soldier was killed in the attack and several more suffered nasty injuries. Two soldiers had severe head trauma, and they required evacuation to the air force hospital in Balad for neurosurgical care. However, helicopters could not fly there due to dust storms between Kirkuk and Balad, making Mosul to the northwest the next best option as a place to send the wounded.

Preparing for six injured patients to arrive in less than hour was not a big deal in Baghdad, but resources were significantly different in Mosul. We notified a critical air transport team, or CCAT, stationed at the Balad Air Force Base and asked them to begin moving our direction. Our plan was to receive the critically wounded patients by helicopter and then turn around and place them on the CCAT Air Force C-130 for an emergent trip to definitive care. Upon arrival, each of the hospital's six physicians took a patient, and we all went to work. About thirty minutes after receiving the casualties, we could hear the props of the C-130 taxiing over to our position, signifying the arrival of the critical air transport team. They arrived, made a quick assessment of the patients and their status, and began loading the soldiers onto the plane. Knowing it is always better in the military to ask forgiveness rather than permission, we followed our patients to the back of the plane and began taking video and pictures of the flying intensive care unit, at least until one of the crew members came over and yelled at us. The arrangement of the plane was impressive, as they had spots reserved for patients all the way down the plane, with IV bags and medical equipment everywhere. It was my first exposure to a CCAT team, and I was impressed. I had been told that emergency physicians serving in the air force often served as the sole physician on these teams, and it was a job that I think would have been a lot of fun, especially since my tour in the air force would only have been four months.

After the excitement died down, I began to clear the EMT, and eventually everyone left and went to bed around 1:00 AM. At 4:00 AM, a sharp knock on my door caused me to stir, and as I opened it, one of our EMT medics excitedly told me that one of our secret teams that "does not exist" had been hit and was sending multiple casualties in at any time. We work with a lot of Army Special Forces guys down in Baghdad, so I was not really sure what the medic meant by, "These guys don't exist." I found out soon enough.

Within the hour, two Blackhawks landed and dropped off six patients, with two of them being critically wounded and the other four with minor shrapnel wounds to the legs. One was intubated, with a right-sided chest tube having previously been placed, and after a quick evaluation, we rushed him to the CT scanner and then to the operating room. Another with a leg wound went straight to the OR, and as I moved around the room, I noticed that all of the guys had the typical Special Forces beards, scraggly hair, and civilian clothes that helped them to blend in. However, when I sat down to look at all the x-rays, I noticed they all had the same last name, with only different first names. Puzzled, I thought to myself why that was, and then it hit me like a ton of bricks. I doubted these guys were all brothers with the same last name; of course they were fake. That much was obvious, but why? If I remembered right, our Special Forces soldiers did not hide their identity from their own military. But then I realized that these guys were more than just Special Forces guys; they were likely members of the Army's Delta Force, the most elite special forces and antiterrorism unit in the world. Chuck Norris movies and a popular recent television series called *The Unit* have revealed small glimpses of their nature and helped explain why they "don't exist." All in all, something had to go really wrong for *these guys* to take casualties, since they usually were prepared and equipped for everything. I would hate to see what happened to the bad guys who engaged our Delta Force team, but I will say that *none* of them showed up for hospital care, so I did not imagine they would be around to attack Americans or innocent Iraqi civilians ever again! Overall, the Delta guys were very nice and cordial; one of them even called me sir, as if he was in the real army. We were able to release a few of them, and some had to admitted overnight after their surgical procedures. To this day, I cannot verify who these guys were, but it was an intriguing experience to care for them.

I then went back to my CHU and got some sleep, until I received a page asking me to report to the EMT, as the one soldier killed in the attack on the Delta guys had arrived and a physician was required to officially pronounce him dead. The Task Force Mosul Chaplain, Cpt. Bailey, led me behind a building and we arrived in a nice, well-lit, air-conditioned annex used as the morgue. As I walked in the door, the mortuary affairs soldiers unzipped the body bag, and I looked in the eyes of yet another dead soldier. His lifeless face reminded me that the war had followed me from Baghdad to Mosul, and our troops were never truly out of harm's reach. Both his right arm and leg were partially amputated and mangled, and I ceremonially checked for a pulse and placed my stethoscope on his chest to listen for a heartbeat. After a few seconds, I pronounced him deceased at 9:10 AM, and then went on to do my paperwork and back to my CHU to rest.

I was able to manage a couple of hours of sleep this time, until receiving an urgent page to get to the EMT as soon as possible. Throwing on my shoes and running, I arrived to see a fifty-something-year-old Turkish man being transferred from a stretcher and onto one of our trauma beds. I quickly looked at his paperwork and noticed he was having a ST segment elevation myocardial infarction, or STEMI, otherwise known as a heart attack. Apparently, he had collapsed while driving a bus on a small American outpost and run the bus into a concrete barrier. Witnesses at the scene performed CPR and shocked him back to life using the automated external defibrillator located on the bus.

Upon interviewing him, I discovered he was still having chest pain, so I quickly began my STEMI management protocol. In the United States, at most hospitals I would arrange for him to undergo emergent heart catheterization by a cardiologist, but that obviously would not be an option here. In more rural places back home, a clot-buster drug can be given, the same one I had administered several times in Baghdad, and it was my only option. However, he had just undergone an automobile accident, knocking him unconscious. How did I know that he did not have bleeding arteries in his head or abdomen that would blow open once the drug was given, killing him before our eyes? I had watched a lot of people die since I arrived in Iraq; I could not help that, but I was not ready for another. Time was of the essence, every second I withheld the drug from him, more of his heart could die from lack of blood flow. I did a quick trauma assessment on him, and not noting any lesions, I performed an ultrasound of his abdomen to look for bleeding, finding none. I then decided to wait another ten minutes and get a quick CT scan of his head to ensure he had no intracranial injuries. After quickly reading the scan, we pushed the medicine.

We were all on pins and needles, waiting to discover the outcome of our treatment, watching his heart enter and exit the normal arrhythmias and irregular beats that we expected to see. Fortunately, no major acute side effects occurred, and he did not die in front of us. But he also did not improve. We arranged an urgent flight to the hospital in Dihok, Iraq, close to the Turkish border, where a cardiologist was waiting for him. I was not sure exactly what a cardiologist was in Iraq, but we sent the man to the physician working as a heart specialist. He needed an emergency catheterization, and I am not sure if they even did that in Iraq. When our flight nurse returned a few hours later, she told us he had done well on the flight. Who knows what happened to him, but we did the best we could and sent him off to live or die. Just like the others, we will never know.

The next day in morning report, one of our surgeons mentioned he wanted to send the Delta Force guys requiring further medical care on the previously scheduled patient evacuation flight to Germany later that morning. However, the patients wanted to leave and care for their belongings prior to leaving Iraq. These guys were not hurt badly, and they were in position to easily call and get a flight any time they wanted and could essentially go anywhere they desired. They did not play by army rules; they played by their own rules and had an unlimited array of options at their disposal. The surgeon, Dr. Matt MacDonald, totally understood this and told them he recommended they take the flight to Germany, but they could do whatever they wished.

However, our deputy commander for clinical services (DCCS) in Mosul did not see it that way. I had been warned before arriving that he was a know-it-all, and he lived up to his reputation! He started saying things like, "They follow orders, just like we do." I wanted to say, "Yes, that's true, but they don't follow orders from those of us in the regular army, sir." Then he raised his voice and stated, "They are not in a position to negotiate; we are in a position to negotiate." My thoughts went like, "Uh, actually, sir, they could easily get a plane to take off from Germany and pick them up here anytime they wanted. I think they can negotiate all they want." And then my favorite line of his was this, "I'm a colonel, and I'll talk to their colonel and tell him how it is." By this point, I was thinking to myself, "Sure, like this Delta Force full-bird colonel would give a rat's *** what you have to say ... sir."

Apparently, their colonel had come in the day before, when one of his boys was in the operating room, and walked right in, placing a surgical mask over his face and making himself right at home. When informed of this, our DCCS was livid. "Why wasn't I notified?" he said. "I'd have kicked him out of there and told him how it works!"

To this, I was thinking, "Sure you would. There's a reason these guys don't have names, and they don't exist ... sir." During his entire tirade, I was leaning over talking to Lt. Col. Dave Jones, another one of the docs on a six-month tour in Mosul, and asking him, "Is this guy for real? Is he aware of how stupid he looks and sounds right now?" Dave just laughed and told me this was his usual behavior, and he just shrugged it off. I would do the same, but not after getting a good laugh first. The patients were gone in one hour, and they did not go back to Germany on that plane.

Later that day, we were informed that the Eighty-sixth CSH suffered the first death of one of its own. I fully expected us to endure several casualties from the nonstop rocket onslaught of a few weeks prior, but now one of our soldiers in Baghdad had apparently just killed himself. I did not know the story behind it, but I did know that he routinely led the Gospel service every Sunday at the chapel down in Baghdad; I was confident he went to be with the Lord. He had just been reassigned a couple of months prior to a different area, but he was still a part of the unit. He was always very helpful and cordial to me.

Who knew what caused him to make that terrible decision. A poem I found written on one of the bathroom stall doors in Mosul seemed appropriate at the time. I still have no idea who the author is, but when thinking back on the carnage, pain, and suffering I had witnessed and the destruction I had yet to face, I think it is very appropriate:

I knew a simple soldier boy
Who grinned at life in empty joy
Slept soundly through the lonesome dark
And whistled early with the lark
In winter trenches cowed and glum
With crumps and lice and lack of rum
He put a bullet through his brain
And no one spoke of him again
You smug faced crowds with kindling eye
Who cheer when soldier lads march by
Sneak home and pray you never know
The hell where youth and laughter go.

— Author Unknown

Much of my remaining time in Mosul was quiet. However, my usual black cloud did indeed follow me to northern Iraq, as an elderly Iraqi man was shot in the back by our forces as he made an aggressive move toward them. The bullet wound tracked straight through his liver, trashing it, along with his colon and kidney in the process. He arrived to the ER with severely low blood pressure and in obvious shock from blood loss. I placed a femoral central line into his right groin, and we pushed several units of blood into him. I then rotated up to his head and secured his airway by intubating him. I then noticed he had a small pneumothorax, or collapsed lung, on the right side and placed a chest tube into it to correct the problem.

Our surgeons then took him to the operating room and removed at least half of his mangled liver. He was placed in the ICU and continued to bleed during the night, and he required all the blood products we had in the small hospital. At 2:00 AM, soldiers from our FOB were called in for a whole blood drive, and while he continued to receive unit after unit of blood, the bleeding just would not stop. After several days and hundreds of units of blood later, he finally died. Hello, black cloud!

My good friend from residency, Dr. Dave Kaylor, was currently serving as the regimental surgeon with the Third Armored Cavalry Regiment in Mosul. It was the identical job to the one I had with the Second Cavalry Regiment, although I did not deploy overseas when serving with them. One day he picked me up and drove me around FOBs Diamondback and Marez. Hills of the brown, familiar landscape of Iraq laid under and around FOB Marez, making it a picturesque scene as I looked out to the southwest. Large electrical towers could be seen running off into the sunset, similar to the ones we had back home. The rolling, treeless hills with electrical lines stretching as far as I could see actually reminded me of the western United States, without the green grass of course! We drove by motor pool after motor pool of tanks, Bradley fighting vehicles, Humvees, and MRAPs. It was quite a display of military might, especially for someone used to living in the very nonmilitary Green Zone. We finally stopped at his regiment's TOC to get a tour.

It was impressive, and I even caught a twinge of sadness when thinking that I did not deploy with my cavalry regiment, realizing I could have been part of a fighting force with a similar setup. That twinge was very short however, when I suddenly snapped back to reality and realized that I was much happier getting thumped working at the CSH instead of working on PowerPoint presentations like I used to do as a regimental surgeon! We then came back for burgers and hot dogs at the hospital and sat around smoking cigars and reminiscing about the times we had when we were together at Fort Hood. It was a great day away from the hospital.

The news from Baghdad became more disheartening. One of our ICU nurses apparently had developed quite a relationship with a local Iraqi man. As I had mentioned before, we were always around the local population, with them working with us in the hospital and living around us in the Green Zone. Apparently, she was even going over to his residence and riding in his car! I am sure she was falling in love with her Middle Eastern beau and was surprised when the U.S. government intervened. They had been monitoring communications and discovered that the Iraqi boyfriend was planning to kidnap her and take her over to the bad guys. Could you imagine how bad that would be? What was she thinking? Sometimes it is unbelievable to me how stupid people can be!

I also had bittersweet news coming from home. Laura and I had just celebrated our tenth wedding anniversary, and we were so excited to be going on a cruise to celebrate when I got to go home in a few weeks. She had also enrolled our fourteen-month-old daughter Avery in gym classes, and they were having a lot of fun together. I could not wait to get home to them! However, on the sad side Laura told me that Houston, my trusted beagle of ten years, was getting older. He was beginning to go deaf and show signs of old age. I knew his getting older and breaking down was inevitable, but he was the first dog I had ever owned that actually loved me more than someone else, and even though he was just a stupid animal, I missed him more than I ever thought I could.

Several weeks later, my time in Mosul was coming to end as Jason Cohen and Sam Matta loaded on a C-130 and began working in my direction. They said they had a good flight, other than having to be rapidly loaded onto the plane only to sit for two hours without the engines or air conditioning on while wearing full body armor to wait for some of Gen. Petraeus's staff to arrive and load. I was excited to leave a few days later and go back to what I knew best, Baghdad ER. The last week in Mosul had been interesting as we had taken a few casualties in our Special Forces community locally, the latest of which resulted in two soldiers showing up with extremity gunshot wounds a night before I was scheduled to leave. The next day, I noticed the task force's Stryker vehicles cruising by and rolling into the city. This marked the first time I had seen them go during daylight hours, as they truly did own the night when it came to combat operations. I figured they had found a high-value target, likely a local Al-Qaeda leader, somewhere in the city and were trying to strike while they had the opportunity, even without their usual cover of darkness.

We did have a guy injured in a similar way to the injury that started the mayhem in Somalia in 1993, the incident that inspired the book and movie *Blackhawk Down*. That started when a fast-roping U.S. Army

Ranger free-fell and injured his spine, marking the first injury in a battle that would leave eighteen soldiers dead and seventy-three wounded in the war-torn streets of the African city. Over five hundred Somalis were killed in the battle. Like the battle of Mogadishu, a few nights prior I cared for a nineteen-year-old Army Ranger who was fast-roping from a Blackhawk and free-fell down to the ground. Fast-roping is a procedure used by the Special Forces community to drop from helicopters to the ground rapidly, dropping down a long rope from the bird to the ground. They jump to the rope and slide down, controlling their descent speed with their bodies. He lost control and hit the ground hard, breaking his tibia in the process. However this time, unlike in Somalia, our forces owned the streets as well as the air, and they were able to get vehicles to him and load him quickly without him becoming trapped in the city without the firepower to evacuate him. Informing him that he would be sent to Germany, he became frustrated and tried as hard as he could to figure out how long it would be until he could get back into the fight and rejoin his brothers.

A vehicle-borne IED killed three soldiers from the Third Armored Cavalry Regiment during this time as well, and their bodies were flown to our mortuary affairs team collocated with the hospital. Dr. Danielle Bird, a neonatologist who specialized in neonatal critical care, was the on-call physician and had to go to the morgue to pronounce the soldiers deceased. Unfortunately, it was the first time she had to deal with the carnage and death of our guys, and it was not easy for her. I wish she did not get the call and that I would have done it, just to spare her having to suffer through the event. But it was her turn, and I guess everyone had to get at least some exposure to the horrors of war while they were there.

An Angel Flight ceremony took place the next day, and almost the entire hospital watched at the flight line to pay their respects to the fallen heroes. Instead of our procedures involving Blackhawks in Baghdad, in Mosul an air force C-130 pulled up and the regiment held a ceremony before they were loaded onto the plane. The leadership of the regiment was present and conducted the procedure, and it was reported to me as very somber and touching. I could not bring myself to go, as I had seen so much death since my arrival that my defense was to block it out. The death of a soldier was much less frequent in Mosul, so naturally, the ceremony was a bigger deal for everyone. Unfortunately, for those of us in Baghdad, it was just part of everyday life.

Just before I left Mosul to head back to Baghdad, I was informed that the soldier who survived the 95 percent burns to his body, the one who touched me so, had just died in the burn center in San Antonio, Texas. After numerous surgeries, and the amputation of three of his four limbs, he finally succumbed to infection and passed away. The news brought tears to my eyes, as I still have never been touched so much by a patient in my career. I just have to remember that he got the chance to go home and see his wife, child, and family before he died. We gave him that much, a chance to say good-bye. As depressed as I became about his death, I rejoice to this day and thank God that he was able to say good-bye. One of my colleagues planned to visit the gravesite of each soldier he pronounced dead in Iraq at some point in his life. After several months, he lost track, and I guess he gave up on the idea. Likewise, my goal was to go see this kid when I got back, but now I had to find something else for my focus.

I did learn that the city of Mosul encompassed the ancient Biblical city of Nineveh. On overhead maps, I could see the walls of the historic township in downtown Mosul, many of which were apparently still intact. In Genesis 10:11, it mentions that Nimrod, a descendant of Noah, founded the city. Later, in the book of Jonah, chapter three speaks of the prophet Jonah's travel to the city to warn them of God's impending wrath for their sins. According to the chapter, after the message they repented, and God spared the city of his wrath. These writings, compared with the monastery I had toured, sure gave an amazing history to this place, even if the place was a crap-hole at the present! I would like to think it was not a hot, dusty, and downright miserable place back in Biblical times, but it sure seemed to be when I was there.

I would miss some aspects of Mosul. The Internet connection was better, and I was able to webcam with Laura and even got a chance to talk with my mom for a few minutes. The best part was getting to see Avery on the webcam, and I so enjoyed watching her over the Internet. When I would raise my hands in the air on the camera, sometimes she would mimic my actions—the same with clapping my hands. It was the first interaction I had with my fourteen-month-old daughter in almost nine months, and I enjoyed it very much. I knew I would miss our reservist orthopedist, Cpt. Dave Sheppard, who was planning to take some antiworming medicine as he headed home to be sure and "get Iraq out of his system" after his ninety-day tour. I also would miss the Saturday night grilled hamburgers and hot dogs by Matt McDonald. But I gladly turned the pager over to Jason Cohen and looked forward to another great day of C-130 travel to my "home" in Baghdad, somewhat refreshed from my month-long change of pace in Mosul.

A busy trauma room

Back in Baghdad

July 2008

I was thrilled to be back in Baghdad! It was quite the trip getting there, and although a patient met me with burns to 55 percent of his body and in bad shape soon after my arrival, I was happy to see all of the team I had the privilege to work with during the first eight months of my deployment. As I flew in, I even noticed Ann Gockley, one of our outstanding nurses, had listed my name up on the EMT board as one of the patients coming on the transfer flight from Balad. Everyone was excited, and I got a lot of hugs, but I must admit it was a long trip back!

I was scheduled to fly from Mosul to Baghdad International Airport on July 1, and I arrived at 7:15 AM with my bags packed as I had been directed. Lugging my gear to the airport terminal from the CSH in Mosul, I sat for about six hours until we were finally notified that our flight was cancelled due to sandstorms in the Baghdad area. I checked back into the CSH and waited two more days for the next flight. On July 3, I was notified that I could catch a flight to Balad Air Force Base/FOB Anaconda, set to leave in three hours. I grabbed my gear, and on my way out I stopped by our movement personnel to get manifested on the Balad to Baghdad nightly patient transfer run as an extra. After waiting on the tarmac for a while, we were finally allowed to walk to the back of the hot-loading C-130. When approaching these planes from the rear, the prop wash hits you hard about one hundred yards behind the loading ramp with air that feels like it has to be at least 150 degrees. Combining that with the 110 temperatures outside made for long walk to the plane!

Our flight made it to Balad uneventfully. Sgt. Little and I immediately tried to fly on the regular Blackhawk shuttle service called Catfish Air directly from the terminal, but we were told that it was a three-day wait to catch a bird down to Baghdad due to the backlog created by the sandstorms. Flagging down an air force guy in a pickup and catching a ride over the hospital, we checked with the patient movement guys there to see if we would have better luck. Discovering there was not room for the two of us, they housed us in the hospital, and we were set to catch a ride the next night. There was only one problem.

Out of clothes, patience, and time to get back to cover the ER, we found ourselves just two hours away from stealing a ride on the patient movement bird when the guy who regulated the movement of patients throughout Iraq stepped up to the desk and tried to get a ride as well. I do not know where he came from, but he happened to be in Balad. I had met with him before as we routinely fought over patient movement in Iraq, me from my clinical position and he from an administrative standpoint. I knew he would throw a fit if he became aware we had weaseled our way onto one of "his" flights, especially knowing that Sgt. Little was not a direct hands-on patient-care person. I figured I could talk my way into staying on the flight, telling him I need to get to the ER in Baghdad to work, but I did not think Sgt. Little would be so lucky. I quickly got Sgt. Little to disappear until right before flight time, and when the birds arrived, he stepped right up and we walked on without saying a word! I am not sure if he ever figured out we were stowaways, but we did not give him the chance until it was too late. Arriving on our CSH's landing zone that night, I felt a huge sigh of relief to finally be home.

Several big events had occurred since I left for Mosul. I have already written about the suicide of one of our members, as well as the nurse getting caught by the FBI dating a local and being the target of a kidnapping plan. A few other things had occurred:

1) One of our soldiers physically assaulted another, attempting to choke her right at the front desk of the hospital. They were dating, and he was sent home for psychological issues.

2) On a different tone, a soldier came in with about 30 percent burns to his body from a generator accident. He was awake and alert, and upon speaking with our burn surgeon, he asked, "Sir, how f***ed up am I?" The surgeon's response was classic gallows' humor, as he replied, "Oh, I'd say about medium f***ed up." The soldier laughed and apparently did very well.

3) The patient census was still low compared to our previous several months.

There were a few other issues as well, but those were the major events. The good news was the rockets were still not flying, and the cease-fire was holding true.

The day I arrived back from Mosul, Laura sent me a framed picture of Avery posing for her twelve-month photo. She was so beautiful, and I really enjoyed showing off my kiddo to every one in the ER! Also, my official get-out-of-the-army date was June 30, 2008, so even though I was still stuck in Iraq, I began telling everyone that I was now a civilian and had been released from the army last week. I told them I was now a contractor for the defense department, so they tripled my salary like the other civilians.

After a week in Baghdad, I was angry again and ready to confront almost every surgeon, anesthesiologist, and command element in the hospital. While violence in Iraq remained low, we received several soldiers early in the week who had rolled over an IED in their Stryker as it detonated through the bottom of the vehicle. Having seen so many of these types of injuries over the past nine months, it was becoming much easier to figure out what happened by looking at the nature of the wounds. One solider lost both of his legs and unfortunately died despite us giving him everything we had. Another suffered extensive lower-extremity injuries. One of them had his foot pushed up the shaft of his tibia, almost in the manner of a fireman sliding down a pole, only in this instance, the foot slid up the leg and the tibia ended up sticking out the bottom of the foot through what was left of his boot. This injury pattern usually told us that the blast came through the floor of the vehicle from a bomb buried under the road. The next day, we did CPR for a good while on a little girl who fell in a pond or water source of some sort. We got her heart beating again, but she died the next day in the ICU. Even with violence down overall, death still did not escape the clutches of Baghdad ER.

I also cared for a very frustrating snakebite case during my first week as well. A four-year-old Iraqi girl was apparently bitten by a saw-scaled viper, a snake similar to the vipers in the United States yet with much more toxicity in their venom. Her father took her to an Iraqi hospital, where she received an unknown dose of antivenin, or antidote. There are many types of antivenins in the world, and each is effective against a particular group of snakes. I had no idea if the correct type was used or even available at that hospital. She apparently sat in the hospital for four days and progressively became worse before her father decided to take her to the front gate of the American base in his area. She was then brought into the American facility where the surgeons performed a highly controversial procedure where they cut the skin and muscle on the leg to decrease the pressure in the tissues, in theory saving the tissue from ischemia, or lack of blood flow. Afterward, they flew her to us and into our EMT.

Upon arrival, she was ill-appearing and had suffered from copious blood loss from her wound site. Blood was beginning to ooze from her gums and other areas as well as the snake venom had thinned her plasma over the course of four days. I placed a call back to Fort Hood, Texas, and got in touch with Dr. Missy Givens, a toxicologist and friend of mine, for any words of wisdom as she was specially trained to deal with snake envenomations. Heeding her advice, we gave the child sixteen vials of anti-venin specific for saw-scaled vipers over the course of the next eighteen hours, with the first dose in the ER. Her blood thinning began to resolve overnight, and she was sedated and placed on a ventilator for respiratory support. During the night, she developed kidney failure, and our ICU docs worked hard to get her transferred to a local hospital that could perform life-saving dialysis for a child.

Once an accepting Iraqi physician was obtained, she was transferred to the accepting hospital, where an all-too-common for Iraq event occurred. The accepting physician changed his mind and refused admittance. I am not sure if he wanted the money up front from the girl's father or what, but she was not allowed inside the building and stayed in the back of the ambulance. Phone calls to recoordinate care were placed, and her oxygen supply began to run low for her ventilator. During the cantankerous process of trying to get her inside, she ran out of oxygen and died in the ambulance outside the Iraqi hospital. How tragic for her to turn the corner, require a procedure that we could not perform, have everything set up to help her get better, and then have someone change their mind only to result in her demise. Anyone who says people cannot have access to care in the U.S. needs to open their eyes and see what medical care is like in a Third World country like Iraq.

We also had other injuries that week. In my career, I had never seen a fractured testicle before, but we had three in one day! The first patient was an Iraqi gentleman who apparently got in a fight with a goat and lost. He came in with an open scrotum and a bloodied testicle inside. I cannot say why this man's scrotum was involved with a goat. A few hours later, an unfortunate soldier came in who was tending to a fire, apparently burning refuse. Someone got the great idea to throw an aerosolized can of compressed air into the flame, only to have it shoot out and tag him in the right side of his scrotum. Ouch! What bad luck for him! The third patient was a bad guy who was beaten severely by the Iraqi National Police. They left their mark by bloodying up his feet, side, and leaving his genitals in a bruised, bloodied mess. Luckily, our urologist, Col. Richard Stack, was on the "ball" and was able to surgically repair all three guys.

We had many other interesting patients over the previous several months, like our dermatologist Maj. Scott Henning's favorite, "Gen. Itchy Balls," an Iraqi general who was in his office every month with chronic itching to his genitals. Numerous salves and ointments had not done the trick, and Scott said the biggest issue was that the guy needed to stop scratching and touching himself. For a potential cure this time, he brought in a female translator for the exam on purpose, trying to shame the guy into ceasing to touch himself, as he had apparently embarrassed the clinic waiting room by putting his hand down his pants and scratching himself incessantly in front of the other patients. Maybe that behavior was normal in Iraq, and these guys did have some strange customs.

I was now ten months into my tour and was set to go on leave in just about three weeks. Time could not move fast enough! When our current group of surgeons, anesthesia providers, and other specialists arrived six months before, we bent over backwards to be flexible and give them a say as to how we worked trauma and similar cases. Sure, we had been there three months and had it figured out, but in the grand scheme of things, three months was not that long. By this point, we had been there three times that long, so we were not going to put up with crap anymore. During the first week the new guys were there, and while they were overlapping with the previous crew, one of our surgeons made a snide comment to me, and uncharacteristically for me I yelled at him. Later, one of our anesthesiologists apparently came down to the ER and caused some confusion and other issues. Upon hearing what happened, I stormed down the hallway and started yelling at the chief surgeons and anesthesiologist. I was sure they were furious with me, but they were leaving in two weeks after their six-month tour ended, and I told them we were preparing to fight a whole new group of rotators as they attempted to take over. We were not very passive six months prior and did not give the new group much room when they wanted to take over our ER during trauma, and we decided to give the next group even less. At times I had to be inappropriate and a jerk just to get my bluff across, but mostly I think I just needed to go home for a break.

While the trauma volume continued to be low, plenty of interesting and amazing events were still taking place around us every day. Maj. Hamilton Le, one of our six-month rotating general surgeons, departed us to redeploy home. The night before he left, as we were saying our good-byes, he said something to me that I have not forgotten, "We've had some crazy times and seen some crazy patients over the past six months, but hopefully we saved more than we let die." I think that summed up our entire deployment.

The hospital had been buzzing over the past few days, as Senator and Democratic presidential nominee Barak Obama was in Baghdad and was scheduled to come by the hospital. All of the administrators were anxious, practicing the tour and walkthrough time after time. Deb Chappel was even given a script to memorize! The day before, while walking in the IZ, Garrett Gore and I saw two Chinook helicopters landing while being escorted by two Marine Cobra gunships, and we both assumed that Obama and his delegation were on board. Later, at the PX parking lot, we witnessed six Blackhawks fly into the LZ, followed moments later by about fifteen SUVs speeding out, marking his likely return to the Green Zone after flying around Baghdad. But about three hours before his scheduled arrival, his visit was cancelled abruptly. The mood around the CSH lightened somewhat, just because our command finally relaxed and we were able to start acting normally again.

We were not given an explanation for the cancellation, but I was sure he and the two senators traveling with him had a very tight schedule to keep on their whirlwind tour of Iraq. A few hours later, just after hearing that we had casualties coming our direction, our guard at the front gate stated into their radio, "The eagle has landed." Not exactly realizing what that meant, we all looked up to see Sen. Obama and his entourage coming through the main doors underneath the American flag and "Baghdad ER" sign. Having been instructed by our command not to shake hands with the VIPs, I was taken aback for a moment when he walked straight through the doors then came right up to me and shook my hand. He asked my name, what I did, and where I was from before moving on down the line to some of the others. After a quick presentation and tour, he was led from the EMT to other parts of the hospital. He was taller than I had seen him on television, a bit skinnier, and even had a few gray hairs on his head. After seeing what being president of the United States did to Bill Clinton's and George Bush's hair, I bet he will have many more gray hairs before his time in office is done! I actually am not a big fan of President Obama, but it was still fun to get to meet the soon-to-be president.

Many transitions and changes were occurring in the CSH. Our group of six-month rotators, comprised of our surgeons, anesthesia providers, and various other physicians, were all departing for home after their 180-day tours. The war in Afghanistan was accelerating, according to the media. Violence in Iraq was down to 2004 levels. The news focus seemed to indicate there would be further reductions of American troops and a likely transition to a focus on Afghanistan. The medevac flight crews, with call signs "Medicineman," "Ventilator," "Crucial," and "Morphine," were being replaced with "Galvanized," "Oasis," and "Eagle Dustoff" as their combat brigades were sent home. New medics were continuing to rotate into our ER. It was a different country than the one we had arrived at almost a year earlier.

A few days earlier, we had been called to the front gate for a triage of a host-nation patient. An Iraqi colonel had pulled his brother from the Baghdad Neurosurgical Hospital, procured an Iraqi ambulance, and driven him to the CSH for us to help. The only problem was that his brother had been shot in the left side of the head, execution style, and was dying with no hope for survival. His brainstem was the only part of his brain keeping his heart beating and lungs breathing, so we discussed our options. Behind us, the Iraqi colonel began yelling and became extremely agitated upon learning of the futility of his trip. He pulled out his pistol and slammed it on the street out front of the hospital. Our guard force quickly and skillfully took care of the situation while we brought the dying man into our specialty room, realizing that we could not just let him die on Haifa Street in front of our hospital. I ordered a morphine drip for him to be pain-free and comfortable while waiting for death to arrive.

We had four new medics rotating with us at the time, and the difference between them and our trauma-hardened and experienced medics was incredibly obvious just by the look on their faces. I explained to them why we could not do anything to help the man and how we were providing comfort measures only. He vomited some, and a couple of the kid's faces brightened as they thought maybe it was a sign that I was wrong, maybe we could save him after all. But I unfortunately had to explain away their hope. I told them not to stay in the room unless they had to, but all four remained with him and watched a man die for the first time in their lives. Overall, they did okay and would be fine—after all, we were all the same way just nine months before.

A few days later, one of our best medics, Sgt. Thomas Clise, was notified that we were about to receive six urgent surgical patients who had been injured in a bomb blast or IED. At that time, many people from the CSH were lined up outside to show their respects for a soldier who had died earlier in the day in our EMT from an IED. The Angel Flight helicopters were coming in soon, and Sgt. Clise hightailed it out to our landing zone where they were awaiting the Angel Flight, as our EMT personnel had to abort the tribute and snap back into business mode to accept the next wave of casualties. As he sprinted by the command sergeant major, the CSM asked him if he had an update on the Angel Flight. Clise told him no, but casualties were coming in, and he ran to notify our personnel.

The CSM actually had the audacity to become offended because Clise "did not show him proper respect" by not researching and providing an update about the Angel Flight. Sgt. Clise was later forced to give two different presentations on proper military respect and bearing as punishment, and eventually he was sent away to a smaller unit. Upon discovering this story, I flew off the handle, but I was told to stay out of it because our hospital commander would not support me if I went against the CSM. This was one of several examples of how the command sometimes did not understand what we did. If casualties were incoming, we had jobs to do, from our docs down to our medics. There was no time to research situations and "give proper military" respect. I even had to close the doors to the ER at one point to keep a command-guided VIP tour out while we were treating traumas. They were well intentioned, but I do not think they truly understood our mission at times.

———

It was the last week of July 2008, and it would be exactly eight days until I left to go home for eighteen days of relaxation. It had been a little over ten months since I had seen Laura and Avery, and the days dragged slowly by. I had warned Laura and my family that I would be in Kuwait for two or three days in the August heat before I made it back home, so I would likely look and smell pretty rough by the time I make it back to Arkansas!

Simultaneously, most of the physicians in the hospital had changed over yet again, and the docs who had been there six months were leaving to go home. We were beginning to break in the new crew. The ER leadership had been pretty rowdy in our meetings, partially in a show of frustration as we watched *another* group of docs leave before us, and partly to get our bluff on the new crew. Up until this point, they had been quiet during trauma resuscitations and for the most part did not get in our way. The day before, while working on a bad guy who was shot in the neck by the Iraqi Army, one of the new trauma surgeons came in and was actually pleasant to deal with. One morning, in our daily morning report, we reported that we had one death in the EMT overnight, to which Marti Roellig quickly stated to the group, "But I didn't kill him!" All of the fresh new faces looked at her in surprise and then looked at me in horror when I answered, "Yeah, it was me. I killed him." The man did die on my shift, but he was a host-nation person who had amputations of two extremities and severe head trauma. He was dead when he came in, and I led the resuscitation to get his heart beating again, but even after twelve units of blood and multiple life-sustaining medications, we realized his head injuries were too severe for him to live. I obviously did everything I could to keep the man alive, so I did not kill him of course, but I did get interesting looks from the new crew when I said that in morning report! That would break them in nicely to Baghdad!

As our latest group of physicians left for home, it was a somber event, as I would miss many new friends I had made. I enjoyed watching movies with guys like Bill Ralston, Steve Svoboda, Mike Myer, and Mark Aierstock. I also knew that I would long for my rooftop cigar-smoking buddies like Tony Allen, Jon Stineman, and Scott Henning. However, just like six months prior, we would have some guys leave we would not miss, like our favorite surgeon who liked to jump in front of everyone, performing rectal exams that were not required on patients who were not expecting them. I was sure we would have some of both with the new guys as well.

First it was Guitar Hero, and later Rock Band became a staple of Baghdad ER. One of our medics, Sgt. Justin Ubert, had an Xbox 360 system complete with two guitars, a drum set, and a microphone. Our nurses and medics played it in the break room whenever they got a chance, and when I joined in, I tried to figure out some sort of rhythm while playing the guitar or the drums. Usually, I successfully kept alive and did not get my band booed off the stage by the raucous crowd in the game, but each time I tried to sing it was not pretty. I quickly began to face reality: God did not give me any musical ability, even for video games. But that was fine—it was fun to play, even if I was terrible!

At one point, I mentioned to our crew that I was writing a book about our times in Baghdad, and somehow the idea morphed into *Baghdad ER: The Movie*. I was not sure how that would work, but our guys went on to create a long list of famous actors and actresses to play each of our parts. I was flattered at first to find my role had been assigned to Brad Pitt, but then disappointed to see whoever suggested that was overruled, and some other skinny, goofy guy I did not know was substituted in Pitt's place. However, later my role was assigned to the comedian Jeff Foxworthy, and while I do not think he is the heartthrob that Brad Pitt is, I think he is funny, so I figured that would work. The cast of characters assembled was quite noteworthy, with actors from Harrison Ford playing Col. Rowe to Farmer Fran from *The Waterboy* playing the role of Sfc. Richard. It looked the star power of the movie would cost millions and millions of dollars to cast, so we would not make many proceeds from the film unfortunately due the expense of the cast.

On an unfortunately more depressing note, a few days before an eleven-month-old boy was brought to our back door by an American unit. He had a condition known as hydrocephalus, caused by the inability of the fluid inside the brain to flow up and down the spinal column in its usual manner. This anomaly resulted in a head the size of about two full-sized basketballs put together from front to back. I had never seen a human's head this large, especially when attached to a tiny eleven-month-old, malnourished body. The child's eyes were both rolled downward and sunken into their sockets, resulting from the pressure in the brain squeezing on the cranial nerves controlling eye movement. He had a large protrusion in the midline of his lower back, a sure sign of a myelocele, a condition from birth causing the paralysis of his legs and associated with the problems causing his enlarged head.

His mother and father had taken him to the neurosurgical hospital in Baghdad, and they were told a shunt could be placed to drain the fluid from the child's head, shrinking it to a normal size. However, they demanded $10,000 before they were willing to perform the much-needed surgery. I knew the poor child would require multiple surgeries and would have a very tough time surviving, even if he resided in the United States. I gave a quick call to our pediatrician Mike Mulraney, and unfortunately he concurred with my thoughts and could not assist.

The boy's mother cried when I gave her the news, and my heart broke as the father begged me for $4,000, saying that he could come up with the rest to get the surgery done. I referred the family to NIAC, the National Iraqi Assistance Center, an agency specializing in these cases. Unfortunately, I also knew this child would require far too many surgeries and most likely would not survive despite everyone's best efforts, so I seriously doubted that NIAC would take him. Tears flowed as we watched helplessly as the mother wrapped her blanket around the child's enormous head, and they were escorted to the army unit's vehicle waiting to take them back to the gate.

I also had a poor Iraqi Army soldier in who had been shot earlier in the month by a sniper. Both of his eyes had been enucleated, or removed by the ophthalmologists at the air force hospital in Balad. He was blind and did not have the family support at home to help him eat or care for himself.

I was not sure what would happen to the man; he signed up in the Iraqi Army, was gravely wounded while fighting for his country, and afterward his country apparently had nothing to offer him. What a terrible tragedy, but yet another depressing and harsh reality of war.

Marti posing with six of our amazing nurses

Eighteen Days in Paradise

After a little over nine months in Iraq, and exactly ten months and six days after kissing my wife and daughter good-bye, I began my journey home for leave. Sitting in the terminal at Baghdad International Airport, I saw soldiers from all over Iraq sleeping on the floor, under chairs, on seats, and in every nook and cranny waiting on their chance to see their loved ones back home. I was allotted three days to make it home—sometimes it took more, sometimes less, but my trip was going well. Our flight to Kuwait was pushed back by four hours, and I spent some time sitting in the BIAP terminal reflecting over the past weeks.

In the month of July 2008, only eleven soldiers were killed in Iraq, the lowest monthly total since the war began. Actually, only three of those were combat related, with six being related to accidents and such and two being the bodies of the soldiers who had been kidnapped the year before. Of course, that was still eleven deaths too many, but compared to what we had been used to seeing, it was indeed great news. However, I did have a typical Baghdad ER sendoff when I headed out the door, with four unfortunate Iraqi women flown to us from a house fire. A gunshot wound (GSW) to the abdomen arrived at the same time, so Marti and Jason took one of the burns and the GSW in the trauma room and I took three burns in the back. Moving to the first patient, I witnessed a middle-aged Iraqi woman rolling around on the bed in pain, moaning and crying for help. The nurse and I quickly estimated her to be about 70 percent burned, and we both knew what that meant. I moved to the next bed to find a slightly younger woman lying on the bed with 60 percent burns, and I once again realized she would inevitably die. I rotated to the third bed to see a ten-year-old girl with about 30 percent burns to her face and extremities. I tried to make the women comfortable with morphine and let them die peacefully or transfer to the Iraqi hospitals, whichever came first. The little girl with 30 percent burns had a chance, so I intubated her and we moved her rapidly to the ICU to begin her long-term care. We knew she might still die in a month or two once she was transferred to the Iraqi health care system, but I was thrilled to be able to give someone a chance to live.

Later in the day, when talking with Deb Chappel, we thought about all the people we had placed on morphine drips and watched die. I estimated I had done that personally over twenty times by that point, and I told her that it bothered me incredibly. I had to remember there was nothing we could do for these patients, as they were burned too badly or blown up too much. Would I wake up a year later in the middle of the night, seeing their faces, hearing their moans, and question if I had done everything I could? Time would tell. While waiting at the heliport to leave the war zone, it dawned on me that for the first time in over nine months, I would not be facing death for a few weeks. I let my guard down for the first time, and the harsh reality of my job set in. Flying over the city in a Blackhawk from the International Zone to the airport, staring out the window I felt numb; I was leaving it behind. As I sat in the terminal, I could feel a huge weight on my shoulders, the weight of death, suffering, and agony. Did I make the right decisions? Should I have let so many people die? Did I really have a say in the matter? Objectively, I knew and understood these questions had an obvious answer; we were in a combat zone and could not save everyone. But would this weight, this feeling of immense pain I felt inside, ever go away? I still feel to this day that I made the right decisions regarding my patients; I made ethical decisions, and I did not let anyone die without pain relief. But why do I still feel at times that I need to ask God forgiveness for what I have done?

Talking to Laura about the realities of war a few days before, she made a profound statement to me, saying, "Todd, you have to realize that where you are at is not reality; reality is being home with Avery and me." It took several days for that statement to sink in because Baghdad ER was the only reality I could imagine. I seemed to wake up angry every day. One day, I would be angry at our surgeons, especially the new group that had just arrived. One of them was very egotistical, telling us he was from Harvard on a daily basis and telling us how to do trauma. We had been doing it for nine months with a 95 percent U.S. survival rate. He had never deployed before. We really did not care what he had to say. A couple of days prior, we had a patient with an amputated leg, and this particular surgeon came to the ER to lay eyes on him, and then he had the audacity to go eat dinner before taking the patient emergently to the operating room! It was the worst move I had ever seen in medicine. The ER doc covering at the time just put on more tourniquets and gave the patient more blood. Finally, he sent the patient to the OR without the surgeon. I reported it up the chain of command, and this particular individual was sent out to a remote FOB for the rest of his tour. I think his punishment should have been more severe, and I was embarrassed that this guy called himself a physician. It was horrible.

On another note, as more and more of our medics were taken away by the command to fill administrative positions, like secretary for the commander and command sergeant major, I began writing risk management documents that were reported to our headquarters. I did not want to make waves, but I could not let our EMT become less safe because one of the senior NCOs of the hospital wanted a medic to check his email for him. My prayer was that the eighteen days of leave I was about to get would remind me of what I had to look forward to back home, the life I would lead after just four more months of deployment once I returned to Baghdad. I prayed for the life that would be reality and that kept me going.

Just before my departure, two notable events occurred:

1) Our dentist decided to go to one of the many parties in the IZ one

night, so she took off her uniform, put on civilian clothes, and got drunk. Of course, we were not allowed to drink alcohol there, but I guess she did not worry about that. To make matters worse, when confronted by the local military police, she resisted arrest and fought with them. As the MPs were struggling to get her handcuffed, she actually bit one of them! How great is that? A dentist bit a police officer. We all chuckled under our breath as she was brought in to the EMT in handcuffs one night about 2:00 AM for a legal blood alcohol draw.

2) While several of us were at the range qualifying with our weapons, the hospital prepared for a six-member group of congressmen and senators who were scheduled to come through and tour. Upon our return from the range, we walked into the ER and were greeted with a gigantic "BAGHDAD ER" sign hanging over the nurses' station. It jumped out like a billboard or a huge neon sign at a beer joint, and we all felt it was tacky, gaudy, and downright terrible. We were embarrassed to have it there, as it seemed to brag to everyone who entered that WE were special because we were Baghdad ER. I requested it be taken down, but I was told the commander and command sergeant major wanted it and I had no right to remove it from my own ER. As the head physician of the ER, did I not have any say in anything? Those guys did not work in the ER! I went to the colonel's office and told him it was terrible and requested it be removed. He came down, just five minutes before the delegates were to arrive, and let us take it down, much to the ire of our sergeant major. He pouted and went straight to my boss, Col. Rowe, and told him that I need to "be kept in line." I guess he really did feel I had no say as to what occurred in my ER, but Col. Rowe set him straight and let him know differently. The sign came down, and we won the battle.

With all of that said, Baghdad was still Baghdad. We were having a ceremony for Sam Matta's promotion from first lieutenant to captain, and while we were on the landing zone, an Australian vehicle resembling a Stryker came rolling in, just to turn around and drive out. Upon hearing the distinct engine of the vehicle rolling our direction, and then seeing the front end and two of the eight tires come around the corner, we began sprinting toward the ER expecting blown up and dead soldiers to come piling out like they had so many times in the past. The gunner of the vehicle saw the commotion and starting waving his arms and putting his hand across his throat in the universal stop signal, but it was too late. We all got a good laugh out of it, and we began to wonder if we would have flashbacks every time we see a Stryker in the future back home!

After mentally preparing for a long, sweaty journey home, my trip from the hospital all the way to Arkansas went flawlessly. Going on leave at the same time as our optometrist Cpt. Angie Baker, we waited in the terminal at Baghdad International Airport for the flight to Kuwait. After heading outside to check on my duffel bag, I walked back into the terminal to find one of the attendants finding me and saying, "Major Baker, you need to get on the plane right now! Where have you been? " I told him that our flight did not leave for several more hours and we had been sitting in the terminal. After discussing it at the R&R desk, I was informed that our flight to Kuwait had been cancelled. They had not told those of us on the flight that we had been bumped up to an earlier flight, and ten minutes of scrambling later found us walking up the back ramp of an air force C-17 jet.

This was my first experience on a C-17, and compared to a C-130, this was first-class travel! We sat in nice airline style seats and enjoyed our quick flight down to Ali Asalim Air Base in Kuwait. However, at the end of the flight the joy subsided somewhat as our pilots began performing the usual evasive maneuvers prior to coming in for landing. At one point in my life, I did not know that a large C-130 cargo plane could rotate almost 90 degrees onto its side, but my previous landing in Mosul taught me differently. Likewise, I quickly learned that a much, much larger C-17 could do similar turns. The feeling returned in my feet an hour or two after the flight, and we were bussed over to large terminal buildings and processed through.

We turned in our body armor and helmets, sat though several in-processing briefs, and only had to spend one night in the transient lodging in Kuwait. The next day we left Kuwait, and sixteen hours later we arrived in Dallas, Texas! The plane erupted in a cheer when the wheels touched down and the pilot announced our arrival back into the United States. While taxing down to our gate, the pilot pointed out the large airport fire trucks positioned on either side of our plane at 90-degree angles to us. As we drove between them, they shot water over the jetliner with their large water cannons, a gesture the pilots described as a "traditional heroes' welcome home."

As we departed the plane, we were taken to a walkway upstairs and separated from the passengers in the terminal below us until we had cleared customs. Everything was glassed in, and despite being separated from the crowds below, the hundreds of passengers waiting at their gates gave us a rousing standing ovation, beginning with the first and continuing until the last of us had passed through. I tried to fight back the tears of pride and joy as I walked through the terminal. After clearing customs, the welcome ceremony only grew. I picked up my duffel bag from the luggage belt and walked into a large room where an older woman greeted me dressed in red, white, and blue as she gave me a huge hug. She directed me into a room filled with approximately three hundred people lining an aisle cheering, shaking our hands, and welcoming us home.

I felt like a movie star or a professional athlete walking down the red carpet to glorious fanfare! One five- or six-year-old boy even stepped out into the pathway and saluted me. I stopped and saluted him back, and I continued to try to keep in the tears as I passed though the masses. Volunteers stepped up and handed us cell phones to call home once we reached the end of the receiving line, and then several more volunteers shuffled us onto busses where we were taken to our departing stations. It was an incredible welcome home and an event I will never forget!

The eighteen days of leave were spectacular. Laura and I took a cruise to the Caribbean for the ten-year wedding anniversary I missed in June, and I was able to get reacquainted with Avery. She obviously trusted and loved her mother much more than the strange man who had moved in for a few days, but we knew she would come around eventually. I was amazed at how much she had grown in ten months! We had the best time playing and watching her dance, and I believe my favorite part of the time home was sitting on the couch and giving her a bottle of milk every night. She would drink the bottle down and then drift off to sleep in my arms. It was so touching and one of the aspects of parenting for which I had always longed. Also, she was not sick, blown up, or even burned. She was just my little girl. I was not used to seeing children who were healthy. Most of the children I had touched over the previous eleven months were standing at death's doorstep or had already walked through. I could not wait to get home and let her fall asleep in my arms routinely! Laura and I grew much closer over those eighteen days as they were just what we needed. We both felt at the time—and still feel to this day—that our future would be so bright, and we just needed survive another four months to get started!

Eighteen days later, I was sitting in the terminal at the Dallas/Fort Worth International Airport waiting to manifest for my flight back to Iraq. A local USO volunteer took us to lunch prior to our departure, and I am still grateful to all of the volunteers who made my homecoming so special. It was nice to get to know my family again, but it was time to head back for a few more months in Baghdad ER. Four months seemed like nothing when considering that eleven were behind.

The sixteen-hour flight from Dallas to Germany to Kuwait was only a blur, as I slept most of the way thanks to Ambien. What I remember of our civilian flight crew was nice, although upon arrival in Kuwait, one of the stewardesses opened the door to the blistering August heat in Kuwait and gasped, "Oh my stars, it's so hot!" One of the soldiers on the plane behind her sarcastically said, "Thanks," and I felt bad for her as she had a very embarrassed look on her face. We were quickly and efficiently processed back into the system, and I only had to stay one night before loading onto a C-130 and flying back to Baghdad. While I did land in one of the worst seats on the plane, the dreaded wheel-well seat, I could not complain as we only had to wait at the airport forty-five minutes before a Blackhawk arrived to take us over to the IZ. Compared to all of the sitting around and waiting for days on flights that my EMT colleagues had been forced to do to get home, it was obvious that God truly blessed me with a smooth trip home and back from leave!

Back on the Ground

As I arrived back to the EMT, I noticed a few changes. The POW flag that we all loved so dearly had been put back up on the wall, sergeant major's opinion be damned I guess. I loved it! This dated back to the sign incident that took place before I left, as others in the hospital were finally beginning to stand up to the guy. Reportedly, the chain of links representing our number of days left in Iraq was back up in the ICU as well, after being removed by demand of the sergeant major. I found a pile of Beanie Babies that had several surgical changes to them in the EMT, leading me to learn that our medics wanted to practice their suturing skills. They put wings on lions, tiger heads on alligators, zebra bodies on fish, and so on. They all had a good time doing it, even if it did surprise people who passed by and saw them. I just hoped that none of the mutated toys fell into the hands of Iraqi children, or they may not know what to think about the Americans and our education!

I also found two brand-new SonoSite Turbo ultrasound systems sitting in the EMT, evidence that we had finally won the battle and received the critically required technology update. I knew they had been ordered before I left, but I did not know how many months it would take to get them. I quickly put them to use, using one to perform a lumbar puncture, or spinal tap, on a soldier in whom I had trouble finding the right spot. I contacted my good friend Ron Dickson at SonoSite and prepared to ship the life-saving Micromaxx ultrasound he had loaned us back to him. It was actually a depressing event to carry the battle-worn machine from the ER and prepare it for shipping; it certainly had been to hell and back for a piece of medical equipment. Despite its blood-stained screen, broken frame, and nonfunctioning buttons, it had helped to save the lives of countless Americans and Iraqis.

I also received a package of no less than five stethoscopes from the Littmann Corporation. I had contacted them earlier about my old trusty stethoscope, which had finally broken just before I left. Instead of only sending me a replacement, they sent me five scopes, all worth more than $200 or $300. I distributed them between Jason, Marti, Deb Chappel, and one of our medics who was planning to go on to PA school upon our return. What a great donation! My first Litttmann stethoscope lasted over ten years, and with this kind of service and support of our military, I will buy their products for the rest of my career.

While I was on leave, Jason Cohen had an article published in *Newsweek* magazine. It was printed just after I returned, and I read a wonderfully written saga about our ER's care for the soldier who came in after being hit by an IED who was a former classmate of Ann Gockley's. His words leaped from the page at the reader and conveyed the feeling of helplessness we all felt when these guys came in. Sure, we could save most of them, but sometimes God wanted them to come home right then. All we could do was try our best, cry our tears, and move on to the next patient. Jason's article brought out those feelings in many of us, and I could not imagine if that next patient coming through was someone I knew personally!

I received a gentleman from Peru who had suffered a heat stroke. He had been outside at the weapons range all day, and evidently had collapsed and become violently agitated. His rectal temperature had been registered at 108 degrees Fahrenheit, and he was carried into our ER on a stretcher, held down by four men. When we transferred him over to our trauma bed, it took six of us to hold him down as he thrashed, kicked, and clawed at us, reminding me of someone who was on a violent, out-of-control trip from cocaine or PCP. Being at the head of the bed, I reached down on either side of his ears and dug my fingertips around his jaw on both sides of his face. Leaning back and putting my weight into it forced him to keep his head down on the bed and not rise. I learned that trick when dealing with drunken soldiers during residency at Fort Hood, as people do not want to sit upright when their head and jaw are being pulled into the bed below them.

One of the medics who brought him to us successfully cannulated the external jugular vein in his neck, and after 20 mg of etomidate and 100 mg of succinylcholine, I intubated him and we safely were able to provide him care and cool him down. The next day, I learned the breathing tube had been removed and he was sitting up in bed eating breakfast and acting normally, and I joked with our ICU doctors that we would hear fighting and maybe even gunfire later in the day when he went crazy again. Evidently, he recovered perfectly, making this case a simple demonstration of how the human brain does not work well when the body is 108 degrees!

The day before, a cold front came through and made the weather much nicer. A small thundershower appeared, and even though the rain was soft and short-lived, the few cracks of thunder coming from the sky sent everyone scrambling to any bunker or building they could find, thinking the rockets were beginning to rain shrapnel down again. I said for months that my first Midwestern thunderstorm back home was going to freak me out, and everyone's response to the thunder showed me I would not be the only one with that reaction.

The night, several of us sat on the roof and smoked cigars as usual, but this time the temperature was a cool 95 degrees, and the slight breeze blowing felt wonderful. It was the equivalent to me of a 70-degree night back home. I do not think I remember a night that nice and cool in several months, and we could not get over having a cooling wind versus the blow-dryer wind we had become accustomed to. It reminded me of the days back in the winter and early spring when I would go upon the roof and read during the daytime. I had not been able to do that in a long time, but it was early September and that opportunity was only a month or so away! While sitting on the roof, a loud explosion startled us, and we began to run for cover before we realized that it was not a rocket but rather a car bomb in the red zone. That used to be a several-day-a-week occurrence, and it was nice to realize that building-shaking explosions did not seem to be a part of our daily lives like they were just a few months prior.

I still could not sleep two weeks after my return from the United States to Baghdad. I found myself lying awake all night until 5:00 am, tossing and turning before I could fall asleep. On the flip side, I had no problem sleeping after my night shifts, as rest during the daytime was coming very easily for me. My first thought was that my body was used to the time zone back home in Arkansas from my eighteen days of leave, but I had been in Iraq for two weeks; I should have been adjusted and back to the sleep patterns I had grown used to over the past year. I began relying on Ambien to sleep at night, and Provigil, a FDA-approved stimulant for shift work, to stay awake on my day shifts. I was sure our schedule of two twelve-hour day shifts followed by two twelve-hour night shifts had something to do with it, but we were stuck with that to keep the shifts even between the three ER docs. I was thrilled I had made it twelve months before my bad sleep habits caught up with me.

Our numbers began to pick up over the next week somewhat, and I participated in and led several major resuscitations of both U.S. and Iraqi personnel. A few days before, I cared for a seven-year-old Iraqi boy with third-degree burns to both his hands. We placed him in our back treatment room, only to find severe bruising and whelps all over his back and legs. The marks were linear and resembled lesions made when someone is beaten with a stick, rod, or other long, slender object. We continued to ask the child who did this to him, to which he consistently replied that his older brother had beaten him and then pushed him into a hot tub of water, resulting in the burns on his hands. The boy's father was present as well, and he backed up the story. Our surgeons operated on his hands, but unfortunately, I was sure he would return home to the same abusive brother once he was released, as the Iraqis have no Child Protective Services or social work system. I never caught the age of the older brother, but the impression I received was that he was around eleven or twelve years old. It sure seemed like the father could help him some; maybe this event would mark a turning point in the poor boy's living situation. That was all I could hope and pray for. Actually, I hoped it was not really the father abusing the boy.

Although we had been seeing a few more patients that week than the past two months, we did have one crazy day where no one came into the ER and got admitted to the hospital. We saw a few patients in the ER and sent them out, but usually most of our patients are quite ill, and our admission rate for the people we cared for was typically around 80 percent, a rare acuity level compared to the United States. However, that day, we had zero sick patients. Amazingly, our other site in Mosul had zero as well, although that was not necessarily a strange occurrence for them. I supposed that with all five of the surge combat brigades home by this point, we had twenty thousand fewer soldiers in our area to get sick or injured. I figured that fact, and the reported 80 percent decrease in violence over the past year, were contributing to our lower numbers, which of course made us happy.

The next morning I was awakened around 5:00 AM by the CRAM incoming mortar or rocket fire alert system, only for it to be a false alarm. Two hours later, I hit the ER, and we began to make up for the easy day we had enjoyed the day before when our day shift began with a soldier coming in who had collapsed. The flight medics were performing CPR on him en route, always an ominous sign. We placed him in bed one, and I quickly suctioned out the vomit from his mouth and airway and intubated him. We continued CPR for a good while, and despite shocking him, pushing epinephrine, atropine, and other cardiac medications, we finally gave up and I pronounced him dead. I am still not sure what made him collapse or what killed him. He was relatively young, and it was still hard to watch soldiers die, whether killed by a terrorist or natural causes.

An hour later, two Iraqi Army men came in after being hit by an IED, and I went to work on the more severely wounded one. He had massive trauma to the right side of his head, and it quickly became apparent that he was gone. We worked on him for a while, but to no avail. After a good two weeks, I had two deaths within an hour! That definitely reminded me of our earlier months over the past year. But death had not released its grip on our ER, and two hours later I found myself intubating and directing the resuscitation of yet another soldier. He had significant head injuries, and once again, despite our best efforts it was not to be. I did not reach my personal high of four deaths on one twelve-hour shift, but three was enough for me. Thank God that was it. The busy and fateful shift reminded us all how lucky we were that things had slowed down significantly, and it also reminded us once again how quickly life can be taken away.

The next day, I got a unique experience as our local army veterinarian brought in a large German Shepherd force protection dog for a CT scan. Apparently, he was having severe hip and back problems, and despite being only six years old, an attack dog that could not attack would likely have to be euthanized. The vet wanted to make sure there was nothing that could be done for him. He had to be sedated for the scan, and I got to help the veterinarian put him down with the sedative medicine propofol while he demonstrated to me how easy it was to intubate a canine. He essentially just pulled on the dog's tongue slightly, exposing his large vocal cords at the base. He easily inserted the large tube into his trachea, and that was it. I wish people, with the tough angle created by the chin and face, were that easy to intubate! It was a fun learning experience for me, and I enjoyed getting to pet and work with a dog for a change.

Over the next few weeks, the days and nights at Baghdad ER became quite monotonous. Needing something to curb the boredom, we were able to arrange a few entertaining excursions for several members of our crew. Working with 1st Lt. James Lorenz, the physician assistant stationed close to us in the International Zone, we got a firsthand tour of some of the checkpoints, or entry control points, that separated the International Zone from the Red Zone in Baghdad. First Lt. Lorenz and his NCO picked us up in their heavily armored ground ambulance, or HAGA, and we drove to one of the pedestrian IZ access points. Arriving ten minutes later, we were given a tour of the checkpoint from the NCOIC. He took us through all of the processing areas, metal detectors, and screening stations that separated the more secure International Zone from the Red Zone. Once we walked to the edge of the checkpoint, we found ourselves standing underneath two Iraqi soldiers with crew-served automatic weapons, protecting the entry. One by one, we walked into the Red Zone and took pictures and watched both the pedestrian and vehicle traffic flow by. It was our first excursion to the edge of the IZ on the ground, and it was informative and a great learning experience.

Next we stopped at the Tomb of the Unknown Soldier, an Iraqi national monument that was usually closed to American forces. However, having a couple of female nurses with us did the trick as Nathan, the Iraqi soldier guarding the tomb, welcomed us in and gave us a tour after getting a chance to talk to the American women. He was sure to include himself in our group photos, and I did not realize how large of a monument it truly was until I was standing on top of it looking down into the Crossed Sabers parade ground. Nathan was most generous to us and allowed us to go all over the monument.

For our last stop, we drove across the Fourteenth of July Bridge, named for the army's birth date, and stopped at the entry control point on the other side. The NCOIC took us into the guard tower, where we were able to look down the barrel of their M240 automatic weapon at the traffic and learn about the entry and exit procedures. I was amazed to see our young soldiers working in full body armor in the late summer heat, checking every car that approached. Iraqis attempting to enter the IZ were initially checked by Iraqi soldiers and eventually by our forces, along with canines from private security companies. I would not like to be one of the Iraqi soldiers at the first checkpoint, just waiting for the car bomb to appear! Overall, we had a fantastic time, and I once again gained a true appreciation for how hard and under what adverse conditions the soldiers of our military truly work while deployed.

The next day, I was able to go with a small group to the famous Al Rashid Hotel, located in Baghdad, tucked away just inside the International Zone. The lobby of the building reminded me of any other hotel, with bellmen in uniforms standing by to help guests, desk clerks dressed in nice clothes answering phones, and restaurants serving fine meals in several locations throughout the building. However, those were about the only similarities to any American hotel that I could remember. The windows of the main part of the building all had shields on them to prevent shrapnel from penetrating the glass. Several had large holes that were caused by the fragments from rockets or mortars hitting Iraq's premier hotel. The water in the swimming pool was green, and while that was not to far-fetched from some American places I had stayed in the past, the helipad on the lawn was a unique twist. Being the choice for many foreign dignitaries during their stays in Baghdad, I guess it made sense to have a helipad there. Amazing carpet and souvenir shops lined the inner walls, and we even ran into Maj. Gen. Barbero, one of the high-level commanders in the country. I bought a couple of nice rugs as keepsakes from one of the shops, and we sat in the lobby for a while and watched important people and their bodyguards move about before we made our way back to the CSH.

Later in the week, we were picked up by one of my paramedic friends from Triple Canopy, one of the main security contracting groups in Baghdad, and he drove us over to one of the weapons ranges in the IZ. He had arranged for us to shoot a couple of their automatic weapons, the M240 and M249 squad automatic weapon, or SAW. Our military forces carried these weapons, and even some of our medics carried them for security during our transit time between Fort Campbell and Baghdad. I fired the M240 first, which was a heavy 7.62 mm machine gun that replaced the famous M60 from the Vietnam War. It was a lot of fun, and as I fired my six- to nine-round bursts in one or two seconds, I found myself having a blast. Next I moved to the SAW, or M249. It was a smaller and lighter weapon chambered in a 5.56 NATO caliber, and it proved to be just as entertaining to shoot. Despite being in the army for seven years, this was my first time to fire these weapons, and we all had a great time, although I sure would not want to carry one around everywhere due to their weight, especially the M240. I decided to be happy with my M16 for the time being!

Despite the 80 percent drop in violence, we still received our share of interesting and amazing patients. We received sniper casualties occasionally throughout the year, but we suffered a several-week rash of soldiers being hit by snipers. One brigade in particular stationed around Sadr City had been taking most of the casualties. One soldier I cared for had been shot in the shoulder, and after discovering that he was only nicked and would recover, we began talking about what happened. After hearing the story, we discovered he was most likely the sniper's next victim, but by the grace of God he had turned at the last moment, moving his body from the bullet's path. He looked up to see the sniper on a rooftop and returned fire before he realized he was hit. Perhaps it was one of the professional snipers, or maybe it was someone else more poorly trained since his victim laid eyes on him. Either way, this soldier would live and recover well, making him a walking miracle to me.

On a lighter note, Triple Canopy brought in one of their Peruvian guards with a large foreign body lost in his rectum. This is a common complaint in emergency departments back home, but I must admit I did not expect to see this problem over here! He had taken a ten-inch bicycle seat post and told us that he was "massaging his prostate" with it. I was not sure how he lost it in there, but his reward was a trip to the operating room and a surgical removal. Col. Febinger, the surgeon who removed the rod, told me the patient would not get it back. I did not blame him; he probably did not want to have to remove it again a few days later!

We finally reached the ninety-day point, with only three months to go before we would be able to head for home. The large tuff boxes provided to us by the CSH were turned in for shipment back to Fort Campbell. Packing and sending off my tuff box was my first step toward going home, and it was an absolute pleasure. Jason Cohen was currently on his eighteen-day leave, and he made the mistake of trusting Deb Chappel and I with the task of inventorying and turning in his box for shipping. After counting everything in his tuff box with Sfc. Richard, we found a few nice additions that we thought would be funny to ship home with his gear. Deb added a large box of tampons, another box of maxi pads, and other feminine products we found in our supply areas. She also found a small Christmas tree, and since he was Jewish, we decided to add that in as well for his enjoyment. Of course, he did not know anything about it until he was back home at Fort Monmouth, New Jersey, and opened his tuff box. I would love to know what questions his wife Amy had for him after they discovered what was inside! We were getting closer to heading home, and this was just the first of many steps we would go though in the process. It was September 30, 2008, exactly one year after I drove away from my beautiful wife and daughter with tears in my eyes and a heavy heart. I will never forget that day; the sadness and fear of the unknown combined with the relief of having the several-year wait to get moving and deploy finally ending. We had only three months to go!

The next day, we received casualties from a helicopter crash. Two Blackhawks were attempting to land when the one in the rear somehow collided into the first. As one bird rolled over, the Special Forces guys inside were banged around quite a bit. One had an open ankle fracture, and another had a dislocated elbow. An Iraqi Special Forces soldier on one of the birds suffered the worst fate, as somehow the rotor blade transected his body, essentially cutting him in half. Jason Cohen pronounced him dead, and told me he was amazed to see the soldier's upper body laying face up in the body bag, with his lower half lying face down. He said he did a double take at first and was blown away by the sight, despite all of the carnage we had witnessed over the past twelve months. I am sure the two halves of his body moved around in the body bag while being transported from place to place, as I doubted they would have placed him in the bag in that manner. According to reports, this Iraqi Special Forces member had killed several enemy snipers personally over the past few days! We hoped he took out the guys who had been killing our troops over a few weeks, although I would imagine a sniper who was very good at his trade would be harder to find than some of these other guys must have been. We heard Al-Sadr had sent many members of his militia to Iran for sniper and other militant training over the summer, and they were beginning to filter their way back in.

One of our outstanding ER nurse's mom sent us an amazing gift about this time. Ann Gockley's mother spent an incredible number of hours during our tour hand making quilts for each of us. With the gracious financial assistance of the Lititz, Pennsylvania, Veteran's of Foreign Wars chapter and the Ephrata, Pennsylvania, American Legion, every medic, nurse, and physician in our EMT received one. Listed below is an excerpt from the letter she included with each quilt:

The Story of Your Quilt of Valor

The mission statement of the Quilts of Valor Foundation is "to cover ALL war wounded and injured service members and veterans from the War on Terror, whether physical or psychological wounds, with wartime quilts called Quilts of Valor." When I read the mission statement I was touched by the fact that the foundation recognizes that service members can be wounded psychologically as a result of their involvement in the War on Terror. Immediately, I thought of you who are caring for the sick and injured U.S. and coalition troops and civilians during your deployment. I find that I cannot possibly understand how you are able to cope with the volume and severity of the injuries you see on a daily basis. Many years of working in a trauma center as an operating room nurse has given me numerous opportunities in dealing with severe injuries and illnesses, but my experiences cannot even come close to the magnitude of the experiences you are having. I know very well the feelings that result after working with extreme intensity and commitment for hours, only to have outcomes that are not what you had hoped for. I know how every one of those experiences impacts one's emotions, and I truly cannot imagine how your experiences have or will affect your souls. For this reason, I became committed to find a way to offer you, as one health care professional to another, a means to comfort you and acknowledge the enormous sacrifices you have made for all Americans. Additionally, I would like to honor you for the outstanding care you provide for the many patients who present with overwhelming challenges. Because of your expertise, dedication, and determination, they are examples of the "miracles" you help to perform. Words cannot really express the respect and admiration I have for you both personally and professionally. My hope is that this Quilt of Valor will comfort you when needed and remind you of the enormous amount of gratitude and admiration I have for you as a person and a professional.

Each quilt had a label with the following words:

> *This quilt was created for you, an EMT member of the U.S. Army Eighty-sixth CSH stationed in the ER of Ibn Sina Hospital, Baghdad, Iraq. It is a token of thanks, gratitude, pride, and honor for the countless acts of valor you performed while caring for the sick and injured U.S. and coalition troops and civilians during your deployment, October, 2007–January, 2009. Stitched and quilted by Sue Gockley, Lilitz, PA. January, 2008–September, 2008.*

The quilts and incredible words left me speechless. What an incredible act of thanks by Ms. Gockley! We will always cherish these quilts; they will always have a place close to our hearts, and she has no idea how appreciated they truly were then and still are today.

The media began reporting that Iraqi civilian deaths had decreased by 91 percent since the year before. It seemed that Al Qaeda was now on the run, afraid of the local communities that had grown tired of cowering and began standing up to their brutal tactics of the past several years. It was reported that most of the foreign fighters were now pouring into Afghanistan rather than Iraq, helping with the resurgence of the Taliban and Al Qaeda there.

The reduction in violence against civilians also resulted in a change of tactics from our enemies. Recent operations hampered the flow of EFPs, and it seemed the bad guys realized that most IEDs did not work too well against our heavily armored vehicles. The days of poor Iraqi citizens being paid to place IEDs quickly and efficiently were not gone, but they had at least become fewer and further between. It seemed their new tactics involved precision hits by snipers and assassins against our forces and Iraqi government officials. While I was ecstatic to say that we had not seen the devastating effects of an EFP killing or maiming any of our soldiers for a while, the sniper attacks continued to increase in a troubling manner.

Just a day or two before, we worked exhaustively on a soldier who was shot in the chest, just above the bulletproof plate that protected him. He had no vital signs upon arrival to our trauma room, and while Marti intubated him, Col. Tom LeVoyer, one of our surgeons, cracked his chest while I placed a central line into his right subclavian vein beneath his clavicle. After several units of blood, multiple rounds of medications, and shocks directly to his heart with paddles, we pronounced yet another soldier dead.

The next shift, word came through our radios that casualties were coming in our back gate unannounced. Visualizing immediately the usual deaths, amputations, and dismemberments we always pulled from the vehicles in these situations, I called in Jason and Marti to help. Triaging at the door to the ER, I noticed most of the soldiers were walking wounded and sent them to the back, keeping our trauma room open for the critically wounded men I was expecting at any moment. Their Iraqi interpreter was not as lucky, and we placed him in the trauma room first. However, thank God, when it was all said and done, all of these guys only had minor flesh injuries, and they all turned out to be okay, including the interpreter. Upon interviewing the soldiers, they told me there had been some type of explosion at an Iraqi police station, and they had been called in to investigate. Once inside, a suicide bomber detonated himself in an effort to kill as many Americans and Iraqis responders as possible. I did not discover how many Iraqi casualties there were, but I was much happier for the results of our guys in uniform. I would take the unannounced arrival of nondying soldiers any day of the week versus what we used to get routinely!

Two days before, we received an Iraqi Army soldier from our forward surgical team based in Al Kut, a smaller town in southeastern Iraq. They had operated on his abdomen and left it open to facilitate further surgery once he was at the CSH. They had also informed us that he had a severe pelvic fracture, but upon arrival, he did not have a pelvic binder or sheet wrapped around his hips to help bind his hipbones together to compress the bleeding vessels. We received him from the helicopter in stable condition, but after we rolled him on his side to evaluate his back, blood began to ooze out the dressings on his abdomen. His blood pressure began to tank, and we ended up giving him twelve units of blood before we could bind his pelvis back together with a sheet. After fixing his pelvis, his blood pressure maintained and he did well. Despite the year of trauma I had done in Baghdad, that was the first time I had seen a sheet binding a pelvis together work so well.

The next week brought a return of the hot weather unfortunately. After enjoying nice, cool days in the low to midnineties, the midday temperatures that week began peaking back over 100 degrees. We knew we were still in Iraq, but the cooler weather prior to this heat wave had us thinking we had escaped the heat. It was mid-October, so we just readjusted and hoped it would be cooler by the end of the month. I still could not complain, however, as the days of 125-plus degree weather with a ten-mile-per-hour, oven-like wind were our norm only a few short weeks ago. I did remember beautiful weather back in November 2007 when we arrived in Baghdad, and I looked forward to its return.

One night, we received an Iraqi man who had been critically wounded in an IED blast, stabilized, and kept at the Air Force Hospital for a while. Strangely, however, he was sent to us with only a small dressing covering his open abdomen. When we removed the abdominal pad, his intestines and omentum leapt from of his belly. Many times, a surgeon will leave an abdominal incision open if the patient will be making repeated trips to the operating room over the course of several days, but they usually put special dressings called wound vacuums or other types of sterile drapes over the wound. This poor guy only had a pad taped down to keep his guts from pouring from his abdomen. It looked like someone just took a knife and sliced him right open from sternum to his pubic area, but then did nothing to close the wound. Dr. Jason Johnson, our surgeon on call, arrived from upstairs after I told him that I had a train wreck for him. He was amazed to see the shape the patient was left in, but he immediately took him to the OR and provided good care. I was not sure what the story was behind this patient; did he loose his dressings in flight? Who knew, but nothing surprised me anymore.

The next night, the Green Zone KBR ambulance brought in a patient they had told us was unresponsive. Meeting the ambulance at the back door, we climbed into the back of the rig to find an American Department of Defense civilian employee in cardiac arrest. He had lost control of his bladder, causing the entire back of the rig to smell like urine. Rushing him into our trauma bed, our nurses used our drill to place a quick line into his left tibia. As they pushed epinephrine, atropine, and other lifesaving medications, I intubated him and noted both of his pupils to be fixed and dilated, a sign of brain death. All of us knew he was dead, but without good IV access we did not want to give up our efforts before we gave him every chance. Sam Matta worked on an IV line in his arm while medic Amy Rice continued pumping on his chest doing CPR. "Hold CPR, check pulse," I stated as I placed a large needle into his chest to find his subclavian vein. Getting a flash, I fed the wire through the needle into the vein, made a stab incision with the scalpel, and then stated "Continue CPR" once I knew the compressions would not ruin my efforts. Once we had access, we noticed him to be in ventricular tachycardia. Several shocks later, amazingly he had a pulse! We treated him with additional medications and later got him over to the CT scanner. Unfortunately, he had a large bleeding vessel into his brain, and a discussion with the neurosurgeon in Balad confirmed our fears that nothing else could be done for him. We took him upstairs to the ICU, where he died shortly afterward. This is a common emergency medicine case back home, but these types of codes were few and far between in Iraq, as we usually found ourselves doing CPR after a trauma code rather than a medical one.

The United Nations mandate justifying the Coalition's presence in Iraq was set to expire on December 31, 2008. Our government had been working very hard with the Iraqi government to set up a status of forces agreement, similar to the ones we share with other nations like South Korea, Germany, and Italy. The agreement would justify and define our presence in the future, as well as set guidelines and boundaries for our nation's actions. As with any agreement, there would have to be compromise on both sides, but troublemakers like Muqtada Al Sadr did not want the long-term agreement signed and desired to force our troops out immediately. He had thousands of his followers marching in the streets of Sadr City during that time, trying to push the government to say no to the agreement that would justify our presence over the next few years.

Reports began telling us that the bad guys had been shipping in more and more rockets from Iran over the last few months and would unleash them on the Green Zone again if the status of forces of agreement was signed and ratified by the Iraqi Parliament. We were told to get ready to begin receiving indirect fire daily again once the agreement was signed. We had been given a break for a while, but figured it was only a matter of time before the natives got restless and found some type of excuse to start lobbing shells in our direction again. Who knew if that day would come again, but until then we continued to enjoy the downtime and decided to worry about it when the first rocket struck the IZ again.

Dena George worked on a project consisting of taking the pictures of the eyes of people she had met and worked with in Iraq over the past year. She then had each person write a one-page summary about their experiences. She solicited input from physicians, nurses, and medics from all over the CSH, as well as military members from various units throughout the International Zone. She also included several of our Iraqi friends, including interpreters, maintenance workers, and others. It turned out to be an amazing piece of work, and below is my one page summary of "What My Eyes Have Seen." The main word that came to mind when trying to organize my thoughts was the term "struggle."

These Eyes Have Seen

What have these eyes have seen over the past fifteen months? ...

The struggle.

The struggle for a soul to hang on to life and refuse to die.

The struggle for a heart to continue beating against all odds, with no blood to keep it going.

The struggle for a friend to let go of their dead buddy, the parent to let go of their dead child.

The struggle to stop the bleeding before it stops on its own.

The struggle for a physician to keep it together; don't cry in front of my team.

The struggle for a physician to keep composure; don't lose your cool now.

The struggle to get the central line placed before the patient bleeds to death.

The struggle for a chaplain to support people of various faiths as they mourn their loved one's death or dismemberment.

The struggle of a young medic to understand why they are having to stand by, watch, and do nothing while another soul takes his last breath.

The struggle of a young medic to understand why that dying soul is another innocent child.

The struggle of a soldier to cope with the realization that he will never have arms or legs again.

The struggle of a squad leader to keep it together while learning of the death of his buddies, his best friends, his brothers.

The struggle of a physician to be nice to a patient asking for sore throat medicines just after pronouncing yet another soldier dead after working on him exhaustingly.

The struggle to sleep with the knowledge that the next rocket to hit at any given moment may have your name on it.

The struggle to lie to your family when they ask you if the rockets are landing "close to where you are located."

The struggle to live with yourself after watching so many people die. Sure, you did all you could, but you still failed in the end.

The struggle to remember that this is not reality; you have a family at home to go to, where there will be no death and destruction.

The struggle to eat at the same restaurant, with the same menu, three meals a day for fifteen months.

The struggle to cope with seeing your peers come and go home in short stints while you are here for the long haul, missing your family more and more by the day.

The struggle to keep your humanity after witnessing some of the most evil acts that man can do to each other; the struggle for sanity.

I did not mean to be so somber and morbid, but when thinking back over the past year, these words flowed through my fingertips to the keyboard.

It did seem to appear that our guys took care of the enemy snipers, or at least forced them into hiding for a while. In the two months after I returned from leave, we had seen several sniper victims, sometimes one a day for several days in a row. While that had fortunately died down, old-fashioned IEDs began coming back into vogue. Several times we would receive calls telling us of several "urgent surgical" U.S. soldiers inbound, spinning up the hospital to prepare for several critically ill casualties, only to have several patients come walking in under their own power with just bruises and small shrapnel injuries. What a blessing! However, our surgeons who had only been there a few months would all look at us funny when we would get excited and anxious while waiting on the casualties to arrive. Many of them seemed to think we were overreacting. Why did we need blood in the ER before the patients arrived, or why did we alert the OR ahead of time? Those of us who had been here over a year all knew at some time the EFPs would be in use again, likely after approval of the status of forces agreement. When Al Sadr's guys began using those instruments of death again, we knew the new guys would see for themselves why we spun into motion so quickly each time we prepared for incoming IED injuries.

Those of us caught outside in bunkers and involved in the mortar attack back on Thanksgiving 2007, as well as those present when we were working in full body armor while caring for patients in the EMT during our close rocket impacts several months before, received the Combat Action Badge. It is an award given to those who have been engaged by the enemy and performed their duties throughout the engagement. I was very proud of our guys for the work they had done while in danger's way, and I was thrilled the command had recognized that fact and obtained this award for our crew. Our enlisted soldiers actually got promotion points for the award, and I was incredibly excited for our guys to receive the recognition they deserved for their incredible performance throughout the several week period of daily bombardment by rocket fire.

Jason Cohen, Marti Roellig, Deb Chappel, and me at our front desk

Halloween 2008:
The Naughty Nurse

On Halloween, October 31, the command allowed us to drop the dress code for a few hours and wear Halloween costumes. I was not sure what they were thinking, but thirteen months of pent-up frustration and personality came out that day! People I had worked with twenty-four hours a day, seven days a week for over a year put on clothes other than scrubs, a PT uniform, or army fatigues for the first time. Any type of character imaginable appeared and ran all over the CSH. Our commander's wall, with pictures of each of the colonels, the command sergeant major, and other important figures, was vandalized during the night by our EMT crew, and they had beards and pirate costumes drawn on their pictures when they came to work on Halloween morning. Other pirates were running around everywhere, and several guys dressed as pimps roamed the halls. Our EMT nurses all dressed as flappers, a term I had never heard of before that refers to the way women dressed in the 1920s. The guys in the EMT, except for one, all were dressed as mobsters, with suits, cigars, and hats. They got me the boss mobster outfit, complete with huge shoulder pads and a mask. It was the first time I had dressed up for Halloween since I was a kid.

However, two costumes stole the show. First, for some stupid, obscene, and incomprehensible reason, Jason Cohen let the nurses talk him into wearing a naughty nurse costume if they bought it for him. And yes, unfortunately, he did wear it. He only planned to put it on for a few moments to fulfill his promise, but when he walked through the door of the physician's office, he was swept upstairs and ended up walking throughout the hospital. I did not know whether to laugh or cry. Interestingly, pictures of him in the outfit kept popping up throughout the EMT several days after the event. He would take them down quickly, but then more would appear. I would not know anything about that …

The other costume that stole the show actually stole my heart. After the event, Laura sent me pictures of my little angel Avery in her mouse costume. The head on the outfit was huge, but Laura said she had so much fun watching all of the kids walk up to the front door and ask for candy, even trying to leave with some of the groups. Laura had to tell them, "If you see a mouse in your group, she belongs to me" each time a group of kids would come to the door for candy. That was so funny, and although I hated the fact that I missed her first two Halloweens, I was fired up because I knew I could be around for the rest of them.

We also learned the story of the most unfortunate, unluckiest Iraqi man I met throughout my tour—but first I must provide a touch of background. When the United States invaded Iraq in 2003, Saddam had his air force MiG fighter jets spread out all over the country to keep them from being knocked out in one easy attack. After the invasion, and to this day, several still sit beside the roadway, or in the middle of nowhere, mostly out of working condition. Recently, this poor Iraqi soldier in question was working close to one of them when he decided to get into the cockpit and see what it felt like to be a fighter pilot. I do not blame him, I would likely do the same thing if given a chance. As he sat in the control center of the dead fighter jet examining the instruments, he found the red lever. For those who do not know, the red lever is attached to the ejection mechanism, designed to eject the seat out twenty-five or so feet in the air to free the pilot from the plane in case it was shot down. While all of the electrical and engine-operated systems were nonfunctional after a few years of rotting in the desert, apparently the ejection mechanism worked well.

He apparently pulled the lever, shot who knows how many feet into the air, and then landed on his face, shattering it on the desert floor. He suffered multiple facial fractures and diffuse axonal injury intracranially, or DAI. It is caused from blunt trauma, high force, high velocity injuries, like when someone is ejected from a fighter jet cockpit and lands on their face, for example. It is a separation of the grey matter from the white matter of the brain. Essentially, the neurons in his brain were sheared apart, and he would likely die soon from this freak accident. After this year of trauma, I guess I had not seen it all yet. This poor guy was doing nothing wrong; he was just curious like many of us would have been in that circumstance.

—

The status of forces agreement between the U.S. and Iraq was eventually signed by both parties. We were concerned with Muqtada Al-Sadr's response, as he vowed once again to combat American forces in Iraq and scheduled a mass protest to keep the Parliament from voting the agreement into law. His threats to "bring back the war" on American forces and the International Zone were not taken lightly, and we all waited on pins and needles to see if the rockets would start flying toward us and the EFPs would begin hitting our troops again. The leading Shiite cleric in Iraq, Ali Al-Sistani, publicly announced his approval of the measure, and we hoped his influence would keep Al-Sadr from stirring up too much trouble. Our first wave of nurses and medics were set to redeploy home in less than a month, and we hoped they would not have to go out with a flurry of rockets chasing after them.

Before we left Fort Campbell, we all had lectures on compassion fatigue. We had been mentally and physically exhausted and had been feeling it for a while, and I think it boiled over for me one day when a fifty-year-old American contractor was brought in for chest pain with an episode of fainting. When I began to interview him, he would not answer my questions. I tried again using a different tactic, and all I could get out of him were vague answers. I became quite irritated and redirected to a third approach. Still nothing. That was it. "Why won't you talk to me?" I yelled at him. Nothing. "Why are you acting like a four-year-old child? We are here for dying and critically wounded people, and you are wasting my time by not talking to me!" I was screaming at him, and some of our staff appeared from out front and came back to see what was going on. "Talk to me!" Still nothing, he just kept shaking his head. Finally, I walked up to him, pointed at him, and yelled, "Are you having chest pain RIGHT NOW?" He shook his had no, and I left the room. Once his labs and studies were back, I admitted him upstairs to receive a cardiology evaluation, and I never went back in the room with him. Later, I discovered he did not want to be sent home and miss out on the tax-free money he received for being in Iraq, which was surely much more than I made. I was just trying to provide him care, and he would not cooperate because he did not want to be sent home. Was that more important to him than his health? It took me a long time to cool down, and all of my nurses and medics said they had not seen me that angry in months. I was not proud, but that seemed to be a recurring theme for all of us as we trudged on, day by day toward the finish line.

The next shift, I cared for a transfer, or "snatch and grab" as we called them, from the Iraqi hospital complex we sent many of our host nation patients to once they were stabilized. He was some sort of VIP who was approved for transfer to us by an American general way above my head. Blown up by an IED four days prior, he had received surgery at the Iraqi hospital on his abdomen and had drains placed into his belly. His bladder was gone, and a catheter placed into his penis drained grossly bloody urine. His right arm was splinted, and upon removing the splint, he told us his wounds had been bandaged on the day of the injury, but not touched since. Pouring water on his dressings to help pry them from his flesh, we pulled the cotton from the gaping holes on his right arm to reveal the stench of rotting muscle. Radiographs revealed that his radius and ulna were both fractured in many places, and he still had shrapnel scattered throughout his wounds. I had seen several cases of terrible care from just about every Iraqi hospital around the greater Baghdad area over the past year, and this was no exception. If he had not been brought to us, there was no doubt in my mind that he would have at least lost his arm, and the horrible medical care likely would have killed him eventually.

All of my patients were not on death's doorstep, however, as I had entertaining encounters as well. I walked downstairs to begin my day shift one day to find a British contractor sitting in bed four, the bed most commonly used for cardiac issues, with chest pain. Not having the older, overweight American contractor look to him, I discovered from his accent that he was a forty-something-year-old British security contractor with crushing chest pain. His paratrooper tattoo and attitude quickly told me he was in great shape, and he had just exerted himself and led his team through several miles of exercises earlier in the morning, but now he was in my ER and clutching his chest in severe discomfort. Our stellar nurse and medic crew had already shot an EKG on him and recognized the typical ST segment elevation pattern of a large heart attack. Springing into action, I questioned him through his cries of discomfort, and within minutes, we gave him the clot-busting drug I had used to help so many in the past. Twenty minutes later, his pained speech and expression transformed into jubilation as he realized we had opened his arteries back up and saved his heart from further damage. With his pain relieved and his EKG back to normal, he said, "Spot on! Jolly well! Cheers, mate!" He repeated the phrases again and again to us and kept smiling and greeting and thanking everyone who walked by who was involved in his care. It was so nice to be back with not only an appreciative patient, but another life saved or least altered for the good.

An urgent surgical head injury call later that shift got us moving, and after the birds landed, we watched a poor Iraqi man get carried into the EMT on a litter with a face that was bloodied, broken, and essentially unrecognizable. The flight medics told us he had suffered a four-story fall. Placing him into bed one, a quick search for vital signs revealed no pulse, so we began CPR and started pushing drugs to get his heart moving again. He had a King LT airway placed, which was basically a big tube placed blindly into the esophagus to help ventilate and get air into the lungs. It was not a definitive airway, and he required a regular endotracheal intubation, but with the massive swelling and disfiguring of his face, the prospects of that going smoothly were low. I asked one of our guys to call anesthesia to come down, as I did not want to attempt intubation without their backup if things got ugly.

His heart was restarted quickly with our medications, and his blood pressure actually returned to normal. Knowing his severe head wounds would cause brain swelling that could rapidly lead to his demise, I ordered antiseizure medications, hypertonic saline, and other drugs to help shrink his brain and decrease the certain edema that would help kill him. Anesthesia arrived as backup, and I pulled the King LT airway from his throat as our medic sucked the air from the balloon that held it in place. Looking in with the laryngoscope, his floppy face obscured most of my view of his vocal cords or the cartilages I look for when trying to intubate someone. He had suffered a LeFort III type fracture, meaning that his face was essentially disconnected from his skull, and it took serious pressure from me lifting on the laryngoscope blade to get the view I needed. Once obtained, I was able to pass the tube and get him intubated smoothly.

Once he was somewhat stabilized, we took him over to CT to discover a large, depressed skull fracture, serious intracranial swelling, and evidence of diffuse axonal injury, or the nonrecoverable shearing apart of the neurons in the brain. Remembering he was dead when he arrived to us, and that after revival he did not move or demonstrate any objective signs of brain activity, we reluctantly decided there was nothing more we, or the neurosurgeons in Balad, could do for him. He was the first patient in a month or so I had to put on a morphine drip and make expectant and watch die.

Later, I cared for a few guys who were not injured badly from another attack. The gunner told me he saw the attacker run out in front of the vehicle and throw a projectile at their vehicle. Just before the detonation, he told me he did "an Irish folk dance" in the turret to get himself out of harm's way. How ironic it seemed to me he could laugh and make light after a narrow escape with his life, but that sense of humor will serve him well in the future, wherever he is today.

Two days prior, a sniper had shot one of our soldiers in the right flank. The trauma was described to us as an "abdominal evisceration," and I welcomed the young twenty-something-year-old soldier into bed one awake, alert, and fully aware of what was going on around him. This surprised me, as patients with bowel eviscerations were usually barely maintaining their mental and respiratory abilities, much less looking as good as he was. I noticed that about half of his small intestine had been pushed through the left side of his abdomen and was exposed, lying outside his body under a large dressing. While our team worked on him, I leaned down to him and asked him where he was from and told him that our colorectal specialist, Dr. Jamie Mayoral, just happened to be the surgeon on call for trauma and that he had the best taking him to the OR. Beneath the fog of his oxygen mask, his smile warmed my heart. As we gave him blood, antibiotics, and other meds to prepare him for the OR, I kept leaning down to talk and comfort him. He was quiet and appeared to be scared of what he had to endure, yet determined to face his fears and meet them head on. His determination really resonated with me, and while I never got his name, for some reason or another he stuck with me. I hoped and prayed that he did well, as it was an honor to care for him, just like every other soldier I worked on in Iraq.

It was mid-November 2008, and we all remembered the wonderful weather that greeted us upon landing and moving into Ibn Sina Hospital the year before. What we did not remember, however, were the flies. I am not sure if this phenomenon occurs every other year, every few years, or what, but the flies were amazing! Our preventive medicine teams placed flytraps everywhere, and they stunk to high heaven. Each trap contained some sort of liquid medium that smelled horrendously, but apparently the flies loved the stuff. Around each trap lay literally thousands of dead flies, with thousands more lying inside the traps, and yet thousands more could be seen and felt hovering around them. Our Ugandan guards stood out front with AK-47s in one arm and fly swatters in the other as they combated the insects while watching their posts. Cob-style flytraps could be placed outside, and they would be filled with hundreds of dead bugs after only a few hours. It was like a plague! After a few weeks the plague passed, but I found myself with a fly swatter in hand anytime I got a chance, inside or out!

Boredom leads people to do stupid things, and I am no exception. The Danish Army, part of the NATO contingent in Iraq, put on a Dancon

March each year they were in a deployed environment. They had done it several times, both in Iraq and Afghanistan, since 2003. The march had been a tradition of the Danish Royal Army since 1972, when they were deployed on the island of Cyprus. It was both an event to demonstrate preparedness and a social gathering. About five hundred of us paid $25 to donate to Iraqi charities and to march 13.75 miles around the IZ. We all arrived at the U.S. Embassy at 4:45 AM in our ACU uniforms with our weapons, and fifteen minutes later we were off and walking. Some people took it as an endurance event and went as fast as they could, but most of us were just there to participate. We took five large laps around the main part of the International Zone, and thank God no rockets, gunfire, or car bombs got in our way! We did see several large Iraqi Army convoys parked on the side of the road, loading up to head out into the Red Zone for their daily missions. Many of the vehicles were Humvees with large automatic weapons on top, but full-size pickup trucks made a large contingent as well. Walking by these trucks, we could see that each had Iraqi soldiers sitting in the truck beds, getting ready to ride behind whatever armor they had fashioned onto the trucks in a homemade manner. Some trucks had copious armor, while others had none. Looking into the smiling and waving faces, the respect I had for these guys was rekindled. They were out front now, with their poor armor, more dangerous vehicles, and knowledge that the Iraqi health care system would not be able to help them if they were injured. I pondered yet another time, "What is this country doing with all of its money? Can they not afford good armor for their troops? God bless these men, these soldiers fighting for their independence from terror." The tide had turned by this point. The surged had worked, violence was down, and the Iraqi Army had stepped to the front of the fight.

Checking out a vehicle from the CSH, the next day Will Smith and Scott Bier, ER docs who were working with us, Dena George, and I drove over to the Crossed Sabers monument, searching for the NATO IZ golf course we had heard so much about. Easing slowly into the checkpoints to keep from accidentally being shot by the Nepalese security guards, we pulled into the checkpoint and asked, "Golf?" They smiled and pointed ahead, and a few minutes later we found ourselves on the first tee of the official Baghdad Country Club par three nine hole golf course. None of our group enjoyed golf, and we only made it through hole two of the nine-hole course before we got tired of it. Of course, there was no grass, so it was not exactly as pretty as I remembered golf courses back home, but it was just as difficult! We got several pictures and were proud to claim we had officially played golf in Iraq. I never thought I would do that when I was getting ready to deploy!

After golf, we talked to a KBR employee who worked at the NATO complex bordering the old zoo. He was from the Houston, Texas, area, and before we knew it, he took us into the zoo to see the sites. Apparently, Saddam enjoyed a good safari every now and then, and our guide told us how Saddam would have a lion released into a neighborhood and then go into the area and shoot it as a hunting trip. Who knows if any of the citizens in the neighborhood were injured or killed? We toured the area, walked down the overgrown walkways, and climbed onto the old Babylonian-looking statue of horsemen pulling a chariot with a wounded lion behind. Making our way to the north side of the zoo that bordered the Red Zone, we looked at a walkway that was blocked off with barbed concertina wire to keep anyone from crossing. A smaller wire could be seen in front, and we traced it down to a grenade hanging on the fence! We had walked upon an old booby trap. We had no idea how long it had been there, but I had never seen one before. It was hidden quite well, and thank God we did not get too close before we had a big problem! The KBR tour guide was surprised as well, as he had not seen it before.

Marti had to go on emergency leave for family issues, leaving us with just two ER docs for a while, Jason and myself. Sure, there were several more working in grossly overstaffed aid stations all over the greater Baghdad area, but most of them were not allowed to come see patients at the CSH as their commanders did not want to let them go. Alas, they wasted away seeing zero to five patients a day with complaints such as athlete's foot, head colds, and requests for physicals, while Jason and I were now providing twenty-four-hour, seven-day-a-week coverage in a place with the potential for disaster and mass casualties at any given moment. I have said it before, we had enough physicians in Iraq: they just were not in the right spots in my opinion! Col. Rowe sent us a list of the physicians and PAs doing their four-month tours at the air force hospital in Balad at the moment, and we counted ten ER providers. All we could do was laugh and tell everyone that the two of us apparently equaled ten air force ER docs, as we had the same trauma volume they did. However, we only had one month left to see patients, as the Tenth Combat Support Hospital would replace us and be up and running thirty days from that point. Even if Jason and I had to work a twelve-hour shift every day without a night or day free, we were fine with it, because we were getting so close to the end! "Just get there, baby," kept running though my head every day.

An IED hit a soldier the next day, and he was treated in the field before being flown into us. At the scene of the injury, his high-speed medic put not one but two tourniquets on the top of his left thigh, just above his wound. Shrapnel had torn through the femoral artery in his left leg, and this medic successfully stopped the bleeding by applying multiple devices to cut the blood flow. Upon his arrival in bed one, I took down one of the tourniquets only to have pulsatile blood shoot out at me. Stuffing gauze rolls into the wound, Megan Solberg and I reapplied the tourniquet tight enough to stop the bleeding, and he was rushed to the operating room. His arterial laceration was repaired successfully by Dr. Mike Weber, our vascular surgeon.

Moments later, I found myself on a conference call with this soldier's battalion commander and his staff. I always enjoyed giving young, lower-enlisted medics major props when they did great work on the battlefield, and this was no exception. I talked extensively to those guys about how that medic in the field, without a doubt in my mind, saved this soldier's life. I pushed as hard as I could to get them to tell me they would recognize the medic formally, and I finally had to give it up after requesting they tell the medic specifically that the ER doctor said he saved that soldier's life. I always blush and get incredibly excited when someone tells me I saved a life, and I can only imagine how excited a young kid with minimal medical training would feel when being told the same thing. I never caught the medic's name, but he did a fantastic job; he was a hero in my book. I am sure the wounded soldier would agree!

About that time, Ann, the translator who watched her son die from an insurgent attack a couple of years ago, finally received her visa to go to the United States. She came quietly to Jason and me beaming with the news, but she did not want to rub it in to the other translators who were still enduring the waiting game. She was set to leave in a few days and could hardly contain her excitement. She planned to stay with a son who already lived in the United States.

However, she came to me later privately and asked me questions that literally blew me away. Incredibly concerned about how to get from the airport to her son's home, she asked me, "Dr. Baker, can I trust a taxi driver? What about a bus driver in America? Will he kidnap or kill me?" I was dumbfounded. Even after being in Iraq for fourteen months, I still had no idea how dangerous it must have been to live there. And how lucky are we in America, where we can put faith in total strangers to safely help us live our daily lives? I wanted to be honest and tell her that you cannot trust *everybody* in the U.S., but how was I to convey that message to a woman who was terrified that any random taxi driver may murder or kidnap her? I struggled to tell her she could trust these people, and then she asked me another question that blew me away: "Dr. Baker, I know that I cannot trust policemen. What do I do in United States? Can I trust policeman not to harm me?" Wow. Having grown up in an era when Officer Friendly was every child's best friend, and being taught all of my life that I could trust the police to take care of me when I was in trouble, I was amazed at the difference in our cultures. I felt so sorry for her! I said, "Ann, you can *always* trust the police when you get to the United States. If you ever need help, you go to them for assistance." She expressed relief and gratitude, and I felt incredibly lucky that I would be able to teach Avery about Officer Friendly when I got home, rather than tell her to run and hide from the men in blue.

The status of forces agreement (SOFA) was to be voted on by the Iraqi

Parliament for ratification on November 25. In the few days prior to that, we had been getting credible threats to the IZ and our forces throughout Iraq, and we prepared for the potential violence to come. We were told about a "spectacular attack" set to come our way at some point, and we began implementing security plans throughout the hospital and in the EMT in case evildoers penetrated our front gate. I highly doubted the bad guys would get the opportunity to break into our compound, but our medics and team all were willing to suddenly turn from caregivers to killers in a heartbeat to keep our patients safe if the situation became dire. While jogging on the compound beside ours the day before, I watched one F-16 fighter jet after another fly over Baghdad and Sadr City. Air traffic was heavier than usual, with multiple Apache attack helicopters and fighters flying constantly. With everything going on around us, the tension and dread of the expected violence to come was becoming palpable.

Thanksgiving 2008: Going Out With A Bang

Thanksgiving has always been my favorite holiday. Cooler weather, beautiful fall colors, family and friends … who could ask for more? The previous Thanksgiving, we got more in the form of mortars raining down on us from above, as insurgents wanted to tell us Happy Thanksgiving in their own way. With the boredom we endured over the past five months, in a strange way, it would almost be welcome again. It would be a nice change from the monotony that had us all questioning, "Why are we still here?" Massive trauma patients had almost become a thing of the past, almost as if the bad guys had given up. "Casualty! Casualty! Casualty!" being screamed over the radio from our guards at the front gate had transformed itself from the usual severely blown up American convoy into some Iraqi VIP with a snotty nose. We still sprang into action at the words, and my heart still skipped a beat every time I heard the air ambulance radio crackle, but we just were not busy anymore, plain and simple. Sure, the SOFA agreement would be signed at any time, and we thought that would make Al-Sadr's guys come after us again; it was only a matter of time. The Shiite madman's followers did flex their muscles over the next few days, but Mother Nature kept us busy as well.

A naked Iraqi man was carried into the EMT from a helicopter one day, and I was puzzled as to why in the world this man did not at least have a blanket or sheet providing him some privacy and warmth. He had some sort of ailment that I cannot remember, but I could not figure out why anyone would be transported this way. Being late November, fall and winter had finally begun to announce their presence with cooler temperatures, and I was sure this guy was cold, and we all know about the embarrassment that comes with shrinkage for a man.

"How long has he been that way? Hopefully not the entire flight," I thought. The answer presented itself when I asked my medics about it. Evidently, the flight medic had placed a blanket over the naked patient on the bird, but forgot to strap it down. The blanket did not last long once the patient was hot loaded off the Blackhawk with its blades spinning. It was immediately sucked up into the rotors and shredded into hundreds of pieces on our landing zone. The pilots actually had to shut down and inspect the bird before they were able to leave, but there was no serious damage. After fourteen months, you would think that would not be the first time something like that occurred, but I guess there is a first time for everything.

Later in the week, an insurgent was sent to us from the prison hospital down at Camp Bucca, near the town of Basra. He had suffered a penile fracture, and you can guess what could cause that, especially for someone in jail. His penis was black and blue from internal bleeding and swollen to several times its normal size. However, his story was he was urinating, and somehow it "broke" that way. He adamantly denied any intercourse that could have caused his malady, and he stuck to his story, I guess assuming we would finally believe it. Our urologist took him to the OR and repaired it surgically. I wonder what his boyfriend thought? We all joked that we would never urinate again if that truly were a possible outcome!

Later, a Pakistani man was brought into our trauma room with a closed fracture of his right lower leg, just below the knee. Apparently, he had suffered a rollover motor vehicle accident, and his fracture was pretty nasty. He was placed into bed one of our trauma room, and he began screaming at the top of his lungs, and it seemed to get louder and louder as time passed. Not speaking Pashtu myself, I could not communicate verbally with him at all, and with his eyes closed and mouth open, he could not hear me even if I could speak in his native tongue. Not being able to talk to my trauma team over his yelling, I needed him to be quiet so we could care for him. I began popping him on the forehead, trying to get him to open his eyes and look at me, so that I could gesture "quiet" to him, but he would not open his eyes. While our medics were attempting to get IVs into him, I knew I had to get the situation under control for everyone's safety. Therefore, I chose the only option available to me: scream over him. I knew he could not understand what I was saying, but an angry man leaning over you while you are in a hospital bed seemed to convey a universal language. "QUIET!!!" I screamed in his face. His eyes opened for the first time, and he looked at me, continuing in his quest to make us all deaf. "Quiet! Shut up! I said SHUT UP!" I yelled, my face inches from his. He stopped screaming and looked up at me. I gave him thumbs up, our medics got a line, and he got some pain medicine in the form of morphine. He never yelled again, and we were able to take great care of him. Later, my medics told me they had never heard someone yell so loud in a trauma. I agreed and echoed the sentiment that he was very loud, but they told me they were actually talking about me! Whatever it takes I guess!

All of us who work in emergency medicine have heard of the patients that have a condition known as flash pulmonary edema. For a variety of different causes, a patient's heart can fail to the point that their lungs fill up with fluid, not allowing them to breathe. A fifty-one-year old Iraqi interpreter was flown emergently to us around midnight that same shift with respiratory distress. He was placed into a bed in our treatment room, and he was only able to talk one word at a time due to his inability to breathe. Within ninety seconds, his heart had stopped, and he was in full cardiac arrest. Our team began CPR by pumping on his chest, and I placed my laryngoscope into his mouth to try to intubate him. All I could see was clear, frothy fluid consistent with pulmonary edema. Placing the suction catheter into his mouth, I began to suction the fluid, finally getting enough out to see his vocal cords. Removing the catheter to grab the endotracheal tube with my right hand took about two seconds, and by that time more fluid had poured from his lungs, obscuring my view once again. I put the tube down and resuctioned him, trying desperately to get a view, as he was going longer and longer without oxygen. Every second counted, and I began ordering the cardiac-restarting drugs epinephrine and atropine while I was suctioning. Once again, I obtained the view I needed, only to lose it again when I grabbed the ET tube to place into his trachea. I knew I had to adjust fire to save him, so I just aimed for the spot in his throat where I could see the air bubbling through the fluid and placed the tube. Our medics suctioned his lungs to get out some of the fluid, and his heart immediately began beating on its own again. We gave him typical medications for someone in flash pulmonary edema, and I called Jeremy Pamplin, our intensive care physician, for admission. Later that night, I heard he began to wake up somewhat, so hopefully his short downtime was not enough to cause anoxic brain injury and make him comatose or kill him. His heart was a different story, and unfortunately I will never know how he turned out as he was shipped to the local Iraqi hospital the next morning. But however the outcome, it was a great save, and we were all excited to know that we were able to resuscitate him successfully. Another life saved, at least long enough to leave the ER.

Overall, it had been an interesting, but not too crazy Thanksgiving Week, especially compared to the year before when we were introduced to mortar fire for the first time. However, it all changed over Saturday and Sunday of Thanksgiving weekend.

Working my last of four night shifts, the ER was empty so I laid down about 4:30 AM in the physician's office to catch a nap. Falling asleep easily, I was excited to get to turn in my JLIST nuclear, biological, and chemical protective equipment at 6:00 AM, since that would mean I did not have to carry it home on my back when we left in a month. However, my alarm did not wake me up, but rather I was awakened by the all-too-familiar BOOM of a rocket crashing into the International Zone. A second one rapidly followed the first, and despite the impacts being a good distance away from us, our building shook and rattled, jolting me from sleep. I jumped up and walked from the physician's office to find people scrambling into the EMT from outside after waiting in the JLIST line, and I proclaimed, "They're back, baby!" It had been several months since we had been rocketed and suffered so many hits on our compound, and we were all thinking, "Here we go again."

No casualties came in for about twenty minutes, and we all began to think the bad guys must have missed and that we would not see any injuries from the impacts. Once the all-clear was given, several of us went outside and got in line to turn in our gear. After standing for about five minutes, one of our nurses came to get me, telling me that casualties were coming through the back gate. I pawned my stuff off to someone else and sprinted inside to meet a third-country national who had suffered shrapnel wounds to his right pelvis and flank. He was in bad shape and was thrown into bed one and we went to work. Medics on both sides attempted to get IV access to no avail, so Joey Campbell, a reservist ER doc rotating with us, began placing a central line into his chest. Joey and I tag-teamed the central line and intubation, and we pounded blood into him, but to no avail. Dr. Amel Graf, the surgeon on call, arrived and cracked his chest. As we kept trying to revive the man, a nurse told me we had fifteen more coming and some were critically wounded. After a quick conference with Amel, we decided we could not go on, and I pronounced the patient dead. Ten minutes later, we were in full-blown mass cal mode with ambulances and vehicles pouring into the back. We stationed physicians, nurses, and medics at each bed we had available, and our team quickly worked to remove the body and free up space for more casualties to arrive.

Our charge nurse, Pat Smith, and I went out to the first ambulance and triaged patients, finding more third-country nationals with holes everywhere. I sent one with a bowel evisceration into bed three, a penetrating chest wound into bed seven, and others with open leg fractures, back, and buttock wounds to other beds. Talking to medical personnel transporting patients in, I was informed there were no more survivors at the scene and that, pending further attacks, we should not be receiving any more patients. I came back into the EMT to notice the usual chaos of a mass cal situation, although this time patients were moved more rapidly to the operating rooms upstairs than I had seen in the past. Within about an hour and half, the ER was empty once again, and after completing the death note on my patient from earlier, I was gassed and ready to get some sleep, especially if days of constant bombardment were back in store.

Getting to bed about nine, I fell asleep quickly. On hour later, I heard Jason's phone ring, and he got up and took off quickly to the ER, so I assumed there was more carnage en route. I quickly drifted off again, only to be awakened by my phone at 10:15. Answering it, I head one of our younger enlisted members from the laboratory tell me about a urine culture I had ordered a few days ago on a patient with an infection. Writing the information down to peruse later, I went right back to sleep, only to have my phone ring in another five minutes. After hearing more about the urine culture results, again I tried to lie back down. However, the rotor noise from multiple air ambulances landing on our pad kept my mind racing, so I gave up on any chance I had of sleeping. I got dressed and went to the ER to find another mess.

Hearing the birds fly away as I was walking downstairs, I thought nothing of it and made my way to the ER. In the trauma room I found Jason, Joey, and Guyon Hill, another rotating ER doc, working on a soldier who had been critically wounded by an IED. He had partial amputations of three extremities, and he was being stabilized after getting some life-saving blood in the trauma room. Less than one minute after I arrived, he was wheeled to the OR. Right as he was wheeled out, four people rushed through the EMT doors carrying a litter with a dining facility worker from our DFAC who was unconscious and having a seizure with blood pouring from his head. Throwing him into bed three, we ripped off his clothes and went to work on him. Jason ran his resuscitation, and I placed lines and served as the "procedure boy" as we had done all year long when we had more than one ER doc present. Once intubated and stabilized, he went to the CT scanner, and I went outside to see what had injured this gentleman.

Finding 1st Sgt. Leonard in the motor pool, I asked him for the story, and he told me an amazing tale. Apparently, the Blackhawk helicopter that had brought in the wounded American soldier had taken off at a very low trajectory from our pad, and then hovered over our motor pool for some reason. The incredible rotor wash sent our guys who were working outside scrambling for shelter, and several of them were hit with debris, leaving them with minor scratches. The sleeping cots they were cleaning outside at the time became airborne projectiles in the windstorm created by the rotor wash, and some were thrown into the large garage doors where our mechanics worked, denting them up. Others were slammed into the back of one of our SUVs, breaking out the rear window. As the low-flying bird moved forward, the rotor wash lifted an awning panel from a building and sent it flying, landing on the poor DFAC worker who was brought into us as he was taking down the "Happy Thanksgiving" sign, resulting in his serious head injury. As if once was not enough, when the birds came to evacuate *that* patient to the neurosurgeons, they once again hovered too low and blew five different air conditioner pieces down from the roofs of our buildings. Luckily, our guys outside knew to run for cover earlier this time, and no one was injured.

By this point in the day, we had endured rocket attacks, a mass cal situation, and had survived our own helicopters trying to kill us. It was not a bad day's work, all by noon. But it was only the beginning!

Having given up on sleep after the morning's excitement, four of us went to the palace for lunch and then to run a couple of errands. Our half-mile walk was uneventful. However, while eating, a huge thunderstorm blew in, and the first cracks of thunder startled us, at first making us think we were being rocketed. A torrential downpour followed, and we decided to wait at the embassy rather than get too wet. A few inches of rain and twenty minutes later, we gave up waiting and struck out for the KBR compound, where we were to pick up end-of-tour gifts for our nurses and medics. The flooding in the streets had already grown several inches deep, and it did not take long for us to be wading in water up to our midshins. As we would wade across the deeper side streets, Iraqis driving by would wave and yell, "Way to go," and sign thumbs-up to us, I guess for braving the storm. Who knows what they were thinking.

About an hour later, we trudged our way back to the CSH, only to find sandbags keeping the standing water from flowing into the hospital. The CSH personnel told us most of the hospital was dry, but they said, "You don't want to see the ER, it's underwater." We rushed to the ER at the back of the hospital to find many of our ER staff and others from the hospital tossing sandbags, using shop vacs to suck up standing water, and pushing the water out with brooms. The entire place was a madhouse, and we would have been in bad shape if critical patients began flowing in during that time as we were not ready to accept patients during the mêlée.

We jumped in and went to work, and three hours later, the ER was dry and likely cleaner than it had been in years. No desk, piece of equipment, countertop, or gurney was left in place as the entire ER was essentially disassembled and reassembled in a matter of three hours. Walls were scrubbed, shelves washed, and nothing was left untouched.

The flooding had begun in a small washroom just off to the side of our trauma bay, where two floor drains attached to our large reservoir tank buried outside backed up. The water gushed up through the two drains in the floor, and it flooded the ER within minutes. The large tank outside was apparently designed to drain into the street, but there were no check valves installed, so if the street flooded, it could also flow backward into the tank, and evidently into our trauma room.

Now having survived the flood, we were all exhausted by shift change at 7:00 PM. One crazy thing had led to another, and it had taken its toll on us. Once again, though, it started pouring down rain around 9:00 PM, but this time we were ready. I pulled my boots from the patient warming system I was using to dry them out on, and we sprinted outside to grab the sandbags and cut off the small washroom from our trauma bay, hoping to ebb the flow of brown water pouring from the drains below. Sgt. Kelly Yates, one of our medics, and I jumped over the sandbags into the muck and began bailing water, while Sam Matta set up the shop vac systems quickly to suck the water from the room. About forty-five minutes later, we were making progress and eventually we got the water out without flooding the trauma room and ER again.

Eventually, our facilities workers produced a bilge pump for us to use, and we all began taking bets as to whether the "poop water" or the bilge pump would prevail in round three. The sewage lines ran above the clean water lines in Baghdad, so we all knew there was likely some truthfulness to the term "poop water." Round three did come an hour later, but it was minor and did not even get deep enough to engage the bilge, so we never discovered which entity would win the struggle.

By 1:00 AM, the rain stopped, and we knew we were safe from the water below, if not the rockets from above. I eventually gave up and went to bed. Rocket fire, a mass cal, a helicopter of death, and a flood all made this one of the craziest days of my life, and one none of us would forget it. Even though our ER family was incredibly close, this day's events brought us even closer, working hand in hand to keep our facility open and available to treat anyone at a moment's notice and to be there for our soldiers on the streets whenever they needed us.

A week later, there was a buzz in the air as everyone was packing their gear, mailing stuff home, and preparing to leave Iraq. The Tenth CSH was currently en route to Kuwait from Colorado, meaning there was no turning back for them! Our unit was leaving in waves over several weeks, and the first wave was set to depart by Chinook helicopter in only a few more days, meaning those of us left behind could begin counting down until it was our turn to fly. It was early December 2008, and the colder weather had finally made its way into the desert. The rainstorm of ten days prior had taken a toll on the Baghdad power grid, and we had been running on our backup generators since that time. The smell of exhaust fumes pouring through the window of my office in the EMT, along with the constant whine of the diesel engines of the generators, told my senses that we were still running on backup, but that was fine with us. We felt for the poor Iraqis out in the community who had no heat. Our heating system in the hospital was all hot, with no warm setting, so the exhaust fumes pouring through an open window were a small price to pay for the cooler air blowing in with them.

The prior week, after the rainstorm, Cpt. Dena George, Cpt. Kris Varga, and I received a real treat as we were invited by Iraq's Vice President Adil Abd Al-Mahdi and his National Security Advisor Dr. Mowaffak Al-Rubaie to dinner. Not wanting to pass up a chance to mingle with world leaders, we readily jumped at the invitation, and we were picked up by two assistants just outside the front gate of the hospital one evening. After being dropped off at the vice president's residence, we were greeted in royal fashion by men in suits and a large number of Iraqi soldiers. As the staff guided us upstairs to meet first with the national security advisor, it amazed me to see each Iraqi soldier jump to his feet and snap to attention when we walked by.

We met Dr. Al-Rubaie first and sat with him for about twenty minutes talking about everything imaginable. Later, the vice president made his way into the room, followed by a throng of security staff and a photographer. Action pictures were taken by the crew as we sat and talked, getting to know each other. Both men spoke excellent English, and before long, I felt much more comfortable with them. They both talked about how much work they had put into the SOFA agreement, and at one point the vice president looked at me and said, "Dr. Baker, are you happy with the SOFA agreement? What is your view?" What a question! Whether I liked the agreement or not, as a soldier I did not have the right to tell my opinion on the matter, at least not to outside parties. Especially not to the party my nation was negotiating the deal with! I told him I was happy with the agreement, and that I was enthusiastic the only result so far from the bad guys had been the two rockets sent into the IZ.

After small talk for an hour or so, dinner was ready, and we were escorted to an elegant, 1960s-era dining room. The furniture was nice, but the feel and style reminded me of my late grandmother's home, with older chairs and decor. The chef had done an amazing job, with no less than twelve entrée's laid out for us to choose from. We ate family style, with everyone taking portions from the plates in the center. I expanded my culinary horizons by chowing down on liver, sheep, and a plethora of the truffles grown in Iraq. The meal was wonderful, but the conversation that took place blew us away.

There we sat, with two world leaders. These were men who were on the world news regularly, in the newspapers, and on the Internet. They talked about our nation's leadership, people I will never meet. They told us about their multiple interactions with Secretary of State Condoleezza Rice, about her mannerisms, speech, and personality. After discussing several of America's leaders these men knew so well, one of our hosts became solemn, and said, "There is one man, above all of these others, that we hold in highest esteem. The best word I can think of to describe him would be determined. That man is George W. [Bush]. He could have given up on us, but he did not. He did not quit us, and to that we will be forever grateful." What a statement! Of course I would expect these men to feel that way, but the words resonated off the walls and furniture and made their way to my heart. Agree or disagree with the forty-third president of our great nation, he did demonstrate incredible determination to stay the course in Iraq, to not give up on these people. They obviously had not forgotten.

An hour later, the three of us sat in amazement on the short drive back to the CSH. We all pondered to each other, "Here we are, three people who grew up blue collar, in small towns, sitting with the leaders of thirty million people, people who talk about the president of the United States and his staff like they were old friends." Before we departed the vice president's compound, they implored us to return to Iraq someday, saying that we "would always have somewhere to stay when we are here." We laughed, thinking, "How does that work? Do I just show up on the front doorstep of the government and say, 'Remember me?'" I did not think I ever in my life expected to have an open invitation to crash with a nation's leadership anytime I got a chance!

Unfortunately, it did not take long for reality to return. The next morning, while on shift, a helicopter landed on our pad. As had been the disturbing trend since the changeover of the medevac crews, they did not call ahead and tell us what they were bringing like the previous crews did regularly. One medic went on one of our gators to see what she needed to pick up. She loaded six boxes of blood onto the gator and let the three soldiers being dropped off walk the two hundreds yards on their own as they were all there for routine doctor's appointments and had no trouble walking.

Meeting them at the front door to the EMT, I asked for their paperwork as usual, noticing that one of the three soldiers was a full-bird colonel. We had eleven of them at the CSH, so that was not a big deal to me, although apparently it was to him. He immediately jumped down my throat and chewed me out for not having "someone at the LZ to meet me."

Any outsider badmouthing my EMT set me off, so I angrily told him, "Sir, when the helicopters come in, not telling us they are coming, we don't know if there is CPR going on, soldiers with amputations, or what. We only send one gator and keep our other medics here to prep the EMT for casualties!"

"Well, you need to get your act together! There was no one to meet me, and I had to walk all this way! That is unacceptable. I am a colonel, and I am so angry right now! You people need to get it together!"

"*Yes, sir!*" was all I could muster. The last thing I wanted was to be accused of insubordination just before leaving the army, and I knew there was no fixing this guy. What a pompous, self-serving jerk. We did not have enough staff to send both of our gators out every time a bird landed unless we *knew* we needed them, but he would have none of it. "Oh well, can't win them all," I thought. It was then I noticed the colonel's uniform. Of all things, he was an army chaplain! I stared at him dumbfounded, and I could not help but laugh at what had just transpired. I had just gotten into an argument with a chaplain! I spent the next week trying to live that one down, as everyone from the EMT who witnessed the altercation harassed me tremendously about it, saying it must be time for me to go home if I was getting into fights with chaplains. I think they were right.

An Iraqi man was brought in later that day with a gunshot wound to the calf. His wailing and moaning could be heard down the hallway, but I gave him the benefit of the doubt—he had been shot, after all. When examining him, I noticed a very superficial abrasion to his left forearm, along with another superficial abrasion from a tangential gunshot wound to his calf. Both injuries were very minor scratches, and I would expect most five-year-old children to man up, dry their tears, and stop crying once their fears were abated. Not this guy. We would not give up that easily. Trying to evaluate the neurologic status of his hand, I squeezed all over it and asked him to wiggle his fingers. Through the translator, he told me he could not. Not discovering any injuries that would cause this ordeal, I kept engaging him, trying to get him to give me something. *Stop wailing and be a man!* Time and time again, I tried to get him to move his fingers ... nothing. Knowing he had no injury that could cause this complaint, I finally broke down and utilized his fears against him.

"Tell him that if he won't move his fingers, we will be forced to cut his arm off at the shoulder," I mentioned to our translator. She snickered, realizing my tactic, and translated the message. Suddenly, he stopped crying, and his fingers began to move. It worked! Not wanting to lose the momentum, I said, "We will have to cut off your leg if you can't move your foot." First the toes, then the foot began to wiggle. Once his radiographs came back negative, and we had explored his wounds and essentially given him a couple of Band-Aids, I knew he would be fine. I asked our interpreter to tell him, "Be a man. Stop crying. You are going to be fine. You will walk out of this ER. There is no alternative, so grow a pair and get up!" Our interpreter laughed and translated the words, and a few minutes later he was on his feet walking through out the door. I felt bad talking to him that way, but it was the only choice I felt I had to get him moving and keep us ready for real casualties.

The next day, the EMT had our formal end-of-tour awards ceremony. During the ceremony, the hospital commander made several nice comments about our staff and accomplishments. He mentioned how we were the first hospital since Vietnam to be specifically targeted and engaged by rocket and mortar attacks by enemy forces, and that we had endured the most indirect fire any hospital had sustained since Vietnam. I had assumed those facts, but that was the first time I had heard them from the command element. After the commander gave his thoughts, the sergeant major spoke and even tried to crack a joke. No one laughed. It was obvious we did not really want these guys in our section. Over the previous fifteen months, we had become very possessive of our area and staff, and we had become very uncomfortable when "others" were down there.

At one point late in the tour, the EMT even decided to secede from the CSH, with Sgt. Sion Ledbetter using his creative writing skills to write a "Declaration of Independence from the Eighty-sixth CSH." We named ourselves "The First of the Last Baghdad ER." I guess, like all army units, we had to have some sort of numerical description in our name, so we chose "The First of the Last." We did not take our grievances to the command; they were unaware we had left the CSH and formed our own unit. We decided we would not tell the command about it until we were home!

After the command gave their speeches, Deb Chappel and I each were given the opportunity to say a few words. Deb spoke first, and after I finished heaping my well-deserved praise onto our crew, the colonel went from person to person, pinning their awards onto their uniforms. All the way around the room he went, purposefully leaving Jason Cohen, Marti Roellig, Deb Chappel, and myself out since we were to receive different awards at a later date. The colonel went through all our crew, and then he stopped with only two to go. We knew that one of the last two was to receive a lesser award, as she had only been with us for a couple of months. All of our medics received the Army Commendation Medal. However, as the Army Achievement Medal, a lesser award, was presented to our final medic, we all stood in disbelief. He had been with us the entire fifteen months. He was an outstanding worker, very gifted both intellectually and clinically. Why would he get shafted? And in front of his peers no less?

We were furious when we discovered what had occurred. The sergeant major, who was usually the culprit behind attacks on our enlisted crew, swore his innocence. He stated he had nothing to do with the downgrading of this medic's award. We had put him in for the same award as the rest of crew, and he deserved no less. We finally figured it out when we put two and two together. Several months prior, during a sensing session, a special town hall–type meeting with the commander designed for soldiers to comfortably bring up their issues, this medic had made a comment the commander did not like. He was crushed and berated by the sergeant major immediately. Thinking that was the end of it, he continued to do amazing work for us, only to not receive the award he deserved at the end. I cannot say how many soldiers' lives he touched with his amazing skill and compassion. But the command did not care, and we were furious as we watched him walk over to the trashcan and throw his medal away.

While it did not surprise us by that point for our hospital command to be so petty, why in the world would he downgrade a deployment award for a medic, a junior enlisted person? We should have been lifting these guys up, celebrating them! As an officer, it was my job to let these guys go first, eat first, and give them the best praise I could. A junior enlisted member in the military has a tough life, especially during wartime, and I held these guys in the highest esteem. It was a commander's job to put them first, not to punish them for speaking their minds in a forum designed for that very thing! Where did that type of leadership go? I understand that as an officer in the military, sometimes you have to order your troops to charge over that hill, regardless of the potential casualties. But I believe that if you treat your soldiers right, they will *want* to charge the hill for you. That is leadership in my humble opinion, not what we witnessed that day.

On my last shift prior to the arrival of our replacements, I treated a British contractor who fell victim to an IED and a soldier with appendicitis. The injuries suffered by the contractor were not bad, and as usual, I enjoyed taking care of the British guys. They seemed to always be so talkative and jovial, even when they had a large open leg fracture like this guy. Hearing words like "Cheers, mate," and "Jolly fine job!" always cracked me up, and it reminded of all of my new British and European friends who worked with us there. They all worked for contractors or other military services and came in to volunteer their medical skills, as well as to get the Baghdad ER experience for themselves.

To be honest, by this time, we were depending on those guys just to stay afloat. Due to a serious room crunch when the Tenth CSH arrived, our command decided to send our unit home in three different waves of about one hundred soldiers each. This move would allow the soldiers of the first wave a chance to get home and be with their families for Christmas, keeping them from missing their second holiday season in as many years. The rest of us stuck around for about fifteen more days and covered for them. All three of our EMT physicians remained behind to leave on the third or fourth wave, but our nurses and medics were hurting due to their losses. We fought with the command for months regarding how many nurses and medics we required to stay behind to keep us safely staffed, and we were at the minimum level by this point. On one of the first days without our full crew, patients came in, and we quickly had to call for help from the understaffed areas upstairs to come down. We even asked Tony Steele and Dane Richardson, two of our favorite UK volunteer medics who worked with a British private contractor, to come help each night until the Tenth CSH arrived to relieve us. It was a great thing that one-third of our CSH was able to make it home for Christmas, but it was a huge gamble to assume we could handle the mission with only two-thirds of our staffing! As commander, I would not have been comfortable with that, but others and I let our objections be known and then drove on with the command's decision.

After our daily morning report the week before, several of us were called forward to receive our end-of-tour awards. Deb Chappel, Marti Roellig, Jason Cohen, Dena George, and I all were fortunate enough to receive the Bronze Star Medal for our service during our combat tours. While my colleagues and I shared much frustration with the command while trying to obtain the same awards for our flight nurses, I must admit I was honored to receive a Bronze Star. However, my story goes back much further than that. My friend Steve Bryant's father, Steven Bryant Jr., served as a captain in the air force for a year during the Vietnam War, living at an air base in Thailand. As I've written, their family took me in as one of their own when I was in high school, and we are close to this day. He was a munitions officer charged with loading the bombers and fighters as they went into combat. He left the service after his tour, and to this day I vividly remember the display of medals he had in a shadow box in his living room. Several medals and ribbons were included, but the highlight of the collection was the Bronze Star awarded for his service. I cannot explain why it meant so much for me to have received the same combat award that he did; maybe it was because I respect him so much. I understand it is nothing more than a ribbon and piece of metal, but that Bronze Star means more to me than any award I have ever received.

At this point, I could also proudly say that the malpractice claim filed against me the year before had now been officially closed! The professional review board found that my care was the standard practice and I should not have done anything differently; in their opinion, I was not at fault in the case. The claim was dropped, and the statute of limitations had expired. How much pain and turmoil that caused! Once again, when I prepared to deploy to Iraq I did not expect to have to deal with a lawsuit, but that is life. Like all physicians, I knew to keep doing the best I could for each patient I saw and worry about the next lawsuit when it came. Emergency physicians are sued an average of once every few years, so hopefully I would be off the hook for a while.

Jason, Dena, and I received a rare treat the next day when we were picked up by an American Special Forces colonel and taken over to the Adnon Palace. The palace was built for Iraq's vice president back in Saddam's day, and it rested on the edge of the IZ with one side open to the red zone and one open to the green zone. The palace tour was great, and then we had the pleasure of eating at Michael's Restaurant, the establishment made famous a few years earlier, earning it the nickname the Baghdad Country Club. An Olympic-sized swimming pool sat just behind the building, and apparently back in 2004 and 2005, the American contractors would park in the grass lot beside the building and have tailgate parties and with lots of booze and other fun stuff. Ambassador Paul Bremer of the Coalition Provisional Authority eventually made it off-limits to Americans for a while. It was slowly becoming safe to eat there again, and I must say the food was very good. I was nervous, however, about forgetting to take the antibiotic I regularly swallowed before eating on the local economy, but I was spared any diarrhea or vomiting from this endeavor.

The last ten days in Baghdad flew by, with several crazy trauma patients followed by the arrival of the Tenth CSH, our replacements. Christmas Eve and Christmas Day were spent, unfortunately, just like the year before with us working in vain trying to save lives and fighting tears as we watched more dead soldiers being flown away into the nighttime sky on Angel Flights. As usual, however, there were good times as well, as our EMT crew all played Rock Band together every day in the break room while standing by in case our replacements required assistance.

During the previous week, five Iraqi civilians were brought in after a serious t-bone vehicle collision somewhere in Baghdad. A convoy of MRAPs happened to be passing by at the time, and our guys stopped to render first aid to the Iraqis. Twenty minutes later, multiple birds began landing on our pad with the beat-up casualties, and Jason called me to come help. My patient had a severely fractured face, with multiple breaks to his upper and lower jaws, as well as most of the bones beneath his eyes. All of his teeth were broken, and his mouth was filled with rows of one to three teeth in a line still attached by tissue to some aspect of his head. Realizing he required airway intervention sooner rather than later, I asked our crew to call one of our anesthesia providers to come down because I expected this airway to be ugly. Unfortunately, it turned out I was right.

After anesthesia arrived, we sedated the man, and I used the laryngoscope blade to take a look. I could see my target, his vocal cords, between the broken teeth and bleeding tongue only after I suctioned copious amounts of blood from the back of his throat. Time after time, I attempted to pass the tube, but I could not get it through all of the mangled teeth and bone. I dropped the tube and began grabbing loose teeth, but found most of them still attached by tissue to his head somewhere. Before it was over, he began to desaturate, or lose oxygen to his brain and body. Dr. Jamie Mayoral, the surgeon on call, immediately began cutting on his neck to place a surgical airway while I continued to try to get the endotracheal tube placed. Jamie was able to place the surgical airway, and the man was oxygenated so we were able to breathe for him.

Over the previous fifteen months, I had been fortunate enough to place more than seventy endotracheal tubes without having to perform a cricothyroidotomy, or cutting the neck open to place a tube. I had intubated multiple patients with massive facial fractures, and two with total facial disjunction from their skull. But this was the first time I needed a cric, and I was thankful we were able to get it done without harm to the patient. The man was taken to the OR the next day by our facial surgeon, and his long road to recovery was initiated. These five men, most with serious injuries, were extremely fortunate their accident occurred in front of an American convoy. I was convinced that at least three of them, including my patient, would have lain in a bed and died had they been transported to an Iraqi hospital rather than the CSH.

Knowing our replacements would arrive the next day, and depressed that my last intubation in Iraq would be a failed one, I did not long for anyone to be sick, but I did wish for a chance to redeem myself before I stopped working. I did not have to wait long as the next night a seventy-five-year old Iraqi woman collapsed at our front gate. Seeing our team performing CPR while wheeling her down the hallway toward our trauma room, I cut Jason off by jumping to the head of the bed and grabbed the laryngoscope blade to intubate her. Jason did not protest as he placed a central line and ran the code, and I was happy to get another chance to finish on a high note. Once I had intubated her, I assisted Jason with the code, and we were able to keep her alive until she got to the ICU. She expired a few hours later, but not before the EMT and ICU teams had given her every chance at life that we could. She would prove to be the last code our team would work on in Baghdad before the Tenth CSH took over.

The Tenth CSH arrived the next day, and seeing my good friend from residency, Maj. Lisa Hile, walk in and give me a hug was a very welcome sight indeed. The end had come, and the only thing keeping me from going home to my beautiful family was now a few days of training for the new crew. However, in typical "First of the Last Baghdad ER" fashion, we all knew we needed to go out on a high note.

That night, led by Kristy Bischoff, our guys decked out the gators under the cover of darkness. Reflective tacky stickers were placed all over them, with sayings like "EMT Rocks," "Eighty-sixth Rules," and other things. Steering wheel covers shipped from the U.S. were placed, leather gearshift covers installed, and aluminum foil "bling-bling" wheels were installed. Tony and our British friends helped out, and "God save the Queen" even made its way onto the back of one of the machines, accompanied by the

Union Jack, or British flag. Sam Matta even created and attached a pair of truck nuts that hung from the back bumper of the ATV like a pair of testicles. No space was spared, and these two machines were totally transformed into the tackiest ATVs any of us had ever seen. Everyone had a fun time doing it, and it was a great going-away event for our staff as we turned the machines over to the Tenth CSH the next day.

Over the next few days, we hammered our replacements with mock trauma after mock trauma. Surprising them with bilateral amputations, gunshot wounds, and other critically ill patients helped them learn where supplies were located, practice large-bore IV sticks, and helped to get them ready for real patient care. A few actual trauma patients came in, and I sat back and watched Lisa Hile run a code for an Iraqi contractor who had been shot in the head by a sniper. It was so hard to stand back and not jump in and help, to do it my way. But I had to stop. She knew what she was doing, and Baghdad ER did not belong to me anymore. It was not my baby. At one point later in the day, Jason and I were in our room reading when the noise of Blackhawks getting louder indicated that birds were landing on our pad.

"Fight it, Todd. Don't you go down there. If they need you, they will call," Jason said. Of course he was right, but it took several days for me to give it up, for my heart to stop skipping a beat every time I heard a bird landing. As chief, I was ultimately responsible for every patient who came through those doors for so long. But it was not mine anymore; I was now a nobody, a has-been. Overall, that was a great thing because it meant I could go home to my family, but it was much harder to let go than I expected.

———

Jason Cohen and Kristy Bischoff were big-time runners throughout our stay, as demonstrated by Kristy's winning of the army ten mile run at BIAP during the year and the fact that they got together and ran the entire length of the IZ every other day or so before daylight. Lisa Hile was a runner as well, and what better way to show her around than a running tour? On Christmas Eve, they dragged me along for an eight-mile jaunt that covered the entire Green Zone. We left the CSH at 7:30 am, all unaware that we had been locked down on the compound because three car bombs had been smuggled into the IZ. A mile into our run, we were jogging beside Washington LZ, where two Blackhawks were drifting down to land. When they were about fifty feet over our heads, I screamed through the deafening noise and thunderous rotor wash, "Welcome to Iraq!" to Lisa. It was a quote that seemed straight out of a movie. We noticed the extra checkpoints all over the IZ as we ran, and a lot people looked at us like we were crazy. Our trek took us by the palace, the new American Embassy, and over to FOB Prosperity where we stopped and posed for pictures in the giant Saddam head sculptures that had been removed from the palace. While running back, one stretch put us on a narrow sidewalk in front of the Crossed Sabers monument and the Tomb of the Unknown Soldier memorial. Running against traffic on the thin strip, cars passed us going forty, fifty, and sixty miles an hour only two to four feet away.

At one point, a car passed us, stopped, and began to back toward us. As they slowly backed our way, I became very nervous they were coming back to blow us up, shoot at us, or try to kidnap us. Thankfully, they stopped and pulled into a parking space close by, getting out of the car. I did not see men carrying rifles, and we were moving away from them rapidly, so I breathed a sigh of relief and kept moving. A good while later, we arrived back at the CSH, only to find out we had been locked down due to the bomb threat. Whoops!

The next day, Christmas Day, the car bomb threat in the IZ became more realistic. Intelligence reports told us the CSH was one of the targets, and we actually had IZ security forces block the road in front of us and search all vehicles with dogs throughout the day. Concertina wire and barriers were stretched across the road on each side of our compound, but nothing ever materialized from the threat. After that, we were locked down after dark each night, because I guess the car bombs were still out there somewhere in our 3.2-square-mile home called the IZ.

While the threat level outside was high on Christmas Eve and Christmas Day, the ER was chaotic much of the time as three soldiers drowned in an overturned Humvee close by. Two were flown into us, and the Tenth CSH guys worked very hard to resuscitate them to no avail. The third soldier took much longer to extract from the vehicle, and he unfortunately expired before getting to us. I was not proud to say that my eyes had witnessed so much death during the past months. I was not as upset as I used to be when people died; I guess it was only natural. But the tears streaming down the faces of the new guys from the Tenth CSH brought out the emotion. It was as if I was preparing to leave and go back home, to a place where death was unexpected rather than the norm. The Tenth CSH gave these guys their all to revive them. Later that night, almost the entire hospital stood outside and saluted the birds as the Angel Flights pulled away with the three deceased heroes, a chilling wake up call for the new guys, and a scary reminder of the past fifteen months for those of us going home.

I spent most of the next day following Jason around as he packed up his gear to go home. Most of our nurses, along with Jason, Marti, and Dena, were heading for Kuwait on the next wave that night. At this point, our mission was totally transferred over to the Tenth CSH, and Drs. Lisa Hile, Martin Lucenti, and Dave Barry were now responsible for Baghdad ER. As our guys prepared their gear for an imminent departure, the few of us left behind for another week were at a loss. Sure, we did not want to be too mushy, but these guys had become family. They had endured multiple near-death experiences with us, celebrated with us, and cried with us. Jason was my roommate for a year, and he and I enjoyed playing video games, watching movies, and doing just about everything else together. Most of all, these guys had missed their families at the same time we were missing ours, and we all will always have a bond that will be hard to break.

Before everyone was to be in formation at 9:00 PM, we all went to the rooftop of the EMT for one last chance to sit and smoke cigars. Puffing on Cubans, we all laughed about the good times and talked about how we all looked forward to getting together for Ann and Sam's wedding in August 2009. While we were on the rooftop, the National Guard medevac birds came in from Balad for a few routine patient transfers. With the birds sitting on the pad, Jason, Marti, Pat, and Sam decided to give Baghdad one final salute. Knowing they were leaving in two hours and were untouchable, they all formed up in a line on the roof and dropped their drawers and mooned the Blackhawks! Of course, pictures were taken, but I am sure the event would be denied if they were ever asked about it.

It truly killed me to watch them go. Do not get me wrong, I was the chief and Deb Chappel was the head nurse, and we should be the last to leave after our soldiers departed. But hugging each of them as they loaded the bus, I could not speak. Words would not come out. My choices were to speak and cry, or just be quiet and hold it together; I chose the latter. Of course, Dena George, the sage of our group, saw what I was going through and said after I had silently hugged her good-bye, "It's okay. I think you need another hug."

Deb Chappel, Heather Brown, and I all stood by as we watched them load on the Rhino busses and head for the landing strip where the Chinooks would take them to BIAP. We still had some of our amazing medics, Sgts. Brunelle, Desillier, Soltis, and Ubert with us, but the seven of us were now the last of our EMT crew. Our freedom would come in a few short days.

Our amazing medics handled a multitude of major injuries on their own until a nurse or doctor could arrive.

The Beaches of Kuwait

Fifteen months, almost to the day, since driving away from Laura and Avery on September 30, 2007, I sat in a Starbucks coffee trailer overlooking a sandstorm blowing through Camp Virginia, Kuwait. As usual, the trip to Kuwait from Baghdad had its share of interesting moments, but we were there and simply waiting a few more days for the flight back home to the U.S. and our families.

Back on December 25, after watching most of our crew climb onto busses and head for home, the few stragglers left behind in Baghdad pretty much waited around with baited breath for the December 30 to arrive. After enduring several briefs on procedure and plan, we all understood that the biggest thing required of us was flexibility. Weather could cancel our flights, as could an increase in violent activity. Apparently, one of the car bombs known to be roaming the IZ was discovered; the other two were still at large and waiting for the right opportunity to strike. Anything could still go wrong and ruin our trip.

When the big day finally came, we were to load the baggage truck at 8:00 AM and then wait for another formation at 1:00 PM. I spent that time showing Dave Barry and Lisa Hile the palace, discovering that it had been gutted overnight as embassy crews frantically tried to get everything shut down and transferred to the new embassy complex by the next day in preparation for the turnover of the palace to the government of Iraq on

December 31. The sandwich bar was gone, as well as the coffee shop and lounge. Cranes out front effortlessly picked up the several ton, twenty-foot-high reinforced concrete blast walls and removed them from the front of the building. Peruvian Triple Canopy guards could be found everywhere, taking pictures of the building they had spent the last several years guarding. Several of them waved us over and wanted us to pose with them, saying, "My American friends!" time and time again in broken English. We must have taken ten or more shots with different guards. Once the tour was complete, I returned to the CSH to wait for my ride out.

A few hours later, assembled outside in the supply area, we heard a speech from our commander, followed by a moving tribute from Maj. Middlebrooks, the Tenth CSH chaplain who had replaced our chaplain, Maj. Felix Sermon. We then gleefully loaded busses and took a quick ride over to Washington LZ to wait for our flight to BIAP.

Growing up with eighties and nineties war movies like *Platoon*, *Full Metal Jacket*, and *Predator*, I had always remembered rock music playing in the background during scenes that depicted them in helicopters flying over the war zone. For some reason, I always remembered a few songs from Credence Clearwater Revival being played in the background of many of the flicks. I had flown over Iraq several times over the past fifteen months, but I had worn my earplugs rather than listening to CCR like soldiers did in the movies. Knowing this was my last chance, I immediately pulled out my iPod once we loaded on the CH-47 Chinook helicopter and put in the earplugs. Once we lifted into the Baghdad sky, "Fortunate Son" blared through my headphones. Turning the volume as high as it would play so I could to hear it over the noise of the twin jet engines powering overhead, "Traveling Band," "Run through the Jungle," and a few others made the cut before we landed at Baghdad International Airport and filed into the terminal. My dream of jamming to war music while flying over a combat zone was complete, now I could go home.

We crashed in the transient lodging tents at BIAP that night, and then jumped up at 2:00 AM to pack and load busses to prepare for our flight at 8:00 AM. I was thrilled to see the giant tailfin of a C-17 waiting for us as we walked out onto the tarmac, and several of us in the long line of soldiers heading out jumped at the explosions in the background. Quickly realizing they were controlled detonations that had been announced to us earlier, we continued our jaunt and happily walked up the rear ramp into the belly of the huge cargo plane. Lucking out and drawing a jump seat on the side of the beast rather than the midsection, I enjoyed a leisurely hour-long flight to Kuwait.

As we walked up the cargo ramp, Col. Rowe walked behind me. Seeing the cargo roller wheels built into the ramp a few feet beside him, he just could not help himself and turned back to step on one of the wheels and act like he was falling off the jet back down the ramp. The crew chief saw some guy with his back to him goofing off while we were loading and quickly chastised Col. Rowe, saying, "You'll have to stay if you want to goof off since the nearest hospital is here." Laughing, Col. Rowe turned around and said, "Oh no, please don't take me back there!" Seeing the eagle rank on the colonel's chest made the crew chief do a double take, and he quickly became quiet and let the playful colonel go on his way. As I sat on the flight, leaving Iraq behind for the safety of Kuwait, the phrase I would repeat to myself each morning during our weeks-long rocket barrage the past spring came to mind: "Fingers and toes." I realized I was leaving Iraq with all of my fingers and all of my toes. What more could I ask for?

Waiting several days in Kuwait for our flight home, we all went about our ways, eating well, working out, and having fun. We witnessed several units arrive one night and catch a plane to go home the next day, only hours later. While that was frustrating to watch, those guys were indeed the warriors who were pounding the streets everyday. Many of them were from the units we worked with around Baghdad. While I hated to sit and watch them come and go, they had earned the opportunity to go home first, even if we had to wait longer. None of those of us left in our EMT crew questioned waiting longer than the guys doing the actual fighting.

Not many things happened while we were sitting in the Kuwaiti cold for those seven days. They were all sunny, without too many clouds to be seen— par for the course in the Middle East. At times the wind blew twenty or thirty miles an hour, dropping the wind-chill factor well below 35 degrees. We did have one interesting event occur during our time in purgatory. My traveling battle-buddy Deb Chappel messed up and got in trouble, misplacing her M16 for a few minutes only to find it quickly afterward. Even being a senior major in the army, she had to endure her punishment. I could not let her labor alone in her punishment, so I volunteered to help her.

Our task was to ensure the full-bird colonels and the command sergeant major, six of them in all, had their bags loaded on the bus in a certain spot when we departed and then taken to the correct location at our staging base while waiting on our flight home. She and I carried their gear, with each person's weighing about one hundred pounds, over to the bus and loaded it, with them watching us work, other than Col. Rowe. As usual, he would not let others do work before himself, so he ordered us not to touch his gear as he carried it himself. Upon our arrival to Ali Alsalem Air Base, Deb and I jumped off and carried the five administrators' gear over to the correct spot for the VIPs. Col. Rowe carried his own and helped, while the others watched us work for the most part. One even asked, "Why is my gear loaded over here instead of there?" My answer was that we did not have enough room and had to move it, but at that point it finally dawned on me. "These guys have the chief physician and head nurse of the ER carrying their stuff for them." Apparently, that was not a big deal to them. Deb and I did not mind doing it; we were not above carrying someone's gear, but I would have been humiliated if someone carried my stuff for me. I would feel like a real slime bag. Technically, as a major I could have demanded that some poor soldier carry my heavy gear, but most others and I would never dream of doing so! What a fitting end to this deployment! None of these guys ever got their hands bloody throughout fifteen months of trauma. Sure, that was not their job, but you would think they would pitch in and show better leadership. I guarantee that some of the colonels I worked with on the green side of the army would be appalled to see their subordinates running in circles to carry their bags after serving under them for fifteen months!

As I sat on the flight home, I could not help but reminisce over the past fifteen months. It had been 464 days since I drove away from my family. Jason, Marti, and I were always on call and ready to work twenty-four-seven, and I could not begin to count how many patients we each cared for when we were not on duty, but we each spent over twenty-five hundred hours in the department on shift, waiting for the worst to come. I had performed countless intubations, central lines, and chest tubes, with countless others that I let rotating physicians perform to keep up their skills. I did not want to count how many people, Iraqis and Americans alike, I had pronounced dead; likewise, I could not begin to count how many lives our team saved from the brink of death.

I laughed and I cried. I made several new friends, and likely I made the same number of enemies. Many times, I had turned over in my bed, facing the wall to keep from being hit in the face by flying shrapnel when the rockets came. I spent countless hours in outside bunkers waiting for the all-clear. My nose had discovered the sulfur-like smell and my eyes had seen firsthand the smoky appearance of the air resulting from mortar rounds exploding a few feet away, and my body had palpated the rumbling of the building and rattling of windows from a rocket landing nearby. I had awakened to car bombs in the distance and rockets landing closely, as well as gunfire at the checkpoints to the IZ. Through it all, even when working on patients in full body armor, I never witnessed *one* of my nurses, medics, or physicians back away from danger if it meant interrupting patient care. I cannot count how many times our nurses and medics put on their body armor and went outside to take a patient to get a CT scan, and then rush back in when the shrapnel came too close. I never saw any of them back away from a patient triage at the front or back gate, knowing that any of those patients could have a bomb or pose a threat.

I had witnessed every kind of atrocity I could imagine regarding violent trauma, grievous medical conditions, and faulty Third World medical care. I had seen all that I wanted to see, lived all that I wanted to live of war. War is necessary at times, a required evil that has been around since the fall of man. It brings out the best and the worst in mankind. I could not have been more proud of any group of people than I was of the Baghdad ER crew,

"First of the Last." We served together for two Christmases, Thanksgivings, and New Year's holidays in Iraq. I would serve with them anytime, and many of us will continue to be friends for a long time.

However, looking out the window of our plane, I could see the beautiful coast of the United States creeping over the ocean's horizon. Laura, Avery, and my family were waiting for me there, and that was the only thing on my mind for the rest of the flight.

Acknowledgments

I would like to take this opportunity to thank everyone who helped turn this book into reality. First and foremost, to God, who kept my family and our Baghdad crew safe during our tour. Thank you to my wife, Laura, who ran the ship back home throughout deployment and has pushed me to work on this endeavor. I would like to thank my family, friends, and current co-workers for putting up with my stories over and over again.

Thank you to Anthony Knighton, Justin Powell, Marc Shepherd, Jake Roberts, Ray Brovont, Carl Baker, Judy Anthony, Andy Baker, Clarence Baker, Bernice Burns, Lawrence Burns and countless others for pushing me to finish this task. Thank you to my daughter Avery Grace, who patiently waited with her toys for daddy to come play time after time.

Thank you to attorneys Elizabeth Powell, William Kircher, and Chuck Brown for your legal guidance, and to Jerry Burns, Julie Holloway, and Betty Kinser for your editing skills. Thanks to Jimmie Clunn and Mike Crandall for your contributions, and to Maya Alleruzzo for your amazing photography skills. Last I would like to thank Jonathan Gullery for your guidance as I have put this project together.

To Jason Cohen, Marti Roellig, Deb Chappel, and the crew of Baghdad ER: you will always be family, and I would serve with you again anytime.

Last I would like to thank you, the reader, for supporting this project. Please remember to support our fighting warriors and their families back home. They are our heroes.

How to Contact the Author

To reach Todd Baker, MD
Regarding a speaking engagement,
Upcoming seminar,
Consultation,
Or any other issues
Please visit his website at

www.BaghdadER.net